04

Google·pedia

The Ultimate Google Resource

Third Edition

Michael Miller

800 East 96th Street,
Indianapolis, Indiana 46240

Google® p ... source,
Third Edition

ISBN-13: 978-0-7897-3820-2
ISBN-10: 0-7897-3820-1

Library of Congress Cataloging-in-Publication data is on file.

Printed in the United States of America

Second Printing: February 2009

Trademarks

Warning and Disclaimer

Bulk Sales

Que Publishing offers excellent discounts on this book when ordered in quantity for bulk purchases or special sales. For more information, please contact:

U.S. Corporate and Government Sales
1-800-382-3419
corpsales@pearsontechgroup.com

For sales outside the U.S., please contact:

International Sales
international@pearsoned.com

Associate Publisher
Greg Wiegand

Acquisitions Editor
Rick Kughen

Development Editor
Rick Kughen

Managing Editor
Patrick Kanouse

Project Editor
Seth Kerney

Copy Editor
Water Crest Publishing

Indexer
Ken Johnson

Proofreader
Paula Lowell

Technical Editor
Karen Weinstein

Publishing Coordinator
Cindy Teeters

Designer
Anne Jones

Page Layout
Gina Rexrode

Table of Contents

About the Author

Michael Miller has written more than 80 non-fiction how-to books over the past twenty years, including Que's *Photopedia: The Ultimate Digital Photography Resource, iPodpedia: The Ultimate iPod and iTunes Resource, Absolute Beginner's Guide to Computer Basics, YouTube 4 You*, and *YouTube for Business*. His 1999 book, *The Complete Idiot's Guide to Online Search Secrets*, was one of the first books to cover Google (then in beta testing).

Mr. Miller has established a reputation for clearly explaining technical topics to non-technical readers, and for offering useful real-world advice about complicated topics. More information can be found at the author's website, located at www.molehillgroup.com.

Dedication

To Sherry—my search is over.

Acknowledgments

Thanks to the usual suspects at Que, including but not limited to Greg Wiegand, Rick Kughen, Seth Kerney, and technical editor Karen Weinstein.

We Want to Hear from You!

As the reader of this book, *you* are our most important critic and commentator. We value your opinion and want to know what we're doing right, what we could do better, what areas you'd like to see us publish in, and any other words of wisdom you're willing to pass our way.

As an associate publisher for Que Publishing, I welcome your comments. You can email or write me directly to let me know what you did or didn't like about this book—as well as what we can do to make our books better.

Please note that I cannot help you with technical problems related to the topic of this book. We do have a User Services group, however, where I will forward specific technical questions related to the book.

When you write, please be sure to include this book's title and author, as well as your name, email address, and phone number. I will carefully review your comments and share them with the author and editors who worked on the book.

Email: feedback@quepublishing.com

Mail: Greg Wiegand
          Associate Publisher
          Que Publishing
          800 East 96th Street
          Indianapolis, IN 46240 USA

Reader Services

Visit our website and register this book at www.quepublishing.com/register for convenient access to any updates, downloads, or errata that might be available for this book.

Introduction

I use Google every day. I've been using it every day since it first launched—before it launched, actually, when it still had the word "beta" on its home page. I use Google because it's easy to use, and because it delivers quality results.

I'm not unusual, of course. Google is the most-used search site on the Web, and most people choose it for the same reason I do—ease-of-use and effectiveness. That's not news.

What is news, for a lot of users, anyway, is that Google is more than just simple search. Most users don't know that they can fine-tune their search in a number of interesting ways, or that they can use Google to find pictures and news articles and compact discs, or that they can use the Google search box to perform mathematical calculations and conversions, or that Google can function as a spell checker or dictionary.

It's also news to most users that Google offers a variety of products and services that have little or nothing to do with web search. Google runs the largest blogging community on the Web, hosts a must-see video-sharing community, distributes a top-notch picture-editing program, and provides free web-based email services. You might not get all this from looking at Google's attractively austere search page, but it's there, nonetheless.

IN THIS CHAPTER

- What's in This Book
- Who Can Use This Book
- How to Use This Book
- There's More Online…
- Get Ready to Google!

All these "hidden" features are what makes Google so interesting, at least to me, and are why I wrote this book. I wanted to show other users all the cool and useful stuff I've discovered in the Google family of sites, and to share some of the tips and tricks I've developed over the years for getting the most out of Google's various products and services.

That's what *Googlepedia* is—a guide to everything that Google has to offer. It's not just web search (although I cover that, in much depth); *Googlepedia* also covers Gmail and Google Maps and Picasa and every other application and service that has come out of Google's headquarters—as well as services that Google acquired along the way, such as Blogger and YouTube. There's plenty of how-to information, of course, but also a lot of tricks and advice that even the most experienced user will appreciate.

I should note, however, that although I know a lot about what Google does and how it works, I'm not a Google insider. I don't work for Google, and had no official contact with Google while writing this book. That means I don't always take the company line; I'll tell you, as honestly as possible, when Google gets it right, when Google needs improvement, and when Google just plain sucks. (The company isn't perfect.) I'm not obligated to put on a positive face, which means you'll get the straight poop, good or bad.

What's in This Book

Google isn't just web search; the company offers a lot of different products and services, all of which I discuss somewhere in this book. Because of everything that Google does, this is a long book—46 chapters in all, organized into 10 major sections:

- **Part I: Getting to Know Google** provides an inside look at Google (the company and the technology), and then shows you how to use Google's various tools to personalize your computing and web browsing experience.

- **Part II: Searching with Google** is all about what Google does best—search for information. You'll learn the best ways to use Google's famous web search, as well as when to use Google's other more-targeted search services.

- **Part III: Communicating with Google** shows you why Google isn't just about search; we'll discuss emailing with Gmail, instant messaging with Google Talk, blogging with Blogger, and virtual chatting with Lively.

- **Part IV: Working with Google Applications** presents Google's web-based applications, including Google Docs, Google Spreadsheets, Google Presentations, Google Calendar, and Google Reader.
- **Part V: Viewing Images and Videos** is all about pictures and videos, courtesy of Google Images and the uber-popular YouTube video-sharing site.
- **Part VI: Working with Google Maps** is all about Google Maps, Google Earth, and creating your own Google Maps mashups.
- **Part VII: Using Other Google Services** discusses a wide variety of useful and information-rich services, including Google News, Google Finance, Google Health, Google Checkout, and Google Sites.
- **Part VIII: Using Google on the Go** is all about using Google on your mobile phone—including the Apple iPhone and the upcoming Android Google phone.
- **Part IX: Making Money with Google** shows you how to optimize your website for Google search, advertise your site with Google AdWords, and put advertising on your site with Google AdSense.
- **Part X: Google for Web Developers** discusses Google's tools for developers and businesses, including how to add Google to your website, analyze your site traffic, develop applications with Google's APIs and developer tools, create Google Gadgets, create OpenSocial gadgets, and take your web-based applications offline with Google Gears.

There are also two appendixes that present useful reference information, and a third that covers one of Google's most exciting new applications. Appendix A is the Google Site Directory (a complete listing of URLs for all of Google's websites), while Appendix B lists Google's advanced search operators. Handy references, both of them. And Appendix C covers Chrome, Google's very own web browser, the one that has everyone in the industry talking.

If you're wondering what's new in this third edition, the answer is "a lot." That's because the Googleverse is constantly changing; not a week goes by without some new feature being added or some old function being improved upon. To name just a few examples of new features covered in this edition that weren't around when the last edition was published, one needs to look no further than Google Knol, Google Health, Google Presentations, Google Sky, Google Sites, Google's iPhone applications, the Google phone, Lively, the OpenSocial API, and the Chrome web browser. And that's just the new stuff from Google; I've updated all the coverage in the book to reflect Google's current status quo and beefed up the coverage of Google's developer's tools.

Who Can Use This Book

Googlepedia can be used by any level of user; you don't have to be a search expert or application developer to find something of value within these pages. That said, I think this book has particular appeal to more experienced or interested users, as a lot of advanced features are presented. Still, even if you've never used Google (or Gmail or Google Maps or whatever) before, you'll find a lot of useful information here.

How to Use This Book

I hope that this book is easy enough to read that you don't need instructions. That said, there are a few elements that bear explaining.

First, there are several special elements in this book, presented in what we in the publishing business call "margin notes." There are different types of margin notes for different types of information, as you see here.

In most chapters, you'll also find some personal commentary, presented in the form of a sidebar. These sections are meant to be read separately, as they exist "outside" the main text. And remember—these sidebars are my opinions only, so feel free to agree or disagree as you like.

note This is a note that presents information of interest, even if it isn't wholly relevant to the discussion in the main text.

Obviously, there are lots of web page addresses in the book, like this one: www.google.com. When you see one of these addresses (also known as a URL), you can go to that web page by entering the URL into the address box in your web browser. I've made every effort to ensure the accuracy of the Web addresses presented here, but given the ever-changing nature of the web, don't be surprised if you run across an address or two that's changed. I apologize in advance.

tip This is a tip that might prove to be useful for whatever it is you're in the process of doing.

caution This is a caution that something you might accidentally do might have undesirable results.

The other thing you'll find in various places throughout this book is HTML code. A snippet of code might look like this:

```
<p>
This is a line of text.
</p>
<img src="URL">
```

When part of the code is italics (such as the *URL* in the previous example), this means that you need to replace the italicized code with your own individual information. In the previous example, you would replace *URL* with the full URL and filename of an image file you want to include in your auction template.

If you're a web page developer, you'll know what to do with this code. If you're not, you might want to skip over those sections. (You don't have to be a developer to use Google, of course.)

There's More Online...

I urge you to move outside the Google universe from time to time and visit my personal website, located at www.molehillgroup.com. Here you'll find more information on this book and other books I've written—including an errata page for this book, in the inevitable event that an error or two creeps into this text. (Hey, nobody's perfect!)

While you're on the Web, check out Googlepedia: The Blog (googlepedia. blogspot.com). This is my own blog devoted to the topic of Google and *Googlepedia*. I post about the latest developments in the Googleverse, as well as updates to this book. Visit it regularly.

And if you have any questions or comments, feel free to email me directly at googlepedia@molehillgroup.com. I can't guarantee that I'll respond to every email, but I will guarantee I'll read them all.

Get Ready to Google!

With all these preliminaries out of the way, it's now time to get started. Although I recommend reading the book in consecutive order, that isn't completely necessary, as each part of Google exists independently of the other parts; just as it's okay to skip around through Google's various products and services, it's also okay to skip around through the various chapters in this book.

So get ready to turn the page and learn more about using the Google family of sites. I know you'll discover features you haven't noticed before, and hopefully become a more effective searcher.

Getting to Know Google

Inside Google

You probably know Google as a web search engine—*the* Web search engine, perhaps. But Google is a lot more than just a simple search engine. It's a collection of technologies (most of which are search-related, to be fair) that helps users find and use all manner of information, both on the Internet and on their own computers.

Google is also the company behind the technology. It might surprise you to know that Google actually makes very little money from its search technologies. What Google does to make money is sell advertising based on its search results. When you look at its income statement, Google doesn't look much like a technology company; instead, it looks quite a bit like an advertising company.

So if you only know Google for its famous search page, you have a lot of catching up to do. Read on to learn more about what Google really is—and what it does.

Getting to Know Google, Inc.

Google the website is just one product of Google, Inc., the company. It's the primary product, to be sure, but it's just one facet of a multifaceted organization.

Google's Mission

If Google is about more than simple web searching, just what does the company do? Well, we can get a clue by examining Google's mission statement:

> **Google's mission is to organize the world's information and make it universally accessible and useful.**

As mission statements go, this one is properly high-minded and vague. But it's also somewhat descriptive of what the company actually does on a day-by-day basis. By using its proprietary search technology, Google does help organize information and make it both more accessible and more useful.

Note, however, that the mission statement doesn't use the word "search." Instead, Google says it wants to "organize" information. It just so happens that the way it chooses to organize this information is via searching. So, in terms of Google's business, organizing data is the mission; searching is the chosen strategy to achieve this mission.

COMMENTARY

GOOGLE'S BUSINESS MODEL

You may have noticed that Google's mission statement is a little vague about how the company expects to make money at this endeavor. In fact, a "a little vague" is an understatement; Google doesn't say one word about how it plans to generate revenues and income.

As you'll learn later in this chapter, Google doesn't make any money from its main search site or technology—at least, not directly. Google generates all its revenues from selling advertising, which is something you wouldn't guess by reading its mission statement. After all, the mission statement doesn't say anything about "selling advertising based on search results" or "generating revenue from the sale of advertising links" or the like.

In reality, even Google's execs don't use the mission statement to describe what the company does. In an interview with *Wired* magazine,

Google CEO Eric Schmidt was asked what kind of business Google is; here's how he responded:

> "Think of it first as an advertising system. Then as an end-user system—Google Apps. A third way to think of Google is as a giant supercomputer. And a fourth way is to think of it as a social phenomenon involving the company, the people, the brand, the mission, the values—all that kind of stuff."

Not a single mention of "search" in that response. As Schmidt says, Google's primary business is advertising. So much for that mission statement.

To be fair, the folks at Google are allowed to take a little license with their own mission statement; there's no law that says you have to lay out all your goals and strategies for the public (and competitors) to see. But I feel it's important for us as consumers of Google's products to realize how the company is monetizing its technology. It's also important if you're thinking about investing in Google stock; you need to know that the number of site visitors or web pages indexed has no direct bearing on the company's revenues or profits—save for the fact that the more visitors to its site, the more advertising revenues Google can generate from its *real* customers.

Google's History

How did Google get to be Google? It all started at a 5,000-watt radio station in Fresno, California...

Okay, not really. But it did start small, and it did start in California.

Google was the brainchild of two Stanford University graduate students. Larry Page, 24 at the time, had just graduated from the University of Michigan and was visiting Stanford on a campus tour. Sergey Brin, then 23, was one of the students assigned to show around the potential students. Legend has it that when they first met on that weekend in 1995, they didn't get along. That changed, however, as they both entered Stanford's computer science graduate program and began to collaborate. (The two happy fellas shown in Figure 1.1 are Larry and Sergey as they look today.)

FIGURE 1.1

The brains behind Google: Larry Page (left) and Sergey Brin. (Photo courtesy of Google, Inc.)

Their first collaboration, in January 1996, was a simple search engine they called BackRub. It was unique in that it based its search results on the number of "back links" pointing to a given website—more or less the same approach later used by the Google search engine.

BackRub was also unique in that it was designed to work on a network of low-end PCs, instead of the expensive mainframes used by the major search engines of the day. Larry and Sergey grew their search capacity by adding more and more consumer PCs to the network that was housed in Larry's dorm room.

By 1998, Larry and Sergey were trying to sell their technology to Yahoo! and other search portals, but they had no takers. So they moved out of the dorm, wrote up a business plan, and found an angel investor in the form of Andy Bechtolsheim, one of the founders of Sun Microsystems. Bechtolsheim wrote Larry and Sergey a check for $100,000, and Google, Inc. was born.

Additional investors followed (mainly family and friends), and the company soon had an initial investment of close to $1 million. That was enough to rent an office (actually, the garage of a friend) in Menlo Park, California, which is what they did in September 1998. The company stayed in the garage until February 1999, when they moved to a real office in Palo Alto. At that time, Google had a total of eight employees.

By then, the Google.com website was up and running and handling more than a

> **note** The word "google" is a play on the word "googol," the mathematical term for the number represented by a 1 followed by 100 zeros. The term was coined by Milton Sirotta and was popularized in the book *Mathematics and the Imagination* by Edward Kasner (Sirotta's uncle) and James Newman.

half-million queries a day. (Figure 1.2 shows the original Google website from December 1998; it doesn't look a whole lot different from Google's current site!) Users loved what they found, which helped Google garner a lot of press attention, which in turned helped increase site traffic, which in turn garnered more press, and so on and so on. The increased traffic and increased press also helped attract additional investors, which helped finance the hiring of more employees and the purchasing of additional hardware.

FIGURE 1.2
Google's original home page, circa December 1998.

Google was a hit.

As time went by, Google continuously expanded the size of its website index and introduced additional features and services. By the turn of the millennium, Google was competing for the titles of both biggest search index and most popular search engine—and it continued to grow.

Amazingly, Google was able to finance this growth with nothing more than venture-capital money, resisting the urge to go public during the late 1990s dot-com boom and resulting early 2000s dot-com bust. But the pressure to go public kept building, and on August 19, 2004, Google issued its initial public offering, listed on NASDAQ under the GOOG symbol. Like all things Google, the IPO had its unique qualities; the initial stock was offered through a little-used Dutch auction process, designed to attract a broader range of small investors than what you find with a normal IPO.

Today, Google continues to grow, and its stock continues to rise—from an initial price of $100 a share to a high of near $500 a share in mid-2008. (It's dropped a bit since then, but it still remains significantly higher than the initial price; Figure 1.3 is a graph of Google's stock price through July 2008.) Google is one of the five most popular sites on the Web, and it ranks as the number-one search engine in the U.S., the U.K., Canada, Australia, and numerous other countries. The Google site attracts close to 400 million unique users every month. (And the number of employees has risen from the initial two—Larry and Sergey—to more than 10,000 today.)

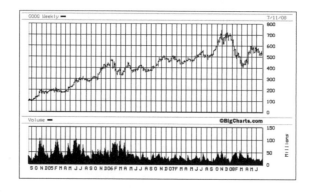

FIGURE 1.3

Google's life-to-date stock price, from 2004 through July 2008. (Courtesy of bigchart.com)

Google's Revenues

Google not only attracts a lot of visitors to its website, it also generates a lot of money. How much money? Table 1.1 details Google's revenues and profits for the years 2002 through 2007.

Table 1.1   Google Revenues and Profits 2002 to 2007

	2002	2003	2004	2005	2006	2007
Advertising Revenues	$410,915,000	$1,420,663,000	$3,143,288,000	$6,065,002,000	$10,492,628,000	$16,412,643,000
Licensing and Other Revenues	$28,593,000	$45,271,000	$45,935,000	$73,558,000	$112,289,000	$181,483,000
Total Revenues	**$439,508,000**	**$1,465,934,000**	**$3,189,223,000**	**$6,138,560,000**	**$10,604,917,000**	**$16,593,986,000**
Net Income	$99,656,000	$105,648,000	$399,119,000	$1,465,397,000	$3,077,446,000	$4,203,720,000
Income as % of Revenues	23%	7%	13%	24%	29%	25%

That's right—in 2007 Google generated more than $16 billion in revenue, and $4 billion in profit. *Four billion dollars in profit.* That's not bad. Not bad at all.

Is Google a Search Company or an Advertising Company?

Let's take another look at Table 1.1 and focus on how Google's revenues were generated. In 2007, Google generated more than $16 billion in advertising revenues versus just $181 *million* in licensing and other revenues. In other words, Google generated just 1% of its revenues from direct technology-related activities. Fully 99% of its revenues came from selling advertising.

What's that, you say? What is a technology company like Google doing selling advertising?

Well, my friend, it's all about monetizing the technology—and when it comes to search technology, you monetize it with ads. Since you can't charge users for searching, you charge advertisers for placing their ads (or "sponsored listings") on the search results pages. So although Google appears to be a company focused on search services and technologies, it's really a highly targeted advertising company.

What does that mean to you, a loyal Google user? Maybe nothing. Or maybe it's possible that Google focuses at least as much on how to increase advertising revenues as it does on improving search results. Or maybe the two activities go hand in hand.

After all, Google's advertising-based revenue model is not unlike what you find in the magazine business. Magazines may charge you a bit on the newsstand, but they generate the bulk of their revenues from advertisers. And the more copies of the magazine they sell, the more they can charge their advertisers for a full-page ad.

It's the same with Google. The more eyeballs Google can deliver to its advertisers, the more it can charge for those "sponsored links." So as Google increases the number of site visitors, it ends up making more money from its advertisers. Google makes the experience better for users, it attracts more users, it charges more for advertising, it makes more money. That's the formula.

And how, exactly, does Google run its advertising business? There are actually two components to the business: *Google AdWords* and *Google AdSense*:

- AdWords sells targeted keywords to advertisers; when someone searches Google using one of those keywords, the advertiser's "sponsored listing" is displayed. Google gets paid (a penny or so) whenever someone clicks the advertiser's listing.

- AdSense is the flip side of AdWords. The AdSense program places small ads on non-Google websites. (So if you run your own website, you can sign up for the AdSense program to put ads on your site's pages.)

Google generates an appropriate ad based on the page's content; when a visitor clicks the ad, both Google and the site owner get paid.

> **note** There's a lot more to say about the AdWords and AdSense programs. To learn more, turn to Chapter 39, "Advertising with Google AdWords," and Chapter 40, "Profiting from Google AdSense."

Life at the Googleplex

So Google is a technology company that makes money from selling advertising. This kind of split personality is evident in Google's many offices around the world—some of which are strictly technology-based, and others of which are strictly sales-based.

> **note** The Googleplex is located at 1600 Amphitheatre Parkway, Mountain View, CA 94043. The main telephone number is 650-253-0000.

Google's world headquarters in Mountain View, California, is called the Googleplex. The Googleplex combines technology offices and sales offices, although it has a decidedly Silicon Valley flavor.

The Googleplex has been described as "a joint founded by geeks and run by geeks." I've never been there, myself, but I've been told that it has a decidedly nonhierarchical feel, kind of an anticorporate atmosphere, where employees move from project to project regularly and frequently. Walk down the hallway and you'll see everything from lava lamps to large rubber exercise balls; the typical office is a "high-density cluster" like the one shown in Figure 1.4, where three or four staffers share couches and computers. During lunch, employees of all levels socialize at the Google Café, and there's a workout room, massage room, washers and dryers, video games, a pool table, and a baby grand piano available for anyone's use. Google's a big company, but the Googleplex still has a small-company feel.

Of course, the Googleplex isn't the only Google office. Google has dozens of offices all around the world, including a handful of engineering-only offices (several in India), considerably more sales-only offices, and a few offices that, like the Googleplex, combine engineering and ad sales—all of which emphasizes the technology/sales dichotomy that drives the company.

FIGURE 1.4
A typical employee "cluster" at the Googleplex. (Photo courtesy of Google, Inc.)

How Google Works

Now that you have a better idea of what Google is and what it does, let's take a look at how it does what it does—in particular, how a Google search works. There's a lot of sophisticated technology behind even the simplest search.

How a Typical Search Works

The typical Google search takes less than half a second to complete. That's because all the searching takes place on Google's own web servers. That's right; you may think you're searching the Web, but in effect you're searching a huge index of websites stored on Google's servers. That index was created previously, over a period of time; because you're searching only a server, not the entire Web, your searches can be completed in the blink of an eye.

So what happens when you enter a query into the Google search box? The process looks something like what's shown in Figure 1.5.

note Google uses more than a half-million servers, located in clusters in its technology centers around the world. All of these servers run the Linux operating system. Google uses three types of servers: *web servers* (which host Google's public website), *index servers* (which hold the searchable index to the bigger document database), and *document servers* (which house copies of all the individual web pages in Google's database).

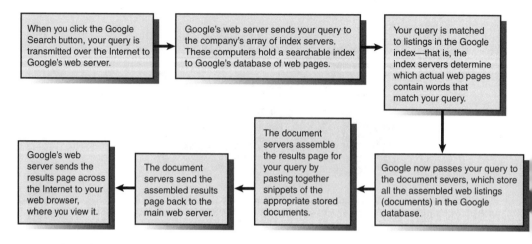

FIGURE 1.5

How a typical Google search is performed.

Of course, you're unaware of all this behind-the-scenes activity. You simply type your query into the search box on Google's main web page, click the Google Search button, and then view the search results page when it appears. All the shuffling of data from server to server is invisible to you.

How Google Builds Its Database—and Assembles Its Index

At the heart of Google's search system is the database of web pages stored on Google's document servers. These servers hold literally billions of individual web pages—not the entire Web, but a good portion of it.

How does Google determine which web pages to index and store on its servers? It's a complex process with several components.

First and foremost, most of the pages in the Google database are found by Google's special spider software. This is software that automatically crawls the Web, looking for new and updated web pages. Google's crawler, known as GoogleBot, not only searches for new web pages (by exploring links to other pages on the pages it already knows about), but it also recrawls pages already in the database, checking for changes and updates. A complete recrawling of the web pages in the

note Google's document servers store the full text of each web page in the Google database. Snippets of each page are extracted to create the page listings on Google's search results pages. In addition, these stored documents provide the cached pages that are linked to from the search results page.

Google database takes place every few weeks, so no individual page is more than a few weeks out of date.

The GoogleBot crawler reads each page it encounters, much like a web browser does. It follows every link on every page until all the links have been followed. This is how Google adds new pages to the database—by following links GoogleBot hasn't seen before.

> **note** GoogleBot is smart about how it updates the Google database. Web pages that are known to be frequently updated are crawled more frequently than other pages. For example, pages on a news site might be crawled hourly.

The pages discovered by GoogleBot are copied verbatim onto Google's document servers—and copied over each time they're updated. These web pages are used to compile the page summaries that appear on search results pages; they can also be viewed in their entirety when you click the Cached link in the search results. (These cached pages are a good way to view older versions of pages that have recently changed or been deleted.)

COMMENTARY

WHAT GOOGLE *ISN'T* GOOD AT

As big as Google's database is, there are still lots of web pages that don't make it into the database. In particular, Google doesn't do a good job of searching the "deep web," those web pages generated on-the-fly from big database-driven websites. Google also doesn't always find pages served by the big news sites, pages housed on web forums and discussion groups, blog pages, and the like.

These are all web pages with "dynamic" content that change frequently and don't always have a fixed URL; the URL—and the page itself—is generated on-the-fly, typically as a result of a search within the site itself.

This lack of a permanent URL makes these pages difficult, if not impossible, for GoogleBot to find. That's because GoogleBot, unlike a human being, can't enter a query into a site's search box and click the Search button. It has to take the pages it finds, typically the site's fixed home page. The dynamically generated pages slip through the cracks, so to speak.

This is why it's possible to search for a page that you know exists (you've seen it yourself!) but not find it listed in Google's search results. It's not a trivial problem; more and more of the Web is moving to dynamically generated content, leaving at least half the Internet beyond the capability of Google's crawler. Google has technicians working on this challenge, but it's a big-enough challenge that you shouldn't expect significant improvements anytime soon.

In order to search the Google database, Google creates an index to all the stored web pages. This search engine index is much like the index found in the back of this book; it contains a list of all the important words used on every stored web page in the database. Once the index has been compiled, it's easy enough to search for a particular word and have returned a list of all the web pages on which that word appears.

And that's exactly how the Google index and database work to serve your search queries. You enter one or more words in your query, Google searches its index for those words, and then the web pages that contain those words are returned as search results. This is fairly simple in concept but much more complex in execution—especially since Google is indexing all the words on several billion web pages.

How Google Ranks Its Results

Searching the Google index for all occurrences of a given word isn't all that difficult, especially with the computing power of more than a half-million servers driving things. What is difficult is returning the results in a format that is usable by and relevant to the person doing the searching. You can't just list the matching web pages in random order, nor are alphabetical or chronological order all that useful. No, Google has to return its search results with the most important or relevant pages listed first; it has to rank the results for its users.

Matching Pages to Queries

How does Google determine which web pages are the best match to a given query? I wish I could give you all the details behind the scheme, but Google keeps this core methodology under lock and key; it's what makes Google the most effective search engine on the Web today.

Even with all this secrecy, Google does provide some hints as to how its ranking system works. It has three components:

- **Text analysis.** Google looks not only for matching words on a web page, but also for how those words are used. That means examining font size, usage, proximity, and more than a hundred other factors to help determine relevance. Google also analyzes the content of neighboring pages on the same website to ensure that the selected page is the best match.

- **Links and link text.** Google then looks at the links (and the text for those links) on the web page, making sure that they link to pages that are relevant to the searcher's query.

- **PageRank.** Finally, Google relies on its own proprietary PageRank technology to give an objective measurement of web page importance and popularity. PageRank determines a page's importance by counting the number of other pages that link to that page. The more pages that link to a page, the higher that page's PageRank—and the higher it appears in the search results. The PageRank is a numerical ranking from 0 to 10, expressed as PR0, PR1, PR2, and so forth—the higher the better.

Understanding PageRank

Although the other factors are important, PageRank is the secret sauce behind Google's page rankings. The theory is that the more popular a page is, the higher that page's ultimate value. While this sounds a little like a popularity contest (and it is), it's surprising how often this approach delivers high-quality results.

The actual formula used by PageRank (called the *PageRank Algorithm*) is super-duper top-secret classified, but by all accounts it's calculated using a combination of quantity and quality of the links pointing to a particular web page. In essence, the PageRank Algorithm considers the importance of each page that initiates a link, figuring (rightly so) that some pages have greater value than others. The higher the PageRank of the pages pointing to a given page, the higher the PageRank of the linked-to page. It's entirely possible that a page with fewer, higher-ranked pages linking to it will have a higher PageRank than a similar page with more (but lower-ranked) pages linking to it.

The PageRank factor on the linking page is also affected by the number of total outbound links on that page. That is, a page with a lot of outbound links contributes a lower PageRank to each of its linked-to pages than a page with just a few outbound links. As an example, a page with PageRank of PR8 that has 100 outbound links will boost a linked-to page's PageRank less than a similar PR8 page with just 10 outbound links.

It's important to note that Google's determination of a page's rank is completely automated. No human subjectivity is involved, and no person or company can pay to increase the ranking of their listings. It's all about the math.

note PageRank is page-specific, not site-specific. This means that the PageRank of the individual pages on a website can (and probably will) vary from page to page.

note If you run a commercial website, it's in your best interest to optimize your site in whatever ways are necessary to maximize your Google PageRank. In fact, an entire website optimization industry has sprung up to help sites improve their PageRank scores. To learn more about manipulating Google's PageRank, see Chapter 38, "Optimizing Your Site for Google Search."

The Bottom Line

Google is one of those tech companies that started small (literally in a dorm room) and grew exponentially over the years. Its success is due to a focus on simplicity—a simple home page, a simple search process, and simple (yet relevant) results. There's a lot of complex technology behind the simplicity, of course, but however Google does it, it works.

And, to Google's credit, it has discovered how to make money (and lots of it) from what is essentially a free service. The searching may be free, but Google turns a profit by selling targeted ads (those "sponsored links") connected to specific search terms. Google makes money from its advertising customers without alienating its consumer customers—a very neat trick.

Google Labs: How Google Develops New Applications

A s you read through this book and discover all the various products and services currently offered by Google, it's tempting to think that the folks back at the Googleplex might be ready to sit back, relax a bit, and take a break. But you'd be wrong, because Google has even more search projects in the works, in an incubator it calls Google Labs.

Google Labs (labs.google.com) is where Google's search experts concoct all manner of cutting-edge search projects. It's like a mad scientist's playground—and it's where the *next* Google features are often found.

Projects That Started in the Labs

Google Labs is, for all intents and purposes, a research and development (R&D) lab. The intent is to create new products and services that can be launched publicly within the Google universe. Granted, some of these projects are more theoretical than others and eventually fall by the wayside. But many Google Labs projects have graduated into full-blown products and services that are now presented alongside Google's more established offerings.

Which Google services first saw life in Google Labs? Here's a short list:

- **GOOG-411.** Search for local businesses by voice from your cell phone (dial 1-800-GOOG-411).
- **Google Desktop.** Search data on your computer's hard disk.
- **Google Docs.** Create and share word processing and spreadsheet documents over the Web.
- **Google Glossary.** Look up definitions for specific words.
- **Google Groups 2.** Create and join topic-specific discussion groups.
- **Google Maps.** View maps and driving directions.
- **Google News Alerts.** Receive email alerts when new news stories appear online.
- **Google Notebook.** Clip and collect information as you browse the Web.
- **Google Personalized Search.** Get search results more relevant to you.
- **Google Reader.** Automatically display the latest articles and headlines from blogs and websites that offer RSS and Atom feeds.
- **Google Scholar.** Search scholarly journals and articles.
- **Google Search by Location.** Restrict your search to a specific geographic area.
- **Google SMS.** Search Google via your mobile phone.
- **Google Spreadsheets.** Create your own web-based spreadsheets.
- **Google Transit.** Plan trips using public transportation.
- **Google Video.** Search and download TV programs and videos.
- **Google Web Alerts.** Be notified of new web pages that match your search criteria.
- **iGoogle.** Create your own custom start page.

What's Cooking in Google Labs Today

At any given point in time, Google Labs has a dozen or so new projects percolating on the virtual test bench. Some of these projects will graduate into normal distribution; others will be incorporated into other products; and there will always be a few

> **note** The researchers at Google Labs are always working on new projects, so the projects available when you're reading this book may be different from the projects listed here.

that just don't cut it and eventually wither away. With that in mind, let's take a quick look at what's currently being tested in Google Labs.

Accessible Search

This is web search for the visually impaired. Try it out at labs.google.com/accessible/.

Experimental Search

This is where Google works to fine-tune your search experience. There are always several projects bubbling in this part of Google Labs, all having to do with different ways to present search results. Check out what's happening at www.google.com/experimental/.

Google Code Search

This is Google for programmers, located at www.google.com/codesearch. It lets you search the Web for publicly available source code.

Google Dashboard Widgets for Mac

If you like the gadgets in Google Desktop but currently use a Macintosh computer, you're in luck. Google Dashboard Widgets for Mac (www.google.com/macwidgets/) translates several popular Google Desktop sidebar gadgets into widgets for the Apple Dashboard.

Google Extensions for Firefox

If you're using Mozilla Firefox instead of Internet Explorer as your web browser, Google Extensions for Firefox (www.google.com/tools/firefox) lets you add a variety of browser extensions to provide new functionality.

Google Mars

If you like Google Maps and have an eye for the stars, you'll love Google Mars. Google Mars (www.google.com/mars) is essentially Google Maps for the red planet, using detailed Martian maps, as supplied by NASA.

Google Product Search for Mobile

Google Product Search for Mobile (labs.google.com/productswml.html) lets you do comparison shopping in the real world. Just whip out your mobile phone when you're in a store, and query Product Search for Mobile to see if the current price is a good one.

Google Ride Finder

Google Ride Finder (labs.google.com/ridefinder) is a Google Maps mashup that lets you view the locations of taxis, shuttles, and limousines. Google Ride Finder contains real-time information for 13 major cities—Atlanta, Baltimore, Chicago, Dallas, Los Angeles, New York, Phoenix, Portland, San Francisco, San Jose, Seattle, St. Louis, and Washington, DC.

> **note** Also available is a U.K. version of Product Search for Mobile (labs.google.com/intl/uk/productswml.html).

Google Sets

Google Sets (labs.google.com/sets) is a way to find words related to a given word. The idea is to enter a few words that make up a type of list, and then let Google try to predict other items in the list.

> **note** Learn more about Google Maps mashups in Chapter 28, "Creating Google Maps Mashups."

Google Suggest

Google Suggest (www.google.com/webhp?complete=1&hl=en) is a technology that offers keyword suggestions as you enter a Google search query.

> **note** Learn more about Google Sets in Chapter 13, "Searching for Specialty Information."

Google Trends

Google Trends (www.google.com/trends) builds on the top searches compiled in the Google Zeitgeist to form a huge database of user information. Using a variety of data-mining and analysis techniques, Google Trends lets you sort through search query data to determine the popularity of a given topic over time.

Lively by Google

Lively (www.lively.com) is a kind of 3D virtual world or social community. You pick a cartoon-like avatar to represent yourself onscreen and then interact with other users in real time.

> **note** Learn more about Lively in Chapter 17, "Chat in Virtual Worlds with Lively."

2

COMMENTARY

THE MOVING TARGET

Writing a book about Google is kind of like shooting at a moving target. That's because Google is constantly adding new features, services, and products—and updating all its existing ones. That's why this third edition of *Googlepedia* has so many new or revised chapters: The ever-changing Googleverse makes it necessary.

All these changes not only keep me on my toes as a writer, they also make it difficult for the average user to keep up with all the new stuff that Google is doing. Let's face it: The average Google user doesn't use much more than the basic search page, so it's easy to miss some of the cool new features that get added on a regular basis.

To that end, you should make it a habit to check out or subscribe to Googlepedia: The Blog (googlepedia.blogspot.com). I launched this blog to accompany this book and to keep readers like you informed about the latest changes in the Googleverse.

Another good source of information is the Official Google Blog (googleblog.blogspot.com). As the name implies, this is Google's official blog, which is where all new products and services are officially introduced on launch. This is where I find out about a lot of new features—there's something new every week!

The Bottom Line

Google's newest products and services are often tested first in Google Labs, which functions as Google's R&D arm. Many Google Labs projects have graduated into real-world use; others are still in testing for Google to determine if they appeal to a wide variety of users.

To find out what's cooking in Google Labs, go to labs.google.com. I know you'll find something interesting there!

2

Creating a Personalized Home Page with iGoogle

I f you've used Google search at all, you're undoubtedly familiar and comfortable with the spartan Google home page. But that's not the only way into the Google search engine. Google also offers a separate start page that you can use as a portal not just to Google, but to the entire World Wide Web.

This page is dubbed iGoogle, and it's totally customizable.

Welcome to iGoogle

To view your iGoogle page, go to www.igoogle.com. (You can also access the page by clicking the iGoogle link on the main Google page.) You must have a Google account to create your iGoogle page; you can then log into your account from any computer to see your iGoogle page wherever you are.

When you first visit iGoogle, it looks like the page shown in Figure 3.1. There's not a whole lot there yet, just a sampling of content available. (The available choices might be different for you than they are for me; they're somewhat locally based.) Don't fret; the whole point of creating a personal iGoogle page is to personalize the content—which you'll learn how to do next.

FIGURE 3.1
The default iGoogle page—not much content yet.

Adding Content to iGoogle

Personalizing iGoogle involves choosing which content you want to display, as well as how you want to display it. We'll start with the content-picking part.

To add content to your personalized page, start at the default iGoogle page and click

> **note** For the first year or so of its existence, iGoogle was known by the rather unwieldy title of Google Personalized Homepage. I like iGoogle a lot better.

the Add Stuff link. This displays the Add Gadgets to Your Homepage page, shown in Figure 3.2. This is where all the content resides.

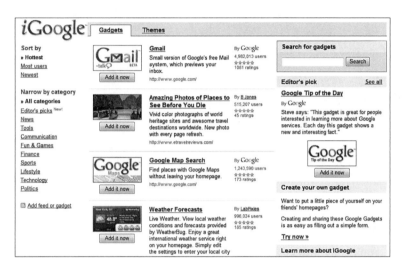

FIGURE 3.2

Displaying available iGoogle gadgets.

iGoogle's content is offered in a series of modules called *gadgets*; select a gadget, and it appears on your iGoogle page. The gadgets on the Add Gadgets to Your Homepage page are organized by type (News, Tools, Communication, and so on). To see modules of a particular type, just click a content link on the left side of the page.

Not surprisingly, Google also lets you search for gadgets to include on the iGoogle page. Just enter your query into the Search for Gadgets box at the top of this page, and then click the Search button; gadgets that match your query are displayed.

To view what a "live" gadget looks like (and to see more details about the content), click the gadget title; this displays a content information page like the one shown in Figure 3.3. To add a gadget to your iGoogle page, click the Add It Now button, either on the main gadget listing or on the detailed content information page.

FIGURE 3.3

Viewing detailed information about a particular iGoogle gadget.

Of course, you can add new gadgets to iGoogle at any time—not just when it's new. All you have to do is open your iGoogle page, click the Add Stuff link, and choose the gadget(s) you want.

Adding RSS Feeds

You're not limited to adding prepackaged content to iGoogle. You can also use iGoogle to display RSS feeds from blogs and other feed-enabled websites (including major news sites). All you need to know is the URL of the RSS feed, and then follow these steps:

1. From your iGoogle page, click the Add Stuff link.

2. When the Add Gadgets to Your Homepage page appears, click the Add Feed or Gadget link.

3. The page expands to include a box that says Type or Paste the URL Below. Enter the URL for the RSS feed into this box, and then click the Add button.

> **note** Some gadgets require additional information, such as your zip code, to work properly. You can add this information from the iGoogle page by editing the gadget in question, as we'll discuss later in this chapter.

Customizing Individual Gadgets

After you've added some gadgets to iGoogle, you may want to customize how they're displayed. Some gadgets let you specify the number of headlines that are displayed; others let you display information for a particular location.

> **note** Learn more about RSS feeds in Chapter 10, "Searching for Blogs and Blog Postings."

You customize a gadget by clicking the down arrow button on the gadget's title bar and then selecting Edit Settings.

If a gadget lets you change the number of headlines displayed, you see a pull-down number list, like the one shown in Figure 3.4. Select the number of stories from the list, and then click the Save button.

FIGURE 3.4
Select how many headlines to display from the pull-down list.

If particular content requires localization, selecting Edit Settings displays the necessary options for your selection. For example, Figure 3.5 shows the editing options for the Weather gadget. You can choose to display the temperature in Fahrenheit or Celsius, choose which country or region to display, and add cities that you want to view. Click the Add button, and the selected cities are added to the Weather gadget's display.

FIGURE 3.5
Adding cities to the Weather gadgets.

Removing Gadgets

It's easy to remove any gadget you no longer want to appear on your iGoogle page. Just click the X in the gadget's title bar, and the gadget is removed from the page. Simple.

Rearranging Gadgets on the Page

With some personalized start pages, you have to access a separate "design" page to rearrange content on the page. Not so with iGoogle. The iGoogle page has a set three-column design, and any gadget can appear anywhere in any column.

To rearrange content on iGoogle, all you have to do is use the mouse to drag a gadget to a different location. The layout of the page is "live" all the time. Just position the cursor in the gadget's title bar, click and hold the left mouse button, and then drag the gadget to where you want it to appear. It's that easy.

Adding New Tabs to iGoogle

Here's something else unique about iGoogle. Instead of putting all the content you want on a single page, iGoogle lets you create multiple tabs, each of which can be filled with different content.

To add a new tab to iGoogle, click the Add a Tab link. This displays the Add a Tab box, shown in Figure 3.6. Enter a name for your new tab, and then decide how lucky you feel.

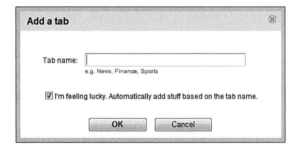

FIGURE 3.6
Adding a new tab to iGoogle.

What do I mean by that? Simple. You can manually add content to any tab, or you can let Google add content based on the tab's name. Let's say, for example, that you want to add a tab with movie-related content. Just enter **Movies** as the title of the tab, check the I'm Feeling Lucky option, and click OK. iGoogle creates a new Movies tab that is automatically populated with movie-related gadgets, as shown in Figure 3.7. Included gadgets include Yahoo! Movies, New York Times Movies, Top 5 Movies at the Box Office,

Fandango Movie Lister, Fandango Movie Showtimes, Netflix New Releases This Week, Rolling Stone Movie Reviews, Movies Opening This Week, and other similar items.

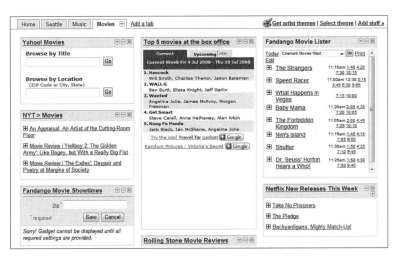

FIGURE 3.7
An automatically created iGoogle Movies tab.

If you don't want iGoogle to prepopulate your new tab, uncheck the I'm Feeling Lucky option. When you click OK, you get a new, empty tab that you can manually fill with gadgets of your choosing.

Customizing the Look of iGoogle with Themes

As soon as all your gadgets are organized the way you want them, you can decide how you want iGoogle to look, color- and graphics-wise. This is accomplished via the use of themes. You can apply different themes to different tabs.

To apply a theme to an iGoogle tab, click the Select Theme link. This displays the Add Themes to Your Homepage page, shown in Figure 3.8. Select the theme you want from the list, and then click the Add it Now button. The theme includes not only a specific color theme, but also graphics for the top of the iGoogle page.

> **tip**
> Find more iGoogle themes by clicking the Get Artist Themes link. These are themes designed by world-class artists.

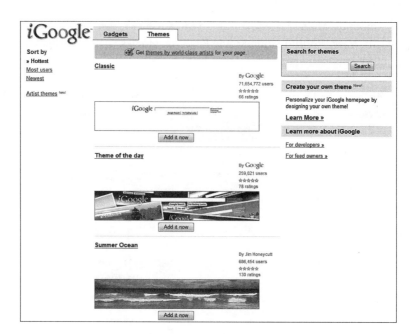

FIGURE 3.8

Choosing an iGoogle theme.

Your Final iGoogle Page

When you're done adding, editing, and deleting gadgets, you have a start page that's as personalized as you like. It's great to have all the content you're interested in assembled on a single page—and still have the handy Google search box at the top. Figure 3.9 shows what my personalized iGoogle page looks like. What about yours?

FIGURE 3.9
A fully customized iGoogle page.

Creating Your Own iGoogle Gadgets

There's one last thing I need to mention about iGoogle. You're not limited to the gadgets that Google and its third-party developers provide. You can actually create your own gadgets to include on your iGoogle page. It's quite easy.

From your main iGoogle page, click the Add Stuff link. When the Add Gadgets to Your Homepage page appears, click the Try Now link in the Create Your Own Gadget section.

As you can see in Figure 3.10, Google lets you create seven different types of gadgets:

- **Countdown**, which displays a countdown to any given event.
- **Daily Me**, which displays information about your current activities.
- **Framed Photo**, which displays a picture of your choice.
- **Free Form**, which lets you display any combination of image and text.
- **GoogleGram**, which displays a special message (along with a "gift" graphic)—one for each day of the week.

■ **Personal List**, which lets you display any type of list—favorite books, tunes, and so on.

■ **YouTube Channel**, which lets you display any number of YouTube videos.

FIGURE 3.10

iGoogle's Make Your Own Gadget page.

To create and add any of these gadgets to your iGoogle page, just click the gadget title. You're taken to a form page for that gadget; fill in the form with the appropriate information, and then click the Create Gadget button.

note After you create your gadget, you have the opportunity to invite others to view your gadget. You're also asked whether you want to publish your gadget to the Google gadget directory or keep it private (the default).

COMMENTARY

PERSONALIZED PORTAL VERSUS PURE SEARCH

For many years, one of the most attractive things about Google was its bare-bones, totally uncluttered home page. Unlike other former search-only sites, such as Yahoo!, Google resisted the urge to turn its search engine into a web portal. Google's search-only page was clean and to the point, whereas Yahoo! and similar sites were crammed with all manner of content.

To be honest, I hate the portalization of sites like Yahoo! and MSN. When I want to search, I want to search. I don't want to be distracted by unwanted and mostly irrelevant content. That's one of the reasons why Google long ago became my search site of choice.

On one level, the adoption of a portal-like approach for iGoogle disturbs me. On another level, I really like it. Oh, to be conflicted!

I'm disturbed because Google is all about purity of search, and throwing all this other stuff into the mix dilutes that purity. On the other hand, iGoogle does the personalized start page thing quite well; the results are at least as appealing as what you get with My Yahoo! (my.yahoo.com) or My Way (www.myway.com). And, to Google's credit, it has kept the personalized portal separate from the standard search page. When you want search and nothing but search, you still go to www.google.com. When you want the portal interface, you go to www.igoogle.com.

As long as Google continues to keep pure search separate from the personalized portal, it will please both types of users—searchers and browsers. Let's hope that the folks in Mountain View never abandon their core search audience, and that iGoogle is merely a supplement to what Google does best.

3

The Bottom Line

Although you can customize the "classic" Google home page somewhat, if you want a true personalized portal, you can turn to iGoogle. You retain the standard Google search box at the top of the page, but what goes below that is entirely up to you. Between Google's in-house developers and a small army of independent programmers, you can choose from hundreds of gadgets to add to your iGoogle page. The potential exists to create a home page that contains all the content you're interested in—a true gateway to the parts of the Web that most interest you, if that's your thing. If not, the traditional Google home page is still there, ready for your next search—and nothing but the search.

3

Creating a Custom Workspace with Google Desktop

You use the Google website to search the Web, but you need to find a lot of information on your own computer as well. So why can't you use Google to search your hard disk?

Well, you can, thanks to the Google Desktop software program. Google Desktop installs on your PC and automatically indexes all your data files, email messages, and the like. When you conduct a Google Desktop search, the program searches this index and returns a list of matching files and messages. It's just as easy as using the Google website, and it lets you find all those "lost" documents that are buried somewhere on your hard disk.

As an added bonus, Google Desktop includes a sidebar that sits on your computer desktop and provides access to different content modules (called *gadgets*—just like the iGoogle gadgets you learned about in the preceding chapter). Assuming that you have the available desktop real estate, the Google Desktop sidebar lets you view your Gmail inbox, the latest news, local weather conditions, your instant-messaging contacts, and lots, lots more, all stacked together on the edge of your computer screen.

I'm not sure what's best about Google Desktop, the local searching or the sidebar content. They're both really cool and very useful, so read on to learn more.

Welcome to the Google Desktop

At first glance, the Google Desktop is a sidebar that sits to the right of your computer desktop, as shown in Figure 4.1. The content of the sidebar is totally customizable. As you'll learn later in this chapter, you can add a variety of gadgets to the sidebar, each with a different and unique function.

FIGURE 4.1

Google Desktop installed on your computer desktop—it's all in the sidebar on the right side of the screen.

The sidebar, however, is just the icing on the cake. The key ingredient in the Google Desktop is a PC-centric version of the Google search engine. After it's installed, you use Google Desktop to search your hard disk (or your entire network) for files and email messages that match a specific query. You do your searching from your web browser, which displays a special Google Desktop page. It works pretty much like a standard Google web search, except that it doesn't search the Web—it searches the contents of your computer's hard disk.

note Google Desktop is available for computers running Windows 2000/XP/Vista; slightly different versions of Google Desktop are available for Linux and the Mac OS.

With all this functionality, you might expect Google Desktop to cost an arm and a leg. Well, you can hold onto your limbs, because Google Desktop is freeware. You can download it free of charge from desktop.google.com.

When you first download Google Desktop, a few things happen. First, the default sidebar is built and displayed on your desktop; you'll be able to configure this to your liking later. Second, the Google Desktop search engine starts up and begins to index the contents of your PC. Depending on the size of your hard disk and how much of it is used, this could take anywhere from a few minutes to a few hours. Although you can use Google Desktop while this index is being created, you probably don't want to conduct any searches until all your disk's contents have been indexed.

What types of items does Google Desktop index? Not every type of file, obviously; for example, it doesn't index executable program files. Here's the complete list of what's indexed:

- Email (including messages from Microsoft Outlook, Outlook Express, Windows Mail, Gmail, Mozilla Thunderbird, and Netscape Mail)
- Chats (from Google Talk, AOL Instant Messenger, and MSN Messenger)
- Web history (.htm and .html files from Internet Explorer, Mozilla Firefox, and Netscape browsers)
- Microsoft Word documents (.doc files)
- Microsoft Excel spreadsheets (.xls and .xlw files)
- Microsoft PowerPoint presentations (.ppt files)
- Adobe Acrobat documents (.pdf files)
- Media files (image files, audio files, and video files)
- Text files (.txt format)
- Other files from Microsoft Outlook and similar programs (contacts, calendar appointments, tasks, notes, and journal entries)
- Compressed files (.zip files—including the full content of each compressed file)

4

Searching Your Hard Disk

Google Desktop is really two applications under a single guise. The sidebar, which we'll discuss later in this chapter, is actually separate from the desktop search engine.

Conducting a Basic Search

There are several ways to search your computer with Google Desktop:

- Click the Google Desktop icon in the Windows taskbar tray, and select Search Desktop.
- Use the Google search gadget in the Desktop sidebar.
- Select Start, All Programs, Google Desktop, Google Desktop.
- Press the Ctrl key twice to display a Quick Search Box on the desktop.

Depending on which method you use to start your search, you may see a Quick Search Box in the middle of the screen, as shown in Figure 4.2, or Google Desktop may launch its own search page in your web browser, as shown in Figure 4.3. This browser page looks almost identical to the main Google web page. The main differences are that you're not connected to the Internet, the search function is set to Desktop, and a few new options appear at the bottom of the page.

FIGURE 4.2

The Google Desktop desktop search window.

FIGURE 4.3

The Google Desktop search page.

Searching your hard disk is as easy as entering a query into the search box and then pressing Enter or clicking the Search Desktop button. (If you click the Search the Web button instead, Google Desktop connects to the main Google website and initiates a traditional web search.)

Viewing Your Results

The results of your search are displayed, as shown in Figure 4.4. This search results page looks a bit different from a standard web search results page, for two reasons.

FIGURE 4.4

The results of a Google Desktop search.

First, the results are, by default, sorted by date instead of relevance, with the most recent results listed first. (You can switch to a relevance list by clicking the Sort by Relevance link at the top of the page.)

Second, the results page contains several different types of results. The type of item found is easily discerned by the icon next to each search result. For example, email messages have an envelope icon, Word files have the Word document icon, and web pages have an icon representing the web page's logo or a generic web page icon.

> **tip**
> Several types of items (such as .jpg files, MP3 files, and some recently visited web pages) also have a thumbnail of that item displayed to the right of the item listing. Click the thumbnail to view the item (or, if it's a web page, a cached version of the page).

For each item listing, Google Desktop displays the item or filename, a brief description of or excerpt from the item, and the location of the file on your hard disk. You can open the file by clicking the filename, or open the folder that holds the file by clicking the Open Folder link. Click the Cached link to view a cached version of the folder contents; click the date link to view all items created on the same date. (This last option is good for finding related email messages.)

Filtering Your Results

By default, Google Desktop displays all items in the same list. You can filter the list, however, to display only a single type of item by clicking the Emails, Files, Web History, Chats, or Other links at the top of the page.

Depending on the type of item displayed, you may have additional filtering options from the view list. For example, if you display just emails, you can filter the results to include only those messages to or from specific users. If you display just files, you can filter the results to include only specific file types. If you display "other" items, you can filter the results to include only contacts, calendar appointments, tasks, and the like.

Conducting an Advanced Desktop Search

Of course, it's often easier to refine your query than it is to filter your results. To that end, Google Desktop offers a Search Options page, accessible by clicking the Advanced Search link on the main page. As you can see in Figure 4.5, this page offers various filters you can apply to your query—although the filters available vary by the type of item you're searching for. Table 4.1 details the available options.

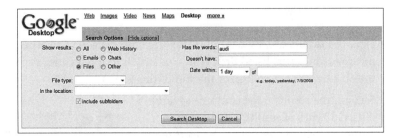

FIGURE 4.5

Fine-tuning your search from the Search Options page.

Table 4.1   Google Desktop Search Options

Type of Search	Available Options
All	*Has the words, Doesn't have,* and *Date within* (search within a date range)
Emails	*To:* and *From:* (restricts the search to emails sent to or from specific users)
Files	*File type* and *In the location* (restricts the search to specific file types or files stored within a specific folder); also, the option to include subfolders in the search
Web History	*In the site* (restricts the search to pages viewed on a specific website)
Chats	No specific options available
Other	*Other types* (restricts the search to contacts, appointments, tasks, notes, and journal entries)

Viewing Items in Timeline View

Searching by keyword is how most people find things on their hard drives, but sometimes it's not the best way to approach the problem. There are times when you remember *when* you sent or received a message or created a file, not necessarily *what* the message or file was about.

For these times, Google Desktop offers the Timeline view. This view lets you see everything created or modified on a particular day.

You access Timeline view by clicking the Browse Timeline link on the main Google Desktop page. As you can see in Figure 4.6, Timeline view lists all your desktop items by date, in reverse chronological order (newest first), starting with today. You can view items from another date by clicking that date on the calendar on the right side of the page. You can also filter items to display only emails, files, web history, or chats.

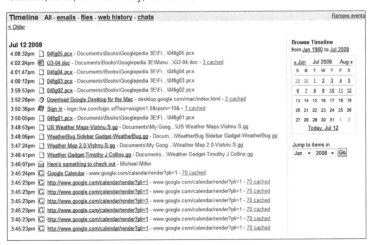

FIGURE 4.6

Viewing items by date in the Timeline view.

Viewing the Contents of Your Index

Want to see exactly what (and how much) Google Desktop has indexed? Click the Index Status link on the main Google Desktop page. This displays the Desktop Status page, shown in Figure 4.7. It lists how many emails, chats, web pages, files, and total items Google Desktop has indexed, as well as the time of the most recent item in each category.

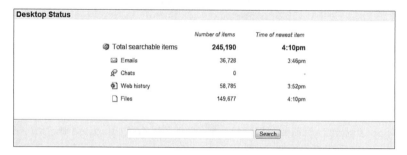

Desktop Status		
	Number of items	Time of newest item
Total searchable items	**245,190**	**4:10pm**
Emails	36,728	3:46pm
Chats	0	.
Web history	58,785	3:52pm
Files	149,677	4:10pm

FIGURE 4.7

Viewing how many items Google Desktop has indexed, on the Desktop Status page.

Searching Within Microsoft Outlook

When you install Google Desktop, it also installs a special search bar in Microsoft Outlook (assuming you're using Outlook, of course). This lets you search Outlook's emails directly from the Outlook program—no need to start up Google Desktop separately.

As you can see in Figure 4.8, the Google Desktop toolbar installs at the far right of the normal Outlook toolbar. Enter your query and click the Search button to search all your Outlook mailboxes; matching emails are listed in a separate search results window, as shown in Figure 4.9. Double-click any item to open and view the email message.

FIGURE 4.8

The Google Desktop toolbar in Microsoft Outlook.

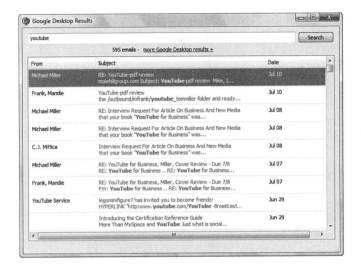

FIGURE 4.9
Results from searching your Outlook email messages.

Searching Other Computers on Your Network

Google Desktop isn't limited to searching your PC's hard disk. You can also use it to search other computers on your wireless or Ethernet network.

To use Google Desktop across multiple computers on a network, you must have a Google account (just one), and you must have copies of Google Desktop installed on all computers you want to include in the search. The reason you need a Google account is that each computer's index is transmitted via the Internet to Google's servers; when you search "across computers" you're actually searching the index for your network, as stored on Google's servers.

To set up Google Desktop to search across multiple computers, follow these steps:

1. Open Google Desktop, and click the Desktop Preferences link. (Alternatively, you can right-click the Google Desktop icon in the Windows system tray, and select Preferences from the pop-up menu.)

tip Because the index information for all your PCs is stored on Google's servers, you can use this feature to view your desktop PC's files and messages from your laptop PC when you're on the road—or vice versa. Just make sure that Google Desktop is running on both PCs, and that they're both connected to the Internet.

2. When the Preferences page appears, select the Google Account Features tab, as shown in Figure 4.10.

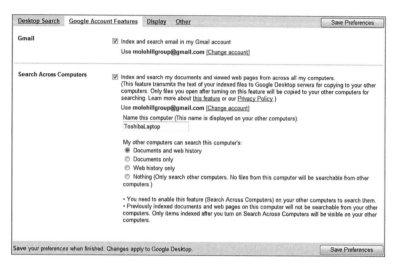

FIGURE 4.10

Configuring Google Desktop to search across multiple computers.

3. From this tab, go to the Search Across Computers section, and check the main option.

4. Enter a name for this computer.

5. Check which items from this PC you want to be able to search from other PCs: documents and web history, documents only, web history only, or nothing. (The "nothing" option lets this computer search other computers but doesn't let them search this PC.)

6. Click the Save Preferences button.

You need to repeat these steps for each computer you want to include in the Google Desktop search. You also need to log onto the same Google account on each PC; this is how Google keeps track of the computers to include in the search index.

Searching the Web from Google Desktop

The Google Desktop program not only lets you search your desktop, it also lets you conduct normal Google web searches—assuming your computer is connected to the Internet, that is. (You don't have to be connected to the Internet to search your own computer, of course.) There are several ways you can do this; we'll look at each in turn.

Searching from the Google Desktop Window

If you have the Google Desktop window open, searching the Web is a snap. Just enter your query as normal, and then click the Search the Web button (instead of the Search Desktop button). Google Desktop connects to the Google website and displays the expected page of search results.

Searching from the Sidebar

The Google Desktop sidebar includes a standard search box, as shown in Figure 4.11. To search the Web from the sidebar, enter your query and wait for the menu of options to appear. From this menu, select Search Web and then press Enter. Your web search results appear in a new browser window.

FIGURE 4.11

The Google Desktop sidebar search box.

Searching from the Deskbar

Another Google Desktop option is to display a *deskbar* on your desktop; this is a search box that appears in the Windows taskbar, as shown in Figure 4.12. You can use this search box to search the Web, just like a sidebar search. Just enter your query, select the Search Web option, and press the Enter key. (If you pause while typing, you see the same menu of search options as you do with the normal sidebar search.)

FIGURE 4.12

Searching the Web from the Google Desktop deskbar.

Using the Google Desktop Sidebar

As I noted in the introduction to this chapter, Google Desktop is more than just a desktop search. It's also about putting more information on your desktop via the Google Desktop sidebar.

The Google Desktop sidebar resides on the far right of your computer desktop (by default, anyway—you can change this) and includes a variety of content modules, which Google calls *gadgets*. You can choose from hundreds of different gadgets to display all sorts of information.

Different Ways to Display the Sidebar

The sidebar is activated by default when you first install the Google Desktop program. You can turn it off by clicking the down arrow at the top of the sidebar to display the pull-down menu and then selecting Close. To redisplay the sidebar, right-click the Google Desktop icon in the Windows system tray and select Sidebar from the pop-up menu.

By default, the sidebar appears on the right side of your desktop. You can move it to the left side of the desktop by displaying the menu and selecting Dock Sidebar, Left. To change the width of the sidebar, just drag the left (or right) side of the sidebar until the sidebar is the desired size.

If you don't want the sidebar taking up all that screen real estate, consider using the auto-hide feature. When this option is selected, the sidebar is hidden until you move the cursor to the far-right side of the screen. When you do this, the sidebar pulls out for your use. To activate auto-hide, pull down the menu and select Auto-Hide.

Working with Sidebar Gadgets

The fun thing about using the Google Desktop sidebar is selecting which gadgets you want displayed. Tons of gadgets are available; you can insert as many as you have room for.

To add a new gadget to the sidebar, click the Add (+) button that appears when you mouse over a category. This displays the Add Gadgets window, as shown in Figure 4.13. From here you can view gadgets in a number of different categories (New, Recommendations, Google Created, News, Sports,

Lifestyle, and so on); click the Add button under a gadget to add it to your sidebar.

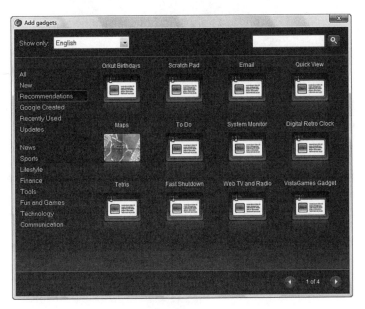

FIGURE 4.13

Selecting new gadgets for the sidebar.

To remove any gadget from the sidebar, click the down arrow in that gadget's title bar, and then select Remove. (You can always restore the gadget by clicking the Add button at the top of the sidebar if you like.)

In the sidebar, any gadget can be displayed at any height, or collapsed to just its title bar. Making a gadget taller or shorter is a simple matter of dragging the top or bottom border up or down using the mouse. You collapse the gadget by clicking the gadget's down arrow and then selecting Collapse.

You can rearrange the gadgets in your sidebar in any order. It's a dynamic process; just grab the gadget's title bar with the mouse and drag it into a new position. The other gadgets rearrange themselves to make room for the moved gadget.

Most gadgets have an expanded view, which you display by clicking the left arrow in the gadget's title bar. This expands the gadget to the left, where (in most cases) more options are available than in the standard gadget. (Using the expanded view is also a necessity when you have the gadget collapsed.) For example, Figure 4.14 shows the expanded view of the Photos gadget.

FIGURE 4.14

The Photos gadget in expanded view.

Individual gadgets can also be undocked from the sidebar. When you click the down arrow in the gadget title bar and then select Undock from Sidebar, the gadget is moved from the sidebar to its own window on the desktop. (Figure 4.15 shows the undocked version of the Weather Globe gadget.) To redock a gadget, click the gadget's down arrow and select Dock to Sidebar.

FIGURE 4.15

An undocked gadget.

COMMENTARY

GADGETS AND WIDGETS

The concept of putting content modules on your desktop didn't start with Google Desktop. The most recent implementation of this concept is Apple's Dashboard, which lets you add a variety of "widgets" to the Mac desktop. It's proven very popular.

On the Windows side, the widget concept was adopted by Konfabulator, which was subsequently purchased by Yahoo! and renamed (not surprisingly) Yahoo! Widgets. Like the Apple Dashboard, Yahoo! Widgets can be placed anywhere on your computer desktop; each widget is a separate mini-application that floats above the desktop, ready for your use.

Even more competition was introduced when Microsoft shipped its Windows Vista operating system. Vista includes its own Sidebar, which looks and feels a lot like the Google Desktop sidebar. The Windows Sidebar, of course, is built into the operating system; like the Google Desktop sidebar, it sits on the side of the screen and is filled with individual gadgets.

All these widgets and gadgets are designed with the same goal in mind—to put more content, information, and functions at your fingertips. It's handier to have these content modules floating on the desktop or docked on a sidebar than it is to dig through layers of menus to open each application individually. For that reason, I'm a big fan of all these sidebars. It's just a matter of choosing the one that has the best gadgets!

The Bottom Line

I liked Google Desktop even before it added the sidebar. The ability to quickly and easily search your hard disk for files and emails is something that should be built into the operating system, but Windows' built-in search function has been notoriously slow and quirky; Google Desktop does it a lot better. (Sorry, Microsoft.) Add the sidebar and all that marvelous gadget content, and you have a winning application—one that's both useful and fun.

Trust me on this one: After you install Google Desktop, you'll use the desktop search a lot, and you'll constantly be trying out new sidebar gadgets. The desktop search is an invaluable tool, and the sidebar is just plain addictive. It's something you'd pay for—except you don't have to, because it's free.

Using the Google Toolbar

Believe it or not, I seldom use Google's website—even though I search with Google a dozen or more times a day. That's because you don't have to go to the Google site to use Google search. If you have the Google Toolbar installed in your web browser, you can conduct all your searches from the Toolbar's search box, so there's no need to open the Google web page.

Even better, the Google Toolbar provides a wealth of direct shortcuts to some of Google's most popular functions and services. If you're a big Google user, installing the Google Toolbar is a must; it will save you a ton of time.

Getting to Know the Google Toolbar

If you use Google a lot (and use a recent version of Internet Explorer), you'll like the Google Toolbar. Everything you normally do on the Google site is right there on the Toolbar, just a click away. It's easy to use and—even better—it doesn't take up much screen real estate.

> **tip** If you use Mozilla Firefox instead of Internet Explorer as your web browser, Google offers a version of its Google Toolbar just for Firefox users. It's quite similar to the IE Toolbar, but with a few Firefox-specific features.

To install the Google Toolbar, go to toolbar.google.com and click the Download Google Toolbar button. Follow the onscreen instructions to download the software and complete the installation.

After it is installed, the Google Toolbar appears just below the other toolbars in your web browser. You can customize the Toolbar to display a variety of buttons; Figure 5.1 shows the default configuration.

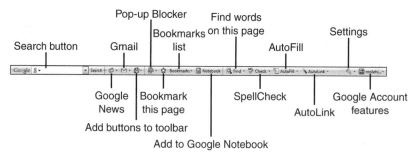

FIGURE 5.1

The Google Toolbar in its default configuration.

We'll look at these and other available features next.

Using the Google Toolbar's Default Buttons

The Google Toolbar, in its default configuration, displays a variety of buttons you can click for direct access to various Google features. And, as you'll learn later in this chapter, you can add even more buttons to the Toolbar than what you see by default.

Let's take a quick look at each of the available buttons for the Google Toolbar.

Enhanced Search Box

Probably the most important part of the Google Toolbar is the search box. This is the thing that I constantly use. Just enter your query into the search box and click the Search button, and you'll conduct a Google web search without having to first go to the Google website.

note This chapter describes version 5 of the Internet Explorer version of the Google Toolbar. If you're using a previous version, upgrade today to get the latest features.

If that's all the Google Toolbar offered, it would be plenty. But what at first glance appears to be a standard search box is in fact an *enhanced* search box, offering more features than what you get on the Google site itself.

tip You can make the Toolbar's search box wider or narrower by dragging the separator to the right of the Search button.

You can see how the enhanced search box works just by entering a new query. As you type your query, the Toolbar displays a list of useful suggestions. This list is based on popular searches from other users, spelling corrections, and your own search history and bookmarks. If your query is displayed in this list, just select it and press Enter.

You can also use the Toolbar to perform more than just standard web searches. Click the G button (with the down arrow) in the search box, and you see a drop-down menu full of other Google searches you can perform, such as searching Google Images, Google News, or Google Maps. Select a search from this list and finish entering your query. When you click Search, your search is directed as noted.

Google News

This one's easy. Click the Google News button, and you go directly to the Google News site.

Gmail

This is another easy one. Click this button to go to your Gmail page and see what messages are waiting for you in your inbox. (Learn more about Gmail in Chapter 14, "Sending and Receiving Email with Gmail.")

note Learn more about Google News in Chapter 30, "Keeping Up-to-Date with Google News."

Add More Buttons

Click the down arrow to choose from a
select list of additional buttons for the
Toolbar. Click a tab to view buttons in a
particular category—Popular, News, Tools,
and More. Or click Visit the Complete
Button Gallery to view all available buttons in a new browser page. (See the
"Adding and Removing Buttons on the Google
Toolbar" section, later in this chapter, for more information.)

note If you're using a version of Internet
Explorer with a built-in pop-up
blocker, you don't need to use
Google's pop-up blocker, too.
They work in pretty much the
same fashion, and one is as good
as the other.

Pop-up Blocker

The Google Toolbar includes its own pop-up blocker, the better to block those
pesky pop-up windows. The "x blocked" number on the button tells you how
many pop-ups it has blocked.

To allow pop-ups on any given page, just click this button. Click the button
again to turn the pop-up blocker back on.

Bookmarks

The Google Toolbar lets you create a set of bookmarks separate from those
normally stored in your web browser. The advantage of these Google bookmarks is that they can follow you from computer to computer; when you log
onto your Google account, your stored bookmarks are displayed in whichever
browser you're using at the time.

To bookmark the current page, all you have to do is click the Bookmark button. (That's the one with the blue star.) To view all your bookmarks, click the
Bookmarks button (that's plural—the one with the down arrow).

Google Notebook

Google Notebook is a way to clip and collect information from the pages you
visit on the Web. Just select the text or image you want to clip, and click the
Google Notebook button on the Toolbar. When the Google Notebook pop-up
appears, select the notebook you want to save to, and click the Clip button.
The text or graphics you selected are pasted into the notebook you selected.

Find

Looking for a particular word or phrase on the current web page? Click the Find button; this opens a new search bar at the bottom of the browser window, as shown in Figure 5.2. Enter the word you're looking for, and click the Next or Previous button to find that word later or earlier on the page.

note Learn more about Google Notebook in Chapter 7, "Saving Your Searches—and Signing Up for Google Alerts."

FIGURE 5.2

Searching for a word on the current web page.

SpellCheck

This isn't one of the most useful buttons, in my opinion—but then, I'm a pretty good speller. What the SpellCheck button does is find any spelling mistakes you've made when typing data into a web form. This in itself isn't that useful, but it also works as a spell checker for any web-based email service, such as Gmail. Click the SpellCheck button to go through the words you've typed one at a time. Click the down arrow and select AutoFix to have the spell checker automatically correct any misspelled words, without your input.

tip You can also highlight the word or phrase in question by clicking the Highlight All button on the search bar.

AutoFill

AutoFill is one of my favorite features of the Google Toolbar. When you activate this feature, clicking the AutoFill button automatically completes web forms with the personal information you've previously entered. Given the increasing number of forms on all manner of websites, it's a great time-saver.

Before you can use AutoFill, of course, you have to enter the data you want to use to fill in all those forms. Here's what you do:

caution AutoFix works only if the spell checker correctly identifies misspelled words—and correctly guesses what word you intended to type. Life being what it is, you might introduce more errors with AutoFix than it actually fixes.

1. Click the Adjust Toolbar Features button, and select Options.

2. When the Toolbar Options dialog box appears, select the AutoFill tab, shown in Figure 5.3.

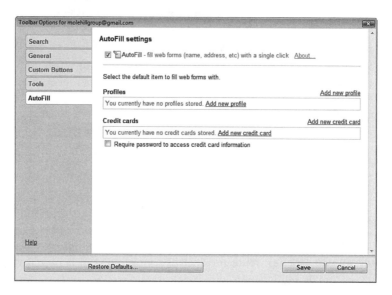

FIGURE 5.3

Entering your AutoFill information.

3. Activate AutoFill by checking the AutoFill option.

4. To add your personal information, click the Add New Profile link, and then fill in the appropriate information—name, email address, postal address, and so on.

5. To enter your credit card data (necessary if you want to use AutoFill for online shopping), click the Add New Credit Card link, and then fill in the appropriate information—card number, expiration date, and so on. If you want to require a password before the credit card info is automatically filled in, check the Require Password to Access Credit Card Information, and enter the desired password.

6. Click the Save button when done.

You enter data with AutoFill simply by clicking the AutoFill button whenever a web form is displayed. If you use AutoFill to automatically enter credit card information, you'll be prompted to supply a password before entering credit card numbers.

AutoLink

When AutoLink is activated, Google automatically evaluates each page you load for addresses, locations, and the like. When it finds these items on a web page, the AutoLink button changes its text label appropriately. For example, if it finds a street address, it changes to a Look for Map button, and clicking the address links to a Google Map of that location. If AutoLink finds an ISBN for a book on a page, it changes to a Show Book Info button, and clicking the ISBN links to that book's page on Amazon.com.

AutoLink can also link package-tracking numbers to delivery status, VINs to vehicle history, and other information. It's kind of cool; give it a try and see what it finds!

Adjust Toolbar Options

This button lets you configure the Toolbar, as we'll discuss in a moment. Click the down arrow next to this button if you need help using the Toolbar or if you want to uninstall it.

Access Google Account Features

If you want to apply your Google Toolbar settings to another computer where you have the Toolbar installed, click the far-right button on the Toolbar. This saves your settings online with your Google Account; when you open the Toolbar in another browser on another computer, it automatically goes online and downloads your saved settings.

Adding and Removing Buttons on the Google Toolbar

So far, we've discussed just those buttons that are displayed by default when you install the Google Toolbar in your web browser. But many more buttons are available—once you know how to add them.

Adding New Buttons

You add and remove buttons to and from the Google Toolbar by clicking the Add Buttons button on the Toolbar. A short list of available buttons is displayed when you click the down arrow next to the Add

tip If you have more buttons activated than can fit horizontally on the Toolbar, a "more buttons" button appears on the far right of the Toolbar, just to the left of the static Settings button. Click this button to display a list of the remaining buttons you have installed.

Buttons button; they are organized by category. Click the tab to view the buttons in each category.

These are just a subset of all the available buttons, however. Click the main Add Buttons button, and then click the View the Complete Button Gallery Link. You're sent to the Web for a page full of Toolbar buttons. As you can see in Figure 5.4, tons of buttons are available from this page; you can search for specific buttons or browse buttons by category.

FIGURE 5.4

Viewing additional buttons for the Google Toolbar.

To add a button to the Toolbar, simply click the Add to Toolbar button.

Removing Buttons

To remove a button from the Toolbar, click the Adjust Toolbar Options button on the Toolbar, and select the Custom Buttons tab. Uncheck the buttons you want to remove, and then click OK.

Other Ways to Search Google from Your Web Browser

The Google Toolbar is just one way to search Google from within your web browser. You also can employ a few other tools—all of which let you search directly, without having to go to the Google website.

> **note** You can even create your own custom Google Toolbar buttons—provided that you know how to program with the Google API. Learn more in Chapter 43, "Using Google's APIs and Developer's Tools."

Making Google Your Default Search Engine in Internet Explorer

As you can see in Figure 5.5, Internet Explorer 7 features an integrated search box at the top-right corner of the screen, next to the address box. You can configure Internet Explorer to send your queries to any specific search engine; just enter a query and click the search button (the magnifying glass icon) to view a page of search results.

FIGURE 5.5

The integrated search box in Internet Explorer 7.

Because this is a book about Google, I'll tell you how to configure Internet Explorer to use Google as its default search engine. All you have to do is click the down arrow next to the search box and select Find More Providers. This displays a page full of search sites; click the link for Google (in the Web Search section) and, when prompted, confirm your selection.

When you next enter a query into the Internet Explorer search box, that query is sent to Google, and IE displays a page of Google search results. It's that easy.

Installing Google Browser Buttons

You can also add special Google browser buttons to your web browser's Links or personal toolbar. You can add these buttons to either the Internet Explorer or Netscape browsers (versions 4.0 and later).

You can add two buttons:

- **Google Search.** Initiates a Google search when you highlight any word on a web page and then click this button.
- **Google.com.** Takes you to the Google home page.

To install these Google browser buttons in your web browser, go to www.google.com/options/buttons.html and click the Get Your Google Buttons Here link. Follow the onscreen instructions to complete the installation.

The Bottom Line

I love the Google Toolbar. I use it several times every day—if not every hour. In fact, I seldom go to the Google home page; instead, I do all my searching from the Toolbar. I also like the Send To button when creating blog entries, the optional Gmail button for checking my inbox messages, and the AutoFill button for automatically entering data into web forms. All in all, I recommend that all Google users add the Google Toolbar to their browsers; it is perhaps the fastest way to do your Google searching.

5

Searching with Google

Getting the Most Out of Google Search

O f all the products and services that Google offers, none is more popular than its original web search engine. In Chapter 1, "Inside Google," you discovered how a Google web search works, from a behind-the-scenes perspective. In this chapter you'll learn how to conduct an effective—and efficient—search, using Google's basic search page, powerful advanced search operators, and the relatively easy-to-use Advanced Search page.

Conducting a Basic Search

One of the things that has made Google so popular is its ease of use. From the spartan nature of the main Google search page to the ease of use of the search feature, a Google search is so effortless that just about anyone can do it, without a lot of effort or instruction.

Behind the simplicity, however, is a powerful search engine that can provide highly refined results. That said, you have to know a little more than "query and enter" to gain benefit from all this power. Read on to learn more.

Navigating Google's Home Page

We'll start our examination of a basic Google search with Google's home page, located at www.google.com. Google's home page, shown in Figure 6.1, is almost shocking in its simplicity. Unlike what you find with Yahoo! and other web search portals, Google's home page has no category listings, no news headlines, no stock tickers, no weather reports, and no blatant advertisements. All you see is the Google logo, the search box, two search buttons (Google Search and I'm Feeling Lucky), and some links to additional search services. It's clean, simple, and fast.

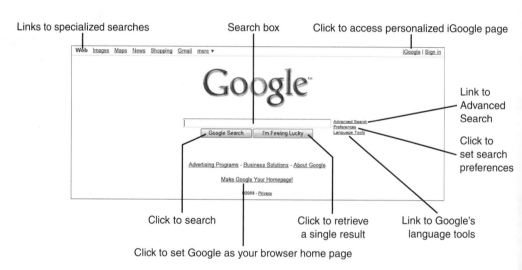

FIGURE 6.1

Google's main search page.

Entering Your Query

Initiating a basic search is incredibly easy. All you have to do is follow these steps:

1. Enter your query, consisting of one or more keywords, into the search box.

2. Click the Google Search button.

That's all there is to it. Enter your query, click the Search button, and wait for the search results page to appear.

Feeling Lucky?

Google is so sure of its capability to generate high-quality results that it puts an I'm Feeling Lucky button on its home page, right next to the Google Search button. When you click this button, you skip the standard search results page and go directly (and blindly!) to the page that is the number-one match to your query. (I don't often use the I'm Feeling Lucky button, I confess, because I seldom want to see just a single result.)

How Google Displays Its Results

After you click the Google Search button, Google searches its index for all the web pages that match your query. Then it displays the results on a search results page, like the one shown in Figure 6.2. We'll look at each part of this page separately.

6

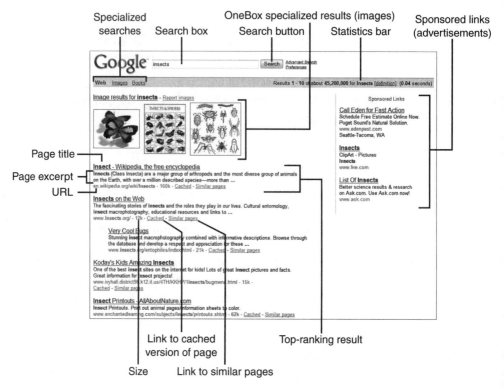

Specialized searches · Search box · OneBox specialized results (images) · Search button · Statistics bar · Sponsored links (advertisements)

Page title · Page excerpt · URL

Link to cached version of page

Size · Link to similar pages · Top-ranking result

FIGURE 6.2

A Google search results page.

- **Search box.** This is where you enter a new search query—just like on Google's home page.

- **Search button.** Click here, after you've entered your query, to initiate the search.

- **Statistics bar.** This bar displays how many results were returned for your query, and how long it took to display those results. In many cases, this bar also includes a link to a definition of the keyword.

- **Specialized searches.** Located on the left side of the statistics bar, click one of these links to narrow your query to a specific type of search. The available searches depend on what you're searching for; in Figure 6.2, you can click to perform an image search or book search.

- **OneBox specialized results.** With some searches, Google displays a short list of specialized search results—images, news stories, maps, and the like. These are displayed near the top of the main search results.

- **Sponsored links.** These are links paid for by Google's advertisers. You should not confuse these links with the main search results; they may have only indirect relevance to your query. These sponsored links typically are positioned to the right of the main search results, and sometimes above the main results.

- **Page title.** For each search result, Google displays the title of the page. The title is a clickable link; click it to view the linked-to page.

- **Page excerpt.** Below the page title is an excerpt from the associated web page. This may be the first few sentences of text on the page, a summary of page contents, or something similar.

- **URL.** This is the full web address of the selected web page. It is *not* a clickable link; you have to click the page title to jump to the page.

- **Size.** The size (in kilobytes) of the selected page.

- **Cached.** Click this link to see the version of the page stored on Google's document servers. Note that the cached page may be slightly older than the current version of the page.

- **Similar pages.** These are pages that Google thinks have a lot in common with the listed page.

- **Other relevant pages.** In some instances, other relevant pages from the same site are listed (and indented) beneath the primary page listing.

- **Related searches.** At the bottom of most search results pages is a list of "searches related to" your current search. Click any of these links to perform a similar search.

Universal Search Results

Before mid-2007, Google presented the results of all its various types of searches separately. When you queried the main Google search page, all you saw were web results. If you wanted to search for images, you had to use Google Image Search; if you wanted to search news stories, you had to use Google News; if you wanted to search blog postings, you had to use Google Blog Search; and so on.

That all changed when Google introduced its Universal Search technology. With Universal Search, relevant results from all of Google's search indexes are shown when you search from Google's main search page. If a query finds a relevant news article, a link to that article is mixed in with the traditional web results. Same thing if a query finds a matching image, or blog posting, or map entry. All the results are presented in a single set of results pages, with no need to query Google's other search indexes separately. (Of course, if you want a specific type of result, you can still query the individual search services, as we'll discuss in later chapters.)

> **tip** Viewing a cached page is particularly valuable if, for some reason, the "live" version of the page is down or otherwise inaccessible. You can also use the cached page to examine recent changes to the page in question, because the cached page is likely a few days or weeks older than the current version of the page.

To display only certain types of results, click the links on the left side of the statistics bar on the results page. For example, if a search returns a mix of web, image, and news results, you see links for Web, Images, and News. To view only the image results, click the Images link; to view only the news stories, click the News link.

Omitted Results

There's one other thing to watch for on the search results page—in particular, on the very last search results page. When you get to the last of the page listings, you're likely to see a message like the one shown in Figure 6.3. This message tells you that Google has omitted some results that are similar to those already listed. In other words, Google is trying to simplify your life by not displaying what it feels are duplicate results.

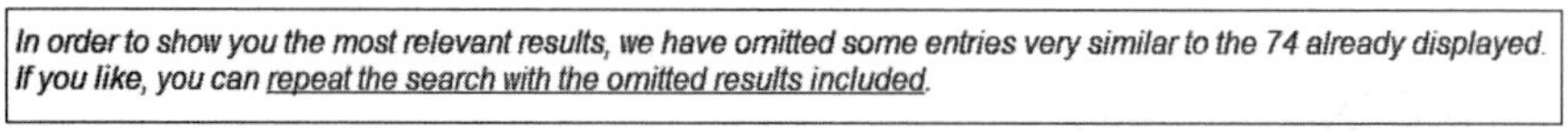

> *In order to show you the most relevant results, we have omitted some entries very similar to the 74 already displayed. If you like, you can repeat the search with the omitted results included.*

FIGURE 6.3
Google sometimes omits duplicate results.

In most cases, this is fine; you don't need to see results that essentially duplicate results you've already seen. But every now and then Google gets it wrong and actually omits results that you might find useful. If you suspect this is the case, click the Repeat the Search with the Omitted Results Included link. This repeats the search and displays *all* results, even those that may (or may not) be duplicates.

> **note** If you're signed in to your Google account, you may see a Note This link next to the Similar Pages link. Click this link and the search result is saved to a Google Notebook. (Learn more about Google Notebook in Chapter 7, "Saving Your Searches—and Signing Up for Google Alerts."

Extending Your Search

For many searches, you can find what you want simply by clicking a few page titles on the first search results page. But you may want to see more results—which, of course, Google lets you do.

First things first. Don't assume that the only relevant results will appear on the first search results page. Some queries return literally thousands (if not *millions*) of matching pages, and even though the most relevant results are supposed to be listed first, it's possible to find much useful information buried deeper in the results. For this reason, make it a habit to at least browse a few pages deeper in the search results. This is easy enough to do; just scroll to the bottom of the search results page and click the Next link. You can also go directly to a specific page in the search results by clicking a page number, as shown in Figure 6.4. And if you want to view a page beyond the first 10 listed, just click the page 10 link, and another nine page numbers are listed. Keep clicking to the right to view more and more pages of results.

FIGURE 6.4

The bottom of a typical search results page; click a page number to jump to that page of results.

Another useful feature is found at the bottom of the search results page. The Search Within Results link lets you narrow your results by refining your query and applying the new search solely to the original results. Here's how it works:

1. Click the Search Within Results link at the bottom of the search results page.

2. When the Search Within Results page appears, as shown in Figure 6.5, enter a new query into the search box.

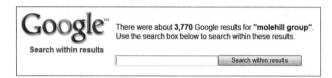

FIGURE 6.5

Refine your query on the Search Within Results page.

3. Click the Search Within Results button.

Google searches the existing results, using your new query. The new, refined results appear on a subsequent search results page.

Conducting a More Refined Search

Most users enter a keyword or two into Google's search box, click the Search button, and are satisfied with the results. This is a rather brute-force method of searching, however, and typically it generates a ton of (mostly unwanted) results.

There is a better way to search—one that generates a smaller, more targeted list of results. To generate fewer, better results, you have to refine your query—using a defined series of search operators.

Don't Worry About Capitalization...

First, let's expose the fact that Google's searches are not case-sensitive. It doesn't matter whether you search for **California** or **california**, the results will be the same—so don't worry about applying proper capitalization.

> **note** An *operator* is a symbol or word that causes a search engine to do something special with the word directly following the symbol.

...But Do Worry About Word Order

In a Google query, the order of your keywords matters. Google weights the importance of your keywords in order of
appearance. The first keyword is considered the most important, the second keyword the second most important, and so on.

note To be fair, in many cases the top results are the same no matter what the word order. The difference tends to come as you move deeper into the result listings.

For example, **hdtv retailers chicago** returns slightly different results than
chicago retailers hdtv.

"And" Is Assumed

Next, know that Google automatically assumes the word "and" between all
the words in your query. That is, if you enter two words, Google assumes
you're looking for pages that include both those words—word one *and* word
two. It doesn't return pages that include only one of the words.

This is different from assuming the word "or" between the words in your
query. As an example, compare the query **bob AND ted** with **bob OR ted**. In
the first query, the results would include pages that mention both Bob and
Ted. In the second query, the results would include pages that mention Bob
alone, as well as pages that mention Ted alone, as well as pages that mention
both Bob and Ted. It's a subtle difference, but an important one.

The upshot is that you don't have to enter the word "and" in your query. If
you're searching for Bob and Ted, all you have to enter is **bob ted**. Google
assumes the "and" and automatically includes it in its internal index search.

Search for One Word or Another

Similarly, if you want to conduct an "or" search—to search for pages that
include one word or another word, but not necessarily both—you can use the
OR operator. For example, to search for pages that talk about either Bob or
Ted (but not necessarily Bob and Ted together), use the query **bob OR ted**.
And when you use the **OR** operator, be sure to type it in all uppercase, or
Google will ignore it as a stop word—which we'll discuss next.

Common Words Are Automatically Excluded

Speaking of the words "and" and "or," Google automatically ignores these and other small, common words in your queries. These are called *stop words*. They include "and," "the," "where," "how," "what," "or" (in all lowercase), and other similar words—along with certain single digits and single letters (such as "a").

Including a stop word in a search normally does nothing but slow down the search, which is why Google excises them. As an example, Google takes the query **how a toaster works**, removes the words "how" and "a," and creates the new, shorter query **toaster works**.

> **note** The **OR** operator is the only Boolean operator that the Google search engine accepts. (Boolean operators come from Boolean logic and mathematics.) The Boolean **AND** operator is assumed in all Google searches; the Boolean **NOT** operator is replaced by the Google – operator, discussed a little later in this chapter.

If you want these common words included in your query, you have two options. You can automatically include them by using the + operator (discussed next), or you can include the common words within a phrase by enclosing the entire phrase in quotation marks (discussed a little later).

Always Include Stop Words

You can override the stop word exclusion by telling Google that it *must* include specific words in the query. You do this with the + operator, in front of the otherwise excluded word. For example, to include the word "how" in your query, you'd enter **+how**. Be sure to include a space before the + sign, but not after it.

Exclude Words from the Results

Sometimes you want to refine your results by excluding pages that include a specific word. You can exclude words from your search by using the – operator; any word in your query preceded by – is automatically excluded from the search results. Remember to always include a space before the –, and none after.

For example, if you search for **bass**, you could get pages about a male singer and/or a fish. If you want to search for bass singers only, enter a query that looks like this: **bass –fish**.

Take Advantage of Automatic Word Stemming

Unlike some other search engines, Google doesn't let you use wildcards to indicate the variable ends of words. Wildcards, as used elsewhere, let you

6

search for all words that include the first part of a keyword. For example, a search for **book*** (with the * wildcard) typically would return results for "books," "bookstore," "bookkeeper," and so on.

Instead, Google incorporates *automatic word stemming*, which is a fancy way of saying that Google automatically searches for all possible word variations. This is a great way to search for both singular and plural forms of a word, as well as different tenses and forms.

For example, a search for the word **monster** returns both "monster" (singular) and "monsters" (plural). A search for **rain** returns "rain," "rained" (past tense), and "rains" (active form). And word stemming works in reverse, too; a search for **rains** returns both "rains" and "rain."

Search for Similar Words

Not sure you're thinking of the right word for a query? Do you worry that some web pages might use alternative words to describe what you're thinking of?

Fortunately, Google lets you search for similar words by using the ~ operator. Just include the ~ character before the word in question, and Google searches for all pages that include that word and all appropriate synonyms.

For example, to search for words that are like the word "elderly," enter the query **~elderly**. This finds pages that include not just the word "elderly," but also the words "senior," "aged," "nursing homes," and so on.

Search for an Exact Phrase

When you're searching for an exact phrase, you don't get the best results simply by entering all the words in the phrase as your query. Google *might* return results including the phrase, but it will also return results that include all those words—but not necessarily in that exact order.

When you want to search for an exact phrase, you should enclose the phrase in quotation marks. This tells Google to search for the precise keywords in the prescribed order.

> **tip** To list *only* synonyms, without returning a ton of matches for the original word, combine the ~ operator with the – operator, like this: **~keyword –keyword**. This excludes the original word from the synonymous results. Continuing with the preceding example, to list only synonyms for the word "elderly," enter **~elderly –elderly**.

For example, if you're searching for Monty Python, you *could* enter **monty python** as your query, and you'd get acceptable results; the results will include pages that include both the words "monty" and "python." But these results will include not only pages about the British comedy troupe, but also pages about snakes named Monty, and guys named Monty who have pet snakes, and any other pages where the words "monty" and "python" occur— anywhere in the page, even if they don't appear adjacent to one another. To limit the results just to pages about the Monty Python troupe, you want to search for pages that include the two words in that precise order as a phrase. So you should enter the query **"monty python"**—making sure to surround the phrase with quotation marks. This way, if the word "monty" occurs at the top of a page and "python" occurs at the bottom, that page won't be listed in the search results.

Use Wildcards to Search for Missing Words in an Exact Phrase

I noted previously that Google doesn't use wildcards to complete missing letters in keywords. However, Google *does* let you use whole-word wildcards within a phrase search. That is, you can search for a complete phrase even if you're not sure of all the words in the phrase. You let the * wildcard character stand in for the words you don't know.

Here's an example. Let's say you want to search for pages that discuss Martin Luther King's famous "I have a dream" speech, but you can't remember whether the correct word in the phrase is "have" or "had." You can use the * wildcard to stand in for the word in question; you would enter the following query: **"i * a dream"**.

You can even use multiple wildcards within a single phrase, within reason. Although **"* * a dream"** might return acceptable results, **"* * * dream"** is a fairly useless query.

Search for Words That Don't Appear Together

Here's another usage of the * whole-word wildcard. If you want to search for documents in which two words *don't* appear side by side, insert the * between the two keywords in your query—while still surrounding both keywords with quotation marks. This searches for instances in which the two keywords are separated by one or more words.

For example, to search for pages where the words "happy" and "holidays" aren't adjacent, enter this query: **"happy * holidays"**.

Narrow Your Search to Specific File Types

Google can search for information contained in all sorts of documents—not just HTML web pages. In particular, Google searches for the following file types and extensions, in addition to normal web pages:

- Adobe Portable Document Format (PDF)
- Adobe PostScript (PS)
- Autodesk (DWF)
- Google Earth (KML, KMZ)
- Lotus 1-2-3 (WK1, WK2, WK3, WK4, WK5, WKI, WKS, WKU)
- Lotus WordPro (LWP)
- MacWrite (MW)
- Microsoft Excel (XLS)
- Microsoft PowerPoint (PPT)
- Microsoft Word (DOC)
- Microsoft Works (WDB, WKS, WPS)
- Microsoft Write (WRI)
- Rich Text Format (RTF)
- Shockwave Flash (SWF)
- Text (ANS, TXT)

If you want to restrict your results to a specific file type, use the **filetype:** operator followed by the file extension, in this format: **filetype:***filetype*. For example, if you want to search only for Microsoft Word documents, enter **filetype:doc** along with the rest of your query.

To eliminate a particular file type from your search results, use the **filetype:** operator preceded by the – operator and followed by the file extension, like this: **–filetype:***filetype*. For example, if you want to eliminate PDF files from your results, enter **–filetype:pdf**.

By the way, when you view a non-HTML document (something other than a web page, such as an Acrobat PDF or Word DOC file), Google displays a View As HTML link in the page listing. Clicking this link translates the original document into web page format—which often displays faster in your browser.

6

Narrow Your Search to a Specific Domain or Website

Maybe you want to search only those sites within a specific top-level web domain, such as .com or .org or .edu—or, perhaps, within a specific country's domain, such as .uk (United Kingdom) or .ca (Canada). Google lets you do this by using the **site:** operator. Just enter the operator followed by the domain name, like this: **site:.*domain*.**

For example, to search only those sites within the .edu domain, you'd enter **site:.edu** along with the rest of your query. To search only Canadian sites, enter **site:.ca.** Remember to put a dot (period) before the domain.

The **site:** operator can also be used to restrict your search to a specific website. In this instance, you enter the entire top-level URL, like this: **site:www.*website.domain*.** For example, to search only within my personal Molehill Group website (www.molehillgroup.com), enter **site:www.molehill-group.com.** Your results will include only pages listed within the specified website.

Narrow Your Search to Words in the Page's Title

Google offers two methods for restricting your search to the titles of web pages, ignoring the pages' body text. If your query contains a single word, use the **intitle:** operator. If your query contains multiple words, use the **allintitle:** operator.

For example, if you want to look for pages with the word "Honda" in the title, use the **intitle:** operator and enter this query: **intitle:honda.** Make sure not to put a space between the **intitle:** operator and the keyword.

If you want to look for pages with both the words "Honda" and "Element" in the title, use the **allintitle:** operator and enter this query: **allintitle:honda element.** Notice that when you use the **allintitle:** operator, all the keywords after the operator are searched for; you separate the keywords with spaces.

Narrow Your Search to Words in the Page's URL

Similar to the **intitle:** and **allintitle:** operators are the **inurl:** and **allinurl:** operators. These operators let you restrict your search to words that appear in web page addresses (URLs). You use these operators in the same fashion—**inurl:** to search for single words and **allinurl:** to search for multiple words.

caution If you enter **intitle:honda element**, Google searches for only the word "Honda" in the page titles; it conducts a normal full-page search for the word "Element." This is why you want to use the **allintitle:** operator if you have multiple keywords in your query.

For example, to search for sites that have the word "molehill" in their URLs, enter this query: **inurl:molehill**. Be sure not to put a space between the **inurl:** operator and the keyword.

To search for sites that have both the words "molehill" and "group," enter this query: **allinurl:molehill group**. As with the **allintitle:** operator, all the keywords you enter after the **allinurl:** operator are searched for; you separate the keywords with spaces.

Narrow Your Search to Words in the Page's Body Text

For all this fuss about searching titles and URLs, it's more likely that you'll want to search the body text of web pages. You can restrict your search to body text only (excluding the page title, URL, and link text) by using the **intext:** and **allintext:** operators. The syntax is the same as the previous operators; use **intext:** to search for single words and **allintext:** to search for multiple words.

For example, to search for pages that include the word "Google" in their body text, enter the query **intext:google**. Be sure not to put a space between the **intext:** operator and the keyword.

To search for pages that include both the words "Google" and "search" in the body text, enter the query **allintext:google search**.

Narrow Your Search to Words in the Page's Link Text

Two more operators are similar to the previous batch. The **inanchor:** operator lets you restrict your search to words in the link, or anchor, text on a web page. (This is the text that accompanies a hypertext link—the underlined text on the page.) The **allinanchor:** variation lets you search for multiple words in the anchor text.

For example, to search for links that reference the word "goose," you'd enter **inanchor:goose**. Be sure not to put a space between the **inanchor:** operator and the keyword.

To search for links that reference the words "goose" and "duck," enter the query **allinanchor:goose duck**.

6

Search for a Range of Numbers

What if you want to search for pages that contain items for sale within a certain price range? Or selected back issues of a magazine?

For these tasks, use Google's ... operator. All you have to do is enter the lower number in the range, followed by the ... operator, followed by the higher number in the range. For example, when you enter **100...150**, you search for pages that include the numbers 100, 101, 102, and so forth up to 150.

List Pages That Link to a Specific Page

Want to know which other web pages link to a specific page? Because Google works by tracking page links, this is easy to find out. All you have to do is use the **link:** operator, like this: **link:***URL*. For example, to see the thousands of pages that link to Microsoft's website, enter **link:www.microsoft.com**.

List Similar Pages

Have you ever found a web page you really like, and then wondered if there were any more like it? Wonder no more; you can use Google's **related:** operator to display pages that are in some way similar to the specified page. For example, if you really like the news stories on CNET's News.com website (www.news.com), you can find similar pages by entering **related:www.news.com**.

Find Out More About a Specific Page

Google collects a variety of information about the web pages it indexes. In particular, Google can tell you which pages link to that page (see the **link:** operator, discussed previously), which pages that page links to, which pages are similar to that page (the **related:** operator), and which pages contain that page's URL. To get links to all this information on a single page (plus a link to Google's cached version of that page), use Google's **info:** operator. This displays a set of links, like those shown in Figure 6.6, that you can click to obtain the desired page info.

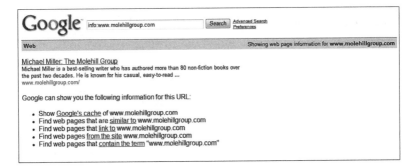

FIGURE 6.6
*The results of applying the **info:** operator to the author's www.molehillgroup.com website.*

Highlight Keywords

If you want to highlight all the instances of the keywords you searched for in a document, use the **cache:** operator, followed by the site's URL. This displays the cached version of the web page, with the keywords in your query highlighted in yellow.

For example, to highlight all instances of the keyword "windows" on the www.microsoft.com website, enter this query: **cache:www.microsoft.com windows.**

Using the Advanced Search Page

Not comfortable learning all those complicated search operators, but still want to fine-tune your search beyond the basic keyword query? You can use Google's Advanced Search page, which performs most of these same advanced search functions, via a series of simple pull-down menus and checkboxes.

You can access the Advanced Search page, shown in Figure 6.7, by clicking the Advanced Search link on Google's home page. The Advanced Search page contains a number of options you can use to fine-tune your searches, without having to learn all those advanced operators. All you have to do is make the appropriate selections on the page, and Google does all the fine-tuning for you.

What options are available on the Advanced Search page? Table 6.1 provides the details.

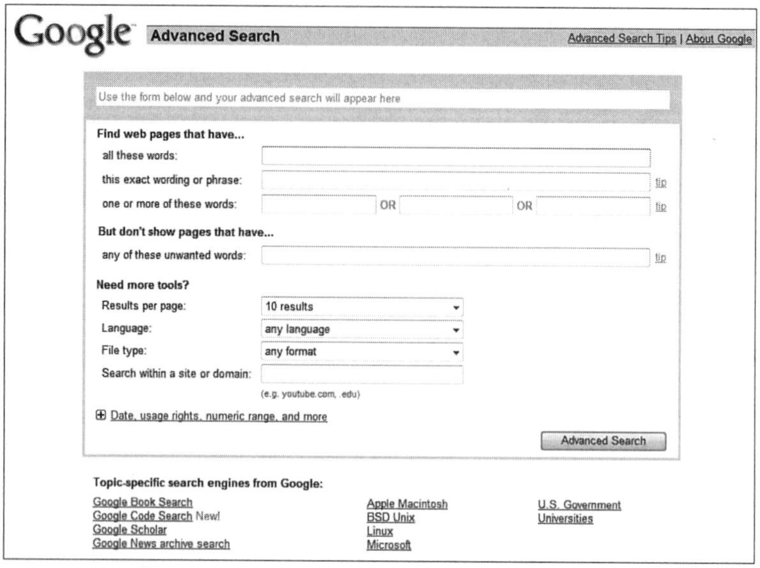

FIGURE 6.7

Google's Advanced Search page.

Table 6.1 Options on Google's Advanced Search Page

Option	Description	Same as This Operator
Find results with **all these words**	Google's default search mode	N/A
Find results with **this exact wording or phrase**	Searches for the exact phrase entered	""
Find results with **one or more of these words**	Searches for either one word or another	**OR**
Don't show pages that contain unwanted words	Excludes pages that contain specified word(s)	–
Results per page	Selects how many listings are displayed on the search results page	N/A
Language	Searches for pages written in a specific language	N/A
File type	Limits the search to specific file types	filetype: and –filetype:
Search within a site or domain	Restricts the search to the specified website or domain	**site:**

Even more parameters are available if you click the Date, Usage Rights, Numeric Range, and More link. This expands the page to include options for Date (search for recent pages), Usage Rights (whether a page is free to use or share), Where Your Keywords Show Up (restricts the search to certain areas of a page), Region (narrows the search to a given country), Numeric Range (search for a range of numbers), and SafeSearch (filters out adult content). There are also options to find pages that are either similar to or link to the page in question.

For many users, it's easier to use the Advanced Search page than it is to learn and enter Google's advanced operators into a standard search query. When you need to fine-tune the occasional search, this is the page to use!

Narrowing Your Search Results with URL Parameters

There's one more way to tweak your Google results—not your queries, mind you, but rather the results that get returned. You can do this by modifying the URL of any search results page, via the addition of what the techno-wizards call URL parameters.

Understanding Google's URLs

What is a URL parameter? It's a technical modifier that appears at the end of a URL; it's essentially the internal code used to generate a particular page of search results. For example, do a basic Google search for **tweeter**, and then examine the URL for the ensuing search results page, which should look like this: http://www.google.com/search?hl=en&q=tweeter. Everything after the www.google.com part of the URL are the URL parameters.

You can see that the first parameter is search?, which tells Google that you're conducting a search. The next parameter is hl=en, which sets the language for the search results to English. The final parameter is q=tweeter, which tells Google that your query is the single keyword **tweeter**.

It's not important that you learn all these URL parameters; they're essential to Google's internal search function, but not to you. However, if you know a few of these URL parameters, you can use them to manipulate the results that Google

> **tip**
> You can also use the URL of a search results page as a bookmark for future searches. Just copy the URL into your favorites list, email it to a friend, or whatever. When you enter the full URL into your web browser, you'll jump to the same search results page, without having to re-enter the original search query.

6

returns from a standard web search. Let's look at a few of the most useful of these parameters.

Displaying the Most Recent Results

If you want to filter your search results to include only pages created within the past few months, you can add the &as_qdr=m# parameter to any search results URL. With this parameter, replace the # with the number of months back you want to search; for example, &as_qdr=m3 refines your results to pages created within the past three months. (You can search back between 1 and 12 months.)

How does this work? It's pretty simple, really. Just follow these steps:

1. Enter your query into the Google search box as normal, and then click the search button.

2. When the search results page appears, move the cursor to the end of the URL in your web browser's address box.

3. Add the following to the end of the URL: &as_qdr=m#, replacing # with a number between 1 and 12.

4. Press the Enter key or click the Go button in your web browser.

Google reruns your search, this time filtering the results to include only those pages created within the past *x* months.

Displaying More (or Fewer) Results

Now let's look at expanding the number of results displayed on a page. Although this is something you can manipulate from the Advanced Search page, you can also do so by adding the &num=*x* parameter to the end of any search results URL. Just replace *x* with the number of results you want to display on a page, and then rerun the search with the modified URL.

Restricting Results to a Specific File Type

We'll look at one last URL parameter—this one is also available from the Advanced Search page but is easily duplicable in the search results URL. If you want to narrow your results to documents of a certain type of file, just add the &as_filetype=*xxx* parameter to the end of the search results URL. Replace *xxx* with the file extension (doc, jpg, pdf, and so forth), and then rerun the search with the modified URL. It's that easy.

Setting Google Search Preferences

Most users are unaware that they can personalize how Google displays search results—and, to a small degree, how the main search page looks. Well, you can, thanks to Google's Preferences page.

You get to the Preferences page by clicking the Preferences link on Google's home page. As you can see in Figure 6.8, you can configure a handful of items; we'll discuss each in the following sections.

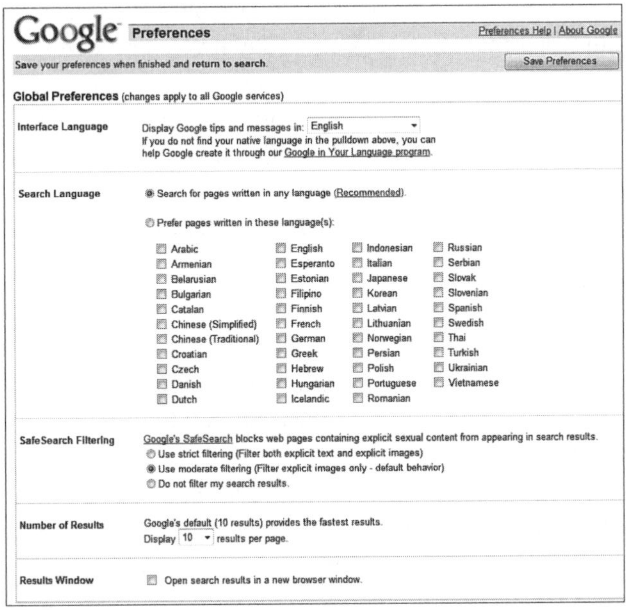

FIGURE 6.8

Customize how Google looks and acts on the Preferences page.

When you're done configuring your preferences, clicking the Save Preferences button applies your choices to your current and all future Google searches across all Google services. That's all there is to it.

Display Google in a Different Language

By default, the Google interface displays with all the text in English. Google can, however, display its main page in dozens

caution Google tracks and applies your preferences via the use of browser cookies. If you have cookies disabled in your browser, or if you delete your cookies, your preferences won't be retained.

of local languages, from Afrikaans to Zulu. To select the interface language, just pull down the Interface Language list and make a selection.

> **tip** Although limiting your search to English-only sites is sometimes useful, it can also limit the information you find. Even if you can't read the text of a foreign-language site, the pictures and graphics you find there can still be helpful.

Search in a Different Language

When you search Google, your query automatically searches for web pages created in any language. You may, however, want to restrict your searches to pages created in a specific language—especially if you speak only that one language.

To that end, you can instruct Google to restrict all your searches to pages created in a specific language. To do this, go to the Search Language section, check the Prefer Pages Written in These Language(s) option, and then click the language(s) you want your results restricted to. The choices range from Arabic to Vietnamese; English is somewhere in the middle.

Search Safely

Like it or not, there's a lot of unsavory content on the Web. When you perform a Google search, some of these undesirable pages can end up in your search results—which is not a great thing if it's your kids who are doing the searching.

Fortunately, Google offers a content filter that you can apply to your Google searches. Google's SafeSearch filter screens the Google index for sites that contain adult information and then eliminates those pages from your search results. Google uses proprietary technology to check keywords, phrases, URLs, and Google Directory categories against a list of objectionable words and topics. When you activate SafeSearch, you're blocked from viewing results that contain these undesirable words and topics.

> **note** Given all the complex algorithms and technologies Google applies to its standard searching, the SafeSearch content filter is surprisingly simple. SafeSearch is nothing more than a filter that looks for the appearance of certain "naughty" words, such as "sex," "porn," and "girls." When a web page contains one or more of these objectionable words (in either the page text or the URL), the page is omitted from Google's search results.

To turn on or off SafeSearch filtering on a global basis (for all future searches), use the settings on Google's Preferences page. You can select from one of three options:

- **Use strict filtering.** Blocks both objectionable words and images.

- **Use moderate filtering.** Blocks objectionable images from Google Image Search results only; it doesn't block any pages based on objectionable text. This is the default configuration.

- **Do not filter my search results.** Disables the SafeSearch filter and displays all pages and images, no matter what content they contain.

> **caution** SafeSearch settings are stored in a cookie on your computer's hard disk. If you have cookies disabled in your browser, you can't use the SafeSearch filter across multiple search sessions.

It's important to note that the SafeSearch filter applies only to results returned from a Google search. Google doesn't block access to any specific web page; it just omits objectionable pages from its search results. You can still enter the URL for an objectionable page into your web browser; Google won't keep you from going directly to that page.

It's also important to note that although SafeSearch does a good job of filtering out objectionable pages, it isn't perfect, and it doesn't catch all obscene material. So it's possible (if not likely) that some objectionable links might creep into your search results, even with SafeSearch activated. To that end, SafeSearch is not a substitute for adult supervision when your kids are searching the Web.

COMMENTARY

SAFESEARCH: HELP OR HINDRANCE?

I'm not a big fan of content filters—especially when those filters are somewhat unsophisticated. Unfortunately, Google's SafeSearch falls into this category.

The problem with an unsophisticated content filter is that it's fairly dumb. All SafeSearch does is look for a list of words to block. Just because a site contains one of those words, however, doesn't automatically mean that the site itself is objectionable. For example, if you want to search for sites about breast cancer, SafeSearch will block your search—because these sites contain the objectionable word "breast."

Google's brute-force approach to content filtering is how almost all content filters used to work—10 years ago. Most third-party content-filtering programs today are more sophisticated in how they look for potentially objectionable sites. They may start with a word filter list, but

6

they apply various algorithms to try to put those words in context on a site. The results are still less than perfect, and they still block a number of legitimate sites, but at least it's progress.

In addition, although Google's SafeSearch filter can easily be enabled by parents, it can just as easily be disabled by their children. There's no "lock" on the setting, no password you have to enter to enable or disable it. That means you can protect your kids only as long as they want to be protected; if they want to see the naughty bits, they can disable SafeSearch and do so.

All that said, if kids use your PC, Google's SafeSearch filter is an okay way to help protect them from seeing things they shouldn't. But if you're searching on your own, you might find the results too limiting. If so, do the smart thing—and turn off the filter.

Display More Results Per Page

By default, Google displays 10 results per page for each search you perform. This allows for a fairly fast display of results. If you want to see more results on your page, go to the Number of Results section of the Preferences page, and change the setting to 20, 30, 50, or 100. As you might expect, choosing a larger number of results per page slows down the display of results—and makes it a little harder to chug through the results.

Open a New Results Window

By default, Google displays your search results in the same browser window you used to initiate your search. If you prefer to have Google open a new browser window containing your search results, go to the Results Window section of the Preferences page, and select the Open Search Results in a New Browser Window option. With this option selected, any time you click the Search Google button, a new browser window opens, with the search results listed.

Tips for More Effective Searches

All the advanced operators aside, most people use Google in a very inefficient and often ineffective manner. If all you do is enter a few keywords and click the search button, you don't get as much out of Google as you could. Read on to learn how to make your searches more effective and more efficient.

Use the Correct Methodology

Whether you're conducting a basic or advanced Google search, you should employ a certain methodology. Follow the proper method and you'll get very targeted results; ignore this advice and you'll get either a ton of irrelevant results or a dearth of relevant ones.

Although there are many different (and equally valid) approaches to web searching, I guarantee that this particular approach will generate excellent results. It's a six-step process that looks like this:

1. Start by thinking about what you want to find. What words best describe the information or concept you're looking for? What alternative words might other people use instead? Can you exclude any words from your search to better define your query?

2. Construct your query. Use as many keywords as you need—the more the better. If at all possible, try to refine your search with the appropriate search operators—or, if your prefer, the Advanced Search page.

3. Click the Search button to perform the search.

4. Evaluate the matches on the search results page. If the initial results are not to your liking, refine your query and search again—or refine your search by switching to a more appropriate search site.

5. Select the matching pages that you want to view, and begin clicking through to those pages.

6. Save the information that best meets your needs.

In other words, it pays to think before you search—and to continue refining your search after you obtain the initial results. The extra effort is slight, and well worth it.

Use the Right Keywords in Your Query

When you construct your query, you do so by using one or more keywords. The keywords you enter are compared to Google's index of web documents; the more keywords found on a web page, the better the match.

You should choose keywords that best describe the information you're looking for—using as many keywords as you need. Don't be afraid of using too many keywords; in fact, using too few keywords is a common mistake made by many novice searchers. The more words you use, the better idea Google has of what you're looking for. Think of it as describing something to a friend—the more descriptive you are (that is, the more words you use), the better the picture your friend has of what you're talking about.

It's the same way when you "talk" to the Google search engine.

If you're looking for a thing or place, choose keywords that describe that thing or place in as much detail as possible. For example, if you're looking for a car, one of your first keywords would, of course, be **car**. But you probably know what general type of car you're looking for—let's say it's a sports car—so you might enhance your query to read **sports car**. You may even know that you want to find a foreign sports car, so you change your query to read **foreign sports car**. And if you're looking for a classic model, your query could be expanded to **classic foreign sports car**. As you can see, the better your description (using more keywords), the better Google can understand what you're searching for.

If you're looking for a concept or idea, you should choose keywords that best help people understand that concept or idea. This often means using additional keywords that help impart the concept's meaning. Suppose you want to search for information about senior citizens; your initial query would be **senior citizens**. What other words could you use to describe the concept of senior citizens? How about words such as elderly, old, or retired? If these words help describe your concept, add them to your search, like this: **senior citizens elderly old retired**. Adding keywords like these results in more targeted searches

note The individual words you enter into a search box are called *keywords*. Collectively, all your keywords (and the operators between them) combine to form a *query*. Just remember that a query is composed of keywords, not the other way around, and you'll have it straight.

tip It's possible to include too many keywords in your query. Google searches only the first 32 words of your query, so anything more than that is just wasted. If you enter a 33-word query (such as **she wore yellow polka dot bikini drove little red corvette around dead man's curve going surfing usa frankie annette muscle beach party southern california hot rod endless summer wipeout tan lotion sand castle**), the 33rd word ("castle," if you're counting) isn't included in the search.

6

and higher-quality results. (Additionally, you can use Google's ~ operator to include synonyms for any selected word, as discussed previously.)

While we're on the subject of keywords, try to limit your keywords to nouns. That's because Google ignores many verbs and conjunctions as stop words, and other words are simply too common to be useful. The key thing to remember is that you're searching for specific things; name those things in your query.

Save Your Results

If you manage to execute a search that results in a perfect set of matches, you probably want to save your results so that you can access them again in the future. If you use Internet Explorer as your web browser, you should save the first results page of your search as a Favorite. (In Internet Explorer 7, click the Add to Favorites button in the toolbar.) If you use another browser, learn how to save the page as a bookmark. This way, you can click the bookmark or favorite and return to that ideal page of results, without the need to replicate the query from scratch.

The Bottom Line

Google's basic web search is a quick and easy way to search the Web. However, you can produce better results by using a variety of search operators, or by using Google's Advanced Search page. Refining your search with these tools gives you a leg up on just about everyone else doing the Google thing; too few users know about or use these effective search tools.

6

Saving Your Searches—and Signing Up for Google Alerts

I f you do a lot of Googling, you may get tired of entering the same searches over and over, trying to find the latest search results. Wouldn't it be great if there were a way to save the data you search for—or even have Google email you when new web pages appear that match your search criteria?

Fortunately, Google has thought of both contingencies. If you want to save the information you find while searching, you use Google Notebook. And if you want to be notified when new information becomes available, you use Google Alerts. We'll look at both services in this chapter.

Saving Your Notes with Google Notebook

Google Notebook (www.google.com/notebook/) is a web-based tool that lets you create an online "notebook" to organize all your web-based research on a given topic. You clip text, images, and links from interesting pages you visit storing them in a topic-specific notebook page. It's a great way to organize typically chaotic web-based research activities.

Getting to Know Google Notebook

As you can see in Figure 7.1, you create different notebooks for different topics. Each notebook holds the notes you make, as well as links to and clips from web pages you select.

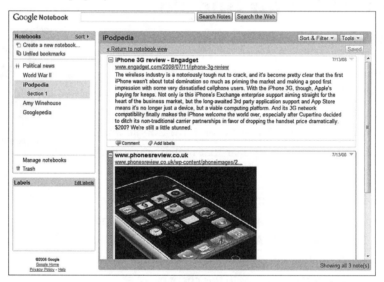

FIGURE 7.1
Organizing notes and web clippings in Google Notebook.

All your notebooks are listed in the Notebooks panel on the left side of the page. Click any notebook to display its contents in the main pane.

The contents of a notebook can be organized by section or displayed independently. Notes are displayed either condensed or in full. To condense a note, click the – button in the top-left corner; to expand the note to display the full contents, click

> **note** To use Google Notebook, you have to sign in with your Google Account.

the + button. Notes can include text that you enter, text clipped from a web page, pictures clipped from a web page, or links to a web page. To view a web page linked to from a note, just click the page's URL.

> **tip** To search your note-books for specific content, enter one or more keywords into the top-of-page search box, and then click the Search Notes button. All matching notes are then displayed as your search results.

Creating a New Notebook

To create a new notebook, click the Create a New Notebook link in the Notebooks panel. This opens a blank notebook with the name "Notebook 1." Place the cursor in this text box, type a new name for your notebook, and click OK. Your new empty notebook now appears in the main section of the page, waiting for you to enter new notes.

Adding a New Note

To add a new note to a notebook, click the New Note button to display the Type, Paste, or Add section, shown in Figure 7.2. Click in this section and start typing; the section changes to a note box. You can enter as much text as you like; the note is complete when you stop. You can add more text to a note at any time by positioning the cursor within the note box and typing some more.

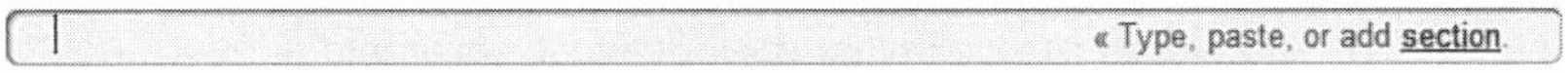

« Type, paste, or add section.

FIGURE 7.2

Getting ready to add a new note.

To format the text in a note, use the formatting controls at the top of the note-book pane. You can create bold, italic, or colored text; you can also change the font and the text size for selected text.

You can also insert web links into a note by clicking the Link button. This displays the Edit Link box; enter the text you want displayed for the link, and then the link URL. Click OK when you are done.

Adding a New Section

One or two notes in a notebook are easy enough to navigate, but when you start adding a lot of notes, it gets a bit cumbersome to later find the information you

> **tip** To insert additional comments below the main note text, click the Comment link and start typing.

7

want. For this reason, Google Notebook lets you organize each notebook into multiple sections; think of a section as a file folder in a filing cabinet.

note Learn more about the Google Toolbar in Chapter 5, "Using the Google Toolbar."

To create a new section in a notebook, click the New Note button, and then click the Type, Paste, or Add Section link. This creates a section header, with the name Section 1. Enter a name for the new section, and then click OK. Your new section is added to the notebook; add as many sections as you like.

Clipping Content from a Web Page

Google Notebook really proves its worth when you clip web page content into individual notes. This is accomplished via the Google Toolbar, which displays a Google Notebook button by default.

Clipping content from a web page is simple. Start by navigating to the web page, and then use the cursor to highlight the area of the page (text or pictures) you want to clip. Then click the Google Notebook button on the Google Toolbar. This displays the Google Notebook pop-up, as shown in Figure 7.3. Select the notebook you want to save to (or create a new notebook), and then click the Clip button. The text or graphics you selected are pasted into the notebook you selected.

FIGURE 7.3

Clipping a selection into a Google notebook.

Managing Your Notebooks

You can manage the content of your notebooks in various ways. Here are some of the most useful:

- To rename a notebook, select the notebook, click the Tools button, and select Rename Notebook.

- To print an individual note, select the note, click the Tools button, and select Print.

- To print all the notes in a given notebook, select the notebook, click the Tools button, and select Print.

- To delete an individual note, click the down arrow on the note and select Delete Selected Note.

- To delete a section of a notebook, click the section header, click the Tools button, and select Delete Section and Its Contents.

- To delete an entire notebook, select the notebook, click the Tools button, and select Delete Notebook.

- To move a section up or down within a notebook, use the cursor to drag the section header from one position to another. (It helps if you first collapse all the sections in this notebook.)

- To move a note into a different section within the same notebook, use the cursor to drag it from one position to another. (You can also click the down arrow on the note, select Move, and then select a different notebook or section.)

- To export a notebook to a Google Docs document, click the Tools button and select Export to Google Docs.

Sharing Notebooks

Another nice feature of Google Notebook is that you can use it as a collaboration tool. That is, you can share a notebook with other users, and let them add their own notes and comments.

To share a notebook, select the notebook and then click the Sharing Options link. When the Sharing Options page appears, as shown in Figure 7.4, enter the email addresses of those with whom you want to share. When you click the Save Settings button, those users receive email invitations to share the notebook, along with links to the notebook. (You have the opportunity to add a personal message to the invitation.)

By default, a shared notebook is a private document, accessible only by those you invite. If you want instead to make your notebook a public web page, go to the Publish This Notebook section of the Sharing Options page and check the Yes option. This expands the Sharing Options page to include a second invitation text box, along with the URL of the shared notebook page. When you make your notebook public, users you invite can view the notebook content, but not edit it (unless they've been separately invited to collaborate, of course). Such a publicly shared notebook is shown in Figure 7.5; it looks a little like a blog.

7

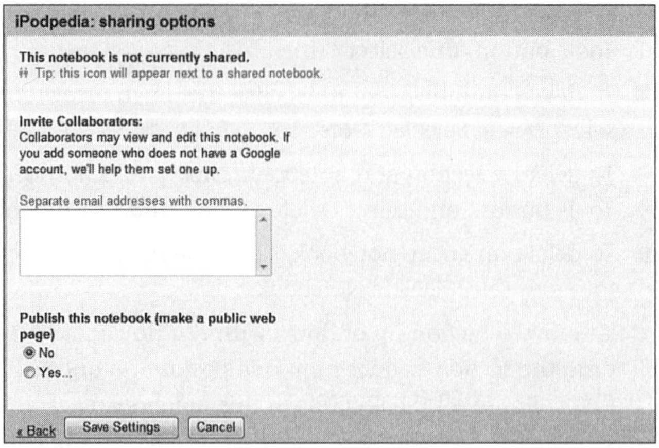

FIGURE 7.4

Sharing a notebook with others.

FIGURE 7.5

A Google Notebook made public.

Keeping Updated with Google Alerts

A Google Alert is an email that Google sends you when it finds new items of interest. It's a great way to keep updated when new web pages or news articles of interest appear. All you have to do is sign up for an alert and then wait for your email inbox to fill up.

Different Kinds of Alerts

Google offers five different types of alerts you can choose to receive. Each type of alert is based on a specific type of Google search:

- **News alerts** search Google News for new headlines that match your query.
- **Web alerts** search Google's web index for new web pages that match your query.
- **Blog alerts** deliver the top ten latest blog posts that match your query.
- **Groups alerts** search Google Groups for new messages that match your query.
- **Comprehensive alerts** aggregates results from multiple sources into a single email alert; this type of alert provides maximum coverage of your topic of choice.

You can opt to receive news alerts once a day, once a week, or "as-it-happens"—as new headlines and pages appear on Google's radar. For most users, the once-a-day option is best; this way, you can see what new information has appeared in the last 24 hours.

Signing Up for Alerts

Signing up for a Google Alert is as easy as entering a search query and then activating the alert service. You do all of this from the Google Alerts home page (www.google.com/alerts/), shown in Figure 7.6. Just follow these steps:

1. From the Google Alerts page, enter your query into the Search Terms box.

2. Pull down the Type list and select which type of alert you want to receive—News, Blogs, Web, Comprehensive, Video, or Groups.

note In most instances, Google Alerts don't notify you of *all* items that match your query—otherwise, you'd receive hundreds of email messages a day. Instead, Google Alerts search only the most relevant results, based on Google's PageRank Algorithm. So if you sign up for News alerts, you're notified only of new stories that make it into the top 10 results for your query. If you sign up for Web alerts, you're notified only of new pages that make it into the top 20 results for your query. If you sign up for Groups alerts, you're notified only of new messages that make it into the top 50 results for your query.

3. Pull down the How Often list and select how often you want to receive alerts—Once a Day, Once a Week, or As-It-Happens.

4. Enter your email address.

5. Click the Create Alert button.

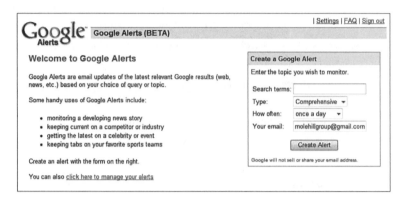

FIGURE 7.6

Creating a new Google Alert.

Customizing and Editing Your Alerts

To manage your existing alerts, you must be signed in with your Google Account. Then, when you access the Google Alerts page, click the Click Here to Manage Your Alerts link. This displays the Manage Your Alerts page, shown in Figure 7.7.

To edit the parameters of an alert, click the Edit link next to that alert. This opens all the fields for editing; you can edit your search query, change the type of alert, or change the frequency of the alert. Click the Save button next to that alert when you're done making changes.

By default, your Google Alerts come to you with fancy HTML formatting. If you'd rather receive plain-text email messages, click the Switch to Text Emails link at the top of the Your Google Alerts page. (You can always switch back by clicking the resulting Switch to HTML Emails link.)

note If you have a Google Account and a Gmail account, your Google Alerts are automatically sent to your Gmail inbox. If you don't have a Gmail account, you need to specify which email address you want your alerts sent to.

tip If you want to view your alert results now instead of waiting for Google to email them to you, go to the Manage Your Alerts page and click the name of the alert. This runs the specified search and displays a normal search results page.

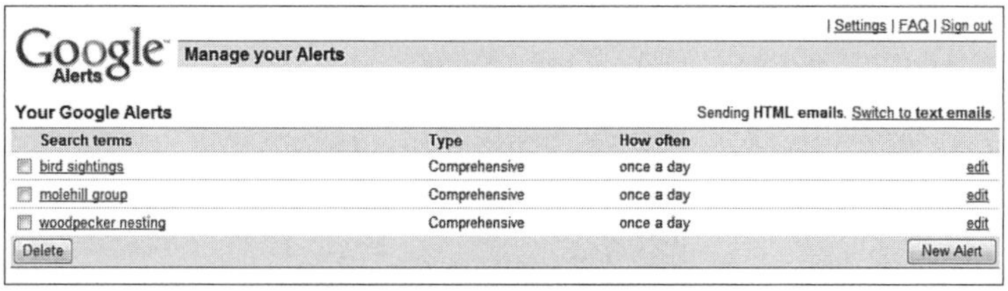

FIGURE 7.7
Getting ready to edit your Google Alerts.

Deleting Google Alerts

There are two ways to stop receiving a Google Alert you've created:

- Go to the Manage Your Alerts page, select the alert, and click the Delete button.
- Click the cancellation link at the bottom of any Google Alert email you receive.

The Bottom Line

Browsing the Web doesn't have to be haphazard and ephemeral. Google Notebook is a great way to organize the content you find on the Web and create notebooks of information for future use—by you or your collaborators. And when you need to keep abreast of new information as it becomes available, nothing beats the ease of notification presented by Google Alerts. Whether you're searching for new web pages, news stories, or group postings, Google Alerts keep you completely up-to-date—from the comfort of your email inbox.

7

Using the Google Directory and Google Knol

G oogle indexes billions of web pages in its search database. That's both good and bad. The huge volume of pages virtually guarantees that you'll find something useful, but all that volume sometimes makes it difficult to separate that one useful page from the thousands (or millions) of less-useful ones. It's kind of a needle-in-a-haystack problem.

By indexing literally billions of web pages, the Google search engine employs a brute-force approach. You get plenty of quantity, but the quality of results isn't always up to par.

When the quality of results matters, it's sometimes better to view a list of pages that have been personally selected for their content and appropriateness (as opposed to letting the GoogleBot and PageRank Algorithm do the gathering and selecting for you). So if it's handpicked results you want, you want a web directory, not an automated search engine.

8

Not surprisingly, Google offers just this type of human-edited directory—
called, also not surprisingly, the Google Directory. And that's not the only
human-edited information available from Google; Google also offers a host of
articles written by human experts, in the guise of what it calls Google Knol.

What the Google Directory Is—and What It Isn't

The Google Directory (directory.google.com), shown in Figure 8.1, is a relatively small database of web page listings (small compared to the main
Google database, that is). Each listing in the Google Directory is handpicked
by a team of human editors; the listings are then annotated and organized
into relevant topic categories. You can browse the directory via category, or
search for specific terms.

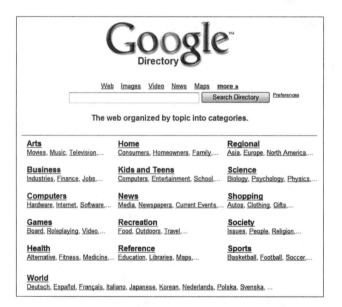

FIGURE 8.1

The Google Directory—ready to browse (by category) or search.

Why a Directory Isn't a Search Engine, and Vice Versa

Most users don't know the difference between a search engine and a directory.
After all, both directories and search engines contain lots of web page listings,
and both are searchable. What's the diff?

The difference between a directory and a search engine is in how the listings are compiled. As you learned in Chapter 1, "Inside Google," Google's search engine works by sending out automated GoogleBot software to crawl the Web, and then it uses a proprietary formula to match the pages to users' search queries. This process guarantees a huge number of results for most queries, but it's all very sterile and automated. There's no good way to truly judge the content or quality of a page; it's all about numbers.

In contrast, a directory is assembled by a team of human editors. That's right—human beings, not machines. They find and evaluate pages on the Web, annotate the page listings, and organize them into relevant categories. Unlike computers, human beings can make qualitative judgments about a page's content and can evaluate the page's actual meaning. It's not about numbers; it's about content.

All of this means that a directory is likely to have higher-quality results than a search engine. It's also likely to have fewer results (far fewer, when compared to Google's gargantuan search index) because of the need to closely examine each individual page before it's added to the directory. Where the Google search index includes billions of listings, the Google Directory contains approximately 4.6 million listings—less than one-tenth of 1% of what's in the search index.

Google's search engine is like casting a wide net and taking everything that's caught. Google Directory is like dropping a single fishing line in the water with the intent of catching a particular type of fish. You get lots of fish with the wide-net approach, but you get the fish you want by using a rod and reel.

The other big difference between a directory and a search engine is organization. A search index has none; those billions of pages are dumped into one big database, with no sense of order. A directory, on the other hand, is all about order; the human editors not only pick the web pages to be included, they also organize the sites into logical categories. So although you can't browse a search index, you *can* browse a directory, simply by clicking through the hierarchy of categories and subcategories.

Because they look at every page included in the directory, the directory's human editors also have the opportunity to annotate those pages. Browse through a directory's category listings and you're likely to see summaries, reviews, and comments about the web pages listed. These annotations are *not* automatically generated from the page's content; they're added by the editors, in what amounts to a very human touch.

A directory's human editors also provide one other important function—they continually check for and remove dead links. This is something that search engines don't always do well; a human being is more diligent about keeping the listings updated.

So what are the final differences between a search engine and a directory? Table 8.1 summarizes them.

Table 8.1   Search Engines Versus Directories

	Search Engine	Directory
Size (Number of Listings)	Large (billions)	Small (millions)
Organization	None	By category
Comments/Annotations	None	Yes
Manually Remove Dead Links	No	Yes
Assembled By	Computers	Human editors

How the Google Directory Is Assembled

The Google Directory works like most other web directories, such as the Yahoo! Directory (dir.yahoo.com) or Best of the Web (www.botw.org). Thousands of human editors sort through sites submitted by users, as well as do their own web browsing, to find the sites included in the directory. As soon as a web page has been accepted for inclusion, the editors write a brief review/overview of the page and assign it to a topic category. It's a totally manual process; there are no bots crawling the Web or linguistic programs excerpting page contents. All the work is done by hand.

But here's the thing. Google doesn't assemble its own directory. No, the Google Directory is actually a customized version of a third-party directory called the Open Directory Project. (Figure 8.2 shows the Open Directory home page—look familiar?)

note You can access the Open Directory directly at www.dmoz.org. (DMOZ is an acronym for Directory Mozilla, which reflects the directory's loose association with Netscape's Mozilla web browser, now owned by AOL.)

FIGURE 8.2
The Open Directory—the basis of the Google Directory.

Google takes the Open Directory listings and grafts the Google interface and search engine to them. So, although the listings in the directory are assembled by Open Directory editors, they're ranked using Google's PageRank technology. If you compare a category in the Google Directory with the same category in the Open Directory, the listings will be the same, but arranged differently.

The good thing about Google using the Open Directory is that it's perhaps the largest and highest-quality web directory available. The Open Directory Project is a huge undertaking, hosted and administered by Netscape (part of America Online), with more than 80,000 volunteer editors submitting reviews and rankings of websites and pages. Google made a good choice in partnering with the Open Directory. Combining Open Directory listings with Google's interface and PageRank rankings makes the Google Directory the easiest-to-use and most useful directory on the Web.

> **note** Sites listed in the Google Directory tend to have higher PageRanks than sites that aren't directory-listed—which makes placement in the directory highly valued.

> **tip** To submit a web page for possible inclusion in the Open Directory/Google Directory, follow the instructions at www.dmoz.org/add.html. To volunteer your services as an Open Directory editor, navigate to any category in the directory that interests you, click the Become an Editor link at the bottom of the page, and follow the onscreen instructions from there.

It's the use of Google's PageRank technology that makes the Google Directory so easy to use. Instead of just browsing through the category listings (which you can do if you want), Google's search technology lets you search the directory listings the same way you search Google's search index. The listings in the directory—and thus the results of your query—are ranked according to relevance, thanks to the use of PageRank. The most relevant sites always appear near the top of the listings, which they don't necessarily do if you access the raw Open Directory listings.

Why You'd Want to Use the Google Directory Instead of Google's Web Search

Now that you know the difference between Google's standard search engine and the Google Directory, which should you use for your searching?

Here are some tips:

- If you want the maximum number of results, use the Google search engine.
- If you want more-targeted results, use the Google Directory.
- If you want to read a little about a page or site before you jump to it, use the Google Directory.
- If you want to browse through all the pages in a category, rather than using the search function, use the Google Directory.
- If you want the "big picture" about a particular topic, use the Google Directory.

The bottom line is that if you want a lot of results, and you don't mind wading through the chaff to find a little wheat, use the standard Google search engine. But if you're tired of search results that aren't quite what you're looking for, and you want more qualified results, consider using the Google Directory. In other words, if you want quantity, use the standard Google search engine. If you want quality—or a good category overview—use the Google Directory instead.

Navigating the Google Directory

Now that you know how the Google Directory gets its listings, let's spend some time using the thing. It's a lot like using Google's regular search feature—with the ability to browse the listings thrown in.

tip You don't have to worry about the Google Directory containing results that don't appear in a standard Google web search. Google's search index includes all the entries in the Google Directory, in addition to the pages added by the GoogleBot crawler.

Searching Directory Listings

Most users opt to use the Google Directory much as they do the regular Google search page—that is, by searching the directory, rather than browsing it. To search the Google Directory, follow these steps:

> **tip**
> When searching the Google Directory, you can refine your search by using any of the search operators discussed in Chapter 6, "Getting the Most Out of Google Search."

1. Go to the Google Directory home page (directory.google.com)—*not* the regular Google home page.

2. Enter one or more keywords into the search box at the top of the page.

3. Click the Search Directory button.

Google displays a search results page like the one shown in Figure 8.3. This page looks a lot like a standard web search results page. Each result listing also features a link to the category in which it is included; click a category link to view all the pages listed in that category.

FIGURE 8.3

A Google Directory search results page.

Browsing Directory Categories

If you're accustomed to using Google to search for information, the concept of browsing might be new to you. It's really quite simple; it all hinges on the concept of hierarchical organization of information into topic categories and subcategories.

You start at the Google Directory home page, where 16 different categories (and a handful of subcategories) are listed. Here are the major categories:

- Arts
- Business
- Computers
- Games
- Health
- Home
- Kids and Teens
- News
- Recreation
- Reference
- Regional
- Science
- Shopping
- Society
- Sports
- World

You start your browsing by clicking a category that matches your interest. This displays a major category page that lists all the subcategories within the major category. (Sometimes a few related categories are listed also.) For example, The Home category lists 25 subcategories, such as Apartment Living, Consumer Information, Cooking, and the like.

Click a subcategory link and you see a subcategory page, like the one shown in Figure 8.4. Some subcategories include even more subcategories (sub-sub-categories?), which are listed at the top of the page. You'll also find a list of related categories; then you see the list of pages within the subcategory.

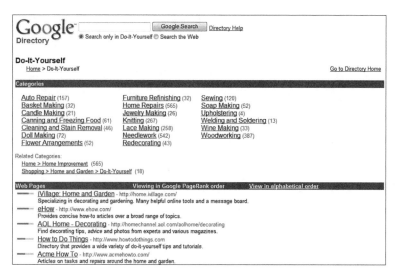

FIGURE 8.4
A typical subcategory page, including additional subcategories and pages listed in the subcategory.

These pages are ranked (using Google's PageRank technology) in order of relevance. The small green bar to the left of each page listing visually indicates the relevance; the longer the green bar, the more relevant the result. Each listing also includes the page's title (click to jump to the page), the page's URL, and the editor's description of the page.

Searching Within a Category

When you stumble across a big category, one with lots of pages listed, it may be difficult to find exactly the page you want. To that end, Google lets you search for pages within a category. All you have to do is navigate to a category or subcategory page, enter your query in the search box at the top of the page, check the Search Only in *Category* option, and then click the Google Search button. Google searches the current category—and only the current category—for the keywords you entered and displays the results on a separate search results page.

Searching within a category can be particularly useful in restricting your search to a particular topic. For example, if you search the entire Google Directory for **lions**,

> **tip** If you'd rather view the listings within a category alphabetically instead of by relevance, click the View in Alphabetical Order link at the top of the listings.

8

Google might return pages about lions (the animal), Lions (the football team), Lions (the public service organization), or any number of other lion-related subjects. But if you first navigate to the Sports, Football, American, NFL category and *then* search for **lions**, you'll see only results related to the Detroit Lions football team.

> **note** According to Google, a "knol" is a unit of knowledge. Thus the name Google Knol, short for (and pronounced like) the word "knowledge."

Getting Expert Results from Google Knol

The Google Directory isn't the only instance of human expertise at work in the Google empire. Google Knol (knol.google.com) is a new feature that offers articles written by human experts; it's the place to go for authoritative information on a variety of popular topics.

Searching for Expert Knowledge

As you can see in Figure 8.5, the main Google Knol page is your gateway to the various articles available. You can browse through the featured articles on the home page, or search for articles using the top-of-page search box.

FIGURE 8.5

Searching for authoritative articles on Google Knol.

An article, or what Google calls a *knol*, is just what you'd expect it to be. Figure 8.6 shows a typical article, complete with a clickable table of contents at the top of the page. A user rating for this article appears at the top; author information and user reviews of the article appear along the right side.

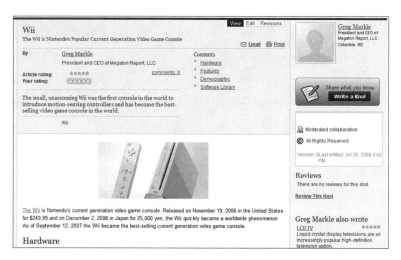

FIGURE 8.6

Viewing a Google Knol article.

To rate an article, just use your mouse to click the appropriate number of stars in the Your Rating section at the top of the page. (It's a one-to-five scale, five being tops.) To provide your two cents' worth about the article's contents, click the Review This Knol link and start typing.

Contributing Your Own Knowledge

In its own way, Google Knol is kind of a contributor to Wikipedia. Like Wikipedia, anyone can write an article; all you need is the desire to do so and a little knowledge of the topic at hand.

To create an article, click the Write a Knol button on the main Google Knol page. Assuming that you've signed in with your Google Account, you now see the page shown in Figure 8.7. From here you start filling in the blanks:

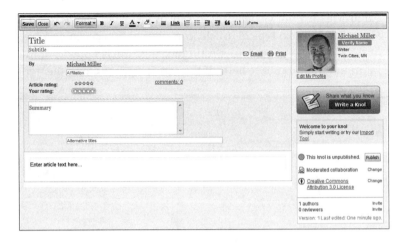

FIGURE 8.7
Writing a Google Knol article.

1. Enter the title of the article.

2. Enter a subtitle, if desired.

3. Enter a brief summary of the article's contents.

4. Enter any alternative titles that might be appropriate for the article.

5. Enter the text of the article; write as much or as little as you want. (You can use the formatting toolbar to format the text as you write.)

6. Set the collaboration setting for your article. You can choose Open Collaboration (anyone with a Knol account can edit or add to your article), Moderated Collaboration (you get to approve all edits), or Closed Collaboration (no modifications allowed by the general public). Moderated Collaboration is the default.

7. Click the Publish button when done.

That's it. Google doesn't edit your article, nor is it checked for accuracy—officially, that is. Also like Wikipedia, Google relies on the user community to rate, comment on, and even collaborate on the submitted articles. That's right, other users can edit your articles, just as you can edit theirs (assuming their articles are configured for open or moderated collaboration, that is). The collaborative nature of Google Knol is supposed to encourage greater accuracy in information, as well as more comprehensive articles.

Editing Other Knols

So what do you do if you find an inaccuracy in an article—or simply want to elaborate on what was originally written? Unless the article was configured for Closed Collaboration, you should see a series of tabs at the top of the article. Click the Edit tab and the article is now editable. That is, you can edit the text of the article as you see fit, in your web browser. Click the Save button to save your edits.

tip To view earlier versions of the article, before the latest edits, click the Revisions tab.

If the article is configured for Moderated Collaboration, your edits have to be approved by the article's writer. If the article is configured for Open Collaboration, your edits immediately appear in the version of the article that the general public sees.

The Bottom Line

The Google Directory is a useful alternative to searching the massive Google web page index. Google Directory results are more focused and of uniformly higher quality than what you find in the larger search index, and they also give you a feel for what's available in any given category. Plus, you get the advantage of browsing by category instead of searching, if that's your style. Kudos to Google for adapting the Open Directory to the Google site and offering users the best of both worlds.

Kudos are also in order for Google Knol, Google's attempt to repeat the success of Wikipedia. Whether you're an expert with knowledge to share or a researcher or student who needs information on a given topic, Google Knol is a great tool. It lets users share their expertise with one another—and provides more authoritative information than you're likely to find from a simple Google web search.

Searching for Products— and Bargains

O ne of the most important developments in the history of online shopping is the creation of the price-comparison site. This is a site that helps you compare prices between multiple online retailers. In essence, you let the price-comparison site do your shopping for you; all you have to do is evaluate the results.

As you might expect, searching for bargains is right up Google's alley; it plays right into Google's strength with search technologies. In fact, Google offers several different ways to comparison-shop online—Google Product Search, Google Catalogs, and Google Base.

Comparing Prices with Google Product Search

note Google Product Search was originally named Froogle (a Googlized play on the word *frugal*). Froogle became Google Product Search in April 2007.

If you're looking for a pure price-comparison site, look no further than Google Product Search. This is Google's shopping search engine, a direct competitor of all the other price-comparison sites on the Web.

How Google Product Search Is Different

Before we get into how Google Product Search works, it might prove beneficial to first understand how the other price-comparison sites on the Web work. That's because Google Product Search works differently from all those competing sites.

If you've ever used BizRate (www.bizrate.com), NexTag (www.nextag.com), Shopping.com (www.shopping.com), or a similar price-comparison site, you might be under the impression that these sites scour the Web for prices from a wide variety of online retailers. That's a false impression; instead, these sites build their price/product databases from product links submitted and paid for by participating retailers. That's right—most price-comparison sites charge retailers to be included in their listings. The more retailers a site signs up, the more products there are for you to search through.

To be fair, these price-comparison sites do appear to honestly present the lowest prices—from participating merchants, that is. The prices presented are legitimate, no matter who's paying what. The only thing is, it's possible that lower prices might exist at a retailer that doesn't sign on to a site's program.

Google Product Search isn't like all the other price-comparison sites. Unique among these sites, Google is completely objective; it doesn't take money for its listings, instead sending its spider software to independently scour the Web for merchants and products.

You see, Google Product Search is a pure search engine, just like its Google parent. Google Product Search searches all the online retailers it can find, and it doesn't accept any paid listings. That makes Google's price comparisons more legitimate than those at other sites. (And, in the name of full disclosure, it should be mentioned that merchants can also submit their product listings to Google—they just don't have to pay for this privilege.)

Not only are Google's results untainted by product placement, but it also typically returns more results for any given item you're shopping for. That's again because of how Google scours the Web for product listings; it's not limited to results submitted by participating retailers. If it's for sale on the Web, chances are Google knows about it.

note Retailers don't actually pay price-comparison sites on a per-listing basis; instead, they pay when customers click their product listings. This is called a *pay-per-click (PPC)* model, and the individual fee is called a *cost per click (CPC)*. CPCs run anywhere from a nickel to more than a buck, depending on the site and the product category.

Searching for the Lowest Prices

The main page for Google Product Search (www.google.com/products), shown in Figure 9.1, bears more than a passing resemblance to Google's main page. You use Google Product Search as you would Google itself, by searching for products you want to buy. (Unlike other price-comparison sites, Google offers no product category browsing capability; it's a search-only interface.)

FIGURE 9.1
The main page for Google Product Search.

Because Google Product Search is an offshoot of Google, it's no surprise that it works so well as a product search engine. In most cases, all you have to do is enter a product description, name, or model number into the search box at the top of the home page and then click the Search Products button.

Understanding Google's Product Search Results

Google displays all matching products on a search results page, such as the one shown in Figure 9.2. By default, the results are displayed in list view. If you click the Show Grid View link, you see the products displayed in a visual grid, which shows more items in the same amount of screen real estate (but with fewer immediate options for each listing).

FIGURE 9.2
The results of a Google product search.

Also by default, Google organizes its results based on relevance, which is measured by customer demand. You can also use the pull-down list at the top of the results listing to sort products by price (low to high or high to low), product rating, or seller rating.

Below the product listings is a section of search refinements you can use to narrow down the search results, as shown in Figure 9.3. These refinements differ by type of product, but typically they include filters that let you restrict your search by category, brand, price range, features, and so on. Click a link to redisplay the results as appropriately filtered.

Comparing Prices

When you find a product you're interested in, click the Compare Prices button. This displays a product page like the one shown

caution Watch out for the advertisements on Google's product search results page. These are the listings in the Sponsored Links section on the right side of the page; they're not really search results, but rather listings paid for by Google's advertisers.

note If you want to display only those items that can be purchased via the Google Checkout payment system, click the Show Google Checkout Items Only link at the top of the search results page. Learn more about Google Checkout in Chapter 33, "Selling Products and Services with Google Checkout."

in Figure 9.4. Here you can read a short description of the selected item, user reviews, or technical specifications. You can also compare prices at competing retailers by selecting the Compare Prices tab. You can sort this list of retailers by relevance, seller rating, price, or if they accept Google Checkout payments. (Although relevance is the default sort, sorting by price is the way to go for most bargain-shopping users.)

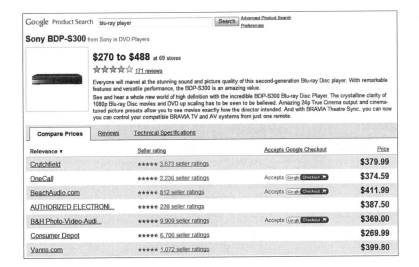

Refine product results for: **blu-ray player**				
Price range	Brands	Stores	Seller rating	Related searches
Under $130	Sony	allmedia9	4 stars and up	blu ray dvd player
$130 - $180	Panasonic	eBay	3 stars and up	blu ray disc player
$180 - $310	Samsung	Japanese Drama Super...	2 stars and up	sony blu ray player
$310 - $400	D skin	valid grooves	Has a rating	panasonic blu ray player
Over $400	Pioneer		More »	samsung blu ray player
$ ___ to $ ___ Go	More »			More »

FIGURE 9.3

Refining a Google product search.

Google Product Search blu-ray player   [Search] Advanced Product Search
                                                     Preferences

Sony BDP-S300 from Sony in DVD Players

$270 to $488 at 69 stores

★★★★☆ 171 reviews

Everyone will marvel at the stunning sound and picture quality of this second-generation Blu-ray Disc player. With remarkable features and versatile performance, the BDP-S300 is an amazing value.

See and hear a whole new world of high definition with the incredible BDP-S300 Blu-ray Disc Player. The crystalline clarity of 1080p Blu-ray Disc movies and DVD up scaling has to be seen to be believed. Amazing 24p True Cinema output and cinema-tuned picture presets allow you to see movies exactly how the director intended. And with BRAVIA Theatre Sync, you can now control your compatible BRAVIA TV and AV systems from just one remote.

Compare Prices	Reviews	Technical Specifications		
Relevance ▾		Seller rating	Accepts Google Checkout	Price
Crutchfield		★★★★★ 3,673 seller ratings		**$379.99**
OneCall		★★★★★ 2,236 seller ratings	Accepts Google Checkout	**$374.59**
BeachAudio.com		★★★★★ 812 seller ratings	Accepts Google Checkout	**$411.99**
AUTHORIZED ELECTRONI...		★★★★★ 239 seller ratings		**$387.50**
B&H Photo-Video-Audi...		★★★★★ 9,909 seller ratings	Accepts Google Checkout	**$369.00**
Consumer Depot		★★★★★ 6,706 seller ratings		**$269.99**
Vanns.com		★★★★★ 1,072 seller ratings		**$399.80**

FIGURE 9.4

Comparing prices from multiple retailers.

Advanced Searching

If you find that Google is returning too many (or too few) search results, you can use the Advanced Product Search page, shown in Figure 9.5, to fine-tune your query. This page is similar to the Google Advanced Search page; you get there by clicking the Advanced Product Search link next the Product Search box.

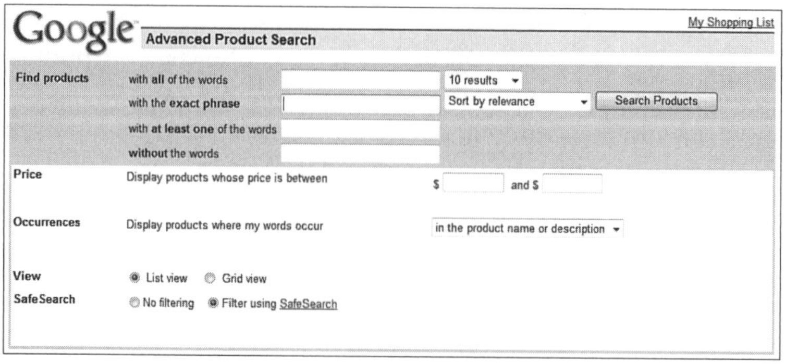

FIGURE 9.5
Advanced product searching.

The Advanced Product Search page offers a number of search parameters, as detailed in Table 9.1.

Table 9.1 Advanced Google Product Search Options

Option	Description	Comparable Search Operator
Find products with **all** of the words	Google's default search mode.	N/A
Find products with the **exact phrase**	Searches for the exact phrase you enter.	" "
Find products with **at least one** of the words	Searches for either one word or another.	OR
Find products **without** the words	Excludes products that contain the specified word(s).	-
Results (pull-down list)	Selects how many listings are displayed on the search results page.	N/A
Sort by (pull-down list)	Selects how results are sorted: Relevance, Price: Low to High, Price: High to Low, Product Rating, or Seller Rating.	N/A
Price	Displays products priced within the specified range.	...
Occurrences	Searches for products where the keywords occur in the product name, description, or both.	N/A
View	Displays results in either list or grid view.	N/A
SafeSearch	Turns on or off SafeSearch content filtering.	safesearch:

Using Advanced Search Operators

Of course, you don't have to go to the Advanced Search page to fine-tune your search. You can use any of Google's advanced search operators to refine your search directly from the Google Product Search box.

For example, you can search for an exact phrase from the main search box by enclosing the phrase in quotation marks, like this: **"sony bdp s300"**. You can also exclude a word from your search by using the - sign in front of the word, or do an either/or search with the **OR** operator.

There's also one product-specific search operator you might want to use. The **store:** operator lets you limit your search to a specified online store. For example, to see what DVD players Best Buy sells, enter the query **dvd player store:bestbuy**. Google lists all matching products offered for sale by the specified merchant.

> **note** Learn more about Google's search operators in Chapter 6, "Getting the Most Out of Google Search."

> **caution** Google's product prices aren't always totally current. Because Google spiders the Web for information, the price data it collects can be several days to several weeks old. Don't be surprised if you click a merchant link and find a different price listed, or discover that the item is no longer available.

Using Google's Merchant Reviews

What do you do if you find a good price for an item on Google but have never heard of the merchant? When the quality of the merchant is as important as the price of the product, turn to Google's merchant reviews. It's a good way to steer your business toward reliable retailers and avoid those that underserve their customers.

Google's merchant reviews, alas, aren't provided by Google—or by Google's users. Instead, they're sourced much like all of Google's content—by spidering the Web. Google's spider seeks out merchant reviews at other product-comparison sites (such as PriceGrabber.com, ResellerRatings.com, and Shopping.com) and then lists and collates them for your shopping convenience. The original reviews, in most instances, are provided by customers of that retailer.

When you search for a product, the first place you see the merchant reviews is on the product detail page. Major merchants are listed with a star rating, on a scale of zero to five stars. Along with the star rating is a listing of many user reviews that merchant has received, as well as a link to view those ratings.

When you click the seller's rating link, you're taken to that retailer's rating/reviews page. As you can see in Figure 9.6, this page displays the seller's overall star rating, along with the most relevant reviews of that seller. (Relevance, in this instance, relates to reviews of products similar to those you searched for.)

> **tip** Obviously, a rating has more weight the more reviews that are attached to it. A one-star rating with just a handful of reviews could imply bias on the part of a few disgruntled customers.

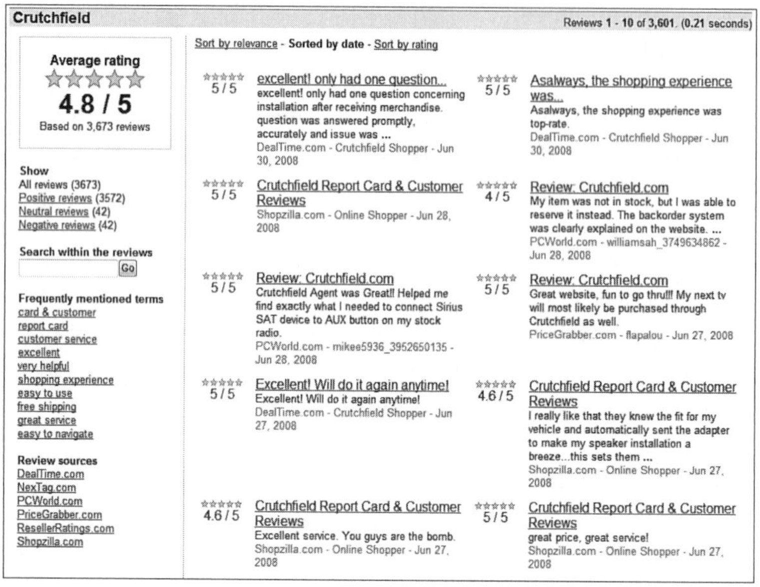

FIGURE 9.6

A seller's rating/reviews page.

If the sheer number of reviews is overwhelming, you can click the appropriate links to

- Show positive reviews only
- Show neutral reviews only
- Show negative reviews only
- Sort reviews by relevance, date, or rating

Google displays only the first few lines of these merchant reviews. To read a full

> **tip** I find it useful to focus on a seller's negative reviews, to see if there are any recurring problems noted. If a seller has a history of slow shipping, for example, this will probably show up in multiple reviews.

review, just click the review title link. This takes you to the original review on its original website. (You can also go to the main page of the reviewing website by clicking the site's name in the Review Sources section of the left column.)

COMMENTARY

THE BEST BARGAIN ISN'T ALWAYS THE LOWEST PRICE

Google does a great job of finding the lowest prices online, but the lowest price doesn't always mean the best bargain. Although it's tempting to base your purchase decision solely on the lowest price, you should consider other factors before you make your purchase:

Product availability. Does the merchant with the lowest price actually have the product in stock and ready to ship?

Shipping/handling costs. Often the merchant with the lowest price also has the highest shipping costs. Look for merchants that offer free or low-cost shipping, and then compare the *total* price—the product price plus the shipping costs.

Product condition. Google's product listings not only display new, in-the-box products, but sometimes also list used or refurbished items. Don't fall for a super-low price on a refurbished product when what you really want is a brand-new one.

Merchant reputation. Not all online retailers are created equal. Some are actually bait-and-switch artists, or offer poor service, or take forever to ship, or otherwise promise to disappoint. This is where you want to take advantage of Google's merchant ratings and compare different retailers by reading the reviews and ratings from previous customers. When you find a low price from a merchant you've never heard of, take the time to read the customer reviews—and skip merchants that rate poorly.

You read a lot of stories about consumers getting cheated or scammed or just being disappointed when dealing with one or another online retailer. On the Internet, just as in the real world, *caveat emptor* is the motto *du jour*. The smarter you shop, the safer and more satisfied you'll be. That means not automatically buying from the retailer with the lowest price—and doing your homework before you click that "purchase now" button.

Buying and Selling Online with Google Base

Google Product Search isn't the only way to find products for sale on the web. Google also offers Google Base, a service that's not easy to describe. Some have described it as a site for online classified ads, like the increasingly popular craigslist. Others have described it as an online marketplace, kind of like eBay without the auctions. Still others view Google Base as a giant database of products and information—and this description probably is the most accurate.

Google describes Google Base as "a place where you can easily submit all types of online and offline content that we'll host and make searchable online." That sounds a lot like a big database to me—which is, presumably, where Google got the Google *Base* name. You can use Google Base to post items you want to sell; other users can search the Google Base database to find items they want to buy. When a match is made, you and the other user arrange payment and shipping between yourselves. (That's why some say Google Base is a lot like eBay, because eBay is also a "middleman" to individual transactions between users.)

Understanding Google Base

Okay, so it's probably best to think of Google Base (base.google.com) as a giant database of products and services. As Google says, the goal of Google Base is to "collect and organize information and to expose it to the world." Of course, most of the "information" that Google talks about is actually physical products for sale by owner; the amount of free information offered in Google Base is a small subset of the total listings.

The reason that Google talks about collecting information is because that's exactly what it collects—information about physical products for sale, as well as other offline and online content. Google deals in the information about the items for sale, not in the items themselves.

The nice thing about Google Base is that it's a totally free service for both buyers and sellers. Items you post for sale on Google Base are available to users of the Google Base site. Depending on their relevance (that is, their popularity vis-à-vis links from other websites), they may also appear on Google proper, Google Product Search, or Google Maps.

What kinds of items can you post on Google Base? Obviously, you can post information about physical items you're selling, from clothing to cars and just about anything in between. You can also post nonphysical items for sale, such as poems, short stories, informational guides, recipes, electronic books, digital artwork, and the like. You can even post items or information for free distribution; Google Base doesn't have to be just for selling.

And you can choose how—or, more precisely, *where*—you sell or distribute your items. If you want to use Google Base as a classified advertising service to sell items for local pickup or delivery, you can. If you want to offer items online for shipment anywhere in the country (or the world), you can. It's your choice.

note When you post an item on Google Base, you describe it by assigning multiple keywords in the form of *labels* and *attributes*. Think of a label as the major product category (automobile, clothing, short story, and so on) and attributes as subcategories or descriptors (Ford, Explorer, automatic, red, and so on). Potential buyers use these attributes to fine-tune their searches.

After you've posted an item, it's available for searching by other Google Base users. It's possible that your item will also show up on Google proper (or on Google Product Search or Google Maps), but don't hold your breath. It has to build up relevance the old-fashioned way, via lots of links from other sites, before Google adds it to its normal search index.

Shopping for Items on Google Base

As you can see in Figure 9.7, the home page for Google Base includes a handful of clickable product categories, links for uploading your own items, and the ubiquitous search box, now located at the bottom of the page. You can find items either through searching (no surprise) or by clicking through the product categories.

Searching for items on Google Base is just like searching for items on Google proper, with the addition of search refinements based on the user-assigned attributes we discussed previously.

To conduct a product search, all you have to do is enter your query into the top-of-the-page search box, and then click the Search Base button. Google Base displays an initial search results page, as shown in Figure 9.8. Unfortunately, the results on this page are probably too broad to use, because it lists all the items posted in all product categories.

tip You can use any of Google's advanced search operators to refine your Google Base search.

FIGURE 9.7

The Google Base main page.

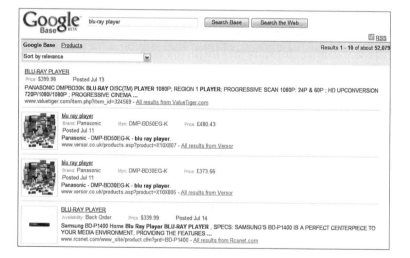

FIGURE 9.8

General results from a Google Base search.

When you want to find out more about a particular item listing, click the title of the listing; this takes you directly to the product page, often hosted off-Google at a third-party site. If you then choose to purchase the item, you

arrange payment and shipping directly
with the seller. Your interaction with
Google Base is now over.

> **note** Many items listed with Google Base are actually eBay auction items. Click one of these items and you're taken to the eBay item listing page.

Selling Items on Google Base

Okay, now you know how you can search
for and purchase items on Google Base. But
what if you have something to sell? Read on to learn how to post your items
for sale on the Google Base system.

Creating a listing with Google Base is a relatively easy process. All you have
to do is follow these steps:

1. From the main Google Base page, click the One at a Time link.

2. The next page, shown in Figure 9.9, prompts you to select an item
   type. This should be the main product category for your listing. You
   can probably find a category that fits by pulling down the Choose an
   Existing Item Type list; if not, enter a new category into the Create Your
   Own Item Type box. Click the Next button to continue.

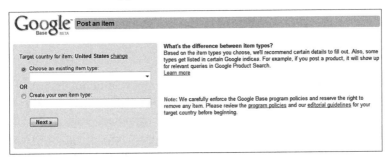

FIGURE 9.9

Selecting an item type.

3. The next page, shown in Figure 9.10, is where you enter all the details
   about what you're selling. Although the specific details will vary by
   item type, you'll probably be asked to enter the item's title, price, price
   type (fixed price, minimum price, or negotiable), quantity, product
   type, condition, brand, and a detailed item description.

FIGURE 9.10

Entering product details.

4. For some items, you see a section for additional details about your item, typically to the right of the Details section. Click any or all links in this section to provide the appropriate details. (For example, if you're selling an article of clothing, click the Apparel Type link; this displays a new Apparel Type list box in the Details section.)

5. Still on the same page, scroll down to the Pictures and Files section and add up to 10 photos of your item. You can add a picture hosted on another website by entering the photo's complete URL, or you can click the Browse button to upload pictures stored on your PC. Click the Attach button after you've entered the information for each photo.

6. Still on the same page, scroll to the bottom of the page and check your Contact, Payment, and Location and Delivery information. Click the appropriate Edit link to change any of this info.

> **note** Most Google Base sellers sign up to accept payments via Google Checkout. Learn more about Google Checkout in Chapter 33, "Selling Products and Services with Google Checkout."

7. Still on the same page, enter how long you want this listing to last into the This Item Will Expire in *XX* Days field. Your listings can run a maximum of 31 days.

> **tip** You need to click the Edit link in the Location and Delivery section to specify your shipping costs for this item.

8. When you're done entering information, click the Preview button to preview your listing or the Publish button to finalize and post your listing.

The resulting listing, like the one shown in Figure 9.11, is now live. Good luck with the selling!

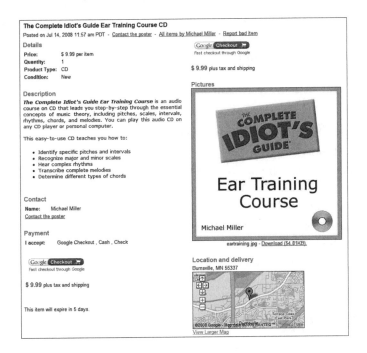

FIGURE 9.11

A live Google Base listing.

Uploading Bulk Items

The process previously described is the way to list individual items for sale. But if you have a lot of items to post, you're better off using Google Base's bulk upload function. You can prepare your list of items offline and then upload them all in a single file.

For bulk uploading, Google accepts information in either tab-delimited spreadsheet or XML (RSS 1.0, RSS 2.0, Atom 0.3, or Atom 0.2) formats. To upload a file of listings, go to the Google Base home page and click the Data Feed link. When the next page appears, click the New Data Feed button, and then follow the onscreen instructions to upload the designated file. See base.google.com/base/howtobulkupload.html for more information on how to create the bulk upload file.

Using Google Base to Submit Store Inventory to Google Product Search

Here's another use for Google Base—it lets retailers submit their store inventory for inclusion in the Google Product Search database. You can use Google Base to submit both online and retail inventory, which means you can then use Google Product Search to drive traffic to your local location.

The best thing about this is that it's the identical process used to upload bulk postings to Google Base. To submit store inventory to Google Product Search, all you have to do is create and submit a bulk-upload file to Google Base.

Using Google Base to Submit Business Location Data to Google Maps

We'll talk more about Google Maps in Chapter 27, "Finding Your Way with Google Maps." If you want information about your local business to be included in the Google Maps database, you can use Google Base to submit that information.

Again, the process to upload business location data is the same for submitting any bulk upload file to Google Base. You need to create a file with your business location information (in tab-delimited or XML format) and then upload that file from the Google Base main page.

The Bottom Line

It should be no surprise that Google offers top-flight product and shopping search services; as you've previously learned, the company's core search technologies can be applied to all sorts of specialized searches.

In the case of Google Product Search, there's a lot to like—and a few things not to like. The big plus is Google's complete impartiality, because it doesn't take any paid listings (as do competing price-comparison sites). That makes it a valuable tool for savvy online bargain hunters.

Searching for Blogs and Blog Postings

One of the most active parts of the Internet is the so-called blogosphere, the home of those public diaries called blogs. A blog—short for "web log"—is a personal website that is updated frequently with commentary, links to other sites, and anything else the author might be interested in. Many blogs also let visitors post comments in response to the owner's postings, resulting in a community that is very similar to that of a message board. It's a 21st century version of self-publishing, enabled by the Internet.

If you want to start your own blog, Google offers its own blog-hosting service called Blogger; we'll discuss Blogger in more depth in Chapter 18, "Blogging with Blogger." But if all you want to do is read blog postings, there are literally hundreds of thousands of blogs you can choose from, covering just about any topic you can think of. How do you find the blog that contains the information and opinions you're interested in?

Again, Google comes to the rescue. When you want to find a particular blog or blog posting, you can use Google Blog Search. This is a specialized subset of the main Google search engine, fine-tuned to search the far-reaching blogosphere. Read on to learn more.

How Google Blog Search Works

Before Google Blog Search, it was a bit of a shot in the dark trying to find information in the blogosphere. There is no single organized directory of blog sites, nor of the frequently updated content of all the blogs that exist today. The blogosphere is quite chaotic, and constantly changing; Google's traditional method of crawling the Web for updated information, which normally takes a few weeks to update, was simply too slow to index blog content.

The solution to this problem came in the form of site feeds. A site feed is an automatically updated stream of a blog's contents, enabled by a special XML file format called RSS (Really Simple Syndication). When a blog has an RSS feed enabled, any updated content is automatically published as a special XML file that contains the RSS feed. The syndicated feed is then normally picked up by RSS feed reader programs and RSS aggregators for websites.

Google hit upon the idea of using these RSS feeds to seed its blog search index. By aggregating RSS feeds into its index, Google Blog Search is constantly (and almost immediately) updated with new blog content. The structured format of the RSS files also makes it relatively easy to accurately search for specific information and date ranges within the blog index.

While some users think that Google Blog Search searches only blogs hosted by Google's Blogger service, that isn't true. Google Blog Search searches every blog on the Internet that publishes a site feed, using either RSS or Atom formats. Google's blog index holds only posts created since the launch of Google Blog Search, however; for most blogs, that means posts made before June 2005 aren't available for searching.

tip Google's Universal Search integrates Google Blog Search results with normal web search results when you search from the main Google search page.

How to List Your Blog with Google Blog Search

If you have your own blog, what do you need to do to make sure it's included in

note Atom is a feed format similar to RSS, with a few extra features.

Google Blog Search results? The answer is, not much. You don't have to submit your blog to Google for indexing; all you have to do is make sure you've enabled a site feed for your blog. You can choose either an RSS or Atom feed; either one works. If you're not sure how to enable the site feed feature, contact your blog host for more information.

COMMENTARY

BROWSING THE BLOGOSPHERE

When you take all the blogs on the Web together, you get something called the *blogosphere*. It's important to think of the blogosphere as separate from the Web, because of all the interlinking going on. Look at any blog, and you're likely to see a list of related blogs (sometimes titled "friends of..."). Bloggers like to link to other blogs that they like— as well as to news stories, photos, audio files—you name it.

In fact, a lot of blogs are nothing more than links to interesting blog entries—there isn't always a lot of original content there. The blogger finds something interesting and then uses his own blog to draw attention to that other posting. In this way, bloggers are a lot like radio disc jockeys, "spinning" links and snippets the same as a DJ spins songs.

These bloggers not only sort through the blogosphere to find the most interesting articles, they also provide some background and organization to these postings, and in many cases add their own commentary. The best blogs have a definite point of view, no matter what content they're linking to.

The way to make the most efficient use of the blogosphere is to find one or two bloggers you really like for a specific topic, and then use those blogs as a kind of guide to the rest of the blogosphere. Let the bloggers lead the way—and be prepared to spend some time jumping from link to link!

Searching for Blogs—and Blog Posts

Now that you know the background, how do you use Google Blog Search to search for information in the blogosphere? It's relatively easy; a simple search returns links to both entire blogs and individual blog postings.

Two Ways to Search

There are actually two different ways to use Google Blog Search.

First, you can go to the main Google Blog Search page (blogsearch.google.com), shown in Figure 10.1. Enter your query into the search box, and then click the Search Blogs button.

FIGURE 10.1

The main Google Blog Search page.

Alternatively, if you use Blogger to host your own blog and you like the Blogger interface, you can use the Blogger Blog Search page (search.blogger.com), shown in Figure 10.2. This page works just like the Google Blog Search page: enter your query into the search box, and then click the Search Blogs button.

FIGURE 10.2

The Blogger Blog Search page.

However you do it, it's the same search, and it returns the same results.

Evaluating Blog Search Results

When you enter your blog search query, Google searches its index of RSS feeds and returns a page of blogs and blog postings that best match your query. As you can see in Figure 10.3, this page has two main parts.

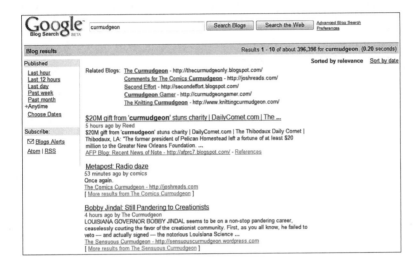

FIGURE 10.3
The results of a Google Blog Search.

At the top of the page is a short listing of blogs that have some relevance to your query. Click the blog name to view the entire blog.

Below that is a listing of individual blog posts. The title of the post is at the top of each listing; click the title to view the full posting. Below the title is a line that tells you when the posting was made, and who posted it. Then there's the first few sentences of the post, serving as a summary. And, finally, there's a link to the blog itself, listing both the blog's title and URL; click the link to view the entire blog.

To view additional postings that match your query, scroll down to the bottom of the page and click the Next link or the Page Number link.

> **tip**
> By default, blog postings are listed by relevance—the best matches are at the top of the list. If you'd rather view the results in chronological order, click the Sort by Date link at the top-right corner of the search results page.

Fine-Tuning Your Blog Search Query

Entering a Google Blog Search query is very similar to entering a standard Google web search query. Just enter one or more keywords into the search box, click the Search button, and you're on your way.

However, you can apply some advanced search options to fine-tune your search results. Read on to learn more.

Using Advanced Search Operators

It's important to know that all the search operators you learned about in Chapter 6, "Getting the Most Out of Google Search," can be used with Google Blog Search. Remember to enclose phrase searches in quotation marks, to use the + and - and **OR** operators, and to use advanced operators such as **link:** and **intitle:** as appropriate.

In addition, Google Blog Search has its own collection of blog-specific search operators that you can use. These operators are detailed in Table 10.1.

Table 10.1   Google Blog Search Operators

Operator	Description	Usage
inblogtitle:	Limits the search to words contained in the blog's title.	**inblogtitle:***keyword*
inposttitle:	Limits the search to words contained in the titles of individual blog postings.	**inposttitle:***keyword*
inpostauthor:	Limits the search to postings by a specific poster.	*keyword:***inpostauthor:***name*
blogurl:	Limits the search to a particular blog, as defined by the blog's web address (URL).	*keyword:***blogurl:** *www.blogurl.com*

Using the Advanced Search Page

If you don't like using search box operators, you can achieve the same results by using the Google Blog Search Advanced Search page. You get to this page by clicking the Advanced Blog Search link on the main Google Blog Search page.

As you can see in Figure 10.4, the Advanced Blog Search page contains a number of search restrictions, all accessible by filling in the appropriate blanks or selecting items from a pull-down list. Table 10.2 details the advanced search options available on this page.

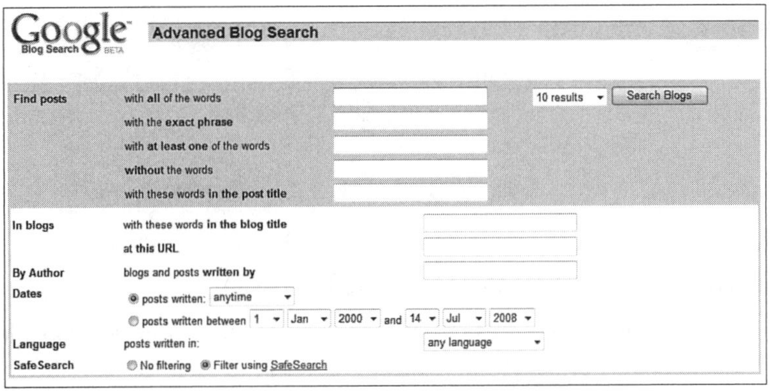

FIGURE 10.4
Google Blog Search's Advanced Blog Search page.

Table 10.2   Google Blog Search Advanced Blog Search Options

Option	Description	Same as This Operator
Find posts with **all** of the words	Standard Google search, assuming the **AND** operator before each keyword.	N/A
Find posts with the **exact phrase**	Searches for exact phrases only.	" "
Find posts with **at least one** of the words	Searches for either one keyword or another.	**OR**
Find posts **without** the words	Excludes words from the search results.	–
Find posts with these words **in the post title**	Searches the titles of blog postings only.	**inposttitle:**
In blogs with these words **in the blog title**	Searches blog titles only.	**inblogtitle:**
In blogs at **this URL**	Searches posts within a specific blog.	**blogurl:**
By Author: blogs and posts **written by**	Searches posts made by a specific user.	**inpostauthor:**
Dates: posts written	Searches only those posts written in the last hour, last 6 hours, last 12 hours, last day, past week, past month, or anytime.	N/A
Dates: posts written between	Searches only those posts written within a specified date range.	
Language: posts written in	Searches only those posts written in the specified language.	N/A

Continues

Table 10.2	Continued	
Option	Description	Same as This Operator
SafeSearch	Turns on or off Google's SafeSearch content filtering.	**safesearch:**
Results	Displays 10, 20, 30, 50, or 100 results per page.	N/A

Subscribing to Blog Search Results

At the beginning of this chapter I talked a little about how Google got its blog search results by using RSS feeds. Well, Google uses this same technology to feed you updates to the postings you find on the search results page. That's right—Google syndicates its blog search results via RSS and Atom.

When you subscribe to an RSS or Atom search results feed, Google automatically notifies you of any new postings that match your search query. The notification can occur via email, via a blog search gadget on your iGoogle home page, or as a feed subscription in the Google Reader application. As new search results are found, you're either notified or they show up as new postings within the feed.

To subscribe to a feed of search results, conduct your blog search as normal from the Google Blog Search main page, and then scroll to the bottom of the search results page. Click the link for the type of notification you want—email alert, blog search gadget for your iGoogle home page, or blog search feed for Google Reader.

The Bottom Line

Blogs are here to stay, and they're becoming an increasingly important medium for the distribution of information and opinions. Google Blog Search came along at just the right time to help users like you and me find specific information in the increasingly large and chaotic blogosphere, which makes it one of the most valuable of Google's new search tools. The additional benefit of subscribing to a feed of your search results is just icing on the cake.

note It should come as no big surprise that Google offers its own feed aggregator called Google Reader. Learn more about this application in Chapter 23, "Using Google Reader."

Searching Books and Libraries

There's a lot of great information out there on the Web. But it pales in comparison to the amount of information available in printed books. If there were a way to create a repository of all the world's book content, it would put the Internet to shame.

For better or for worse, Google is working to create that legendary global book repository. Imagine, if you will, every book ever published, available for searching online, from your web browser. That's what Google is trying to accomplish with Google Book Search, in conjunction with the Google Books Library Project. If Google is successful (and there's no guarantee of that, of course; the project is rather daunting), the collected wisdom of the ages will be just a mouse click away.

The Story Behind Google Book Search

Google's ultimate goal with Google Book Search is to let you search the full text of any book ever published. Then you will have the option of reading that book online (for selected books), purchasing the book (from selected booksellers), or finding out where you can borrow a copy (from participating libraries). To achieve this goal, Google must have the full text of all these books in its database—which is a formidable challenge.

Google is now in the process of adding the contents of as many books as possible to its Google Books database. This book content is coming primarily from two sources—publishers and libraries.

Google Books Partner Program

Publishers can submit their books for inclusion in the Google Books database via the Google Books Partner Program. This program is being pushed as a way for publishers to promote their books online, via exposure to Google's vast user base.

When a publisher signs up for a Google Books account, the company sends Google a list of its books that it wants included in Google Book Search. Ideally the publisher also sends Google a printed copy of each book or the text in PDF format. (The publisher can also just have Google add its books to the Google Books database when they're scanned at a library—which we'll get into in a moment.)

Just because Google has the full text of the book in its database, however, doesn't mean that users can read the entire book online, for free. To protect the publishers' copyrighted content, Google lets readers view only a handful of pages online. In addition, all copy, save, and print functions are disabled, so freeloading readers can't download or print books for free. The only reason that Google archives the full text of the book is so that readers can search the entire book and then read snippets of text.

In other words, Google Book Search is not intended as a way for readers to read entire books online. Instead, you use Google Book Search to discover what books contain the information you're looking for; you can then opt to purchase the book or borrow it from a library.

This explains why many books are listed in the Google Book Search database without detailed content. Many publishers have opted to provide book listings only, as a kind of Amazon-like pseudo-advertisement on the Google site. Click one of these listings and you don't see a synopsis or manuscript; instead, you're shown a list of places where you can buy the book—often accompanied by the publisher's marketing blurb. So it goes.

Google Books Library Project

The other way that Google is obtaining content for its Google Books database is from participating libraries, as part of the Google Books Library Project. To date, Google has agreements with a variety of academic and public libraries across the country and around the globe:

- Bavarian State Library (Germany)
- Columbia University
- Cornell University Library
- Ghent University Library (Belgium)
- Harvard University
- Keio University Library (Japan)
- Lyon Municipal Library (France)
- National Library of Catalonia (Spain)
- New York Public Library
- Oxford University, Bodleian Library (U.K.)
- Princeton University
- Stanford University
- University Complutense of Madrid (Spain)
- University Library of Lausanne (Switzerland)
- University of California
- University of Michigan
- University of Texas at Austin
- University of Virginia
- University of Wisconsin–Madison and Wisconsin Historical Society Library

These partners are scanning the books in their collections and will make them available for searching online. The result is like having all the books from these libraries available in your web browser, with Google Book Search serving as a kind of online card catalog to all that book content.

Of course, the library doesn't own the content of all the books in its collection. Although Google may be able to scan a library's books, it can't legally distribute them (or provide access to them electronically) unless the books' publishers have given Google permission to do so. Unless, that is, a given book is old enough that its copyright has expired.

So the library collections available through Google Book Search contain searchable indexes of all available texts, and full-text versions of works in the public domain. It's not quite the same as having the full content of a library available for reading online, but it's getting close.

note If a publisher or copyright holder doesn't want its books included in Google Book Search, they can ask Google not to scan selected library texts. For more information on excluding titles from the database, see books.google.com/partner/exclusion-signup.

Searching—and Viewing—Book Content

The Google Books database is accessible in two different ways—from the regular Google web search page, or from the dedicated Google Book Search page.

Searching from the Standard Web Search Page

You don't have to go to the Google Book Search page to search for book content. Google Books results can appear as the result of a standard Google web search—assuming that the book(s) in question have something to do with the query at hand. In this instance, matching books appear in OneBox results either at the top or bottom of the first search results page, as shown in Figure 11.1.

Book results for **music history**
A History of Rock Music - by Piero Scaruffi - 567 pages
The Modern Invention of Medieval Music ... - by Daniel Leech Wilkinson - 358 pages
The Music of India - by Reginald Massey - 204 pages

FIGURE 11.1
Google Books results from a standard web search.

Searching from Google Book Search

The other way to conduct a book search is from the Google Book Search page (books.google.com), shown in Figure 11.2. This page functions like Google's standard web search page; enter your query into the search box, and then click the Search Books button.

tip You can also browse for books from the main Google Book Search page. Just click a category on the left and keep clicking till you find something interesting.

FIGURE 11.2
Searching for books with Google Book Search.

Conducting an Advanced Book Search

Google Book Search also offers an Advanced Book Search page, accessible when you click the Advanced Book Search link. As you can see in Figure 11.3, this page offers many of the advanced search options you find on Google's regular Advanced Search page, as well as a few book-specific search options.

All these search options are detailed in Table 11.1.

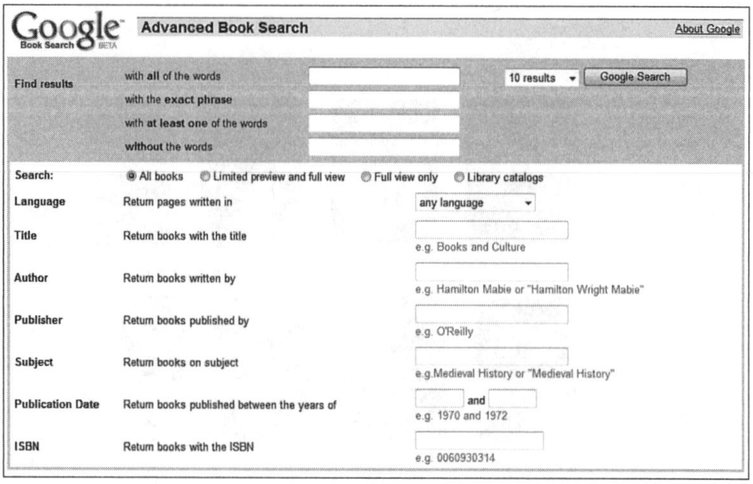

FIGURE 11.3
Google's Advanced Book Search page.

Table 11.1	Advanced Book Search Options
Option	**Description**
Find results with all of the words	Default search mode.
Find results with the exact phrase	Searches for messages that contain the exact phrase entered.
Find results with at least one of the words	Searches for messages that contain either one word or another.
Find results without the words	Excludes messages that contain the specified word(s).
Search	All books in the database, those that offer a limited preview or full view, those that offer full view only, or those listed in library catalogs.
Language	Searches for books written in a specific language.
Title	Searches for words in the book's title.
Author	Searches for books written by a specific author.
Publisher	Searches for books published by a specific publisher.
Subject	Searches for books by the main topic of the text.
Publication date	Searches for books published between two given years.
ISBN	Searches for a book's ISBN.
Results	Displays 10, 20, 30, 50, or 100 results per page.

Viewing Book Content

After you enter your search query, Google returns a list of matching books, as shown in Figure 11.4. You can display the results in Google's traditional list view, or click the Cover View link to see a more visually appealing but somewhat less efficient view of the results, as shown in Figure 11.5.

FIGURE 11.4

List view search results from a Google Book Search.

Books in the search results list can have four different viewing options, depending on the book's copyright status and publisher/author wishes:

- **Full view.** The full text of these books is available for reading online.

- **Limited preview.** These books have only a limited number of pages available for reading online, as kind of a preview to the rest of the book. The full text of the book is not available for reading online.

- **Snippet view.** Similar to limited-preview books, these books offer only a few snippets of text for preview. These snippets show a few instances of the search term in the content; the full text of the book is not available for reading online.

- **No preview available.** For these books, no previews or snippets are available. Obviously, the full text of the books is also not available for reading online—although sometimes a marketing blurb or publisher's summary is posted.

FIGURE 11.5
Viewing search results in cover view.

Getting More Information

After you've accessed a book page (full view or otherwise), you have several options for obtaining more information. Depending on the book, you can

- Read the book online (for full-view books). Click the right and left arrow buttons to turn the pages, or click the links at the left to go to specific sections of the book. (You can also enter a page number below the page window to go directly to a specific page in the book.)

- Search within the book. Use the search box on the left side of the page to search for instances of words and phrases within the book.

- Read bibliographic information about the book (author, publisher, publication date, and so on), located below the book page display.

> **note** Books without their cover art in the Google database are displayed with a generic blue, green, or red "leather" cover.

■ Read more about this book (such as a synopsis) by clicking the About This Book link.

■ Read online reviews of the book. (Click the links below the book page display.)

> **note** The Find It In a Library function utilizes the Online Computer Library Center (OCLC) WorldCat database. Learn more about the OCLC at www.oclc.org.

■ Learn more about the book's publisher by clicking the publisher name below the book page display.

■ Buy the book from selected bookstores; click the bookstore link to go directly to a purchase page.

■ Find this book in a nearby library by clicking the Find It In a Library link and entering your zip code.

Know, however, that not all of these options are available for all books. Many books simply let you see a preview or snippet, some brief bibliographical information, and a link or two to purchase the book online.

COMMENTARY

GOOGLE VERSUS THE PUBLISHING COMMUNITY

As the Google Books Library Project goes about its business of scanning in hundreds of thousands of library books, it's important to note that Google is scanning those books without first seeking the approval of the authors or publishers. This has caused a great deal of friction between Google and the publishing community—and at least one major lawsuit.

The so-called "publishing community" is separate from the library community, and it's the libraries that Google is working most closely with. Publishers and libraries have significantly different mindsets, which is at the core of this conflict.

You see, publishers (and authors), whatever their artistic intent, are ultimately in the business to make money, which they do by selling books. Libraries, on the other hand, exist to disseminate information, most often for free. It's this age-old conflict between generating revenues and distributing information that Google has deliberately walked right into the middle of.

11

When it comes to allowing their books to be available via Google Book Search, publishers are of decidedly mixed minds. Some publishers view it as a promotional opportunity and another potential outlet for book sales; other publishers view it as interfering with their own internal sales plans. That's why you see some publishers cooperating with Google on this project, but many more publishers shying away. These less-enthusiastic publishers want to protect their copyrights and restrict access to the books they publish; they're more likely to partner with an online bookseller like Amazon.com than with a site that, in their view, gives away content.

Authors face a similar dilemma. Should they embrace Google Book Search as a way for readers to find out about their less-visible works, or should they be afraid of Google lessening the value of their content by giving it (or some of it) away?

Opposing Google's effort is the Authors Guild. The Guild, along with individual authors Herbert Mitgang, Betty Miles, and Daniel Hoffman, have sued Google over the Book Search program, alleging that Google is engaging in massive copyright infringement at the expense of the rights of individual writers.

Former Authors Guild president Nick Taylor had this to say about the situation:

> "This is a plain and brazen violation of copyright law. It's not up to Google or anyone other than the authors, the rightful owners of these copyrights, to decide whether and how their works will be copied."

The problem, as many authors see it, is that Google is scanning all library books by default and then requiring disinterested authors and publishers to opt out of the program. A better approach would be to ask permission before scanning, instead of assuming that permission and then allowing proactive opt-outs. As currently constructed, the program can inadvertently include content that authors (or publishers) do not want distributed online.

That said, many authors think that Google Book Search can increase the visibility of the books they've written. For example, here's what author Paul Andrews says about the program:

> "As a longtime dues-paying member of the Authors Guild, I'm party to a lawsuit against Google over its new book-search service called Google Book Search. As an author of two books, though, I'm not sure I want to be suing Google. Every writer wants his or her work to be read. But to be read, a work needs to be found. Digital search is fast becoming the *de facto* way to be found, [and] Google Book Search aims to do for books what Google has done for the Web."

Author Cory Doctorow puts it more succinctly:

> "Thank you, thank you, thank you, Google, for providing a way to put books back into the daily round of average people."

And it looks like the non-Author Guild authors have a point. Recent research has shown that Google Book Search is driving traffic to booksellers—those listed on the Google Book Search pages, of course. People are using Google Book Search to find books and then linking back to booksellers' websites to make their purchases. This should not be surprising.

As an author, I can see both sides of the conflict. On one hand, I really don't want Google or any other entity giving away copies of my books (electronic or otherwise), without paying me any royalties. On the other hand, if only snippets of my books are available for online browsing, what's the harm? In fact, if viewing a page or so online encourages a potential reader to purchase one of my books, I benefit from the exercise.

The spanner in the works, however, is whether readers of nonfiction works can find the information they want from a Google search result snippet, and therefore not have to purchase the printed book. It's possible, for example, that someone searching for information about Google Book Search might be able to read this very page online, and therefore not have to purchase the book. In this instance, Google Book Search becomes a deterrent to book sales, which isn't a good thing. (At least it's not a good thing for authors and publishers; for readers, it might be a different story.)

My gut tells me that as long as Google Book Search shows only snippets of book content, it actually works to promote the sale of printed books, especially those that don't receive a lot of promotion or appear on the bestseller lists. If the program evolves to providing the full text of works online, without the approval of or compensation to the legal copyright holder, the program is more akin to intellectual property theft than it is to providing useful information for web searchers. As pundits are fond of saying, only time will tell the ultimate impact of the Google Books program.

The Bottom Line

The Google Books project is an interesting and ambitious endeavor. Although the prospect of having all the world's books available online is deceptively attractive, it's also somewhat impractical. Google can't, after all, make available copyrighted material without the permission of the books' copyright holders. This means that most of the books in print today won't be available for reading online, at least not for free.

As such, the value of having book content searchable but not readable is debatable. You can try Google Book Search for yourself to see what you think, but be prepared; a lot of the information you find will be tantalizingly out of reach.

11

Searching for Scholarly Information

As great as Google is for the average Internet user, it can also be a librarian's worst nightmare. Many students and researchers are abandoning bricks-and-mortar libraries (as well as proprietary online research services) in favor of Google's free online searches. Almost any piece of information, it seems, can be found with a standard Google web search.

Or can it?

Google's web search engine indexes only that part of the Internet that is accessible to the general public. It doesn't access the tons of information stored in private research databases, or that exists in print journals and reference books found only in university and research libraries. Although you *could* use Google to conduct research or write a scholarly paper, the amount of true scholarly information available to you would be limited—and difficult to separate from all the home-grown information out there. Google, it seems, is more for the hobbyist than for the serious student or professional researcher.

To their credit, the folks at Google recognized this deficiency and acted on it. The result is a relatively new service called Google Scholar. Google Scholar enables anyone—students, researchers, even the general public—to search a database of scholarly journals and articles free of

note Scholars and researchers sometimes refer to Google Scholar as "Schoogle" (pronounced *skoogle*). Searching Google Scholar is known as "Schoogling."

charge. Now students and researchers can conduct their research from the comfort of their dorm rooms and offices, without having to trudge down to the local library.

How Google Scholar Works

Within a few short months of its launch, Google Scholar drew raves from its scholarly audience and established itself as a viable (and free) alternative to the expensive research databases offered by Elsevier, Thomson, and other scholarly publishers. Although some librarians say that Google Scholar doesn't offer quite the quality and quantity of results of its more-established rivals, others praise it for its easy access and simple operation.

As you can see in Figure 12.1, the Google Scholar search page closely resembles the traditional Google web search page. You access Google Scholar at scholar.google.com.

FIGURE 12.1

The Google Scholar main search page.

When you search Google Scholar, you receive a list of matching articles, journals, papers, theses, books, and the like, along with a brief summary of each item. Much of the information displayed on the search results page is available online free of charge. Some is available online only for subscribers to a particular service. Some is available online only for members of a particular library. And some is available in printed format only.

The information in the Google Scholar database is also available via a traditional Google web search, although it's often buried deep in the search results. The advan-

> **note** Another benefit of this citation analysis is a Cited By link next to each search result listing. When you click this link, you see a list of all the pages and documents that point to the current article.

tage of Google Scholar is that it focuses your search solely on the scholarly literature and returns results in a format familiar to students and researchers. The search itself is also fine-tuned for the scholarly crowd; you can confine your search to specific disciplines, authors, and publications.

Put another way, Google Scholar is a way for students and researchers to find academically appropriate and peer-reviewed literature without having to wade through all the nonprofessional information that clutters the public Internet.

Identifying Scholarly Content

To identify content for inclusion in the Google Scholar database, Google uses an algorithm that guesses at what it thinks is scholarly content. As with Google's PageRank algorithm, the Google Scholar algorithm is a closely guarded secret.

What we do know is that the algorithm tries to identify credentialed authors and searches for citations for each article. These citations are extracted and analyzed; at least in part, Google examines the connections between other documents that cite the article in question. This citation analysis is also used to help rank documents within the Google Scholar results. (Google Scholar also takes into consideration the full text of each article, the article's author, and the publication in which the article appeared to make its rankings.)

Searching Beyond the Public Internet

Google Scholar not only searches the public web for scholarly information, it also strives to include articles, journals, and books from major scholarly publishers. If the full text of a document is not available for dissemination via the public web, Google still includes an abstract from the document; you can then choose whether to pay for access (if that option is available; some materials require a subscription to the host library for access).

Some of this nonpublic information is available through Google's partnering with major scholarly research services and libraries. For example, Google Scholar derives some of its content from the Open WorldCat database, which contains records of materials owned by libraries that participate in the Online Computer Library Center (OCLC) project. (You can learn more about OCLC and Open WorldCat at www.oclc.org.)

> **note** When dealing with scholarly literature, it's often the case that the same paper is hosted in more than one database. In these instances, Google identifies what it believes is the "best" version and provides links to other available versions.

Including Print-Only Content

In the case of some scholarly literature, the publication itself is not actually online; only the abstract and citations are available over the Internet. This is a benefit of including information sourced from various library databases—you can find out what documents a library has available, even if you can't download them from the Internet.

> **caution** As useful as Google Scholar is, it searches only a fraction of the published scholarly literature. For more comprehensive scholarly research, use the search function provided by your local research library to search the many field-specific databases that cover scholarly publications, such as ABI/Inform, ERIC, Medline, and Proquest.

COMMENTARY

FINDING "INVISIBLE" INFORMATION

One of the interesting things about Google Scholar is that much of the material included in its database is already available to the general public—if only the public went to libraries. That's because Google Scholar includes listings of articles and books that are available only in print format or via electronic research databases and that are made available only to libraries. The information is out there; you just have to go to the library to find it. And because fewer and fewer people are going to libraries these days, the information becomes invisible to the PC-bound user.

12

That's one of the nice things about Google Scholar—it directs you to use your local library. Yes, you use Google Scholar to determine the availability of information, but then you have to hit the library to read some of it. (Some information, of course, is readily available online.) This is, in my opinion, a good thing; more hands-on exposure to books and literature benefits us all.

Another benefit of Google Scholar is that it provides at least limited access to online information that normally is locked behind subscription barriers. Most search engines—including Google—simply can't search private, subscription-only databases. The information in these databases creates what some call the "deep web," or what others call the "invisible web." The information's there, all right, but you wouldn't know it (and couldn't access it) without a subscription to the proprietary database service.

In some instances, this formerly password-protected information is made available to Google Scholar users, thanks to arrangements made between Google and the subscription services. In other cases only an abstract of the information is available; to read the full text, you have to subscribe to the service or pay a one-time fee to access the article. (You may also have to frequent a library that has a subscription to the service.) In any case, Google Scholar makes you aware of this previously "invisible" information, which is also a good thing.

Understanding Google Scholar Search Results

When you conduct a Google Scholar search, the results returned are limited primarily to scholarly articles, journals, theses, books, and the like. (In fact, articles tend to make up the bulk of Google Search results.) Figure 12.2 shows a typical Google Scholar search results page.

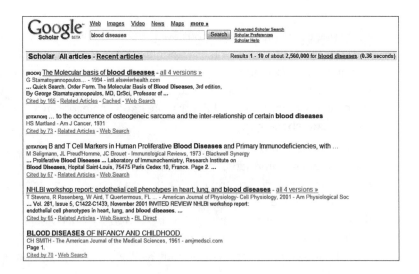

FIGURE 12.2
A typical Google Scholar search results page.

Different Types of Results

The information you see about a particular search result depends on what type of document it is. Let's work through the possibilities.

If it's an article available online, the title is clickable. When you click the title, you're taken either to the full text of the article or (if the article itself is available only via subscription) to the article's abstract. If the article is available for purchase via the British Library, a BL Direct link is displayed; click this link for purchase information.

If it's an article *not* available online, the title is *not* clickable, and the word [CITATION] appears beside the title. In this instance, you may be able to find the information you want by displaying the article's citations.

If it's a book that's available in electronic form online, the word [BOOK] appears beside the title, and the title is clickable. When you click the title, you're taken either to the full text of the book or (if the book itself is available only via subscription) to the book's abstract.

caution Articles marked with [CITATION] are referred to online but are not yet available online. Unfortunately, a large amount of scholarly literature is still available offline only—although this is apt to change over time.

If it's a book that's *not* available online, the word [BOOK] appears beside the title, and the title is *not* clickable. You'll also see a Library Search link; click this link to find a library that carries the hardcopy book.

> **caution** Not every source listed in Google Scholar is free. Many citations link directly to the websites of the articles' publishers, many of which charge a fee for access.

Listing Information

For each item listed on the search results page, you see some or all of the following information:

- Title of the book or article. If the full text or abstract is available online, the title is a clickable link.

- Bibliographic information (in green), including author, publisher, and so on.

- Cited By link, which links to a list of other articles and documents that cite this particular article.

- Related Articles link, which lists other articles on the same topic.

- View As HTML link, which lets you view a PDF-format article in normal web page format.

- Web Search link, which lets you search for information about this article in the main Google web index.

- Library Search link, available when a book is listed, which lets you view a list of real-world libraries that carry copies of the book.

- BL Direct link, available when an article is available for purchase via the British Library.

- Group Of link, visible when an article is one of several in a group of scholarly works. Click the link to view a list of the other articles.

How to Use Google Scholar Results

To best use Google Scholar results, you should first try clicking the article title. If this option isn't available, or if you're taken to an abstract only, you can use the Cited By and Web Search links to search for related articles and information. (You can also try to find the full-text article at your local library, of course.)

> **tip** If you're accessing Google Scholar from a university or research library, you may see a FindIt @ link next to selected search results. Click this link to locate an electronic version of the work via your library's online resources.

If you find a book that looks interesting, and if the book isn't available for online reading (most aren't), it's time to head to the library. Click the Library Search link to find a list of libraries that carry the book, and then put on your jacket and make a visit.

Searching Google Scholar

Now that you're somewhat familiar with the kind of scholarly information that Google Scholar finds, let's dive headfirst into the research waters and learn how to find that information.

Conducting a Basic Search

You can perform most of your research directly from the Google Scholar main page. Just enter your query into the search box and click the Search button, the same as you would a normal Google web search.

Using Advanced Search Operators

Scholarly research, however, is a little more exacting than typical web searching. More often than not you're searching for articles by a particular author, or for articles from a specific publication. To fine-tune your search in this manner, you can use most of the same search operators discussed in Chapter 6, "Getting the Most Out of Google Search"—in particular, +, –, " ", **OR**, and **intitle:**.

One new operator is specific to Google Scholar. The **author:** operator lets you search for articles written by a specific author. To use this operator, enclose the author's name in quotation marks and place it directly after the operator, like this: **author:"m miller"**. If you're interested in finding *references* to works by that author (as opposed to the author's works themselves), skip the **author:** operator and simply enclose the author's name in quotation marks as an exact-phrase search.

The exact-phrase operator is also useful when you're searching for a particular article or publication. Simply enclose the article/publication title in quotation marks, like this: **"discovering peer to peer"**. No other operator is necessary.

tip Given the vagaries of format, you may need to search for the author by first initial, first initial followed by a period, and full first name. For example, to search for me, you could enter **author:"m miller"**, **author:"m. miller"**, or **author:"michael miller"**.

Using the Advanced Scholar Search Page

Even more fine-tuning is available from the Google Scholar Advanced Scholar Search page. You access this page, shown in Figure 12.3, by clicking the Advanced Scholar Search link on the main Google Scholar page.

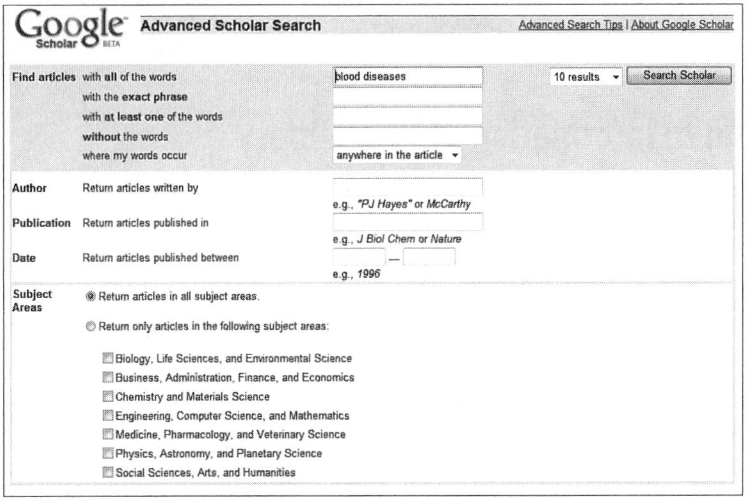

FIGURE 12.3

Using the Advanced Scholar Search page.

As you can see, the top part of this form offers pretty much the same type of fine-tuning available from the normal Google Advanced Search page (or by using advanced search operators). You have the option of searching for all the words (default), an exact phrase (" "), at least one of the words (**OR**), and without the words (–). The new option here is the last one, which lets you specify where in the article to search—in the title only, or anywhere in the article (the default).

The other options on this page include the following:

- To find articles written by a specific author, use the Author option and enter the author's name.

- To find articles published in a specific publication, use the Publication option and enter the publication's name.

- To find articles published within a specified date range, use the Date option and enter the starting and ending year.

■ To limit your search to a specific subject area (biology and life sciences, business and finance, and so on), go to the Subject Areas section and click the areas you want to search. (By default, Google Scholar searches all subject areas.)

caution Searches by publication are often incomplete. This is due to missing or incorrect information included with many citations, which often don't bother to mention where the article was published.

Linking to Information at Your Library

I mentioned previously that some search results might have a FindIt @ link next to the title. This indicates that the article is available for reading from your local or university library.

How does Google Scholar know which library you're using? If you're logging on from a campus computer, this information should be sensed automatically. But if you're logging on from another location, you can manually inform Google Scholar which library you normally use.

This is done from the Scholar Preferences page, which you get to by clicking the Scholar Preferences link on the main Google Scholar page. Scroll down to the Library Links section, enter the name of your library, and click the Find Library button.

You see a list of available libraries. You can select up to three libraries from this list, although you may be prompted to log on to a particular library site before accessing the associated FindIt @ link. Click the Save Preferences button when you're done.

tip It's also a good idea to check the Open WorldCat option so that you can search items listed in the Open WorldCat library database.

Expanding Google Scholar

Google Scholar is a far-reaching service, one that hasn't yet reached its full potential. Let's look at several ways that research professionals can increase access to the Google Scholar database.

Add Google Scholar to Your Website

Any website can add a Google Scholar search box to its web pages. This enables site visitors to search Google Scholar from your website, without exiting and opening the Google Scholar site. All you have to do is go to scholar.google.com/scholar/scholarsearch.html and follow the instructions there.

Google Scholar for Libraries

As you might have gathered from reading this chapter, Google Scholar is particularly useful for school libraries. There are two ways that a library can participate in Google Scholar—by offering Google Scholar access to library users, and by making library materials available to the Google Scholar database.

To make Google Scholar available to a library's patrons, the library needs to contact its link resolver vendor. In some instances, Google Scholar is now an option on the vendor's configuration pages; in other instances, you may need to set up specific procedures. When you've joined the Library Links program, all on-campus users will see FindIt @ links to library materials within the standard Google Scholar search results.

To include your library's materials in the Google Scholar database (so that they appear when a user clicks the Library Search link next to a search result), the library has to join the OCLC Open WorldCat program. You can also contact Google directly for more information at scholar-library@google.com.

And here's something all libraries will appreciate. Both the Library Links and Library Search programs are free! No budget demands here.

Google Scholar for Publishers

If you're a publisher of scholarly content and would like to see your works included in the Google Scholar database, you should contact Google at scholar-publisher@google.com. You can opt to provide full-text articles, abstracts, or even subscription-controlled content—it's your choice.

note If you opt not to provide full-text articles (or to provide subscription-only content), you still have to provide Google with a complete abstract it can display to its users.

The Bottom Line

Google Scholar is a real boon for students and research professionals. Even though much of the information found by Google Scholar isn't available online (or for free), it still opens the curtain to the world of the invisible web. It lets you discover content that you otherwise wouldn't have found via traditional web search engines. Yeah, you may still need to trundle down to the library, but at least you'll know exactly what you're looking for.

Searching for Specialty Information

N ow we get to the really fun stuff. As you've no doubt surmised from reading the previous chapters, Google offers many different kinds of searches. Some of these searches are obscure enough and specialized enough that they don't fit into any easy category—so we'll lump them all together and cover them in this chapter.

What kinds of searches are we talking about? How about searching for street addresses and phone numbers? Or word definitions? Or information about an airline flight? Or mathematical constants and conversions?

That's right—Google can do all of this and more. (My favorite oddball Google function is its ability to perform mathematical calculations directly from the Google search box.) Read on to learn all about these special functions—and how to use them.

Searching for People and Phone Numbers

If you're like me, every now and then you need (or want) to look up information about a particular person. I'm not talking about famous personages here, but rather normal people whose addresses or phone numbers I can't remember.

As far as Google is concerned, a person's name, address, or phone number is just another piece of information stored in the database. The techniques to retrieve this information, however, are a little different from normal Web search techniques.

Searching for People by Name

As part of its massive database of information, Google includes listings for millions of U.S. households in what it calls the Google PhoneBook. You search the PhoneBook listings from the main Google search box using specific query parameters.

You start a PhoneBook search with the **phonebook:** operator, followed by the person's name. To narrow your results, you need to include more information than just the name, such as the person's city, state, or ZIP code. There are six ways you can search for a person or household in the Google PhoneBook. Table 13.1 details each of these methods, along with an example for each.

Table 13.1   Ways to Search for People and Households

Query	Example
First name (or initial), last name, city	**phonebook: john smith minneapolis**
First name (or initial), last name, state	**phonebook: john smith mn**
First name (or initial), last name, city, state	**phonebook: john smith minneapolis mn**
First name (or initial), last name, zip code	**phonebook: john smith 55909**
Last name, city, state	**phonebook: smith minneapolis mn**
Last name, zip code	**phonebook: smith 55909**

13

As you might suspect, the more details you provide, the more targeted your results will be. Searching for all the Smiths in Minneapolis will produce a higher number of results (most of them unwanted) than searching for all the John Smiths. Searching for all the John Smiths in a particular ZIP code would be much more efficient than searching for all the John Smiths in an entire state.

When you enter your query using one of these methods, Google returns a Residential PhoneBook search results page. The top matching names are listed, along with each person's phone number, street address, and a link to a map of this address (via Google Maps).

Searching for People by Phone Number

After Google has captured name, address, and phone number information in the PhoneBook, it's an easy enough task to search that information in a variety of ways. One such approach is to do a reverse phone number lookup, in which you enter a phone number and Google tells you who the number belongs to.

To conduct a reverse phone number search, all you have to do is enter the full phone number, including area code, into the standard Google search box. You can enter all 10 numbers in a row, without hyphens (like this: **1234567890**), or use the standard hyphenated form (like this: **123-456-7890**); Google accepts either method. When you click the Search button, Google displays a single matching PhoneBook result.

caution Because it takes so long to get change-of-address information into the system, Google PhoneBook listings may not always be up-to-date; new numbers may not always be listed, and old numbers may take some time to get removed. In addition, Google can display only names that are publicly available. If a person's phone number is unlisted, it isn't displayed.

tip As soon as you're on a PhoneBook results page, you can opt to conduct a new PhoneBook query by entering the person's name and information into the search box at the top of the page and then clicking the Search PhoneBook button.

tip If you'd rather not have your phone number available for everyone on the Web to Google, you can have your phone information removed from Google's database by following the instructions at www.google.com/help/pbremoval.html.

13

COMMENTARY

GOOGLING YOURSELF

In this Internet age, one of the most popular time-wasters is searching for information about yourself on the Web—Googling yourself, in the common parlance. While this may seem to be a particularly useless and self-indulgent endeavor, there's more to it than meets the eye.

Yes, it's fun to enter your name into the Google search box and see what comes up. You never know who's saying what about you, especially if you have a bit of a public presence.

The real value in self-Googling, however, comes when you discover how much of your personal information is—or hopefully isn't—available for public viewing on the Web. Googling yourself is a great way to find out just how private or public your phone number, email address, and street address are. You can also find out if your credit card or Social Security numbers are floating around the Web. (If they are, it's a sure sign you've been a victim of identity theft.)

To do a full-bore personal security check on your personal information, enter the following items into the Google search box (one at a time, of course), and see what results come up:

- First and last name
- Street address
- Phone number
- Email address
- Social security number
- Credit card numbers
- Bank account numbers

The first item is relatively innocuous; if you've ever posted a comment on a Web forum or blog, your name probably is in Google's database. Even your street address and phone number aren't much to worry about, especially if the results come primarily from the Google PhoneBook. (This just means that your address and phone number are public information, as published in your local white pages telephone directory.)

Discovering that your email address is public knowledge, however, is a bit of a bigger deal. Again, Google is likely to know your email address if you've ever placed a forum or blog posting, or created a web page with a link to your email address. The problem with having an easily Googleable email address is that if you can Google it, so can email spammers. In fact, Googling for email addresses is one of the most common ways for spammers to get your email address. A spammer might search for all email addresses within a given domain; if your address appears in the results, you're added to the spammer's mailing list.

The worst possible situation is if you Google your financial information and get a match. This means that someone, somewhere has stolen your personal info and made it available on the Web for others to use. If you find credit card or bank account info on the Web, contact your credit card company or bank immediately to put a hold on your account, and check for fraudulent use.

If you find your Social Security number online, you should contact the Federal Trade Commission at www.consumer.gov/idtheft/ or 1-877-438-4338. If you think someone is using your Social Security number for work purposes (which you could find out by examining the Social Security statement the government sends you each year), contact the Social Security Administration at 1-800-772-1213.

Searching for Words and Definitions

Want to look up the definition of a particular word, but don't want to bother pulling out the old hardcover dictionary? Not sure of a specific spelling? Use Google as an online dictionary to look up any word you can think of. It's easy, and there are two ways to do it—plus an interesting third approach that helps you generate words on the fly.

Using a "What Is" Search

The first approach to looking up definitions is to use a little-known Google feature, known as a "what is" search. All you have to do is enter the keywords **what is** in your query, followed by the word in question. No question mark is

13

necessary. For example, to look up the definition of the word "defenestrate," enter **what is defenestrate**.

When you use a "what is" search, Google returns a standard search results page (typically with several useful definition links in the list), as well as a single Web definition in a OneBox result at the top of the page. As you can see in Figure 13.1, this OneBox result includes a short definition of the word and two useful links. The first link, disguised as the result title, is actually a link to other definitions of the word on the Web. The second link, Definition in Context, displays an example of the word used in a sentence. (This in-context usage is supplied by the same site that supplies the main definition.)

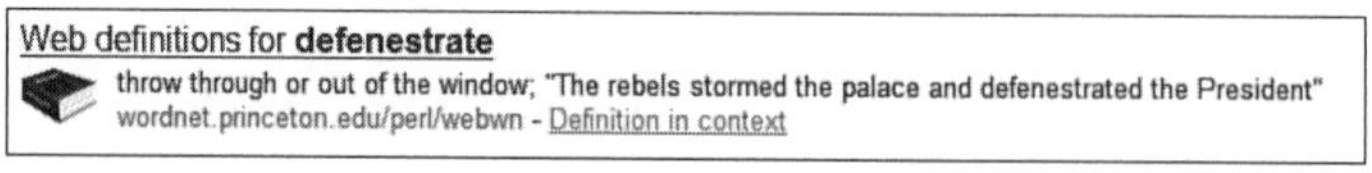

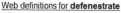

Web definitions for **defenestrate**
throw through or out of the window; "The rebels stormed the palace and defenestrated the President"
wordnet.princeton.edu/perl/webwn - <u>Definition in context</u>

FIGURE 13.1

The special results of a "what is" definition search.

There's something even more useful on the "what is" search results page. If you look in the statistics bar, you'll see the word you searched for displayed as a link. Click this link, and Google displays the full dictionary definition of this word from the Answers.com website. This page includes a pronunciation of the word, as well as one or more definitions.

Using the Google Glossary

Even more definitions are available when you use the Google Glossary feature. Even though it's called Google Glossary, it's really just another advanced search operator that produces some very specific results.

The operator in question is **define:**. Use this operator before the word you want defined, with no space. For example, if you want to define the word "defenestrate," enter the query **define:defenestrate**.

When your query includes the **define:** operator, Google displays a special definitions page, as shown in Figure 13.2. This page includes all the definitions for the word that Google found on the Web; click a link to view the full definition.

note Answers.com (www.answers.com) offers all sorts of information, including—but not limited to—dictionary definitions. Its definitions are sourced from *The American Heritage Dictionary*.

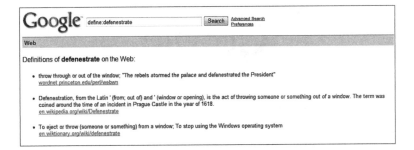

FIGURE 13.2

*Results of a search using the **define:** operator.*

And here's something else to know. If you want to define a phrase, use the **define:** operator, and put the phrase in quotation marks. For example, to define the phrase "peer to peer," enter the query **define:"peer to peer"**. Without the quotation marks, Google would define only the first word in the phrase.

Finding Similar Words with Google Sets

Our final word-related search feature is one that's still in development at Google Labs. I'm talking about Google Sets. You enter two or more related words, and Google Sets displays similar terms to complete the set.

You access Google Sets at labs.google.com/sets. As you can see in Figure 13.3, the main Google Sets page is actually a form.

All you have to do is enter a few terms from the set you want to complete, and then click either the Large Set or Small Set button.

The resulting page displays a longer list of terms predicted from the short list you entered. You can expand this list by clicking the Grow Set button beneath the list.

For example, if you enter the terms **round**, **square**, and **rectangle**, Google Sets returns the terms **triangle**, **oval**, **circle**, **hexagon**, and so forth. If you enter the terms **dog**, **cat**, and **bird**, Google Sets returns the terms **horse**, **rabbit**, **fish**, **snake**, and so forth.

> **tip**
> If you enter the keyword **define**—*not* the **define:** operator—with a space between it and the word you want defined, Google returns the same results as if you entered a "what is" query.

> **note**
> Learn more about Google Labs in Chapter 2, "Google Labs: How Google Develops New Applications."

13

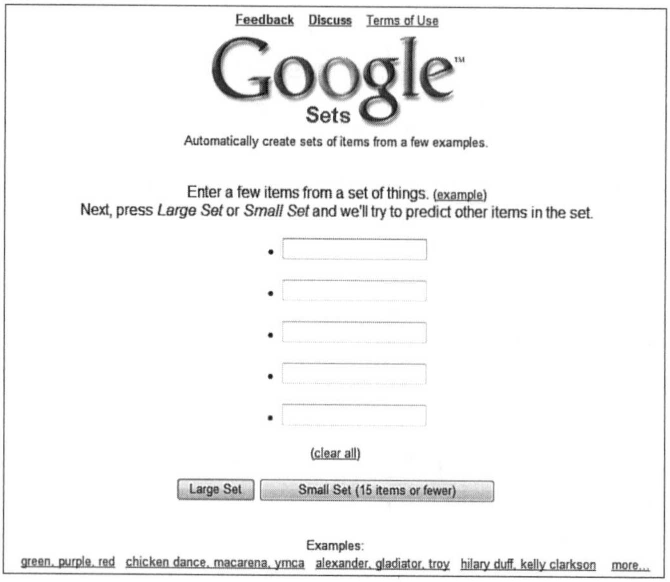

FIGURE 13.3

Searching for related words with Google Sets.

How might you use Google Sets? One use is to help "fill in the blanks" when you're writing or creating lists. Another use might be to expand your own set of query terms when you're using Google to search an unfamiliar subject.

Searching for Facts

When you're looking for hard facts, Google might be able to help. Yes, Google always returns a list of sites that match your specific query, but if you phrase your query correctly—and are searching for a fact that Google has preidentified—you can get the precise information you need at the top of the search results page.

What types of information are we talking about? Fact-based information, such as birthdates, birthplaces, population, and so on. All you have to do is enter a query that states the fact you want to know. For example:

- To find the population of San Francisco, enter **population san francisco**.

- To find where Mark Twain was born, enter **birthplace mark twain**.

- To find when President Bill Clinton was born, enter **birthday bill clinton**.

- To find when Raymond Chandler died, enter **die raymond chandler**.

- To find who is the president of Germany, enter **president germany**.

caution If a fact isn't in the Google Q&A database, it isn't displayed on the search results page.

The answers to these questions are displayed in a OneBox section at the top of your search results page. You get the precise answer to your question, according to the referenced website. Click the associated link to learn more from this source.

This capability to display "quick answers to straightforward questions" is called Google Q&A. The information presented is typical reference information, the kind of stuff you might find in a desk reference or almanac. Google Q&A isn't always consistent about the sources of this info, or about the specific facts that are displayed. For example, searching for **distance to mars** returns no quick fact; neither does **height empire state building** or **size football field**. So accept what you get, and recognize that Google is selective about the facts it knows.

Searching for Weather Information

Did you know that Google can be used to find and display current weather conditions and forecasts? It's a pretty easy search; all you have to do is enter the keyword **weather**, followed by the location. You can enter the location as a city name, city plus state, or ZIP code. For example, to view the weather forecast for Minneapolis, enter **weather minneapolis**.

As you can see in Figure 13.4, Google displays current weather conditions and a four-day forecast at the top of the search results page. Although this is a good summary report, you may want to click through to the more detailed forecasts offered in the standard search results listings below the four-day forecast.

note Google's weather search results are provided by Weather Underground (www.wunderground.com).

13

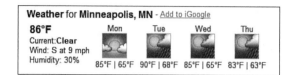

FIGURE 13.4
Google's weather search results.

Searching for Travel Information

Weather information is important to travelers, as is information about flight
delays and airport weather conditions. Fortunately, you can use the main
Google search page to search for this information, just as you did with
weather forecasts.

Viewing Airport Conditions

To search for weather conditions and delays at a particular airport, all you
have to do is enter the airport's three-letter code, followed by the word **airport**
For example, to view conditions at the Minneapolis-St. Paul International
Airport (whose code is MSP), enter **msp airport**. This displays a link to conditions at the chosen airport, as provided by the FAA. Click this link for detailed
information.

Tracking Flight Status

Google also lets you track the status of any
U.S. flight, and many international flights.
All you have to do is enter the flight number
into the Google search box. For example, to find out the status of United
Airlines flight 116, enter **ua116**. Google displays a link to the real-time status
of the specified flight, courtesy of the FlightStats website (www.flightstats.com)
Click this link to view the current status of the flight.

> **tip** To find the code for any
> airport in the world,
> go to www.world-airport-codes.
> com.

Searching for Numbers

Airline flights aren't the only numbers you can look up with Google. Google lets
you enter all sorts of numbers into its main search page and then displays the
relevant information at the top of the search results page.

For example, if you want to track a package that was sent via UPS, all you have to do is enter the UPS tracking number. If you want to see what product is attached to a specific UPC (universal product code), just enter the bar code number. If you have an area code and you want to know which city it serves, enter the area code.

Table 13.2 details all the different types of numbers that Google can look up for you.

note In most instances, all you have to enter is the number itself, with no associated operator. The only exception is if you're searching for an FCC equipment ID or patent number; in these instances, enter the keyword **fcc** or **patent** before the ID number.

Table 13.2   Google Number Lookups

Type of Number	Example
FedEx tracking number	123456789012
U.S. Postal Service tracking number	1234 1234 1234 1234 1234 12
UPS tracking number	1Z1234W123456789012
UPC bar code	123456789012
Area code	123
Vehicle ID number (VIN)	AAAAA123A1AA12345
FAA airplane registration number	a123bc
Patent number	patent 123456
FCC equipment ID	fcc A1B-12345-DEF

Searching a University Site

If you're a student or alumnus, Google makes it easy to search specific university sites using something called University Search. University Search works by limiting your search to pages housed on a specific university website; you're searching a single university site, not the entire Web.

As of this writing, Google lists site-specific searches for more than 600 institutions worldwide, from Abilene Christian University to York University. You can use University Search to search for course schedules, admissions information, and the like. Just go to the University Search page (www.google.com/options/universities.html) and select the university you want to search. When the next

13

page appears, enter your search query and click the Search button. That's all there is to it!

note BSD (Berkeley Software Distribution) UNIX is a specific version of the UNIX operating system developed at the University of California at Berkeley.

Searching for Technology Information

As you've no doubt surmised, Google's University Search works by restricting the search to a specific domain, using the (hidden) **site:** operator. Well, nothing stops Google from using a similar strategy to offer other site- and topic-specific searches—which leads us to our next batch of special searches.

Knowing that a large number of people use the Internet to search for computer- and technology-related information, Google has created several technology-related special searches. You can use these specialty searches to find technical support, software updates, downloadable software, and other computer-related information and services.

There are four of these technology-related searches, each focused on a specific computer platform:

- Google Microsoft Search (www.google.com/microsoft) searches the main www.microsoft.com domain and other Microsoft-related sites.
- Google Apple Macintosh Search (www.google.com/mac) searches the main www.apple.com domain and other Apple-related sites.
- Google Linux Search (www.google.com/linux) searches a variety of Linux-related sites.
- Google BSD UNIX Search (www.google.com/bsd) searches a variety of sites that specialize in the BSD version of the UNIX operating system.

Searching for Government Information

Looking for information about the United States government? Use Google's U.S. Government Search (www.google.com/unclesam). As you might suspect, this search focuses solely on U.S. government websites—which makes it the best place to search for official government forms, information, reports, and the like.

When you access U.S. Government Search, Google directs your search to all the sites within the .gov domain, which includes sites for all major U.S.

13

government agencies, Congress, and the White House. And, so as not to be too federalist, U.S. Government Search also searches all the individual state government sites in the .us and .gov domains. Suffice it to say, if it's government-related, U.S. Government Search will find it.

> **note** Google's U.S. Government Search page also displays information of interest to government workers—White House news, armed forces information, headlines from the *Washington Post*, and Washington, D.C. area weather.

Searching for Solutions

Here's something few Google users know. You can use Google as a calculator, and to perform conversions and look up constants. This is one of the coolest "hidden features" in the Google universe—and you're reading about it here!

> **tip** If you want to search for documents that contain the equation you entered, rather than calculate the results of the equation, click the Search for Documents Containing the Terms link on the search results page.

Performing Basic Calculations from the Google Search Box

To use Google as a calculator, all you have to do is enter your equation or formula into the search box and then click the Google Search button. The result of the calculation is displayed on the search results page, as shown in Figure 13.5. It's that simple.

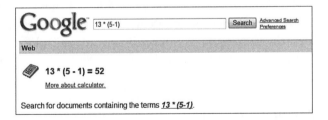

FIGURE 13.5
Using Google as a calculator.

You can use a number of algebraic operators to construct your calculations. Table 13.3 details the operators that Google recognizes.

Table 13.3   Google's Basic Calculator Functions

Function	Operator	Example	Result
Addition	+ *or* **plus** *or* **and**	2 + 1	3
Subtraction	– *or* **minus**	2 – 1	1
Multiplication	X *or* × *or* **times**	2 × 1	2
Division	/ *or* **over** *or* **divided by**	2 / 1	2

Note that several functions have multiple operators you can use. For example, for addition you can use either +, **plus**, or **and**. That means you can add the numbers 2 and 3 in three different ways:

- **2 + 3**
- **2 plus 3**
- **2 and three**

And you don't have to enter spaces between the operator and the numbers (unless you're spelling them out). So **2 + 3** is just as good a query as **2+3**. Google's smart enough to figure out what you mean.

Google also lets you string multiple operations together. For example, if you want to calculate 12 times 5 divided by 4, enter **12 * 5 / 4**. The calculations work from left to right, multiplying and dividing first, and then adding and subtracting. So, using another example, 2 + 3 * 3 equals 11, not 15.

You can also create nesting equations by using appropriately placed parentheses. So, to divide the sum of 4 plus 3 by the sum of 5 plus 2, you'd enter **(4 + 3) / (5 + 2)**. You can get as complex or creative as you want; Google can handle it.

Performing Advanced Calculations

Google's calculator isn't limited to basic addition and multiplication. It can also handle more advanced calculations (detailed in Table 13.4), trigonometric functions (Table 13.5), inverse trigonometric functions (Table 13.6), hyperbolic functions (Table 13.7), and logarithmic functions (Table 13.8). If you know what these functions are, I assume you know the proper way to use them. If you don't, get yourself a good math book, or don't bother with them.

13

Table 13.4 Google's Advanced Mathematic Functions

Function	Operator	Example	Result
Percent (*X* percent of *Y*)	**% of**	20% of 10	2
Square root	**sqrt**	sqrt(16)	4
Root	*n*th **root of**	5th root of 32	2
Exponent (raise to a power)	**∧** *or* **** *or* **to the power of**	4∧2	16
Factorial	**!**	10!	3,628,800
Modulo (finds the remainder after division)	**%** *or* **mod**	15%3	2
Choose (determines the number of ways of choosing a set of *Y* elements from a set of *X* elements)	**choose**	9 choose 3	84

Table 13.5 Google's Trigonometric Functions

Function	Operator	Example	Result
Sine	**sin**	sin(100)	−0.506365641
Tangent	**tan** *or* **tangent**	tan(100)	−0.587213915
Secant	**sec** *or* **secant**	sec(100)	1.15966382
Cosine	**cos** *or* **cosine**	cos(100)	0.862318872
Cotangent	**cotangent**	cotangent(100)	−1.70295692
Cosecant	**csc** *or* **cosecant**	csc(100)	−1.97485753

13

Table 13.6 Google's Inverse Trigonometric Functions

Function	Operator	Example	Result
Inverse sine	**arcsin**	arcsin(1)	1.57079633
Inverse tangent	**arctan**	arctan(1)	0.785398163
Inverse secant	**arcsec**	arcsec(1)	0
Inverse cosine	**arccos**	arccos(1)	0
Inverse cotangent	**arccotangent**	arccotangent(1)	0.785398163
Inverse cosecant	**arccsc**	arccsc(1)	1.57079633

Table 13.7 Google's Hyperbolic Functions

Function	Operator	Example	Result
Hyperbolic sine	**sinh**	sinh(1)	1.17520119
Hyperbolic cosine	**cosh**	cosh(1)	1.54308063
Hyperbolic tangent	**tanh**	tanh(1)	0.761594156

Table 13.8 Google's Logarithmic Functions

Function	Operator	Example	Result
Logarithm base 10	**log**	log(100)	2
Logarithm base 2	**lg**	lg(100)	6.64385619
Logarithm base e	**ln**	ln(100)	4.60517019

Looking Up the Values of Constants

In addition to performing calculations, Google knows a variety of mathematical and scientific constants, such as pi, Avogadro's number, and Planck's constant. It also knows the radius of the Earth, the mass of the sun, the speed of light, the gravitational constant, and a lot more.

13

Let's check this out. Not sure what the value of pi is? Enter **pi**, and Google returns 3.14159265, as shown in Figure 13.6. How about the speed of light? Enter **speed of light**, and Google returns 299,792,458 m/s. What about the radius of the Earth? Enter **radius of earth**, and Google returns 6378.1 kilometers.

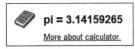

pi = 3.14159265

More about calculator.

FIGURE 13.6

The value of pi.

Now let's get fancy. Try dividing the radius of the Earth by pi. Enter **(radius of earth) / pi**; Google's answer is 2030.21229 kilometers. Or how about multiplying the radius of the Earth by the speed of light and then dividing the answer by Avogadro's number? I'm not sure why you'd want to do this, but the query looks like this: **(radius of earth) * (speed of light) / (avogadro's number)**. The answer is $3.17512652 \times 10^{-09}\,\text{m}^2/\text{s}$.

And what constants does Google know? Here's a short list, with shorthand entries in parentheses:

- Astronomical unit (au)
- Atomic mass unit (amu)
- Avogadro's number
- Boltzmann constant (k)
- Electric constant (epsilon_0)
- Electron mass (m_e)
- Electron volt (eV)
- Elementary charge
- Euler's constant
- Faraday constant
- Fine-structure constant
- Gravitational constant (G)
- Magnetic flux quantum
- Mass of moon (m_moon)
- Mass of *planet* (m_*planet*, as in **m_earth**)

- Mass of sun (m_sun)
- Molar gas constant (R)
- Permeability of free space
- Pi
- Planck's constant (h)
- Proton mass (m_p)
- Radius of moon (r_moon)
- Radius of *planet* (r_*planet*, as in **r_mars**)
- Radius of sun (r_sun)
- Rydberg constant
- Speed of light (c)
- Speed of sound
- Stefan-Boltzmann constant

13

For example, if you wanted to find the speed of light, you could enter **speed of light**, or you could just enter a capital **C**. Google knows the value both ways.

Converting Units of Measure

Another surprise is that Google's calculator also handles conversions. It knows miles and meters, furlongs and light-years, seconds and fortnights, and even angstroms and smoots—and it can convert from one unit of measurement to another.

caution When dealing with mathematical constants, Google's calculator sometimes interprets uppercase letters differently from lowercase letters.

note Google's currency conversion rates are provided by Citibank N.A. and may not always be the most current rates.

The key to using the Google calculator as a converter is to express your query using the proper syntax. In essence, you want to start with the first measure, followed by the word "in," followed by the second unit of measure. A general query looks like this: *x firstunits* **in** *secondunits*.

Let's look at some examples.

Don't know how many feet equal a meter? Enter the query **1 meter in feet**; the result is shown in Figure 13.7. Not sure how many teaspoons are in a cup? Enter **1 cup in teaspoons**. Want to convert 100 U.S. dollars into euros? Enter **100 usd in euros**. Or how about converting 72 degrees Fahrenheit to Celsius? Enter **72 degrees Fahrenheit in Celsius**. Or maybe you want to find out your weight in kilos, or your age in seconds. Enter the queries **180 pounds in kg** or **45 years in seconds**.

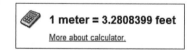

1 meter = 3.2808399 feet
More about calculator.

FIGURE 13.7
Converting meters to feet.

All the formulas necessary for these types of conversions are hardwired into the Google search engine. Just state your query as clearly as possible, and Google does the rest.

What units of measure does Google know? Table 13.9 lists just some of what you can find when you search Google.

Table 13.9   Google's Units of Measure

Type of Measurement	Units
Currency	U.S. dollars (USD), Australian dollars (AUD), Canadian dollars, British pounds (GBP, pounds), euros
Mass	Grams (g), kilograms (kg), pounds (lbs), grains, carats, stones, tons, tones
Distance (length)	Meters (m), kilometers (km), miles, feet (ft), angstroms, cubits, furlongs, nautical miles, smoots, light-years
Volume	Gallons, liters (l), pints, quarts, teaspoons, tablespoons, cups
Area	Square miles, square kilometers, square feet, square yards, acres, hectares
Time	Days, hours, minutes, seconds (s), months, years, centuries, sidereal years, for nights
Electricity	Volts, amps, ohms, henrys
Power	Watts, kilowatts, horsepower (hp)
Energy	British thermal units (BTU), joules, ergs, foot-pounds, calories, kilocalories (Calories)
Temperature	Degrees Fahrenheit, degrees Celsius
Speed	Miles per hour (mph), kilometers per hour (kph), kilometers per second, knots
Data	Bites, bytes, kilobytes (kb), megabytes (mb), gigabytes (gb), terabytes (tb)
Quantity	Dozen, baker's dozen, gross, great gross, score, googol
Numbering systems	Decimal, hexadecimal (hex), octal, binary, Roman numerals

Google even lets you do some nonsensical conversions. You can query **speed of light in knots** or **1 foot in smoots**. You can also use these conversions to create nonsense calculations, such as **(radius of earth) / 3 teaspoons**. It doesn't make any sense, but Google can do it. (And you get the wonderfully absurd measurement of "kilometers per liter.")

tip   Google's calculator has been hardwired to include the answers to some fairly complex—and fairly fanciful—calculations. My favorite is to enter the query **what is the answer to life the universe and everything**. Google's answer, 42, should delight fans of Douglas Adams's *The Hitchhiker's Guide to the Galaxy*.

13

The Bottom Line

Google contains a lot of useful and interesting information, as you've discovered. I've found that if there's something I want to know, from a FedEx tracking number to the value of the dollar versus the euro, there's no harm in entering the query into Google's search box. If Google knows the answer, it displays it in a OneBox at the top of the search results page. If Google doesn't know the answer, you get the standard search results listing—and the information you want is *somewhere* on the Web. You'd be surprised what Google knows!

13

Communicating with Google

Sending and Receiving Email with Gmail

Everybody has an email account—at least one. You probably have a home email account from your Internet service provider (perhaps with additional addresses for your spouse and kids), as well as a work email account. You might also have a Web-based email account from Windows Live Hotmail or Yahoo! Mail, as either a backup or just to have it.

So why would you want yet another email account? And from Google, of all places?

That's right—Google has its own Web-based email service, called Gmail, that competes with Hotmail and Yahoo! Mail. What makes Gmail unique, though, is the massive amount of storage it offers, as well as its insistence on a nonfolder, pure search approach to organization.

Given all the other email offerings available today, is Gmail right for you? That's a good question. You'll have to read this chapter to decide.

What Makes Gmail Unique

At first blush, Gmail (mail.google.com) looks a lot like Hotmail and Yahoo! Mail. It's free, it lets you send and receive email from any web browser, and the interface even looks similar to its competitors.

note If Google's free storage isn't big enough for you, you can purchase additional storage, starting at 10GB for $20/year and going up to 400GB for $500/year.

Despite the visual similarities, Gmail offers a few unique features that set it apart from the Web-based email crowd. First, Gmail doesn't use folders. That's right, with Gmail you can't organize your mail into folders, as you can with the other services. Instead, Gmail pushes the search paradigm as the way to find the messages you want. This isn't a surprise, given Google's search-centric business model. It does take a bit of getting used to, however, especially if you're a highly organized type. This may be one instance where Google's reliance on search technology might not be totally practical for the application at hand.

However, Gmail lets you "tag" each message with one or more labels. This has the effect of creating virtual folders, because you can search and sort your messages by any of their labels.

In addition, Gmail groups related email messages in what Google calls *conversations*. A conversation might be an initial message and all the replies (and replies to replies) to that message. A conversation might also be all the daily emails from a single source that have a common subject, such as messages from subscribed-to mailing lists.

Like all of Google's Web-based services, Gmail is free; all you have to do is sign up for an account. If you already have an account for any other Google service, that account can serve as your Gmail account. When you sign up for your Gmail account, you get assigned an email address (in the form of *name*@gmail.com), and you get access to the Gmail inbox page. As of August 2008, Gmail offered 6GB of storage for users.

COMMENTARY

EMAIL WITHOUT FOLDERS?

The whole bit about "searching, not sorting" deserves special consideration. If you're like me, you're used to storing different types of email messages in different folders within your email program. You might have a folder for messages from family members, another for messages from work colleagues, and still others for specific projects or events.

14

If you want to look back through the messages from that person or relating to that project or event, all you have to do is open the folder. It's how we tend to organize things, as witnessed by the huge sales of file folders at your local office supply store.

Google, however, has thrown that paradigm out the window. You simply can't create folders in Gmail; your messages are all dumped into the same massive inbox (or, in the case of older messages, archived in the All Mail box). If you want to see all the messages from your Aunt Peg, or if you want to read all messages related to a given project, you have to search for them.

(Nitpickers will take this opportunity to remind me that individual messages can be labeled, and that you can assign the same label to all related messages, and that this is sort of like filing your messages. But labeling is like filing only if you happen to throw all your labeled papers into one massive file folder. You still have to search for messages that bear a given label; therefore, the search-not-sort paradigm holds.)

Because Google is the king of search, it should come as no surprise that it tries to push the search paradigm in every service it offers. And, in some instances and for some users, that's fine. But not all users think that way, especially when you're looking at an email inbox that over time might hold tens of thousands of messages. Do you really want to search through that inbox every time you want to view all messages on a given topic? Wouldn't it be easier to sort the messages by topic beforehand, using the tried-and-true folder approach?

I have to give Google credit for sticking with its core search paradigm in everything it offers, even if it doesn't always make sense. (This is, after all, how Google distinguishes itself from its folder-happy competition at Microsoft.) But, in the case of Gmail, don't count me as a complete fan. I like the massive storage capability, I like the interface, I even like the "conversation" grouping. But I don't like not being able to create and use folders to organize my messages. Would it have killed the Google powers-that-be to let their Gmail customers use folders in addition to search? I simply don't see where *not* offering a feature (such as folders) gives Gmail a competitive advantage. A best-of-both-worlds approach would have offered the traditional folder paradigm, as well as Gmail's enhanced search functionality.

Are you listening, Google?

Signing Up (It's Free!)

Gmail is a free service; all you have to do is sign up for an account.

If you already have a Google account, it serves as your Gmail account. When you go to the main Gmail page, just enter your Google account username and password, and you're ready to go.

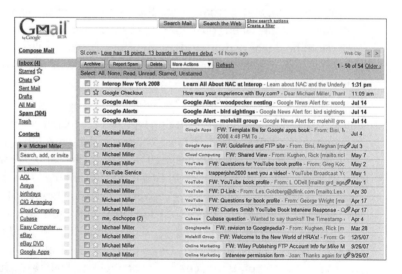

tip If you're moving your email from another account to Gmail, check out Google's Switching to Gmail feature. This lets you import your contact list into Google contacts and announce your new email address to your contacts.

If you don't yet have a Google account, you can sign up for a new Gmail account. Go to the main Gmail page, and click the Sign Up for Gmail link. You're prompted to enter your name, desired login name, desired password, and a security question. After that, click the Create My Account button.

That's all there is to it!

Getting to Know the Gmail Interface

After you sign up for your Gmail account, you get assigned an email address (in the form of *name*@gmail.com), and you get access to the Gmail inbox page, shown in Figure 14.1.

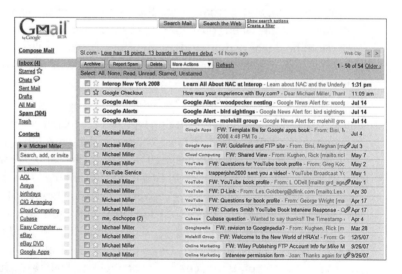

FIGURE 14.1

The Gmail inbox.

The default view of the Gmail page is the inbox, which contains all your received messages. You can switch to other views by clicking the appropriate links on the left side, top, or bottom of the page. For example, to view all your sent mail, simply click the Sent Mail link on the left; to view only unread messages, click the Unread link at the top or bottom.

Each message is listed with the message's sender, the message's subject, a snippet from the message itself, and the date or time the message was sent. (The snippet typically is the first line of the message text.) Unread messages are listed in bold; after a message has been read, it's displayed in normal, non-bold text with a shaded background. And if you've assigned a label to a message (more on this later), the label appears before the message subject.

To perform an action on a message or group of messages, put a check mark by the message(s), and then click one of the buttons at the top or bottom of the list. Alternatively, you can pull down the More Actions list and select another action to perform.

Sending and Receiving Email

Obviously, the Gmail interface is fairly easy to understand. (If Google does nothing else, it creates simple, easy-to-understand interfaces.) Now let's get down to brass tacks, and learn how to use Gmail for basic message sending and receiving.

Reading Messages

To read a message, all you have to do is click the message title in the inbox. This displays the full text of the message on a new page, as shown in Figure 14.2.

If you want to display this message in a new window, click the New Window link. To print the message, click the Print All link. To return to the inbox, click the Back to Inbox link.

14

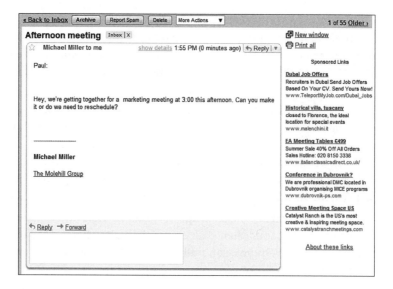

FIGURE 14.2
Reading an email message in Gmail.

Viewing Conversations

One of the unique things about Gmail is that all related email messages are grouped in what Google calls *conversations*. A conversation might be an initial message and all its replies (and replies to replies). A conversation might also be all the daily emails from a single source with a common subject, such as messages you receive from subscribed-to mailing lists.

A conversation is noted in the inbox list by a number in parentheses after the sender name(s). If a conversation has replies from more than one person, more than one name is listed.

To view a conversation, simply click the message title; as you can see in Figure 14.3, only the most recent message is displayed in full. To view the text of an individual message in a conversation, click that message's subject. To expand *all* the messages in a conversation, click the Expand All link. All the messages in the conversation are stacked on top of each other, with the text of the newest message fully displayed.

14

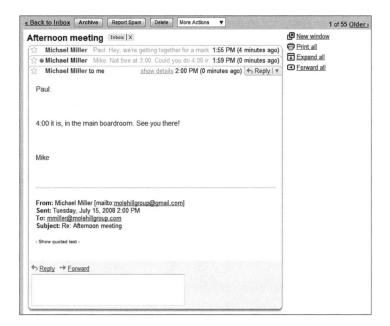

FIGURE 14.3

Viewing a conversation.

Replying to Messages

Whether you're reading a single message or a conversation, it's easy enough to send a reply. All you have to do is follow these steps:

1. In the original message, click the Reply button. This expands the message to include a reply box, like the one shown in Figure 14.4.

2. The text of the original message is already quoted in the reply; add your new text above the original text.

3. The original sender's address is automatically added to the To: line, so click the Send button to send the message on its way.

> **tip** If a conversation has multiple participants, you can reply to all of them by clicking the down arrow next to the Reply button and then selecting Reply to All.

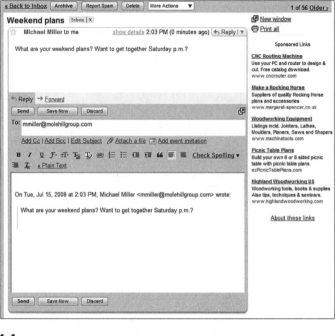

FIGURE 14.4
Replying to an email message.

Forwarding Messages

Sometimes you might want to forward a message to a third party, instead of simply replying to the original sender. You do this by following these steps:

1. In the original message, click the down arrow next to the Reply button and select Forward. This expands the message to include a forward box, like the reply box just discussed.

2. Add the recipient's email address to the To: box.

3. Enter your message into the main message box.

4. Click the Send button to send the message on its way.

Composing and Sending New Messages

Creating a message from scratch isn't a whole lot harder than replying to an existing message. All you have to do is follow these steps:

1. Click the Compose Mail link at the top of any Gmail page.

2. When the Compose Mail page appears, as shown in Figure 14.5, enter the recipient's email address in the To: box. Separate multiple recipients with commas.

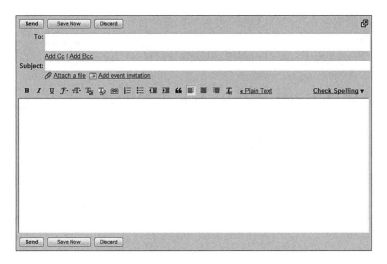

FIGURE 14.5

Composing a new email message.

3. Enter a subject for the message into the Subject box.

4. Enter the text of your message in the large text box. Use the formatting controls (bold, italic, font, and so forth) to enhance your message as desired.

5. When you're done composing your message, click the Send button.

Attaching Files

One of the key features of Gmail is its capability to store large amounts of data. You can use this feature to email files to yourself for backup purposes; of course, you can also email files to other users, as you like.

> **tip** You can cc (carbon copy) and bcc (blind carbon copy) additional recipients by clicking the Add Cc and Add Bcc links. This expands the message to include Cc or Bcc boxes, into which you enter the recipients' addresses. (A bcc sends the message to the intended recipients but hides their addresses from the main recipients; a cc displays the recipients' addresses.)

> **tip** Gmail provides spell checking for all your outgoing messages. Just click the Check Spelling link and misspelled words are highlighted in yellow. You can then accept or reject the suggested spelling changes throughout your document.

14

To attach a file to a Gmail message, follow these steps:

1. Compose a new message, as discussed previously.

2. From the new message page, click the Attach a File link.

3. When the Choose File dialog box appears, navigate to and select the file you want to attach, and then click the Open button.

The file you selected appears under the Subject box on the new message page. To attach another file to this same message, click the Attach Another File link; otherwise, continue composing and sending your message as normal.

Opening or Viewing Attached Files

What do you do if someone sends you a file attached to an email message? First, make sure that you're expecting the attachment, and that it's not a virus tagging along for the ride. If you're confident that it's a legitimate attachment from someone you know and trust, you can opt to either view the attachment (ideal for photos) or save the attachment to your hard drive.

When you receive a message with an attachment, you see a paper clip icon next to the message subject/snippet. To view or save an attachment, follow these steps:

1. Click the message to open it.

2. If the attachment is an image file, the photo appears in the opened message, as shown in Figure 14.6. To view other types of files, or to view a photo in a separate window, click the View link.

3. To save the file to your hard disk, click the Download link. When the File Download dialog box appears, click the Save button, select a location for the file, and then click the second Save button.

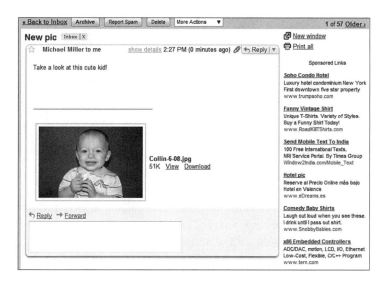

FIGURE 14.6
Attached photos display automatically when you open a message.

Deleting Messages

There are two ways to delete messages in Gmail:

- From the inbox page, check the message, and then click the Delete button.
- From any open message, click the Delete button.

Either of these approaches moves the selected message to the Trash bin. Messages stay in the Trash bin for 30 days; after that, they're permanently deleted.

Searching Your Inbox

As noted previously, Gmail organization is based on Google's popular search paradigm. That is, to find a specific message in your crowded inbox, you have to search for it.

tip You can view the messages in the Trash bin by clicking the Trash link. You can then undelete any message by checking it and then clicking the Move to Inbox button.

14

Basic Search

For most users, Gmail's basic search feature quickly and easily finds the messages
you're looking for. All you have to do is
follow these steps:

1. Enter one or more keywords into
   the search box at the top of any
   Gmail page.

2. Click the Search Mail button.

caution Unlike
Google's Web
search, Gmail search doesn't offer
automatic stemming, which
means that it doesn't recognize
matches to partial strings, plurals,
misspellings, and the like. If you
search for **dog**, Gmail doesn't recognize **dogs**, **dogged**, or **doggy**.

Gmail returns a search results page, like the one shown in Figure 14.7. This
page lists messages in which the queried keywords appear anywhere in the
message—in the subject line, in the message text, or in the sender or recipient
lists. Click a message to read it.

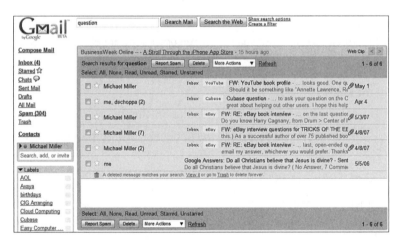

FIGURE 14.7
Viewing the results of a Gmail search.

Searching with Search Options

The more messages in your inbox, the more you need to fine-tune your mail
searches. Fortunately, Gmail makes this easy with a simple checkbox interface. When you click the Show Search Options link (beside the search box),
the top of the Gmail page expands, as shown in Figure 14.8. From here, you
can search according to the parameters listed in Table 14.1.

14

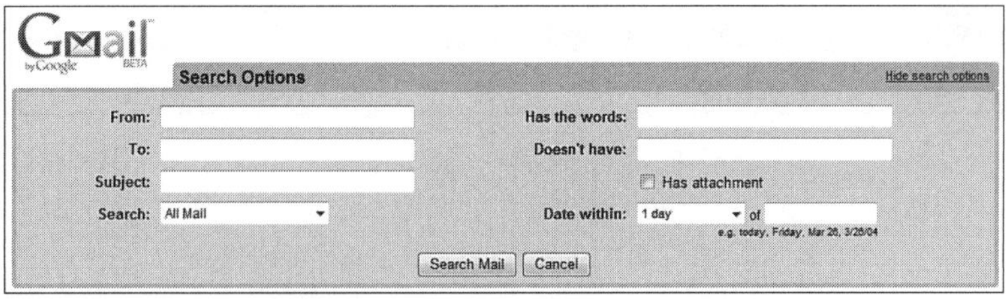

FIGURE 14.8
Fine-tuning your search with Gmail Search Options.

Table 14.1   Gmail Search Options

Search Option	Description
From:	Searches within the sender (From:) field only.
To:	Searches within the recipient (To:) field only.
Subject:	Searches within the message subject line only.
Search:	Pull down to search within All Mail (including archived messages), Inbox, Starred, Chats, Sent Mail, Drafts, Spam, Trash, All Mail & Spam & Trash, Read Mail, or Unread Mail, or by specific label (if you've applied labels to your messages).
Has the words:	Searches for messages that contain all the words listed.
Doesn't have:	Searches for messages that don't contain the words listed.
Has attachment	Limits searches to messages with files attached.
Date within:	Narrows searches to a specific timeframe (1 day, 3 days, 1 week, 2 weeks, 1 month, 2 months, 6 months, 1 year) of the specified date.

Just enter your keywords into the box(es) next to the criteria you want, and then click the Search Mail button.

Searching with Advanced Operators

If you prefer to do your searching from the search box only, Gmail offers a slew of advanced search operators you can employ. These operators work just like the regular search operators we discussed in Chapter 6, "Getting the Most Out of Google Search," except that they're specialized for the task of email searching.

Table 14.2 details the available Gmail search operators.

14

Table 14.2 Gmail Advanced Search Operators

Search Operator	Description	Example
from:	Searches for messages from a specific sender.	from:sherry *or* from:sherry@example.net
to:	Searches for messages sent to a specific recipient.	from:mike *or* from:mike@gmail.com
subject:	Searches for words contained in the message subject line.	subject:meeting
OR	Searches for messages containing one or another word (OR must be in all caps).	sherry OR mike
–	Excludes messages that contain a specific word.	–meeting
label:	Searches for messages by label.	label:friends
has:attachment	Searches only for messages with files attached.	has:attachment
filename:	Searches for attachment by name or file type.	filename:sherry.jpg *or* filename:pdf
" "	Searches for an exact phrase.	"friday meeting"
( )	Used to group words in a query.	from:(sherry OR mike) *or* subject:(dinner movie)
in:*location*	Searches for messages in specific areas of your account: anywhere, inbox, trash, spam.	in:anywhere
is:*state*	Searches for messages that are read, unread, or starred.	is:unread
cc:	Searches for recipients in the cc: field.	cc:melinda
bcc:	Searches for recipients in the bcc: field.	bcc:oliver
after:*year/month/day*	Searches for messages sent after a given date.	after:2008/06/15
before:*year/month/day*	Searches for messages sent before a given date.	before:2008/09/01

Obviously, you can combine any or all of these operators. For example, to search within a certain date range, combine the **after:** and **before:** operators, like this: **after:2008/06/15 before:2008/09/01**. To search for unread messages from a certain person, enter this query: **from:gary is:unread**. And so on.

> **note** When you use the **in:anywhere** operator, it searches for messages anywhere in your account *except* in Spam or Trash.

Other Ways of Organizing Your Email Messages

If searching doesn't get the complete job done for you, Gmail offers a few other ways to organize your messages—short of offering folders, of course. Still, every little bit helps.

Starring Important Messages

If you find a message that you think is more important than other messages, you can "star" that messages. In effect, Gmail "starring" is the same as the "flagging" feature you find in competing email services and programs.

To star a message, just click the empty star next to the message in your inbox. After it is clicked, the star appears in solid colors (a nice shade of gold with a blue border).

The advantage of starring messages is that Gmail lets you display only starred messages, if you like. Just click the Starred link to the left of the message window, and just the starred messages are listed.

Applying Labels

Another way to organize your Gmail messages is to assign each message a *label*, which is akin to attaching metadata to a photo or music file. In Google, this system is supposed to be equivalent to (and superior to) folders, although I'm not so sure. Still, as I said before, every little bit helps.

You can assign one or more labels to every message in your inbox. After they are labeled, you can recall all messages that share a given label—which is kind of like opening a folder.

To assign a label to a message, follow these steps:

1. In the inbox, check the messages that you want to share the same label.

2. Pull down the More Actions list and select New Label. (Or, if you've already created a label, select this label from the pull-down list.)

3. If prompted (via a separate dialog box), enter the label you want to apply to the selected message(s).

To apply another label to the same message(s), just repeat this procedure. After the messages are labeled, the label appears before the message's subject line.

Each of your labels also appears in the Labels box, at the bottom left of the inbox window, as shown in Figure 14.9. To view all messages with the same label, just click the label name in the Labels box; Gmail displays all the messages labeled as such. (You can also use the **label:** operator in the search box to search for messages with a specific label.)

FIGURE 14.9

The Labels box.

Archiving Old Messages

If you're a busy little emailer, chances are your inbox will get very large very quickly. This is particularly so with Gmail, because you can't offload messages from the inbox into folders.

When your inbox becomes too cluttered with messages, Gmail lets you archive older messages. When you archive a message, it moves out of the inbox into a larger store called All Mail. Because all your Gmail searches search the All Mail messages, one strategy is to archive all messages after you've read them, thus freeing the inbox for only your most recent messages.

To archive one or more messages, follow these steps:

1. From the Gmail inbox, check the messages you want to archive.

2. Click the Archive button.

That's it; the messages you marked are removed from the inbox, but they remain accessible from the All Mail link or whenever you perform a Gmail search.

tip To edit or delete a label, click the Edit Labels link in the Labels box, and then click either the Rename Label or Remove Label link.

tip Given Gmail's 6GB storage capacity, Google recommends archiving old messages rather than deleting them—just in case you ever need them. It's kind of a pack-rat approach to email management, but that's what happens when storage is virtually unlimited and search tools are fairly effective.

tip You can return archived messages to the inbox by clicking the All Mail link, checking the message(s) you want to move, and then clicking the Move to Inbox button.

Filtering Incoming Mail

Here's another way to organize your messages—specifically, to manage what happens to them when they arrive in your inbox. Gmail lets you create up to 20 filters that identify certain types of incoming messages and then handle them in a specified manner.

For example, you might want to create a filter that applies a label to all messages with certain words in the subject line. Or maybe star all messages that come from a particular person. Or forward all messages from one sender to another recipient. Or just automatically delete all messages from a particular sender, or on a particular subject.

Gmail lets you choose from five different actions for your filters:

14

- Skip the inbox (automatically archive the message)
- Star it
- Apply a label (choose from a list, or create a new label)
- Forward it to (a specified email address)
- Delete it

Here's how you create a filter:

1. From the Gmail inbox, click the Create a Filter link (beside the search box).

2. The Create a Filter section, shown in Figure 14.10, appears at the top of the inbox page. Enter the search criteria to identify which messages you want the filter applied to, and then click the Next Step button.

FIGURE 14.10

Specifying which messages the new filter will apply to.

3. When the next page appears, as shown in Figure 14.11, select the action you want the filter to initiate.

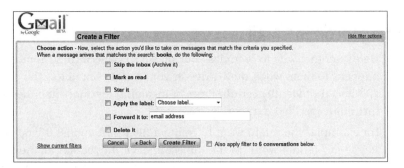

FIGURE 14.11

Specifying the action you want the filter to apply.

4. Click the Create Filter button.

All future messages that match your search criteria (as well as matching messages already in your inbox) will have the specified action performed on them.

tip To view all your current filters (and edit or delete selected filters), click the Settings link at the top of the Gmail inbox page, and then select the Filters tab.

Dealing with Spam and Viruses

Google, like any responsible email provider, offers several features designed to reduce the amount of unwanted spam messages you receive in your inbox, as well as reduce the risk of computer virus infection. These features are applied automatically, but it's nice to know how they work.

Blocking Spam Messages

Google applies a variety of internal spam filters to identify spam as it enters the Gmail system, and thus block it from appearing in users' inboxes. In most cases, you never see the spam; Google blocks it before it ever gets to you.

Sometimes spam makes it past Google's main filter but then is caught on the receiving end. When this happens, the spam message appears in the Spam section of your inbox. You can view purported spam messages by clicking the Spam link.

If Google happens to route a legitimate message to your Spam list (it happens sometimes), just check the message and click the Not Spam button. This moves the message out of the Spam list and back into your general inbox.

If you inadvertently receive a spam message in your Gmail inbox, you can help train Google's spam filters by reporting it. You do this by checking the message in your inbox and then clicking the Report Spam button. This action both removes the spam message from your inbox and sends information about the message back to Google.

Scanning Your Attachments for Viruses

Gmail also takes steps to protect you from email-borne computer viruses. These viruses typically come as file attachments, even more typically as EXE files attached to email messages.

To that end, Gmail automatically blocks the sending and receiving of all EXE files. It's a fairly draconian approach; there's no way around the system to send a legitimate EXE file, so don't bother trying.

14

Google also scans all the attached files you send and receive via Gmail, no matter what the file extension. If a virus is found in an attachment, Gmail tries to clean the file (remove the virus); if the virus can't be removed, you can't download or send the file.

Working with Contacts

Every email program or service offers some sort of address book, a list of your most-frequent contacts. Gmail is no exception; its Contacts list lets you store contact information (including but not limited to email addresses) for thousands of people.

Adding a New Contact

It's easy to add a new person to your Gmail contact list. Just follow these steps:

1. Click the Contacts link on the left side of any Gmail page.

2. When the Contacts page appears, as shown in Figure 14.12, click the New Contact button—the one with the single person next to the +.

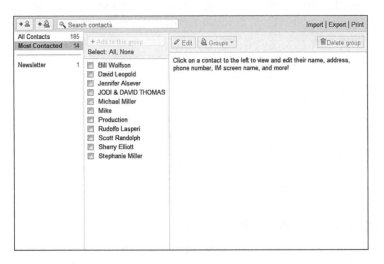

FIGURE 14.12
Gmail's Contacts page.

3. A new panel appears on the Contacts page, as shown in Figure 14.13. Enter the person's name email address, phone number, and street address into the appropriate blanks.

14

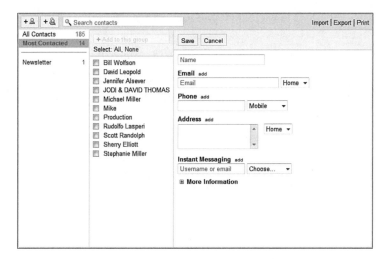

FIGURE 14.13

Adding a new contact.

4. To enter any additional information about this person—title, company, and notes—click the More Information link and proceed as necessary.

5. Click the Save button to create the contact.

Importing Contacts from Another Program

If you already have a lot of contacts entered in another email program or service, such as Microsoft Outlook or Hotmail (and you probably do), you can import those contacts into your Gmail Contacts list. All you have to do is export your contacts from the other program or service into a CSV-format file and then import that file into Gmail.

For example, if you're using Microsoft Outlook as your primary email program, you start by selecting File, Import and Export (within Outlook). Then you use Outlook's Import and Export Wizard to export your contacts into a comma-separated values (CSV) file.

tip You can also add a sender's email address to your Contacts list whenever you receive a new email message. All you have to do is click the down arrow next to the Reply button and select Add *Sender* to Contacts List.

14

After the CSV file is created, you follow these steps to import the contacts into Gmail:

1. From the Gmail inbox, click the Contacts link.

2. When the Contacts page appears, click the Import link.

3. When the Import Contacts dialog box appears, click the Browse button to locate the file you want to import.

4. After you've selected the file, click the Import button and proceed as directed.

Your contacts should now appear in Gmail's Contacts list.

Displaying Contacts

When you click the Contacts link on Gmail's inbox page, you display the Contacts list. This list has three tabs:

- Most Contacted displays only those contacts to whom you send the most messages.

- All Contacts displays all your contacts, even those you never send email to.

- Groups displays groups of contacts you create.

Click a tab to view the contacts within that tab.

Searching for Contacts

If you have a ton of contacts in your Contacts list, you may need to search for the ones you want to use. To search for a particular contact, go to the Contacts list, enter the name of that contact into the search box, and then press the Enter key. You can search by a person's first name, last name, or both; you can also search by domain or email address.

> **note** We'll talk more about groups in the "Using Contact Groups" section in a moment.

Using Contact Groups

Most email programs let you create mailing lists that contain multiple email addresses, which makes it easier to send bulk mailings to groups of people. Gmail also offers a mailing list-like feature, which it calls contact groups. When you want to send a message to all members of a group, you have to select only the group name—not every contact individually.

14

To create a contact group, follow these steps:

1. From the Gmail inbox page, click the Contacts link.

2. When the Contacts page appears, click the Add Groups button—the one with the two people next to the +.

3. A pop-up window appears, prompting you for the name of the group. Enter the group name and click the OK button.

4. The Contacts page is updated with the new group. Select the group name. The Contacts page changes to show the contacts in this group— currently blank, as you can see in Figure 14.14.

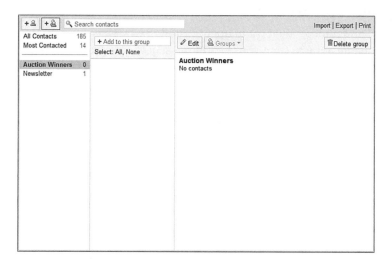

FIGURE 14.14

Creating a new contact group.

5. Enter the contacts you want included in this group into the Add to This Group box; use commas to separate names.

Sending a Message to a Contact or Contact Group

The whole point of creating contacts and contact groups is to make it easier to send email messages—without having to remember all those email addresses every time. It's easy to do.

> **tip** You can also add contacts to a group from either the Most Contacted or All Contacts tab. Just check the contacts you want to add, click the Groups button, and then select the name of the contact group.

14

All you have to do is enter the name of a contact group into the To: field when you compose a new message in the normal fashion. When you enter the group name, it's automatically replaced by the email addresses of all the individual contacts in that group.

> **tip** If you start to enter the name of an individual contact into the To: box, Gmail automatically displays all contacts that start with the first letter(s) you type. Highlight a contact name from this list to select it.

Using Gmail with Other Email Programs and Accounts

Here's another neat thing about Gmail. Google lets you send your Gmail messages to any POP email program, forward your messages to another email account, and even read email from other accounts in your Gmail window. All these options make it easy to use Gmail in conjunction with Outlook, Outlook Express, Windows Mail, and similar email programs.

> **note** POP is short for Post Office Protocol, a technology used to send and receive email from standalone email programs (such as Microsoft Outlook) via web-based email servers.

Retrieving Email from Other Accounts

You can use Gmail to fetch messages from any POP email account. This lets you access your POP email when you're on the road—or just use the single Gmail interface for all your email management.

> **note** You can't use Gmail to fetch other Web-based email—which means that you can't integrate Gmail with Hotmail or Yahoo! Mail.

To set up Gmail to work with a POP email account, follow these steps:

1. Click the Settings link (at the top of any Gmail page).
2. When the Settings page appears, select the Accounts tab, shown in Figure 14.15.

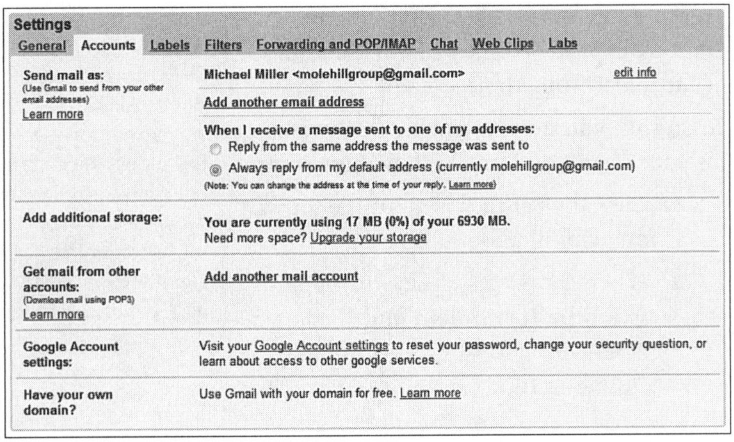

FIGURE 14.15
Managing your Gmail accounts.

3. In the Get Mail from Other Accounts section, click the Add Another Mail Account link.

4. When the Add a Mail Account window appears, enter the email address you want to add, and then click the Next Step button.

5. When the next screen appears, enter that account's username, password, and POP server.

6. If you want to leave copies of all messages on the other email server (so that you can also retrieve these messages with your normal email program), check the Leave a Copy of Retrieved Messages on the Server option.

7. To apply a Gmail label to all messages from this account, check the Label Incoming Messages option, and then select a label from the pull-down list.

8. Click the Add Account button.

As soon as this account is set up, Gmail checks it on a regular basis, and new messages appear in your Gmail inbox.

Reading Gmail in Another Email Program

Just as you can check POP email from within Gmail, you can check Gmail from within your POP email program—any

note You can obtain your POP server address from your Internet service provider.

14

program, including Microsoft Outlook, Outlook Express, Windows Mail, Eudora, or Mozilla Thunderbird.

To do this, you have to enable POP email for your Gmail account. Follow these steps:

1. Click the Settings link (at the top of any Gmail page).

2. When the Settings page appears, select the Forwarding and POP/IMAP tab, shown in Figure 14.16.

> **tip** Because programs like Outlook allow you to put email into folders, this is one way around the lack of support for folders in Gmail. However, keep in mind that any messages moved from your Gmail account into a folder in a separate email client are inaccessible if you access Gmail via the Web.

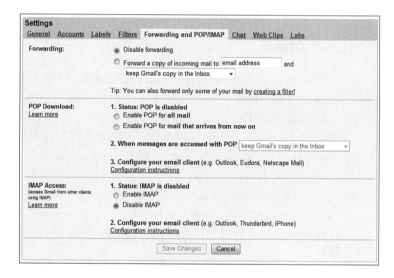

FIGURE 14.16

Setting up POP downloading and Gmail forwarding.

3. In the POP Download section of this page, check the Enable POP for All Mail option.

4. Pull down the When Messages Are Accessed with POP list. Select either Keep Gmail's Copy in the Inbox (so that all messages are still accessible from Gmail over the Web), Archive Gmail's Copy (so that all messages are also sent to Gmail's All Mail list), or Delete Gmail's copy (so that messages do not appear on the Gmail website).

5. Click the Save Changes button.

6. Open your POP email program and create a new account for your Gmail messages. When prompted, enter **pop.gmail.com** as the incoming mail server and **smtp.gmail.com** as the outgoing (or SMTP) mail server.

> **tip**
> If your email client or portable device (such as an Apple iPhone) supports the IMAP protocol, you should use that instead of POP to facilitate two-way email synchronization. Check the Enable IMAP option and then configure your client per Google's instructions.

From now on, you should be able to retrieve your Gmail messages from your existing POP email program.

Forwarding Gmail to Another Account

You can also forward your Gmail messages to another of your email accounts. This is different from reading your messages in another program, in that copies of your messages are sent to your other email address. You then retrieve these copies of your Gmail messages whenever you check the mail in your other account.

To set up Gmail forwarding, follow these steps:

1. Click the Settings link (at the top of any Gmail page).
2. When the Settings page appears, select the Forwarding and POP/IMAP tab.
3. In the Forwarding section of this page, check the Forward a Copy of Incoming Mail To option.
4. Enter the address of your other email account into the email address box.
5. From the pull-down list, select how you want to handle the original Gmail messages—Keep Gmail's Copy in the Inbox, Archive Gmail's Copy, or Delete Gmail's copy.
6. Click the Save Changes button.

The options discussed in this section and the preceding one are great for when you're on vacation. You can forward your Gmail to whichever account you read when you're away from home, or simply use your other email program to read your Gmail messages at your leisure.

14

Putting Gmail into Vacation Mode

Speaking of vacation, Gmail also has a dedicated vacation mode. When you activate vacation mode, anyone who sends you a message automatically gets a response that you're on vacation.

Here's how to activate Gmail's vacation mode:

1. Click the Settings link (at the top of any Gmail page).

2. When the Settings page appears, select the General tab, and scroll down to the Vacation Responder section.

3. Check the Vacation Responder On option.

4. Enter a subject for the messages you want the responder to automatically send out, something along the lines of "I'm on vacation."

5. Enter the text of your vacation message.

6. If you want only your contacts to receive this vacation message, check the Only Send a Response to People in My Contacts option.

7. Click the Save Changes button at the bottom of the page.

That's it. With the vacation responder activated, anyone who sends you a message automatically receives your vacation message in reply. When you return from vacation, return to the Settings page and check the Vacation Responder Off option.

Adding a Signature to Your Messages

If you want to add a personalized signature to the bottom of all your email messages, you don't have to manually enter that signature every time you send a message. Instead, you can configure Gmail to automatically add the signature. Just follow these steps:

1. Click the Settings link (at the top of any Gmail page).

2. When the Settings page appears, select the General tab.

3. Scroll down to the Signature section, and check the second option (the one below No Signature).

4. Enter your signature into the large text box.

5. Click the Save Changes button.

If you prefer not to include a signature, check the No Signature option.

Gmail in iGoogle

Finally, if you're a user of Google's iGoogle personalized home page, you can check your Google inbox directly from iGoogle. As you can see in Figure 14.17, iGoogle includes a Gmail content module that displays the five most recent messages in your inbox, with unread messages in bold. Click the Inbox link to go to the Gmail inbox page, or click the Compose Mail link to create a new Gmail message.

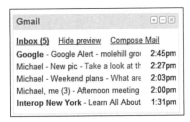

FIGURE 14.17

Viewing new Gmail messages on the iGoogle personalized home page.

The Bottom Line

Although I don't particularly like the lack of folders, I grudgingly admit that Google has created a pretty good Web-based email service with Gmail. I particularly like the huge storage capability, which just encourages my packrattish tendencies. Gmail is a worthy competitor to the more established Hotmail and Yahoo! Mail services.

And there's more to Gmail than just email. Gmail also offers a live chat function, which we'll discuss in Chapter 15, "Instant Messaging with Google Talk." Turn the page to learn more.

note Learn more about the iGoogle personalized home page in Chapter 3, "Creating a Personalized Home Page with iGoogle."

14

Instant Messaging with Google Talk

A merica Online has its AOL Instant Messenger (AIM) service. Microsoft has its Windows Live Messenger service. Yahoo! has Yahoo! Messenger. It should come as no surprise, then, that Google offers an instant-messaging service called Google Talk.

What is surprising is that you can access Google Talk from the stand-alone Google Talk client program (similar to what's offered with both AIM and Windows Live Messenger) or from the Gmail and iGoogle web pages. That's right—you can instant-message your friends from Google's web-based email service. Cool.

Chatting with Google Talk

Google Talk is the name of both Google's instant-messaging network and its IM client. You can download the Google Talk client and learn more about the Google Talk network at talk.google.com.

As with competing IM systems, Google Talk lets you send and receive both text-based instant messages and voice-over-IP Internet phone calls. To use Google Talk as a text-based IM client, all you need is your computer and an Internet connection; to use Google Talk for Internet phone calls, you also need a microphone and a speaker for your PC.

Initiating a Text-Based Chat

Google Talk displays your contacts in its main window, as you can see in Figure 15.1. Those who are online and available to talk are displayed first, with a green ball next to their names. Offline contacts are displayed underneath.

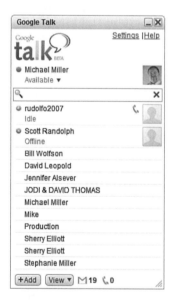

FIGURE 15.1

Viewing your Google Talk contacts.

To start a chat with one of your contacts, just click that person's name. This opens a new chat window, like the one shown in Figure 15.2. Enter a message

15

in the bottom text box, and then press Enter. Your ongoing discussion is displayed in the main window.

FIGURE 15.2
Chatting in Google Talk.

Adding New Contacts

To invite new users to talk, just enter their email address or username into the search box at the top of the Google Talk window. If your friend already has a Gmail account, he'll get an invitation to talk. If he doesn't, you'll be prompted to send a Gmail invitation in addition to the Google Talk invitation.

As for chatting with other Gmail or Google Talk users, all your Gmail contacts are preloaded into Google Talk, with the most frequently emailed contacts first. Contacts who already have Google Talk have a colored ball next to their names. A gray ball means they're offline, a red ball means they're busy, an orange ball means they're idle (away from the keyboard), and a green ball means they're online and available to chat.

Blocking Other Users

Every now and then you run into some jerk online you really don't want to talk to again. Fortunately, Google Talk lets you block incoming messages from selected users. All you have to do is open a new chat window for that person, click the down arrow in that window, and select Block *Contact*.

To unblock a previously blocked user, enter his or her email address into the Search, Add, or Invite box. The blocked user's name should appear in the resulting list; click the name to open a talk tab, and then click the down arrow on the tab and select Unblock.

Sending Files

If the person you're chatting with also has the Google Talk client installed, you can send files back and forth between yourselves. All you have to do is click the down arrow button in the chat window and select Send Files. Select one or more files on your hard drive, and then send them to your chat buddy. The file is received in the Google Talk window; your chat buddy has the option of accepting or declining the file. If he accepts, he can then open or download the file to his computer.

Saving Your Chat History

By default, Google Talk saves copies of all your chats. Some users like this ability to revisit a chat history, just in case something important got discussed that you'd like to refer to again.

Each complete chat session is saved as a message in your Gmail account. When you click the Chats link on the Gmail inbox page, you see a list of all your chats, as shown in Figure 15.3. Click a chat to read the history, or delete the chats you don't really want to keep.

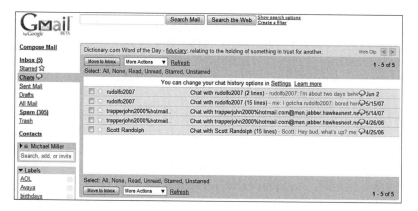

FIGURE 15.3

Revisiting chat histories in Gmail.

At any point in a chat session, you can go "off the record" and halt the history recording. All you have to do is click the down arrow in that chat window and select Go Off the Record. To resume recording the chat history, click the down arrow again and select Stop Chatting Off the Record.

(By the way, as soon as you go off the record with a given user, all your subsequent chats—for this and other users—are off the record until you choose to go on the record again.)

Changing Your Status—and Signing Out

To change your online status, click the Available list under your name in the main Google Talk window. You can choose to sign out, display your status as busy (with a standard message or a custom message), or display your status as available (again, with a standard message or a custom message). You can even opt to show the current music track you're listening to, whether you're available or not. To sign out, select Sign Out.

tip Saving a history of your children's chats is a good way to keep track of what your kids are doing online. On the other hand, keeping a history of your own chats could become a security risk, because everything you discuss can be accessed by others.

Initiating a Voice-Based Chat

Google Talk also lets you conduct voice-based chat sessions with your fellow users. These Internet phone sessions are possible only if both computers are equipped with a microphone and speaker (or, alternatively, a telephone headset).

To initiate a voice chat, open a chat window for the person you want to talk to, and click the Call button. You'll then be connected.

Chatting from iGoogle

One of the most unique features of Google Talk is that you don't need the Google Talk client to instant-message other users. If you use Google's iGoogle personalized home page, you can add a Google Talk gadget to chat directly from that page.

As you can see in Figure 15.4, the Google Talk gadget looks and works just like the freestanding Google Talk client. If you want to move from iGoogle talk to the normal Google Talk window, just click the Pop Out button.

FIGURE 15.4

The Google Talk gadget in iGoogle.

Chatting via Gmail

Here's another unique feature of Google Talk. You can talk to your Google Talk contacts directly from your Gmail page in your web browser.

To start a chat with one of your Gmail contacts, hover over that person's name in the Chat list on your Gmail page. This opens a pop-up window, as shown in Figure 15.5; click the Chat button to initiate the chat.

FIGURE 15.5

Starting a chat from within Gmail.

At this point a message window appears in the lower-right corner of your web browser, as shown in Figure 15.6. If you prefer to view the chat in a separate window, click Pop-out. In either case, you enter your messages in the bottom text box and then press Enter; the full chat is shown in the space above.

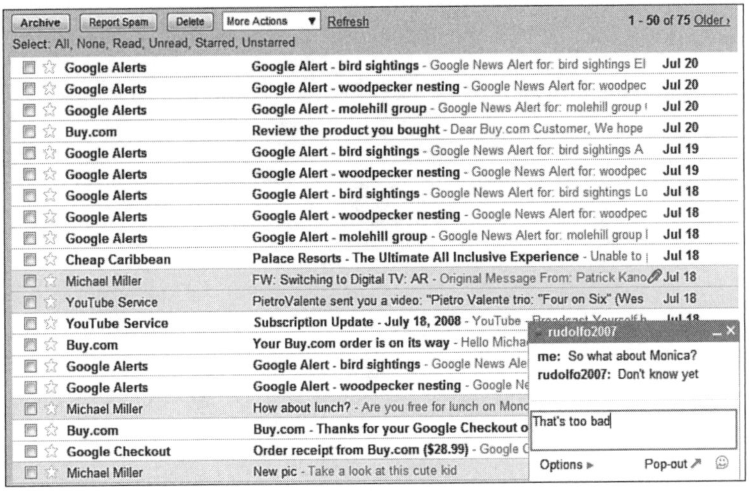

FIGURE 15.6
Chatting from within the Gmail browser window.

And, of course, you can go off the record or block a user the same way you do with the Google Talk client, just by clicking the Options menu.

The Bottom Line

Google Talk works pretty much like AIM and Windows Live Messenger, although it isn't quite as feature-rich as those more-established IM clients. (It has no video chat, for example.) It also isn't nearly as popular; perhaps the biggest drawback of Google Talk is that too few people are using it.

That said, Google has an agreement with AOL to connect Google Talk to the AIM network, but that connection is not yet fully implemented—only through the Gmail Talk component, not through the Google Talk client or iGoogle gadget. So if you want to talk to your AIM buddies, use Google Talk via Gmail. Otherwise, you're limited to talking to only those (few) users who are currently using the Google Talk IM network.

tip You can use the Gmail-based Google Talk to chat with your AIM buddies. In other words, Gmail's Google Talk is fully integrated with and connected to AOL Instant Messenger. That AIM connection is not yet live for either the Google Talk client or the iGoogle Talk gadget, however.

Forming Communities with Google Groups

Google Groups has an odd history. It started as an archive of Usenet newsgroup messages, past and present. But as Usenet began to fade in importance, Google rejigged Google Groups to feature user-created discussion groups so that any user could create a group around any given topic.

And that's what Google Groups is today—a mixture of Usenet newsreader (because Usenet still exists, as does its archive of past postings) and web-based community. It's an interesting mix.

The History of Google Groups

The history of Google Groups starts with Usenet. Predating the World Wide Web—but still using the Internet's underlying infrastructure—Usenet is a collection of more than 30,000 online discussion groups, organized by topic. Usenet ties into Google via Google Groups, which functions as a newsreader for Usenet newsgroups and an archive of historical newsgroup postings—as well as a host of thousands of user-created (non-Usenet) discussion groups.

How Usenet Works

Usenet is a network that piggybacks on the larger Internet. In fact, it was one of the first components of the Internet, predating the Web and the so-called public Internet. The Usenet network is designed to host and convey messages from users organized around topic categories called *newsgroups*.

In essence, a Usenet newsgroup is an electronic gathering place for people with similar interests. Within a newsgroup, users post messages (called *articles*) about a variety of topics; other users read these articles and, when so disposed, respond. The result is a kind of ongoing, freeform discussion in which dozens—or hundreds—of interested users can participate.

Google Groups: Archiving Usenet Articles

Usenet is a kind of living beast, with new articles being posted daily and old articles fading into the ether. Except that you really don't want those old articles fading away, because they contain (among the expected chaff, of course) some very important discussions and information that simply don't exist anywhere else on the Internet.

For that reason, there have long been attempts to archive historical Usenet postings. The most successful of these archives was DejaNews (later called Deja.com), which Google purchased in 2001. Google subsequently turned DejaNews into Google Groups, which continues to function as both an archive of historical Usenet articles and a Web-based newsreader for current Usenet newsgroups. You can use Google Groups to search the newsgroup archives or to browse the current messages in any Usenet newsgroup.

note Unlike some Web-based discussion forums or blogs, most Usenet newsgroups are unmoderated, meaning that no one's watching the message content to ensure that subject discussions stay on track. The result is a kind of only slightly organized chaos, typically with a lot of off-topic messages and thinly concealed advertisements mixed in with the on-topic and useful messages.

Google Groups Today

Today, Google Groups is more than just Usenet. Yes, Google Groups continues to serve as a Usenet newsreader and as a comprehensive Usenet archive, but it's also home to thousands of user-created discussion groups that have nothing to do with Usenet. When you search Google Groups today, you're searching both Usenet postings and postings made within these user-created groups; as far as Google Groups is concerned, one type of group is just as good as the other.

Searching the Newsgroups

In the past, you had to use a newsreader program to browse through Usenet newsgroups and read individual newsgroup articles. This was fine for the time, and it was marginally acceptable if you were only interested in following a handful of newsgroups. But it just didn't cut it if you were power-searching for specific information across multiple newsgroups. For that, you need a more powerful tool, a true Usenet search engine—which is where Google Groups comes in.

Searching for Groups

You access Google Groups, shown in Figure 16.1, by going directly to groups.google.com. From here you can search for specific groups, browse through available groups, or search all groups for specific information.

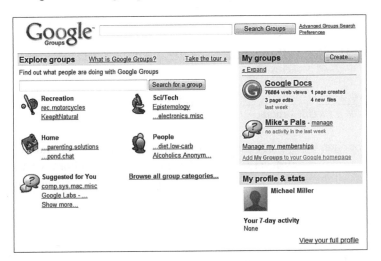

FIGURE 16.1

The Google Groups home page.

When you want to read the current articles or postings in a specific group, you start by searching for that group. To conduct a group search, go to the Explore Groups section of the Google Groups page, enter your query, and then click the Search for a Group button.

The search results page, shown in Figure 16.2, lists several different items. At the top of the page is a series of filters you can click to list only those matching groups within a specific topic, language, activity level, or size (number of members). Below that is a list of the groups themselves, listed in order of activity (high to low).

FIGURE 16.2
Searching for a specific group.

For each group, Google lists the group name, the group's language, the group's activity level and number of users, and whether it's a Usenet newsgroup. (If the word "Usenet" doesn't appear, it's a user-created Google Group.)

Browsing Through the Groups

You can also browse for groups by category. Just scroll down to the bottom of the Google Groups page and click the Browse All Group Categories link. This displays the Group Directory, shown in Figure 16.3. Click through a major category and through the various subcategories until you find the specific group you want.

Group directory		Search for a group
All groups		

Topic
Computers (69865)
Arts and Entertainment (62897)
Recreation (61629)
Society (61221)
Schools and Universities (52710)
People (45175)
Business and Finance (41084)
Science and Technology (28773)
Adult (27943)
Other (27793)
Health (23281)
Home (13513)
News (12465)

Region
Asia (32470)
Europe (32367)
United States (29168)
Latin America (13169)
Middle East (3993)
Canada (3459)
Africa (3315)
Oceania (1883)
Caribbean (1463)
Central America (1298)
Mediterranean (896)

Messages per month
0 (1829855)
1 - 9 (75545)
10 - 99 (48097)

Romanian (4250)
Hebrew (3317)
Swedish (2574)
Danish (2512)
Czech (1996)
Greek (1983)
Finnish (1972)
Lithuanian (1903)
Catalan (1737)
Bulgarian (1613)
Norwegian (Bokmål) (1328)
Ukrainian (1301)
Croatian (1292)
Malay (1264)
Slovenian (1152)
Slovak (1124)
Serbian (968)
Hindi (592)
Tagalog (520)
Tamil (393)
Estonian (382)
French (Canadian) (337)
Latvian (260)
Esperanto (234)
Albanian (228)
Telugu (191)
Abkhazian (182)
Malayalam (170)
Bengali (163)
Urdu (161)
Azerbaijani (150)
Nepali (127)

Assamese (16)
Oriya (15)
Laothian (14)
Zulu (13)
Irish (13)
Kazakh (11)
Sindhi (11)
Interlingue (11)
Sundanese (9)
Yiddish (9)
Faroese (9)
Fiji (8)
Malagasy (8)
Occitan (8)
Kyrgyz (8)
Sanskrit (8)
Tonga (7)
Welsh (7)
Afar (7)
Cambodian (6)
Hausa (6)
Klingon (6)
Moldavian (6)
Bislama (5)
Frisian (5)
(5)
Volapuk (4)
Twi (4)
Tibetan (4)
Guarani (4)
Shona (4)
Inuktitut (3)

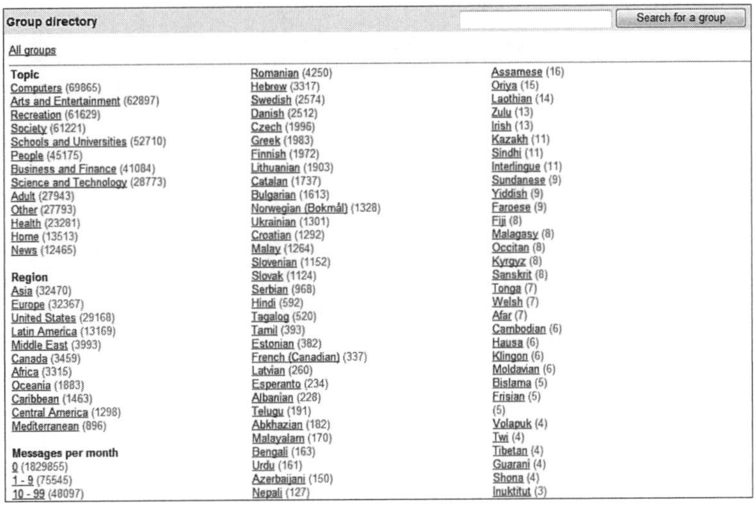

FIGURE 16.3
Browsing through the Group Directory.

Searching Across All Groups

If, instead of reading the messages in a specific group, you want to search for messages about a given topic across all groups, you can do that. Searching the Google Groups archive is as simple as entering a query into the search box at the top of the Google Groups page and then clicking the Search button.

This displays a list of individual messages that match your search criteria. Click a message header to read that message, or click the group name below that message to go to the hosting group.

Using Advanced Search Operators

When you're searching for messages across groups, you can use any of three Groups-specific advanced search operators to fine-tune your search, as shown in Table 16.1. Just enter the operator into the search box.

> **tip**
> To browse through Usenet newsgroups by hierarchy, click the Browse All of Usenet link on the Group Directory page.

Table 16.1	Google Groups Advanced Search Operators	
Operator	Description	Example
author:	Searches for posts by a specific author	author:molehill
group:	Limits your search to a specific group	group:alt.movies
insubject:	Limits your search to the subject lines of messages only	insubject:abba

Performing an Advanced Search

Google Groups also offers a Groups Advanced Search page, shown in Figure 16.4, which lets you fine-tune your search from a simple web form. You access this page by clicking the Advanced Groups Search link on the Google Groups page.

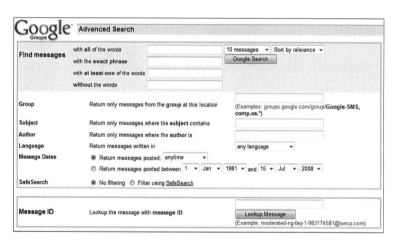

FIGURE 16.4

The Groups Advanced Search page.

Table 16.2 details the search options available on the Groups Advanced Search page.

Table 16.2 Groups Advanced Search Options

Option	Description
Results	Selects how many listings are displayed on the search results page.
Sort by	Sorts messages by relevance or date.
Find messages with all of the words	Default search mode.
Find messages with the exact phrase	Searches for messages that contain the exact phrase entered.
Find messages with at least one of the words	Searches for messages that contain either one word or another.
Find messages without the words	Excludes messages that contain the specified word(s).
Group	Searches for messages within the selected group.
Subject	Searches only within the subject line of messages.
Author	Searches for messages from the specified user.
Language	Restricts the search to messages written in the specified la guage.
Message Dates	Restricts the search to messages created between the specified dates.
SafeSearch	Activates the SafeSearch content filter for this search.
Message ID	Searches for a specific message number.

Make your choices, and then click the Google Search button to initiate the search.

Participating in Google Groups

As soon as you find a group you like, you have a couple of options. You can opt to visit the group and read messages on an infrequent basis, or you can subscribe to the group so that you're notified when new messages are posted.

Visiting Groups and Reading Messages

To view any Google group, all you have to do is search for or browse to the group, and then click the group name. This displays the group's main page.

If you're viewing a Usenet newsgroup, the page looks like the one shown in Figure 16.5. On this page you see a list of the most recent topics (in Usenet parlance, "threads"), with a snippet of the most recent message in each thread. A list of older topics is displayed in the right column. If you like, you also can search the messages within this group by using the search box at the top of the page and clicking the Search This Group button.

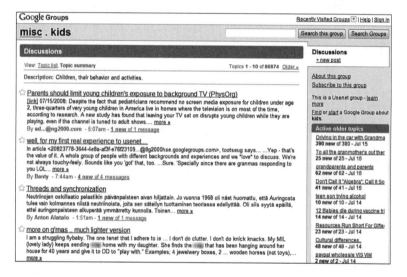

FIGURE 16.5

The home page for a Usenet newsgroup.

On the other hand, if you're viewing a Google Groups group, you see a page like the one shown in Figure 16.6. A list of the most recent topics (in Google parlance, "discussions") is on the left side of the page; a full list of topics can be had by selecting the Discussions tab on the right side of the page. Groups can also contain specialized pages (on the Pages tab) and files for downloading (on the Files tab).

Whichever type of group you're visiting, you can read all the messages on a given topic (in a given thread or discussion, that is) by clicking the title of the thread. This displays the message page, like the one shown in Figure 16.7. Messages are listed in chronological order (the first message at the top and the last at the bottom).

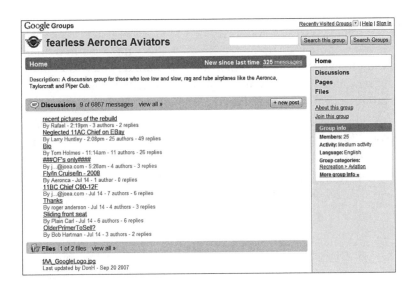

FIGURE 16.6
The home page for a Google Groups group.

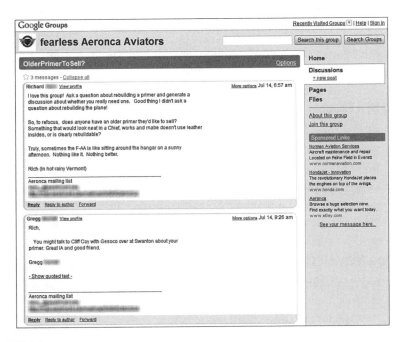

FIGURE 16.7
Reading all the messages in a thread.

Joining a Group

If you want to keep up-to-date on all the new messages in a group, you may want to join that group. When you join a group, you're automatically notified of new messages posted to the group via email; you don't have to visit the group page to read messages.

To subscribe to a group, just go to the main group page and then click the Join This Group link on the right side of the page. When the Join page appears, select how you want to be notified of new messages:

- **No Email.** You aren't informed of new messages; you have to go to the Google Groups site to read the group's messages.

- **Abridged Email.** You get one email a day that summarizes all the new messages.

- **Digest Email.** You get one or more emails a day containing the full text of up to 25 messages. If a group has more than 25 messages in a day, you receive additional digest emails containing the excess messages.

- **Email.** Each new message in the group is sent to you via email as it is posted.

After you've made your selection, enter the nickname you want to use, and then click the Join This Group button.

Posting to a Group

As soon as you're on a group page, you have the option of simply reading messages, replying to messages, or posting a message on a new topic.

To reply to a message, start by opening the message thread. At the bottom of each message in the thread is a Reply link. When you click this link, the page expands to show a Reply box. Enter your reply into the box, and then click the Post button. Your reply is added to the end of the current thread.

Creating a New Message Thread

You're not limited to replying to existing message topics. You can also start a new message thread (also called a discussion) with a new message.

To do this, go to the main group page and click the New Post button at the top right of

tip To unsubscribe from a group, go to that group's page, click the Edit My Membership link, and then click the Unsubscribe button on the bottom of the Edit My Membership page.

the page. This displays the Start a New Discussion page, shown in Figure 16.8. Enter a name for the new discussion into the Subject box, and then enter the text of your message into the Message box. When you click the Post Message button, your new message appears as the first in a new topic/thread on the main group page.

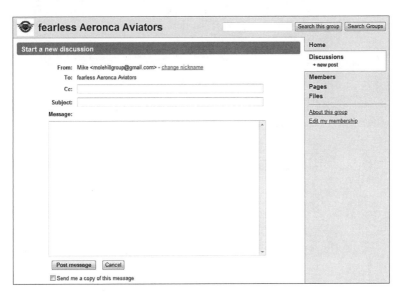

FIGURE 16.8
Creating a new post on a new topic.

Creating Your Own Google Group

With the tens of thousands of groups available on Google Groups, it's still possible that no group is available for a given topic in which you're interested. If this is the case, you can always start your own Google Group, on just about any topic you want.

note User-created groups are not Usenet newsgroups, and they are available only to users of the Google Groups website. In this sense they're similar to the user groups hosted by Yahoo! Groups (groups.yahoo.com).

Setting Up the Group

To start a new Google Group, follow these steps:

1. From the main Google Groups page, click the Create button in the My Groups section on the right side of the page.

2. When the Create a Group page appears, as shown in Figure 16.9, enter a name for your group.

FIGURE 16.9

Creating a new Google Group.

3. Enter an email address for your group. (This is typically the group name, followed by @googlegroups.com.)

4. Enter a brief description of your group.

5. If the group is likely to contain adult content or language, check the option This Group May Contain Adult Content.

6. Select the desired access level for the group: Public (anyone can join, but only members can read messages), Announcement-Only (anyone can join, but only moderators can post messages), or Restricted (only the people you invite can join). For what it's worth, most groups have Public access.

7. Click the Create My Group button.

Inviting Members to Your Group

After you've created your group, it's time to find some members. You do this by inviting people to join your group:

> **note** If you created a Public or Announcement-Only group, your group will appear in the public Google Groups directory. Any user who finds your group in the directory can join at that point.

1. After you click the Create My Group button, the Add Members page appears.

2. Enter the email addresses of those people you want to invite to your group. Separate multiple addresses with commas.

3. Enter an invitation message to send to each person you signified.

4. Click the Invite Members button.

You can also invite new members at a later date. Just go to your group page, click the Invite Members button (at the top of the page), and follow the onscreen directions from there.

Managing Your Group

After you've created your group, you can manage it on a day-to-day basis. When you open your group page, it now looks like the one shown in Figure 16.10. (Only you, as the group owner, see this special page; all visitors see the normal group page.) From here you can invite or add new members, create group-specific pages, upload files, and change your group's settings.

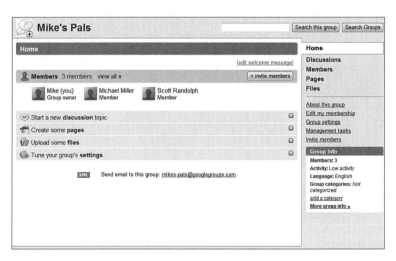

FIGURE 16.10

Managing your Google Group.

16

The Bottom Line

Continuing access to the Usenet newsgroup archive would be reason enough to celebrate Google Groups. The fact that Google Groups also lets you create your own discussion groups is just icing on the proverbial cake. (Notice that it's always the cake that's proverbial, and not the icing?) In any case, if you have a topic that especially interests you, Google Groups is the place to find others who share your interest. I particularly like the ability to receive message summaries and digests via email so that I don't have to visit the actual site if I don't particularly want to—after I've subscribed to all my favorite groups, of course!

Chat in Virtual Worlds with Lively

I f you're a bit of an Internet old-timer, you're probably familiar with the concept of online chat rooms. If you're a younger user, no doubt you're familiar with Second Life and other virtual worlds. Well, Google has a service that's part chat room, part virtual world. It's called Google Lively, and it's what this chapter discusses.

What Is Lively?

Google describes Lively as a three-dimensional chat world. As such, it doesn't have quite the functionality as a true virtual world, such as Second Life. It's more like a traditional chat room where each chatter has his or her own 3D character onscreen.

Like Second Life, the Lively characters (called *avatars*) can be personalized to suit your personality, and they move around onscreen in a three-dimensional virtual space. The Lively site has numerous virtual chat rooms; you can choose to chat in an existing room or create your own new room. Up to 20 people can occupy a room at one time.

note There's a lot more to Lively than what we can cover in this chapter. For example, you can embed virtual rooms in your own website and create your own furniture and other items. If this interests you, spend some time on the Lively site, and get to know what's available.

Lively doesn't require any special software to run; instead, it runs within your web browser (Internet Explorer or Mozilla Firefox). It's flash-based, and you have to download a small browser plug-in before you can start chatting. As of fall 2008, Lively runs on Windows XP and Windows Vista, but not on the Mac

Getting to Know the Lively World

You download the Lively client from the Lively home page (www.lively.com). When you first access Lively, you're asked to choose an ID. After you're logged in, you choose which virtual rooms you want to visit. Figure 17.1 shows the list of available rooms; you can view new rooms, friends' rooms, your favorite rooms (my rooms), or all rooms. You can even search for rooms by name or topic.

When you enter a room, you see a 3D space like the one shown in Figure 17.2. Other users appear as human-like avatars; their comments appear as speech balloons over their avatars.

You look around a room by using the mouse like a joystick. Simply click and drag to move your viewpoint back and forth and side to side. To move your avatar, click your character with the mouse to display the four-arrow cursor, and then click and drag your avatar throughout the room.

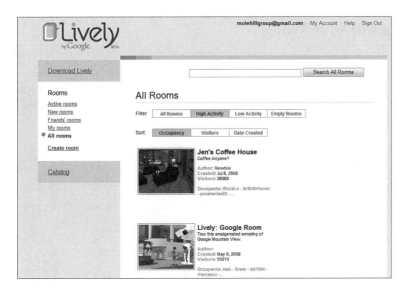

FIGURE 17.1

Browsing Lively virtual rooms.

FIGURE 17.2

Cruising a virtual room.

Designing Your Avatar

To choose or change your avatar, click the My Avatar button on the room's control bar on the right. This opens the My Avatar pane, shown in Figure 17.3. Start by choosing a predesigned character from the Character tab, and then click the Customize tab to personalize your avatar with different hair, skin color, and the like.

FIGURE 17.3
The My Avatar pane.

To change your avatar's clothing, click the My Wardrobe button. The My Wardrobe pane, shown in Figure 17.4, lets you choose from a variety of clothing styles.

FIGURE 17.4

"Shopping" for new clothing.

Chatting with Other Users

Chatting in a Lively room is just like chatting in any other online chat room or instant-messaging program. To talk, enter your text into the chat box at the bottom of the screen, and press Enter. This puts your message onscreen in a speech balloon. This is also how you "listen" to other users—by reading their speech balloons.

To make your avatar perform a specific motion, click your avatar to display your profile, and then select the Animations tab. You can choose from a variety of motions, from angry to "yes," with several dances and rude gestures in between.

You can also view everyone's messages in a text-based chat window. Click the People button in the room's control bar, and then select the Chat tab. As you can see in Figure 17.5, this displays a more traditional text version of everyone's conversations.

> **note** Sometimes your avatar performs an action based on the text you type. For example, if you type "hi," your avatar waves.

FIGURE 17.5

Viewing conversations in text view.

Just remember that when you talk in this fashion, you're talking to everyone in the room, not just to another individual. To have a private conversation with another user—what Lively calls a "whisper"—click that person's avatar to display the profile box, shown in Figure 17.6. This displays the person's profile and lets you initiate a private conversation. Just click the Whisper To button, and you see the dialog box shown in Figure 17.7. Enter your private message, and then click the Send button.

FIGURE 17.6

Viewing another user's profile.

FIGURE 17.7
"Whispering" to another user.

Creating Your Own Virtual Rooms

Most Lively users are content chatting in the numerous preexisting virtual rooms. But if the mood strikes, you can create your own rooms, for your own public or private purposes.

From within an existing room, click the New Room button in the control bar. This opens the Room Properties pane; click the Create New Room button.

You now see the Create New Room pane, shown in Figure 17.8. Here you give your room a title and description, as well as choose a "shell" for your room. (A shell is merely the starting layout for how the room will eventually look.) You can also click the Sounds tab to add background music to your room.

FIGURE 17.8
Designing a new virtual room.

Now click the Sharing tab. If you want your room to be available to the public, check the Include This Room in the Lively Room List Where Anyone Can Find It option. You can also determine whether you want visitors to be able to "decorate" the room. Click the Create Room button, and your room is created

To decorate your new room, click the Furniture & Things button. When the Furniture & Things pane appears, pick out the items you want. Then, when you're done adding furniture and things, click the Move Furniture button; this lets you place your new items within your room.

The Bottom Line

Is Lively a virtual world like Second Life or a traditional chat room with avatars and 3D camera controls? To me, it feels more like an animated chat room—but then, I've never been a big virtual-worlds person. If you're a Second Lifer, however, chances are you'll find Lively interesting but not nearly as versatile as other virtual worlds. (And if you're not familiar with Second Life, go to www.secondlife.com to see how Lively compares.)

However you classify Lively, it's probably worth taking a look. There's no cost involved, and no tricky software to download and install. It runs in any Windows-based web browser, and it's easy to start using, without a steep learning curve. Give it a visit and see what you think!

tip
More items are available when you click the Shop For More button in the Furniture & Things pane. For something really fun, look for items labeled "with video"; these let you display YouTube videos in your virtual room!

Blogging with Blogger

I f you want to create your own blog, you have two ways to go. You can use blogging software to create a blog on your own website, using your own web-hosting service. Alternatively, you can create a blog at one of the many blog-hosting communities.

A blog-hosting community is a site that offers easy-to-use tools to build and maintain your blog and then does all the hosting for you—typically for free. Creating your own blog on one of these sites is as simple as clicking a few buttons and filling out a few forms. After your blog is created, you can update it as frequently as you like, again by clicking a link or two.

Perhaps the most popular blog-hosting community on the Web today is Blogger, which Google just happens to own. Now, you might think that Blogger has very little to do with Google's core competency, search technology, and you'd be right. But Blogger does offer Google lots of opportunities to sell advertising space, and as we've discussed throughout this book, that's how Google makes its money.

Because Blogger is an important part of the Google empire, it gets covered in this book. It also helps that Blogger is very good at what it does, perhaps the best (and definitely the biggest) of all the blog-hosting communities on the Web today. If you want to launch your own blog, you could do worse than using Blogger.

Creating a Blog

After you've registered with Blogger, the home page (www.blogger.com) becomes the Blogger Dashboard, as shown in Figure 18.1. From here, you can manage all your blogs, create new blog posts, manage your Blogger account and profile, and access Blogger's help system.

FIGURE 18.1
The Blogger Dashboard.

Creating a new blog is surprisingly easy. Start by going to the Blogger dashboard and then click the Create a Blog link.

> **note** Blogger was a free-standing site with more than a million users long before Google acquired it in 2003. Since then, it's only gotten bigger—and better. In fact, Blogger is one of the crown jewels of the Google empire; Blogger is host to more than 8 million individual blogs, more than any other blog-hosting service.

You see the Name Your Blog page, shown in Figure 18.2. Enter a title for your blog and a corresponding blog address (the part of the URL that goes before Blogger's blogspot.com domain), and click Continue.

note Before you can create a blog, you have to have a Google account.

You are then asked to do a word verification for security purposes. Type in the word shown on the screen, and click Continue.

FIGURE 18.2

Naming your blog.

Next, you get to choose a template for your blog. As you can see in Figure 18.3, a template is a predesigned combination of page layout, colors, and fonts. Try to choose a template that's easily readable, especially for the types of postings you think you'll be doing. (You can preview any template at full size by clicking the Preview Template link under the template's thumbnail picture.) After you make your choice, click the Continue button.

note By default, Blogger serves as host for your blog, and it assigns you a URL in the blogspot.com domain. If you'd rather host your blog on another website, read the section "Changing Where Your Blog Is Hosted," near the end of this chapter.

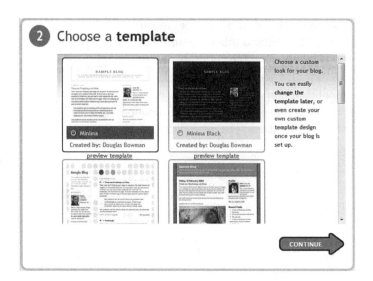

FIGURE 18.3
Choosing a template for your blog.

Blogger creates your blog and displays a confirmation page. If now is a good time to write your first blog post, click the Start Blogging link. Otherwise, you can create posts later.

Viewing Your Blog

You can view your blog by entering the URL that was previously assigned, or by going to the Dashboard (www.blogger.com), clicking the blog name, and then clicking the View Blog tab. As you can see in Figure 18.4, a typical blog includes a Blogger search bar at the top of the page, with the title of the blog just below that. Blog posts take up the balance of the page, with assorted personal information in a narrow column to the right or left of the postings.

note The templates presented on this page are just a subset of the larger number of available templates—but chances are you'll be happy with one of them. If not, you can change—and customize—templates after you've created your blog. Learn more in a moment in the section "Customizing Your Blog."

FIGURE 18.4

The blog for this book—Googlepedia: The Blog.

Each blog post is accompanied by a date and time stamp (sometimes above the post, sometimes below), as well as links to any reader comments or other blogs that have linked to this post. Click the Comments link to read any comments; click the Links to This Post link to see the links.

Although the format of the blog posts themselves is fairly standard, the elements in the narrow column are highly customizable. Most blogs include an About Me section (which may or may not include a photo), a listing of recent posts, a listing of archived posts (typically organized by month), and any other information you choose to include. If you don't like what you see, you can easily customize the contents and layout of your blog page—which we'll discuss next.

> **note** Specific blog elements and the placement thereof differ from blog to blog and from template to template. Your blog will probably look different from the one shown here.

Customizing Your Blog

The blog templates you get to choose from when first creating your blog are nice, but there aren't a lot of them. Fortunately, Blogger offers additional templates for your blog—and lets you fully customize the look and feel of your blog page. Read on to learn more.

Choosing a Different Template

First things first: If you no longer like the template you originally chose for your blog, you can change it. Blogger offers more than 35 different blog templates, and there's no harm in switching from one to another to suit your mood. Here's how to do so:

1. From the Blogger Dashboard, click the Layout link next to your blog name.

2. When the next page appears, select the Layout tab, and click Pick New Template.

3. Doing so puts all of Blogger's templates on display, as you can see in Figure 18.5. This is a larger selection of templates than was visible when you first created your blog; several template styles are available in different color variations. To preview how your blog will look with a given template, click the Preview Template link beneath that template.

4. To choose a new template, select that template's radio button.

5. After you select a template, click the Save Template button.

Personalizing Fonts and Colors

You don't have to settle for the stock templates that Blogger provides. Blogger lets you customize the fonts and colors used in any template, with a few clicks of the mouse.

To customize the look of individual elements in your blog template, go to the Blogger Dashboard, and click the Layout link next to your blog title. When the next page appears, select the Layout tab, and click Fonts and Colors. Doing so displays the Fonts and Colors page, the top of which is shown in Figure 18.6.

caution When you choose a new template, any changes you've made to your previous template are lost.

note Blogger uses CSS (cascading style sheets) to control all the fonts and colors in a template. The style sheet code is at the beginning of the page's underlying HTML code, and it defines the look of each page element. Obviously, this all goes on behind the scenes; when you make a selection on the Fonts and Colors page, you're actually making changes to the CSS code.

18

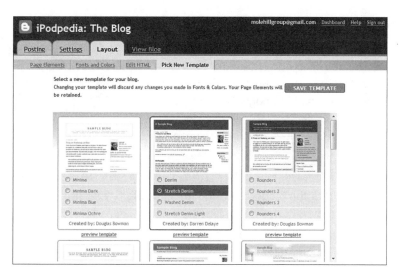

FIGURE 18.5

Choosing a new template for your blog.

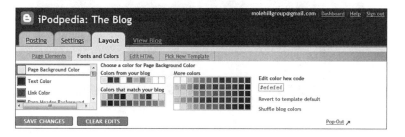

FIGURE 18.6

Changing colors.

From the Fonts and Colors page, you can change the color of all the elements on your page, from the background and main text to the sidebar and links. You can also change the font of the text and the page header.

For colors, making a change is as simple as selecting the element in the list and then clicking the new color in the color picker. To change the text font, select Text Font from the list and choose a font family, font style (normal, bold, or italic), and font size (smaller or larger). The preview of your blog, at the bottom of the page, reflects your changes. When you're satisfied with your changes, click the Save Changes button.

Adding New Page Elements

One of the more useful features of Blogger is the ability to add subsidiary page elements in either the sidebar or the main column of the blog page. You can use these page elements to add descriptive text, pictures, links, lists, and the like to your blog.

tip A fun option for any color element is to shuffle randomly through a compatible color scheme while you display your blog. Just click the Shuffle Blog Colors link to see how this works.

To add a new element to your page, follow these steps:

1. From the Blogger Dashboard, click the Layout link next to your blog name.

2. When the next page appears, select the Layout tab, and click Page Elements.

3. The next page, shown in Figure 18.7, displays all the current elements used in your blog. To rearrange existing elements, simply drag the selected element to a new position on the page.

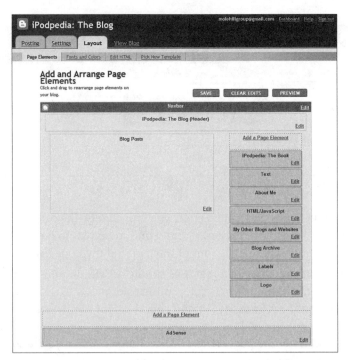

FIGURE 18.7

Viewing the layout of your blog page.

4. To add a new element to your page, click the Add a Page Element link.

5. This displays the Choose a New Page Element window, shown in Figure 18.8. Click the Add to Blog button beneath the element you want to add.

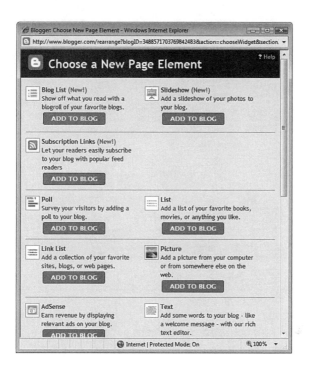

FIGURE 18.8

Adding page elements to your blog.

6. You see a window specific to the type of element you selected. For example, Figure 18.9 shows the Configure Blog List window, which opens when you choose to add a blog list (also called a *blogroll*) to your blog. Fill in the information required in this window, and then click Save.

FIGURE 18.9

Adding a blog list to your blog.

Your blog now contains the element you selected. You can then decide where on the page that element will appear, by dragging it into place on the Add and Arrange Page Elements page.

tip To edit an existing page element, go to the Add and Arrange Page Elements page, and click the Edit link next to the element you want to edit.

What elements can you add to your blog?

Table 18.1 details the page elements that Blogger lets you add.

Table 18.1   Blogger Page Elements

Page Element	Description
AdSense	Displays Google AdSense ads on your blog—an easy way to pick up some extra money, based on click-throughs from your blog visitors.
Blog archive	Use this element to display links to older posts in your blog.
Blog List	Links to your favorite blogs.
Feed	This element displays up-to-the-minute content from another blog or news feed on the Web; all you have to do is enter the feed's URL.
HTML/JavaScript	This element lets you add snippets of HTML or JavaScript code to your blog, which you can use to incorporate additional functionality from third-party sites.
Labels	This element displays a list of all the labels you use to categorize your blog posts.
Link list	Similar to a text list, except that each list item has a hyperlink to another web page. Use the link list element to create lists of favorite websites.
List	A simple text list you can use to create lists of CDs, books, and the like.
Logo	Use this element to display a Blogger logo on your page.
Newsreel	This displays current headlines from Google News. You supply one or more keywords; then headlines (with short synopses) that match that keyword search are displayed in a list.
Page header	This element typically goes at the top of your blog page; it displays your blog title and description.
Picture	This adds a single picture to your blog page. You can upload the picture from your PC or link to it on another site on the Web.
Poll	Enables you to conduct visitor polls on your blog.
Profile	This element displays your Blogger profile.
Slideshow	An automatic slide show of your favorite photos.
Subscription links	Enables visitors to subscribe to a sitefeed for your blog.
Text	Add a block of text anywhere on your blog page. The text block can have a title and description; you can format the text itself with bold, italic, and colored text.
Video bar	Displays selected video clips from YouTube and Google Video. You supply one or more keywords; then thumbnails for matching videos are displayed in a stack in your blog sidebar.

18

As you can see, these page elements add much useful content to your blog. It's a simple matter of clicking a few links and filling in a few blanks, and Blogger adds the element automatically.

Posting New Blog Entries

After you've created and customized your blog, it's time to write your first blog post. Read on to learn how to post.

Posting from the Blogger Dashboard

When you're ready to post, the place to start is the Blogger Dashboard. All you have to do is follow these steps:

1. From the Blogger Dashboard, click the New Post icon for this particular blog.

2. When the Posting page appears, as shown in Figure 18.10, enter a title for this post.

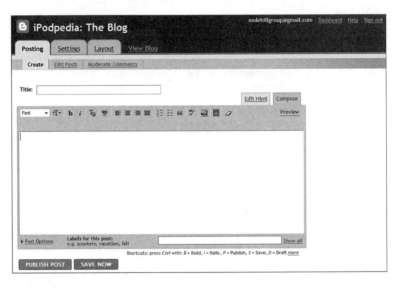

FIGURE 18.10
Creating a new blog post.

3. Enter the text for your post into the large text box. If you like, you can format the text (bold, italic, colors, and so on) using the formatting toolbar above this text box.

4. If you want to apply more sophisticated formatting (and you know how to code in HTML), click the Edit Html tab and enter your own HTML codes.

5. To check the spelling in your post, click the Check Spelling button. Misspelled words are highlighted in yellow; click a word to see a list of suggested corrections.

6. To view a preview of your post, click the Preview link.

7. When you're done writing and formatting, click the Publish Post button.

Blogger publishes your post and displays a confirmation screen. Click the View Blog button to view your blog, with the new post at the top of the page.

Adding Links to Your Posts

One of the neat things about a blog is the ability to link to other pages on the Web, via the use of inline hyperlinks. Fortunately, Blogger makes it easy to add links to your post.

You add links while you're creating the blog post. Just highlight the text from which you want to link, and then click the Link button. This displays the Hyperlink dialog box; enter the URL for the link, and then click OK.

Adding Pictures to Your Posts

Another way to make a visually interesting blog is to incorporate pictures into your blog entries. Again, Blogger makes this relatively easy to do.

You add pictures while you're creating your blog post. Just position the cursor where you want the picture to appear, and click the Add Image button. This displays the Upload Images window, shown in Figure 18.11.

To upload an image file from your computer, click the Browse button in the Add an Image from Your Computer section, and then navigate to and select the image file. You can upload additional pictures by clicking the Add Another Image link.

To point to an image hosted elsewhere on the Web, enter the full web address for that image into the URL box in the Or Add an Image from the Web section. Click the Add Another Image link to link to additional images.

After you select the images to include, you can choose how to display that image in the blog post. In the Choose a Layout section, select how you want the image aligned, relative to the blog text: left, center, or right. In the Image

Size section, select how big you want the image to appear: small, medium, or large.

Clicking the Upload Image button adds the photo to the selected blog post. Blog visitors can click the image to view it full size.

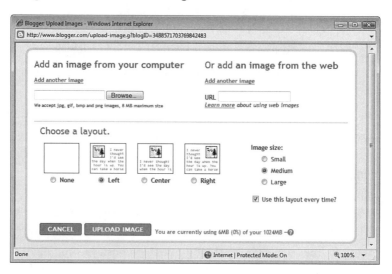

FIGURE 18.11
Adding a photo to your blog post.

Adding Videos to Your Posts

Similarly, Blogger lets you add videos to your blog posts. A video appears in its own video player in the post; visitors click the player's Play button to watch the video.

To add a video to the current post, click the Add Video button. This displays the Add a Video to Your Blog Post window, shown in Figure 18.12. Click the Browse button to select the video to upload, and then enter the title of the video into the Video Title box. Check the box to agree to Blogger's terms and conditions, and then click the Upload Video button. The video is uploaded to the Blogger site and inserted into the current blog post.

note Blogger lets you upload videos in most popular file formats: AVI, MPEG, QuickTime, Real, and Windows Media Video (WMV). Your videos must be 100MB in size or smaller.

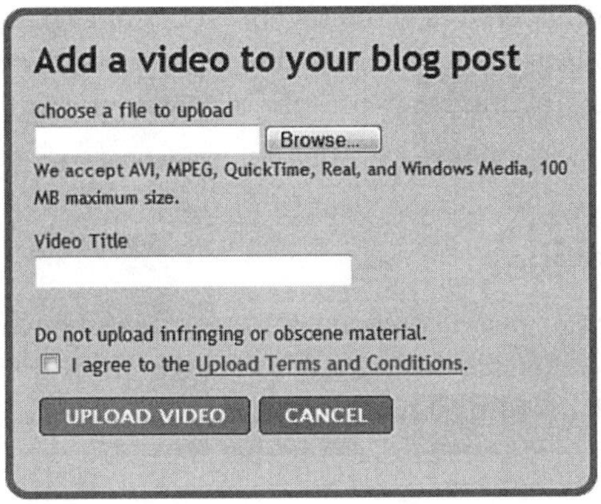

FIGURE 18.12

Adding a video to your blog post.

Adding Labels to Your Posts

When you get a lot of posts in your blog, it becomes increasingly difficult to find a particular post. You can make this easier for your blog visitors by using labels to categorize your posts. Visitors can then click a label in the label list to view all posts related to that particular topic.

To add a label to your post, all you have to do is enter the label into the Labels for This Post box at the bottom of the Create page. You can enter multiple labels for any post; just separate the labels with commas.

Posting via Email

Blogger also lets you submit your posts via email, which is helpful if you're posting from the road. That's right—you can create a post in an email message and then send that message to Blogger to post to your blog.

For this to work, you first have to create a mail-to-Blogger address. You do this by clicking the Settings link next to your blog name in the Blogger Dashboard and then clicking the Email link. When the next page appears, enter or confirm the email address in the Mail-to-Blogger Address section, check the Publish option, and then click the Save Settings button.

> **tip**
> To view a list of all the labels you've previously created, click the Show All link beside the label box.

Now you can open a new message in your email program and compose your post within that message. Email the message to your mail-to-Blogger address, and Blogger automatically uses the text of your email to create a new blog post.

Managing Your Blog

Even after your blog is up and running, you still have to perform a bit of ongoing maintenance. Fortunately, you can do everything you need to do from the Blogger Dashboard—and you don't have to do much.

Editing Your Posts

No one's perfect. Every now and then, you'll post something to your blog and then discover an egregious spelling error, or a bad link, or maybe just something you wish you'd never written. Have no fear, gentle blogger; Blogger lets you edit any post you like.

To edit a Blogger post, follow these steps:

1. From the Blogger Dashboard, click the Manage: Posts link for your blog.
2. When the list of recent posts appears, click the Edit link next to the post you want to edit.
3. When the Edit Posts window appears, edit your post accordingly.
4. When you're done editing, click the Publish Post button.

Limiting Comments

By default, anyone can post comments to your blog postings. These comments appear below each posting when a visitor clicks the Comments link. If you'd rather not have everyone and their brother comment on your blog, you can limit comments to either registered Blogger users or members of your blog. You do this by following these steps:

1. From the Blogger Dashboard, click the Manage: Settings link next to your blog name.
2. When the Settings page appears, click the Comments link.
3. When the next page appears, go to the Who Can Comment? section and select either Anyone, Registered Users, Users with Google Accounts, or Only Members of This Blog.
4. Click the Save Settings button.

Moderating Comments

The Comments tab of the Settings screen also lets you configure several other ways that comments are displayed on your blog. One of the key settings concerns comment moderation. When you choose to moderate comments, you must approve any comments to your blog before they can be posted.

You turn on moderation by checking the Enable Comment Moderation? option on the Comments screen of the Settings tab. This displays a new Moderate Comments link on the Posting tab, which is where all user comments appear. (You also receive an email to alert you to all new comments.) On this page, you can choose to publish or reject any listed comment; click the Publish button, and the comment is posted to your blog.

Fighting Comment Spam

Another problem with blog comments is that, without any moderation, they can be used for spam purposes. Unscrupulous spammers use spam robots to seed blog postings with unwanted spam messages. It's all done automatically. Don't be surprised if you wake up one morning and find a ton of comments to your blog that have nothing to do with your original postings.

There's an easy way to defeat these spam robots. All you have to do is require some sort of human input to post. Blogger does this by adding a word verification section to the comments posting page. Readers have to enter the word verification code before the comment is posted. Because robots can't read graphic images like this, they can't enter the word verification code, and no spam is posted.

You turn on word verification by going to the Comments screen on the Settings tab and checking the Show Word Verification for Comments? option.

Controlling Access to Your Blog

By default, your blog is public, so anyone on the Internet can read it. However, there's a way to make your blog private so that only invited guests can view it. To control access to your blog, follow these steps:

1. From the Blogger Dashboard, click the Manage: Settings link next to your blog name.

2. When the Settings page appears, click the Permissions link.

3. When the next page appears, go to the Blog Readers section and select who can view your blog: Anybody (keeps the blog public), Only People I Choose, or Only Blog Authors.

4. If you select the Only People I Choose option, you have to invite people to view your blog. The page expands to include a new text box; enter the invitees' email addresses, and then click the Invite button. (If the invitee already has a Google account, he's automatically granted access; if he doesn't yet have a Google account, he's sent an invitation via email.)

> **note** A *blog author* is someone like you, who can create new blog postings. Although anyone can add comments to existing postings, only blog authors can create new postings.

5. If you choose the Only Blog Authors option, you have to enable some authors other than yourself. Click the Add Authors button to invite other authors to post on your blog.

Syndicating Your Blog

A *site feed* is an automatically updated stream of a blog's contents, enabled by a special XML file format called *RSS* (Really Simple Syndication). When a blog has an RSS feed enabled, any updated content is published automatically as a special XML file that contains the RSS feed. The syndicated feed is then picked up by RSS feed reader programs and RSS aggregators for websites, so that subscribers are automatically informed of new posts.

Activating Basic Atom Syndication

Blogger uses Atom for its blog syndication. When you activate Atom syndication for your blog, Blogger automatically generates a machine-readable version of your blog that can be read by most feed readers and aggregators.

To activate Atom syndication for your blog, follow these steps:

1. From the Blogger Dashboard, click the Manage: Settings icon next to your blog name.

2. When the Settings page appears, click the Site Feed link.

3. To syndicate the full content of each post, pull down the Allow Blog Feeds list and select Full. To syndicate just the first paragraph (or 255 characters) of each post, select Short. If you don't want to activate a feed, select None.

4. If you want to add a footer that appears at the bottom of each post in your feed, enter that text into the Post Feed Footer section. This is also where you enter the HTML code for any AdSense ads you want to appear in your feed.

5. Click the Save Settings button.

> **note** Google offers its own Google Reader feed aggregator. Learn more in Chapter 23, "Using Google Reader."

Activating Feeds for All Blog Comments

Blogger not only lets you syndicate new posts that you make to your blog, it also lets you syndicate all the comments that visitors make to your posts.

> **tip** If you'd rather use RSS syndication instead of Atom, use the Feedburner service (www.feedburner.com).

Start by going to the Site Feed page on the Settings tab and clicking the Advanced Mode link. This expands the page to display the following new options:

> **tip** Notice the URL for your site feed. It's typically your blog URL with /atom.xml attached, like this: *myblog*.blogspot.com/atom.xml.

■ Blog Comment Feed contains all the comments made to posts on your blog; select either None, Full, or Short.

■ Per-Post Comment Feeds creates a separate site feed for each post on your blog, containing the comments for only that post. Again, you can choose either None, Full, or Short posts.

Make your selections and click Save Settings.

Making Money from Your Blog

Here's something cool—and potentially profitable—about Blogger. Google lets you insert context-sensitive text advertisements into your blog, which (in theory) could generate a bit of income for you. Every time a visitor clicks one of the ad links, you earn a small commission. However, Google doesn't disclose just how much of a commission you earn—which is a bit of an odd way to attract participants to the program, if you ask me.

These Blogger ads are served by Google's AdSense division. This is one of the key revenue-generating parts of the Google empire. It's to Google's benefit for you to add ads to your blog; the fact that you participate in the revenues is the carrot to get you to sign up.

Adding an AdSense Module to Your Blog

To add AdSense ads to your blog, follow these steps:

1. From the Blogger Dashboard, click the Manage: Layout link next to your blog name, and then click the Layout link.

2. When the Layout tab appears, click the Page Elements link.

3. When the Add and Arrange Page Elements page appears, click the Add a Page Element link.

4. When the Choose a New Page Element window appears, click the Add to Blog button for the AdSense element.

5. If you don't yet have an AdSense account, you're prompted to create one. Follow the onscreen directions to proceed.

6. After your AdSense account is created, you see the Configure AdSense window, as shown in Figure 18.13. Pull down the Format list and select an ad format. You can choose from various sizes and shapes of ads; the ad you select is previewed on the page below the pull-down list.

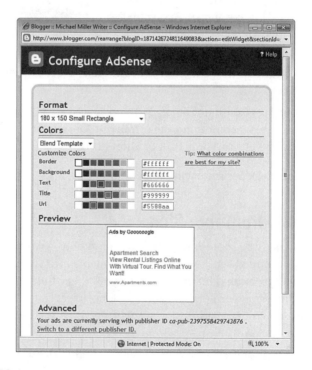

FIGURE 18.13

Adding AdSense ads to your blog.

7. Pull down the Colors list and select a color scheme for your ad. Alternatively, you can select custom colors from the Customize Colors palette.

8. Click the Save button.

> **note** Learn more about Google's AdSense program in Chapter 40, "Profiting from Google AdSense."

AdSense automatically uses the ID previously assigned to your Google Account. If you want to assign your ads to a different ID, click the Switch to a Different Publisher ID link.

> **note** To enable ads in your site feed, you must select the Full option for the Allow Site Feed setting.

After you've activated AdSense for your blog, you can view your ad activity in the AdSense console (www.google.com/adsense/). This console tracks your click-through activity; you can also select the AdSense Setup and My Account tabs to manage the details of your account and ads.

Adding AdSense Ads to Your Site Feed

When you add an AdSense module to your blog, the ads appear only on your blog—not in the syndicated blog feed. Obviously, the more exposure for the ads, the more revenue you can generate, so it's probably a good idea to include AdSense ads within your site feed. That isn't hard to do.

First, you have to copy your AdSense code from the AdSense website. Then go to the Blogger Dashboard, click the Manage: Settings link next to your blog name, and click the Site Feed link. When the next page appears, paste the AdSense code into the Feed Item Footer box. This puts in the ads at the bottom of each feed page. Click the Save Settings button when you're done.

Changing Where Your Blog Is Hosted

By default, your Blogger blog is hosted on the Blogger website and has an address with the blogspot.com domain. You're not limited to using Blogger as a host, however; if you want to, you can host your blog on a different website and give it a unique domain name.

To host your blog on another site, first you have to have another site, provided by a web-hosting service. You also need to have FTP access to that site, because Blogger uses FTP to upload all blog postings.

18

After your website is set up, you can configure Blogger to use that site to host your blog. Here's what you need to do:

1. From the Blogger Dashboard, click the Manage: Settings icon next to your blog name.
2. When the Settings tab appears, click the Publishing link.
3. Click the Switch To: Custom Domain link.
4. When the next page appears, click the Switch to Advanced Settings link.
5. Enter the URL for the blog into the Your Domain box.
6. Click the Save Settings button.

Your blog appears on the website you selected. The blog is physically hosted on the other server, and it appears with the website address you specified.

The Bottom Line

If you want to blog, Blogger makes it easy. Creating your own blog takes less than five minutes, and it's just as quick and easy to create new blog posts. And, if you want a truly personalized blog, Blogger lets you get your hands dirty and tinker with the underlying HTML to your heart's content—or, if you're less technically inclined, to simply choose another predesigned blog template. In any case, blogs are all the rage these days, and Blogger is the most popular blog host for a reason. What have you got to lose? (It is free, after all.)

18

Working with Google Applications

Using Google Docs

As you've no doubt surmised, Google is much more than a search engine. In fact, with all the end-user applications that Google has developed, Google appears to be a software developer, competing with the likes of Microsoft.

This is most apparent when you examine the office application space. Microsoft has owned this market for some time now, with its popular suite of Microsoft Office applications—Microsoft Word, Microsoft Excel, and so on. But Google represents new competition for Microsoft, thanks to Google's Web-based word processor, spreadsheet, and presentation applications, collectively dubbed Google Docs.

That's right—Google competes directly with Microsoft Office. And the best thing is, Google's applications are free!

Introducing Google Docs

The comparison is simple. Google Docs is Google's answer to Microsoft Office. Google Docs is a suite of word processor, spreadsheet, and presentation applications that mimics most of the key features of similar freestanding programs, such as Office.

What's different about Google Docs, however, is that it's all Web-based. The application and all your documents reside on Google's servers, not on your computer. This results in some unique benefits.

note Even though Google Docs is a Web-based application, you can still use it when you're not online, thanks to something called Google Gears. Learn more in the "Working Offline" section, near the end of this chapter.

Benefits of Web-Based Applications

The most obvious benefit of using a Web-based application is that you can access your documents wherever you are, from any PC. With Google Docs, you'll never be disappointed to realize that the document you need is located on your office PC when you're using another PC, either at home or on the road.

caution Given how websites and Web browsers work (or sometimes don't), it's always possible that your latest changes might not make it to Google's servers. Server overload or a slow connection can sometimes cause your changes to take more time than expected to get stored on the server. The bottom line is, even though Google goes to great lengths to avoid data loss, there's always a slight chance of losing your latest data when the Internet is involved.

Also nice is that, by being Web-based, you can easily share your documents with others. That makes real-time workgroup collaboration possible from anywhere around the globe, which is something you don't have with Microsoft Office and similar programs.

Another benefit of being Web-based is that you can't lose your work—theoretically, anyway. After you've named the document you're working on, Google Docs saves your file on its servers. From that point on, every change you make to the document gets saved to the Google servers automatically. Nothing gets lost if you close your web browser, navigate to another website, or even turn off your computer. Google saves everything you do.

The final thing that's unique about Google Docs is that it's free. It costs nothing, unlike the ever increasingly expensive Microsoft Office. Being free makes it easy to take for a test drive, and even easier to add to your bag of applications. Many early users who've tried Google Docs have said that they're likely to switch from Office. It can do almost everything Word and Excel can do,

19

from a basic editing standpoint, which makes it perfect for corporate and small-business environments.

Privacy and Security Concerns

When you use Google Docs, you rely on Google to store your work on its servers. This may raise some concerns about privacy and security; all your data is in Google's hands.

These sound like reasonable concerns, but Google says you shouldn't worry. Although Google stores your documents on its servers, it does not collect other personal information about you. In addition, Google uses a secure authentication method to control access to any document you create. Although you can grant access to others to share your documents, those documents are private by default. Unless you share a document URL, no one else can view that spreadsheet.

Should You Use Google Docs?

Before you jump into the Google Docs waters, you need to consider whether Google Docs is right for your particular needs. Here are the users for whom I'd say Google Docs holds promise:

- **Beginning users.** If you're just starting out with word processing, spreadsheets, or presentations, there's no better place to start than with Google Docs. The slightly limited functionality of Google's applications actually works to the benefit of beginning users; you aren't overwhelmed by all the advanced options that clutter the Word, Excel, and PowerPoint workspaces. Plus, Google Docs is extremely easy to use; everything you need is out in the open, not hidden beneath layers of menus and dialog boxes. I wish I'd had Google Docs 20 years ago, when I was learning how to use PC-based word processing and spreadsheet programs.

- **Casual users.** Google Docs is also a good choice if you have modest word processing, spreadsheet, and presentation needs. If all you're doing is writing memos and letters, totaling a few numbers, or giving a short presentation, Google Docs gets the job done with ease.

- **Anyone who wants access to their documents from multiple locations.** If you work on the same data at work and at home (or on the road), you know what a hassle it is to carry your data around with you from computer to computer—and keep it synchronized. Google Docs

19

solves this problem. Wherever you are (home, office, on the road), you always access the same version of your document, stored on Google's servers. There are no synchronization issues; you work on the same file wherever you go.

■ **Anyone who needs to share their documents with others.** Sometimes you need others to view what you're working on. Maybe you have a family budget that you and your spouse both need to see. Maybe you have a soccer team schedule that other parents need to view. Whatever the need, Google Docs lets you share your documents with anyone you like, over the Web.

■ **Anyone who needs to edit their documents in a collaborative environment.** Sharing is one thing; collaborative editing is another. If you need multiple users to both access and edit data in a document, Google Docs lets you do things that are impossible in Microsoft Office. For example, I know of one entrepreneur who adopted Google Docs for his small telemarketing company. He has five employees making calls at the same time, all from their homes. He has all five employees work from the same spreadsheet; not only do they access the same call data, but they also enter their results into the spreadsheet—live, via the Internet.

All that said, Google Docs isn't for everyone. So who *shouldn't* use Google Docs?

■ **Power users.** If you've created your own custom documents or spreadsheet applications in Microsoft Word, Excel, or PowerPoint, especially those with macros and pivot tables and the like, Google Docs is not for you. Google Docs lacks many of Office's most advanced features and simply won't get the job done.

■ **Anyone who wants to create sophisticated printouts.** Google Docs lacks some of the more sophisticated formatting options that some Office users take for granted. With Google Docs, what you see onscreen is exactly what prints—for better or for worse. If you need fancy printouts, Google Docs will probably disappoint.

■ **Anyone working on sensitive documents.** Web-based applications (and documents stored on the Web) are not good tools if your company has a lot of trade secrets it wants to protect. In fact, some organizations may bar their employees from working on documents that don't reside on their own secured servers, which rules out Google's applications.

So, if you're a beginning or casual user who doesn't need fancy charts or printouts, or if you need to share your documents or collaborate online with other users, Google Docs is worth checking out.

Navigating Google Docs

You access Google Docs at docs.google.com. After you log on with your Google account, you see the page shown in Figure 19.1. This is the home page for all three applications—word processing, spreadsheets, and presentations. All your previously created documents are listed on this page.

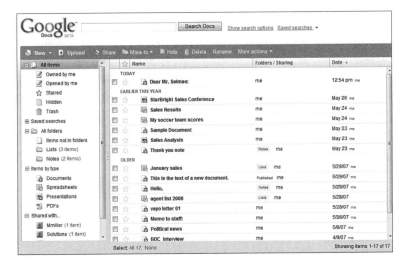

FIGURE 19.1
The main page of Google Docs.

The left pane helps you organize your documents. You can store files in folders, view documents by type (word processing documents, spreadsheets, presentations, or PDFs), see the results of saved searches, and display documents shared with specific people.

The documents for the selected folder are displayed in the main part of the window. As you can see, word processing documents are noted with a document icon, spreadsheets have a spreadsheet icon, and presentations have a slide icon. (And, of

> **tip**
> To create a new folder, click the New button, select Folder, and then give the new folder a name. To move a document to a folder, check the document, click the Add to Folder button, and then select the folder you want to add it to.

course, PDF documents have the requisite Adobe PDF icon.) To open any type of document, click the item's title; the document opens in a new window. To delete an item, select it and then click the Delete button.

Creating New Documents

To create a new word processing document, click the New button and select Document; the new document opens in a new browser window. Ditto to create a new spreadsheet or presentation: click the New button and select either Spreadsheet or Presentation to open a new, empty spreadsheet or presentation window.

Alternatively, you can create a new document based on a predesigned template. When you click the New button and select From Template, Google opens a new Templates Gallery window, as shown in Figure 19.2. You can search or browse for templates; Google has templates for documents, spreadsheets, and presentations. Click the Preview link to see a quick view of the template, and then click the Use This Template button to create a new document based on the template.

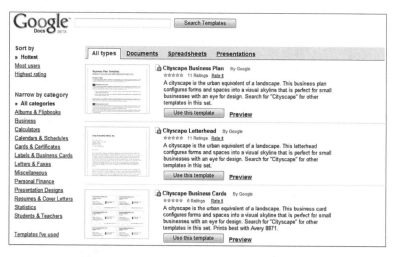

FIGURE 19.2
Browsing Google's Templates Gallery.

Importing Microsoft Office Documents

One of the nice things about Google Docs is that you can use the application to work on files you've previously created in your regular word processing or spreadsheet programs. After they are imported, you can work on these documents in Google Docs, online.

You can import the following file types:

> **note** A template is a combination of text styles, document formatting, and graphics to which you can add your own text, graphics, and numbers. Templates are great for getting a head start on a specific type of document or project; Google includes templates for calendars, photo albums, invoices, letterhead, business cards, business plans, budgets, and the like.

- Adobe PDF files (.pdf) up to 10MB in size (2MB if imported from a website)
- Comma-separated value (.csv) spreadsheet up to 1MB
- Microsoft Excel (.xls) spreadsheet up to 1MB
- Microsoft PowerPoint presentation (.ppt or .pps) up to 10MB (2MB if imported from a website or 500KB if added via email)
- Microsoft Word document (.doc) up to 500KB
- OpenDocument Spreadsheet (.ods) up to 1MB
- OpenDocument Text (.odt) up to 500KB
- Plain text (.txt) up to 500KB
- Rich text (.rtf) up to 500KB
- StarOffice (.sxw) up to 500KB
- Web and HTML documents (.htm) up to 500KB

To import a file, follow these steps:

1. From the Google Docs home page, click the Upload button.
2. When the Upload a File page appears, as shown in Figure 19.3, click the Browse button and select the file to upload. Alternatively, if you want to import a file found on a website, enter the file's full URL into the Or Enter the URL of a File on the Web box.

> **note** A .csv file is a spreadsheet file in text format, with fields separated by commas.

19

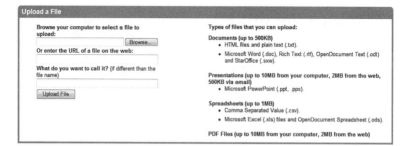

FIGURE 19.3
Uploading an existing file.

3. If you want to rename the file during the upload process, enter a new filename into the What Do You Want to Call It? box.

4. Click the Upload File button.

Google displays the uploaded document in your browser window. You can edit the document as you like; Google automatically saves a copy of the file on its servers for your future use.

Using Google Docs for Word Processing

Now it's time to examine the individual applications included in the Google Docs suite. We'll start with the most obvious application—the Google Docs word processor, Google's Web-based competitor to Microsoft Word.

> **tip** You can also email your documents to your Google Docs folders. Just email a file to the email address displayed on the Upload File page.

Getting to Know the Google Docs Workspace

As you've learned, you open a new word processing document by clicking the New button on the Google Docs home page and selecting Document. The new document, like the one shown in Figure 19.4, looks like a big blank space in a new browser window, one with a menu bar and toolbar at the top.

> **note** Google Docs is based on the Writely Web-based word processor, originally developed by the software company Upstartle. Google acquired Upstartle in March 2006 and subsequently mated it with its home-grown Google Spreadsheets application.

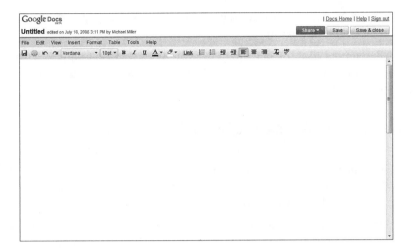

FIGURE 19.4

The Google Docs workspace.

You enter your text into the main window. Each pull-down menu is dedicated to a specific function; for example, you use the Edit menu to perform basic editing functions. And you click the buttons on the toolbar to perform some of the most common file, editing, and formatting functions.

Saving a Document

When you create a new document, you need to save the file. When you first save a file, you must do so manually. After this first save, Google automatically resaves the file every time you make a change to the document. In essence, this means that you have to save the document only once; Google saves all further changes automatically.

To save a new document, click the Save button. Google saves the document and names it according to the first bit of text in the editing window. For example, if you entered the text "Dear Mr. Selman:", your file would automatically be named **Dear Mr. Selman:**.

If you don't like the name Google assigns, you can easily change it. Just pull down the File menu and select Rename; when prompted in the pop-up window, enter the new name and click OK.

note When you create a Google Docs document, you're actually creating an HTML document. All HTML-type formatting is available for your documents through the Google Docs interface.

The document is now saved on Google's servers, and you don't have to bother resaving it in the future.

Remember that the document file you just saved isn't on your PC's hard disk. It's stored on Google's servers, which means that you must be connected to the Internet to access it.

Exporting a Google Document to Microsoft Word

By default, all the documents you work with in Google Docs are stored on Google's servers. You can, however, download files from Google to your computer's hard drive to work with in Microsoft Word. In essence, you're exporting your Google document to a .doc format Word file.

To export the current document, select File, Download File As, Word. When the File Download dialog box appears, click the Save button. When the Save As dialog box appears, select a location for the downloaded file, rename it if you like, and then click the Save button.

The Google Docs file is saved in .doc format on your hard disk. You can now open that file with Microsoft Word and work on it as you would with any Word document. Know, however, that whatever changes you make to the file from within Word affect only the downloaded file, not the copy of the document that still resides on the Google Docs site. If you later want to reimport the Word file to Google Docs, you'll need to return to the main Google Docs page and use the Upload function.

Entering Text

Now to the main event—entering text into your document. It's as easy as positioning the cursor in the blank area of the document window and typing the text. Use the cursor keys on the keyboard to move back and forth through the text, and the Delete and Backspace keys to delete text you've entered.

Formatting Text

Google Docs lets you format your text in a number of ways. Table 19.1 details the formatting options, all available from the toolbar.

> **tip**
> Google also lets you export your document as a PDF file, an OpenOffice file, a plain text or RTF (Rich Text Format) file, and as an HTML file for use on the Web.

Table 19.1　Google Docs Formatting Options

Formatting	Instructions
Bold	Click the Bold button.
Italic	Click the Italic button.
Underline	Click the Underline button.
Change the font	Click the Font button and select a new font (Sans Serif, Serif, Wide, Narrow, Comic Sans MS, Courier New, Garamond, Georgia, Tahoma, Trebuchet MS, Verdana, and Wingdings).
Change the font size	Click the Size button and select a new size (8, 10, 12, 14, 18, 24, or 36 pt).
Change the font color	Click the Text Color button and select a color from the color chooser.
Highlight text	Click the Highlight Color button and select a color from the color chooser.
Indent a paragraph	Click the Indent More button.
Unindent a paragraph	Click the Indent Less button.
Left-align a paragraph	Click the Align Left button.
Right-align a paragraph	Click the Align Right button.
Center a paragraph	Click the Align Center button.

You can also create a numbered list by clicking the Numbered List button, or a bulleted list by clicking the Bulleted List button. Additional formatting options are available from the Format menu, including three levels of headings, strikeout, superscript, subscript, and block quote formats.

Inserting Web Links

Because Google Docs is a Web-based word processor, it's not surprising that you can include links to web pages in your documents. All you have to do is highlight the text you want to use for the link, and then click the Link button. Google Docs displays the Insert Link dialog box, shown in Figure 19.5. Enter the URL you want to link to, as well as any "flyover" text you want displayed when the link is hovered over. If you want the link to open in a new window, click the Open Link in New Window option. Click the OK button to create the link.

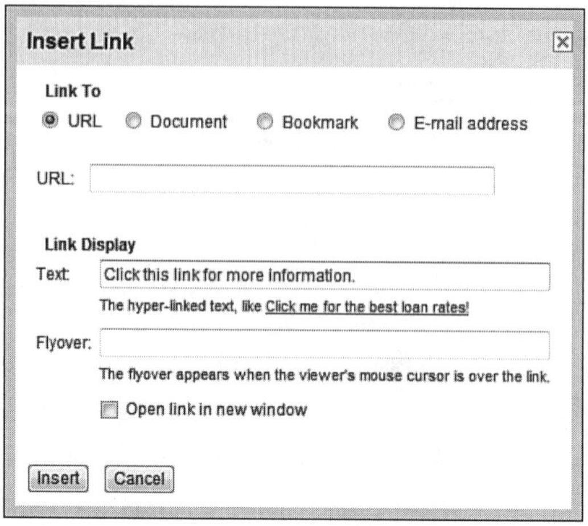

Insert Link   ⊠

Link To
◉ URL   ○ Document   ○ Bookmark   ○ E-mail address

URL: [   ]

Link Display
Text: [Click this link for more information.   ]
      The hyper-linked text, like Click me for the best loan rates!
Flyover: [   ]
      The flyover appears when the viewer's mouse cursor is over the link.
      ☐ Open link in new window

[Insert]   [Cancel]

FIGURE 19.5
Creating a Web link.

Inserting Images

To insert pictures and other images into a document, position the cursor where you want the image to appear, and then select Insert, Picture. This displays the Insert Image dialog box; you can insert images from your computer (click the Browse button) or from the Web (enter the URL of the image).

To see more configuration options, click the More Image Options link; this lets you resize and position the image, as well as wrap the text around the image. Click the Insert button to insert the image.

Working with Tables

Google Docs also lets you insert tables into your documents. Position the cursor where you want the table to appear, and then select Insert, Table or Table, Insert Table.

This displays the Insert Table dialog box, shown in Figure 19.6. From here, you select the following options:

- Number of rows
- Number of columns
- Width of the table
- Whether columns are of equal width

- Height of the table
- Table padding, spacing, alignment, and float
- Border width and color
- Cell background color

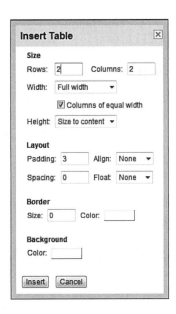

FIGURE 19.6

Creating a table.

After the table is created, you can position the cursor within the cells to enter text. To further edit the look of the table, as well as insert or delete rows and columns, right-click the table and make a selection from the pop-up menu.

Checking Your Spelling

A word processor wouldn't be complete without a way to check your spelling, which is why Google Docs includes its own spell checker. To check the spelling in a document, just click the Check Spelling button on the toolbar. Google Docs checks your document and highlights words that are either misspelled or not in its built-in

note Google Docs offers many more features than we have space to examine here. Most of these features are similar to features in Microsoft Word, so if you know how to use Word already, you should be able to do the same in Google Docs.

dictionary. Click a highlighted word to see a list of suggested spellings or to add this word to the dictionary.

Printing a Document

Printing a Google Docs document is as simple as clicking the Print button on the toolbar. When the Print dialog box appears, make sure the correct printer is selected, and click the Print button.

Sharing and Collaborating

The truly unique feature of Google Docs is the ability to share a document with others—either for viewing or for collaborative editing. The only hitch to this process is that anyone you want to share with must have his or her own Google account to access the Google Docs site. That said, you can easily invite another user to create his or her own new Google account.

To share a document for viewing or collaboration, click the Share button at the top right of that document, and then select Share with Others. This displays the Share This Document panel, shown in Figure 19.7.

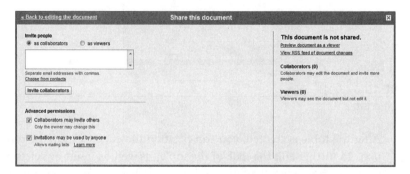

FIGURE 19.7

Getting ready to share a document.

In the Invite People box, enter the email addresses of the people you want to share the document (separate multiple addresses with commas). If you want others to simply view the document without being able to edit it, check the As Viewers option. If you want others to be able to edit the document, check the As Collaborators option. Click the Invite Viewers or Invite Collaborators button to send the invitations.

Your recipients will receive an invitation via email. The invitation contains a link to the document; clicking this link opens the document in a new browser window.

Anyone invited as a viewer can navigate the entire file and also save that file to his or her personal Google Docs online storage area or as a file to his or her PC. Anyone invited as a collaborator can edit the file in real time. (In fact, multiple users can edit the document at the same time.)

Publishing Your Document

Another way to share a document is to publish it as a public web page or blog posting. When it is published, anyone can access the document for viewing; all they have to know is the URL for the page or blog post.

> **tip** If you want your collaborators to invite other collaborators, check the Collaborators May Invite Others option.

> **caution** Google permits more than one user at a time to make changes to an open document; the document isn't "locked" when the first user starts editing. This can create havoc if both users try to make changes to the same data or are unaware of the other changes being made. For this reason, you should always use caution while collaboratively editing a document.

To publish your document, click the Share button for that document and then select Publish as Web Page. This displays the Publish This Document panel, shown in Figure 19.8. To publish the document as a web page, click the Publish Document button. If you want to update the web page as the document is edited, also check the Automatically Re-Publish When Changes Are Made option. You're prompted to let anyone on the Internet see this document; click OK. The web page is now published, and Google Docs displays a link to the document's web page.

19

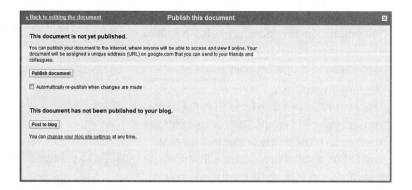

FIGURE 19.8

Publishing a document to the Web.

To post the document to your blog, click the Post to Blog button. The first time you do this, you're prompted to set your blog site settings; you need to provide your blog host, username, password, and the like. The document is then posted to your blog as a new post.

Working Offline

Originally, Google Docs was a Web-only application, meaning that you had to be online to edit a document; if you weren't connected to the Internet, you couldn't access your Google Docs files. That changed with the introduction of Google Gears, a utility that lets you access all your Google Docs documents when you're offline.

To edit your documents offline, you have to install the Google Docs Offline application. Do this by clicking the Offline link at the top of the Google Docs home page and then clicking the Get Google Gears Now button. It's a short and simple installation; just follow the onscreen instructions to do the download.

After Google Gears has been installed, you can open the offline version of Google Docs by entering http://docs.google.com into your web browser, or by clicking the Google Docs shortcut on your desktop. If you're not connected to the Internet, you open the offline version of Google Docs; if you are connected to the Internet, you open the normal online version. Whenever you're online, Google Docs automatically synchronizes the files stored on your computer with those stored online. It's a seamless and relatively invisible process.

note You can use Google Docs offline via the Google Chrome web browser, which has Google Gears built in. Learn more about Chrome in Appendix C, "Introducing Google Chrome."

The Bottom Line

Google Docs is a worthy competitor to Microsoft Word. It's not quite as fully featured, but it includes most features used by most users. It's great for creating everyday documents, and I really like the fact that your documents are accessible from wherever you are, via the Web. This lets you edit your work documents from home or the road, with no file copying necessary.

Should you use Google Docs? Maybe. It's certainly an option for the frugal computer user (it's free versus several hundred dollars for Microsoft Office), as well as the traveling user and the frequent collaborator. It's worth checking out to see if it does the job for you.

19

Using Google Spreadsheets

G oogle Spreadsheets is the spreadsheet application in the Google Docs suite. Unlike the Google Docs word processor and Presentations presentation application, both of which were acquired from third-party companies, Google Spreadsheets was born in Google Labs. It was also the first application in the Google Docs suite, which makes Google Spreadsheets the most fully developed of all the Google Docs applications.

In fact, Google Spreadsheets has evolved a lot over the years, from an "Excel lite" type of application to a fairly robust spreadsheet program that even sophisticated users can appreciate. Unless your needs are overly advanced, you're apt to find Google Spreadsheets a worthy competitor to and replacement for the venerable Microsoft Excel.

Opening and Saving Spreadsheets

You access Google Spreadsheets from the Google Docs home page (docs.google.com). All your existing spreadsheet files are listed there, along with your word processing documents and presentations.

Creating a New Spreadsheet

To create a new spreadsheet, all you have to do is click the New button and select Spreadsheet. The new spreadsheet opens in its own window on your desktop. Alternatively, you can select New, From Template to create a new spreadsheet based on a predesigned template; this opens Google's Template Gallery, from which you can make your choice.

Opening an existing spreadsheet file is equally easy. Just click the file's name on the Google Docs home page, and the spreadsheet window opens.

Saving a Spreadsheet

When you are finished with a spreadsheet, you need to save the file. When you first save a file, you must do so manually—and give the file a name. After this first save, Google automatically resaves the file every time you make a change to the spreadsheet. In essence, this means that you have to save the spreadsheet only once; Google saves all further changes automatically.

To save a new spreadsheet, click the Save button. When the Save Spreadsheet dialog box appears, enter a name for the spreadsheet, and then click the OK button. That's all there is to it. The spreadsheet is now saved on Google's servers, and you don't have to bother resaving it at any future point.

Exporting a Google Spreadsheet to Excel Format

By default, all the spreadsheets you work with in Google Spreadsheets are stored on Google's servers. You can, however, download files from Google to your computer's hard drive to work with in Excel. In essence, you're exporting your Google spreadsheet to an XLS-format Excel file.

To export the current spreadsheet, click the File button and select Export, .xls. When the File Download dialog box appears, click the Save button. When the Save As dialog box appears, select a location for the downloaded file, rename it if you like, and then click the Save button.

The Google Spreadsheets file is saved in XLS format on your hard disk. You can now open that file with Excel and work on it as you would with any Excel

20

spreadsheet. Know, however, that whatever changes you make to the file from within Excel affect only the downloaded file, not the copy of the spreadsheet that still resides on the Google Spreadsheets site. If you later want to reimport the Excel file to Google Spreadsheets, you'll need to return to the main Google Docs page and use the Upload function.

> **note** Google Spreadsheets is similar to Excel, but not identical. Excel-like functionality not available by default in Google Spreadsheets includes macros, pivot tables, and databases.

Getting to Know the Google Spreadsheets Workspace

Not surprisingly, Google Spreadsheets looks and works a lot like every other PC-based spreadsheet application you've ever used. Whether you started with VisiCalc, 1-2-3, Quattro Pro, or Excel, you'll recognize the row-and-column grid you see when you first access Google Spreadsheets. Sure, the buttons or links for some specific operations might be in slightly different locations, but pretty much everything you expect to find is somewhere on the page.

Let's take a quick look at what's where in the Google Spreadsheets workspace, shown in Figure 20.1. The first thing to note is that the workspace changes slightly, depending on which tab (Edit, Sort, Formulas, Form, or Revisions) you select at the top of the page. Each tab in a Google spreadsheet has its own toolbar of options, specific to that toolbar's function.

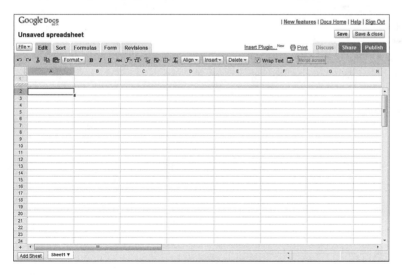

FIGURE 20.1

The Google Spreadsheets Edit tab.

Examining Google Spreadsheets Tabs

The Edit tab displays a toolbar full of editing options. From left to right, there are buttons for undo and redo; cut, copy, and paste; number formatting; text formatting (bold, italic, and so on); cell alignment; and inserting and deleting cells. There's also a button to add a chart to your spreadsheet, based on selected data.

The Sort tab displays an abbreviated toolbar of sort-related options. You can sort the selected cells in normal or inverse order, or opt to freeze the header rows for easier sorting.

The Formulas tab displays a Range Names button, which you can use to name a range of cells. There are also links to insert some of the most common functions (Sum, Count, Average, Min, Max, and Product), as well as a More link that displays all available functions.

The Form tab provides quick access to tools for creating, sending, and embedding spreadsheets, as well as creating forms. Data entered via these forms is automatically inserted into the underlying spreadsheet.

The Revisions tab displays a pull-down list of the various versions of the current file. You can also use the Older and Newer buttons to switch to a different version.

Outside the tabs are a handful of common buttons. For example, the File button lets you open, save, and otherwise manage your spreadsheet files. Likewise, the Print button lets you print your spreadsheet, and the Save button lets you save your work.

Working with Multiple Sheets

Like Excel, Google Spreadsheets lets you work with multiple sheets within a single spreadsheet file. Unlike Excel, which always starts with three sheets per spreadsheet, Google defaults to a single sheet. You can then add sheets to this first sheet.

To add a new sheet to your spreadsheet, all you have to do is click the Add Sheet button at the bottom of the main spreadsheet window. To switch to a different sheet, just click its link.

tip By default, Google names its sheets Sheet1, Sheet2, Sheet3, and so forth. If you'd like a somewhat more descriptive name for a sheet, select the sheet and then click its tab. When the pop-up menu appears, click Rename, enter a new name, and then click OK.

Entering and Editing Data

Google Spreadsheets lets you enter four different types of data, as detailed in Table 20.1.

Table 20.1 Types of Google Spreadsheets Data	
Type of Data	Description
Numbers	Numbers can be in a variety of formats, including currency and percent formats. All numbers can be manipulated mathematically.
Text	Text can contain both alphabetic and numeric characters. Text cannot be manipulated mathematically.
Dates	Dates are specially formatted numbers.
Formulas	Formulas tell Google Spreadsheets how to make calculations using data in other cells.

Entering New Data

Entering data is as simple as selecting a particular cell and typing input from the keyboard. Just move the cursor to the desired cell, using either the mouse or the keyboard arrow keys, and begin typing.

This approach works for all types of data, with the exception of formulas. Entering a formula is almost as simple, except that you must enter an equals sign (=) first. Just go to the cell, press the = key on the keyboard, and then enter the formula.

As to how the individual data is formatted—that is, how Google Spreadsheets interprets numbers and letters—it depends on what type of data you enter:

- If you typed only numbers, the data is formatted as a number (with no commas or dollar signs).
- If you typed a number with a dollar sign in front of it, the data is formatted as currency.
- If you typed any alphabetic characters, the data is formatted as text.
- If you typed numbers separated by the – or / character (such as 12–31 or 1/2/09), the data is formatted as a date.
- If you typed numbers separated by the : character (such as 2:13), the data is formatted as a time.

20

Editing Previously Entered Data

Editing existing data in a cell is a fairly simple exercise; you actually edit within the cell. Just move the cursor to the desired cell and press the F2 key; this opens the cell for editing. Move the cursor to the data point within the cell you want to edit, and then use the Delete and Backspace keys to delete characters, or use any other key to insert characters. Press Enter when you are finished editing, and your changes are accepted into the selected cell.

> **tip** If you accidentally delete data you want to keep, don't panic! Google Spreadsheets includes an Undo option that lets you unwind your last command. All you have to do is click the Undo button at the top right of the workspace. Presto! You've undone your last delete, and your data is back where it belongs.

Inserting and Deleting Rows and Columns

To insert a new row or column into a spreadsheet, start by positioning the cursor in the row or column where you want to insert a new row or column. Click the Insert button, and select whether you want to insert a row (above or below) or a column (to the right or left). Google Spreadsheets does the rest.

You can also delete entire rows and columns, or clear the contents of individual cells. To delete a row or column, position the cursor in that row or column, click the Delete button, and select whether you want to delete the row or column. To clear the contents of a cell, you do the same thing but select Clear Selection when you click the Delete button.

Working with Ranges

When you reference data within a spreadsheet, you can reference individual cells or you can reference a range of cells. When you reference more than one contiguous cell, that's called a *range*. You typically use ranges with specific functions, such as **SUM** (which totals a range of cells) or **AVERAGE** (which calculates the average value of a range of cells).

A range reference is expressed by listing the first and last cells in the range, separated by a colon (:). For example, the range that starts with cell A1 and ends with cell A9 is written like this:

A1:A9

You can select a range with either the mouse or keyboard. Using the mouse, you can simply click and drag the cursor to select all the cells in the range.

Using the keyboard, position the cursor in the first cell in the range, hold down the Shift key, and then use the cursor keys to expand the range in the appropriate direction.

Finally, you can use a combination of mouse and keyboard to select a range. Use either the mouse or keyboard to select the first cell in the range. Then hold down the Shift key and click the mouse in the last cell in the range. All the cells between the two cells are automatically selected.

Sorting Data

Often, you want your data to appear in a sorted order. You might want to sort your data by date, for example, or by quantity or dollar value. Fortunately, Google Spreadsheets lets you sort your data either alphabetically or numerically, in either ascending or descending order.

tip
The A>Z and Z>A sorts don't just sort by letter; they also sort by number. An A>Z sort arranges numeric data from smallest to largest; a Z>A sort arranges numeric data from largest to smallest.

Sorting data in Google Spreadsheets is a two-step operation. First you have to "freeze" the header row(s) of your spreadsheet, and then you identify the column by which you want to sort. Google then orders all the "unfrozen" (non-header) rows of your spreadsheet in whichever order (ascending or descending) you specified.

Start by selecting the Sort tab, and then click the Freeze Rows button and select how many rows you want to include as the spreadsheet's header. Next, identify which column you want to sort by, and move the cursor to any cell within that column. Finally, to sort in ascending order, click the A>Z button; to sort in descending order, click the Z>A button.

Formatting Spreadsheet Data

Let's face it—a basic Google spreadsheet looks pretty plain. Fortunately, you can spruce it up by changing font size, family, and color, and by changing the background color of individual cells. All you have to do is select the cell(s) you want to format, and then use the formatting options on the Edit tab toolbar.

note
Although you can change text attributes for an entire cell or range of cells, Google Spreadsheets doesn't let you change attributes for selected characters *within* a cell.

20

You can also change how numbers are formatted within your spreadsheet. A number can be expressed as a whole number, as a percentage, as a fraction, as currency, as a date, and even exponentially. To apply a different number format, just select the cell or range, click the Format button (on the Edit tab), and then select a format.

Entering Formulas

After you've entered data into your spreadsheet, you need to work with those numbers to create other numbers. You do this as you would in the real world, by using common formulas to calculate your data by addition, subtraction, multiplication, and division. You can also used advanced formulas preprogrammed into Google Spreadsheets; these advanced formulas are called *functions*.

A formula can consist of numbers, mathematical operators, and the contents of other cells (referred to by the cell reference). You construct a formula from the following elements:

- ■ An equals sign (=); this is necessary at the start of each formula.
- ■ One or more specific numbers.

  and/or

- ■ One or more cell references.
- ■ A mathematical operator (such as + or –); this is needed if your formula contains more than one cell reference or number.

For example, to add the contents of cells A1 and A2, you enter this formula:

=A1+A2

To multiply the contents of cell A1 by 10, you enter this formula:

=A1*10

And so on. Table 20.2 shows the algebraic operators you can use within Google Spreadsheets formulas.

20

Table 20.2   Accepted Operators for Google Spreadsheets Formulas

Operator	Description
+	Addition
–	Subtraction
*	Multiplication
/	Division
^	Exponentiation (to the power of)
=	Equal to
>	Greater than
>=	Greater than or equal to
<	Less than
<=	Less than or equal to
<>	Not equal to
%	Percentage

To enter a formula in a cell, move the cursor to the desired cell, type = to start the formula, and then enter the rest of the formula. Remember to refer to specific cells by the A1, B1, and so on cell reference. Press Enter to accept the formula or press Esc to reject the formula.

When you're finished entering a formula, you no longer see the formula within the cell; instead, you see the results of the formula. For example, if you entered the formula =1+2, you see the number **3** in the cell. To view the formula itself, just select the cell and then look in the reference area in the lower-right corner of the spreadsheet window.

tip You can use the mouse to enter cell references into your formulas. Use the keyboard to enter the =, and then use the mouse to select the cell or range of cells to include. Use the keyboard again to enter any operators, and then use the mouse again to select additional cells. Press Enter to finish the formula.

20

Using Functions

A function is a type of formula built into Google Spreadsheets. You can use Google's built-in functions instead of writing complex formulas in your spreadsheets; you can also include functions as part of your formulas.

Functions simplify the creation of complex formulas. For example, if you want to total the values of cells B4 through B7, you could enter the following formula:

=B4+B5+B6+B7

Or you could use the **SUM** function, which lets you total (sum) a column or row of numbers without having to type every cell into the formula. In this instance, the formula to total the cells B4 through B7 could be written using the **SUM** function, like this:

=sum(B4:B7)

This is much easier, don't you think?

Google Spreadsheets uses most of the same functions as those used in Microsoft Excel. All Google functions use the following format:

=*function(argument)*

Replace ***function*** with the name of the function, and replace ***argument*** with a range reference. The argument always appears in parentheses.

You can enter a function into a formula either by typing the name of the function or by pasting the function into the formula from a list of functions displayed on the Formula tab. (You don't have to be on the Formula tab to enter functions manually, however.)

To use the Formula tab to enter formulas, move the cursor into the cell you want to hold the results of the function. Click the More link at the top right of the page and, when the Insert a Function dialog box appears, as shown in Figure 20.2, click the function you want to use. When you click the Close link, the function is pasted into the selected cell.

> **tip**
> Google Spreadsheets includes more than 200 individual functions. These functions are identical to the ones built into Microsoft Excel, so if you're an Excel user, you'll be right at home.

20

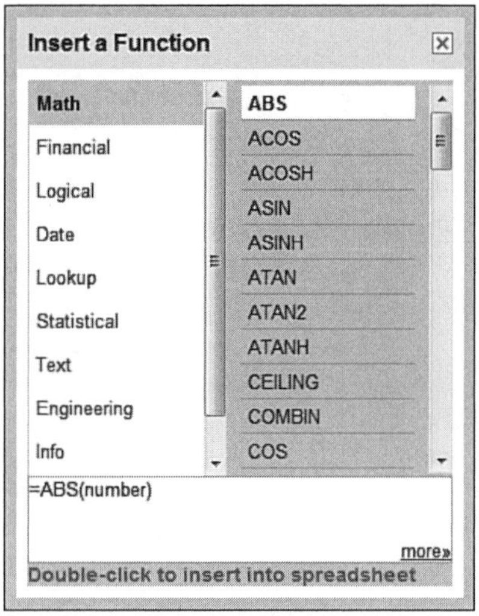

FIGURE 20.2

Choosing a function from the Insert a Function dialog box.

Charting Your Data

Google Spreadsheets also lets you chart your data. This functionality is relatively new; it wasn't in the initial version of the application.

To create a chart, start by selecting the Edit tab, then select the cells that include the data you want to graph and click the Add button and select Chart. This displays the Create Chart dialog box, shown in Figure 20.3. You can create six types of charts—columns, bars, pie, lines, area, and scatter—and different subtypes within each major type. Select the type of chart you want, along with the subtype, enter a chart title, and select any other desired options (such as a chart legend). When the preview looks like you want it to, click the Save Chart button. The chart is created and added to the current spreadsheet, as shown in Figure 20.4.

20

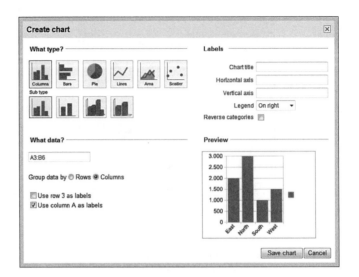

FIGURE 20.3

Creating a chart.

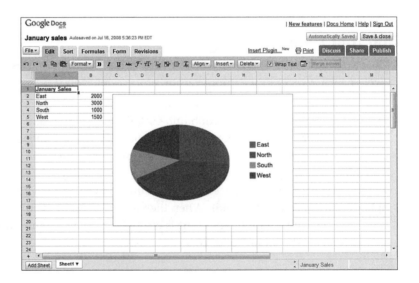

FIGURE 20.4

A chart added to a Google spreadsheet.

Printing Google Spreadsheets

When you're finished creating your spreadsheet, you might want to print a hard copy. This is fairly easy to do. Just click the Print button on the selected spreadsheet page. When the Print dialog box appears, make sure that the correct printer is selected, and then click the Print button.

Expanding Functionality with Gadgets

As noted earlier, Google Spreadsheets doesn't have all the functionality you find in Microsoft Excel. You can increase the functionality, however, by adding various *gadgets* to your spreadsheets.

In the Google Spreadsheets world, a gadget is a plug-in that adds functionality to the basic application. Gadgets are created both by Google and by other users; you can also create your own gadgets if you're so inclined. You can find gadgets that create more sophisticated chart types, add pivot table functionality, and the like. This is a great way for Google to make Google Spreadsheets better without having to alter the core application code.

To add a gadget to a spreadsheet, either click the Insert Plugin link or go to the Edit tab, click the Add button, and then select Gadget. This displays the Add a Gadget dialog box, shown in Figure 20.5. Select the type of gadget you want, and then click the Add to Spreadsheet button to add the gadget.

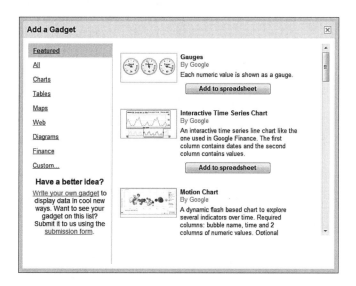

FIGURE 20.5

Adding a gadget to a Google spreadsheet.

Sharing and Collaborating—and Working Offline

One of the key reasons to use Google Spreadsheets is the collaboration function. Because it's a Web-based application, it's relatively easy to share a spreadsheet with others—and to collaborate on a single spreadsheet as a group.

We covered Google Docs' sharing and collaboration functions in depth in Chapter 19, "Using Google Docs." Those functions work pretty much the same in Google Spreadsheets as they do in the word processing application. You find the sharing/collaboration functions on the Share tab and the publishing functions on the Publish tab.

You can also use Google Spreadsheets offline, thanks to Google Gears. This lets you access your spreadsheets even when you're not connected to the Internet. Learn more about this functionality in Chapter 19 as well.

The Bottom Line

I've been using Google Spreadsheets since its launch, and I've been pleased to see how the application has developed over the years. What started as a fairly bare-bones spreadsheet (with no charting function!) has evolved into a sophisticated alternative to Microsoft Excel. That sophistication is only enhanced by the addition of the plug-in gadgets, which promise to add just about any feature you can think of to the core Google Spreadsheets feature set.

20

Using Google Presentations

The final component of the Google Docs applications suite is Google Presentations. As the name implies, Google Presentations is an application, similar to Microsoft PowerPoint, which enables you to create and give slideshow-like presentations. Due to its web-based nature, you can also use Google Presentations to give PowerPoint presentations when you're away from the office; you don't have to take any files with you—all you need is a computer with an Internet connection.

Creating and Saving Presentations

You access Google Presentations from the Google Docs home page (docs.google.com). All your existing presentation files are listed there, along with your word-processing documents and spreadsheets.

Creating a New Presentation

You create a new presentation the same way you create any new Google Docs file. All you have to do is click the New button and select Presentation.

In this activity, you learn how to create a new blank presentation.

Alternately, you can select New, From Template to create a new presentation based on a pre-designed template. This opens Google's Template Gallery, from which you can make your choice.

After you've saved a presentation, reopening it is equally easy. Just click the file's name on the Google Docs home page, and the presentation opens in a new browser window.

Saving a Presentation

After you create a new presentation, you need to save the file. When you first save a file, you must do this manually—and give the file a name. After this first save, Google automatically resaves the file every time you make a change to the presentation. In essence, this means that you only have to save the presentation once; Google saves all further changes automatically.

To save a newly created presentation file, select File, Save. Google saves the presentation and names it according to the first bit of text in the editing window. For example, if you had entered the text "Sales Conference," your file would be automatically named **Sales Conference**.

Importing a PowerPoint Presentation

Many organizations use Microsoft PowerPoint to create their presentations. If you or your colleagues still use PowerPoint, you can import your PowerPoint presentations into Google Presentations for online editing and collaboration.

tip If you don't like the name that Google assigns, you can easily change it. Just click the File button and select Rename; when prompted in the pop-up window, enter the new name and click OK.

21

To import a PowerPoint presentation, go to the Google Docs main page and click the Upload button. When the Upload a File page appears, click the Browse button; then locate and select the file you want to upload. Enter a name for the uploaded file into the What Do You Want to Call It? box; then click the Upload File button. The file now opens in Google Presentations for editing or presenting.

tip
Even if you continue to use PowerPoint to create and edit your presentations, you can use Google Presentations to give those presentations when you're on the road. Just import your PowerPoint presentation into Google Presentations; then you can access that presentation from any computer connected to the Internet. There's no longer any need to take large PowerPoint files (or even your own notebook PC) with you when you travel!

Exporting a Google Presentation to PowerPoint Format

By default, all the presentations you work with in Google Presentations are stored on Google's servers. You can, however, download files from Google to your computer's hard drive to work with in Microsoft PowerPoint.

note
You can import .ppt and .pps format PowerPoint files up to 10MB in size.

Here's how to do it. From within the current presentation window, select File, Download Presentation As, PPT. When the File Download dialog box appears, click the Save button; when the Save As dialog box appears, select a location for the downloaded file, rename it if you like, and then click the Save button. The Google Presentations file is now saved in .ppt format on your hard disk. You can open this saved file with Microsoft PowerPoint and work on it as you would with any PowerPoint presentation.

Getting to Know the Google Presentations Workspace

A presentation is composed of a number of different slides. Each slide can hold text, images, or videos, or any combination of the preceding.

In the Google Presentations workspace, shown in Figure 21.1, the slides in a presentation are displayed in the slide sorter pane, to the left of the main part of the workspace. The larger part of the workspace, called the editing window, displays the current slide for editing. To edit a different slide, just select that slide in the slide sorter.

21

All the application's editing and formatting tools are at the top of the work-space. Formatting commands are found on the application toolbar.

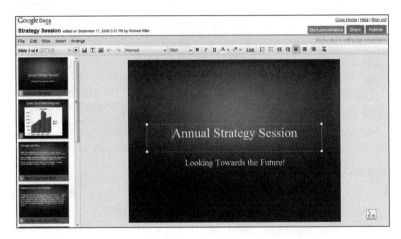

FIGURE 21.1

The Google Presentations workspace.

Managing the Slides in Your Presentation

In Google Presentations, a slide can be based on one of five predesigned lay-outs:

- **Title.** This consists of the presentation title and subtitle only (ideal for the lead slide in presentation, or to signal new sections in the presentation).

- **Text.** This consists of the slide title and a block of text below.

- **Two columns.** This consists of the slide title and two columns of text.

- **Caption.** This has a blank main area (ideal for inserting graphics or videos) and a text caption at the bottom.

- **Blank.** This is completely blank—you can insert anything on this type of slide.

Every new presentation starts with a single title slide. To add a new slide, click the Insert New Slide button (the + sign above the slide sorter pane). When the Choose Slide Layout dialog box appears, as shown in Figure 21.2, select the layout for the new slide. The new slide is now added to the slide sorter pane and displayed in the main window.

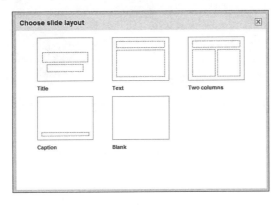

FIGURE 21.2
Choosing a new slide layout.

Of course, you don't always want to keep every slide you create. To delete a slide, simply select it in the slide sorter and then click the Delete Current Slide button.

As your presentation develops, you may need to rethink the order of the slides in the presentation. You rearrange your slides in the slide sorter, using your mouse. Just select the side you want to move, and then drag it up or down to a new position.

Changing the Look and Feel of Your Presentation with Themes

Few people want to give a presentation of black text on a plain white background. You gain more attention by using attractive background colors and graphics, as illustrated in Figure 21.3.

tip If you've created a slide with content or formatting that you'd like to repeat elsewhere in your presentation, you can duplicate that slide and then edit the duplicate. Select the slide you want to duplicate in the slide sorter; then click the Create a Duplicate Copy of the Current Slide button. A duplicate of the selected slide is created after the selected slide in the slide sorter.

21

FIGURE 21.3

A visually interesting slide created with a predesigned theme.

Google Presentations lets you choose from several predesigned themes for your presentations. You can also design your own themes by using custom background images on all of your slides.

Choosing a New Theme

The easiest way to change the look and feel of your presentation is to choose a new theme. You do this by selecting Edit, Change Theme. When the Choose Theme dialog box appears, as shown in Figure 21.4, click the theme you want to use. This theme is now applied to all the slides in your presentation.

Adding Custom Background Colors and Graphics

If you don't like the looks of any of Google Presentations predesigned themes, you can create your own theme by applying a custom background color or graphic to all the slides in your presentation.

Start by right-clicking anywhere on the current slide, and then select Change Background from the pop-up menu. When the Change background dialog box appears, as shown in Figure 21.5, click the Change Background button to select a new background color.

> **note** A theme is a predesigned collection of background images, color schemes, and fonts that are applied to every slide in your presentation.

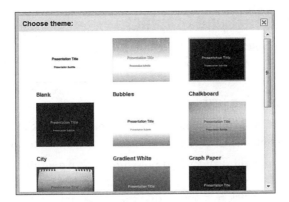

FIGURE 21.4
Choosing a new theme for a presentation.

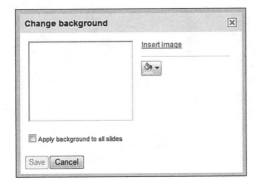

FIGURE 21.5
Changing the background color of your slides.

Click the Apply Background to All Slides option, and then click the Save button. The new background color or image is now applied to all the slides in your presentation.

tip If you'd rather use an image for the background of your slides, click the Insert image link. This changes the dialog box slightly; click the Browse button to find and select the graphics file you want to use.

Working with Text and Graphics

Once you've chosen a slide layout, it's time to start adding content to that slide. Slide content can be in the form of text or images of various types.

Adding and Formatting Text

We'll start by adding some text to a slide. Each block of text is added via a separate text object; select an object to add, edit, or format the text within.

For example, most slides in a presentation have a title that appears at the top of the slide; this title area is an object labeled "Click to add title," as shown in Figure 21.6. Click this object, and then type your title.

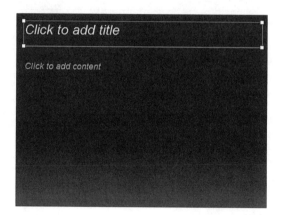

FIGURE 21.6
Adding title text to a slide.

Adding body text is similarly easy. Just click the text object labeled "Click to add content;" then type your text. You can enter a block of text, like a paragraph, or (using the appropriate buttons on the formatting toolbar) bulleted or numbered lists.

Google Presentations also lets you format text on a slide, pretty much the way you'd format text in a word-processing document. Just select the text object on the slide that contains the text you want to edit and then, within the text object, use your cursor to select the text you want to format. Now click the appropriate button

tip A bulleted list is the best way to emphasize individual points or items. A numbered list is best for presenting step-by-step instructions or a sequential to-do list.

tip To add a web page link or email address to the text on a slide, select the anchor text and click the Link button. When the Edit Link dialog box appears, enter the web address (URL) or email address for the linked-to page, and then click OK.

on the formatting toolbar to apply the formatting you want. For example, to change the font of the selected text, select a new font from the Font list; to boldface the selected text, click the Bold button.

Adding Images

Text isn't the only type of object you can add to a slide. Often, you'll want to show a picture of some item on a slide, or just add a graphic for visual interest.

To add a picture to a slide, position your cursor where you want the image to appear and click the Insert an Image button. When the Insert Image dialog box appears, click the Browse button and select the image file you want to include. Click OK, and the image is inserted into your slide as a new object.

> **tip** You can also add graphic shapes to a slide, in the form of boxes, arrows, callouts, and the like. Position the cursor where you want the object to appear; then select Insert, Shape and select the desired shape.

After the image is inserted, you can now use your mouse to drag the image object to a new location on the slide. You can also resize the image, by clicking and dragging the image's corner handles.

Adding Charts

Although Google Presentations does not currently include its own chart editor, you can add a chart created in another program to a Google Presentations slide. The easiest approach is to create a chart in Google Spreadsheets and then copy that chart to Google Presentations as an image object.

Start by creating a chart in Google Spreadsheets; then double-click the chart and select Save Image. When the File Download dialog box appears, click the Save button; when the Save As dialog box appears, make sure PNG Image is selected in the Save as type box and then select a filename and location for this file.

Now switch to Google Presentations and open the slide for the chart. Position the cursor where you want the chart to appear and click the Insert an Image button. When the Insert image dialog box appears, click the Browse button and then navigate to and select the image file you just created. Click OK and the image of the chart is inserted into your slide as a new object.

You can now use your mouse to drag the chart to a new location on the slide, or click and drag the image's corner handles to resize the chart.

> **caution** Charts imported into Google Presentations cannot be edited. They can only be repositioned and resized.

21

Animating Elements on a Slide

While Google Presentations does not currently offer slide-to-slide transitions, you can animate the individual elements on a slide. That is, you can configure one element to appear after another element, via what Google calls *incremental reveal*.

When you choose to incrementally reveal an object, it doesn't appear when you first display the slide during a presentation. To reveal an object, you press the next button as if you were going to a new slide; this displays the first object chosen to reveal. If more than one object on a slide is formatted for incremental reveal, each successive object is displayed each time you press the next key.

tip Google Presentations also lets you run videos from within a presentation, by facilitating the insertion of any video uploaded to Google's YouTube video-sharing site. To add a video object to a slide, you must first upload that video to YouTube. Then position the cursor where you want the video window to appear on the slide, select Insert Video, and choose the video you want.

It's even better when you select a bulleted or numbered list for incremental reveal. In this instance, only the first list item is displayed when you press the next button during the presentation. Continue pressing the next button to display successive items in the list.

To use incremental reveal, right-click the object you want to appear first and then select Incremental Reveal from the pop-up menu. A timer icon now appears next to that object on your slide.

Now select the object you want to appear next and select Incremental Reveal from that object's pop-up menu. A timer button with the number 2 now appears next to that object on your slide. Repeat this second step for any other object you want to be revealed on the slide.

When you give the presentation, all you have to do is click the next button to display each selected item in order.

Printing Handouts and Speaker Notes

Google Presentations lets you print your entire presentation, one slide per page, or create speaker notes for you to use when giving the presentation.

To create printed handouts, select File, Print. When the Print Preview dialog box appears, as shown in Figure 21.7, pull down the Layout list and select how many slides you want to print per page—1, 2, 4, 8, 9, or 12. Click the Print button, and your handouts will be printed as specified.

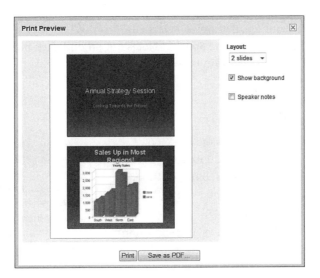

FIGURE 21.7

Getting ready to print handouts.

Beyond simple handouts, presenters like to prepare speaker notes that they can then reference while they're giving a presentation. To do this, go to the first slide of your presentation and click the View Speaker Notes button at the lower-right corner of the workspace. This changes the workspace to reveal a speaker notes pane, as shown in Figure 21.8. Enter your notes for this slide into the speaker notes pane; then move to subsequent slides in your presentation and enter notes for those slides.

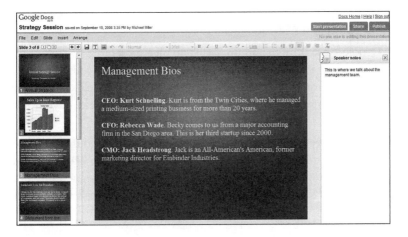

FIGURE 21.8

Entering speaker notes.

To print your speaker notes, select File, Print. When the Print Preview dialog box appears, check the Speaker Notes option and click the Print button. This prints your presentation one slide per page, with speaker notes displayed beneath each slide.

Collaborating Online

One of the key reasons to use Google Presentations is the collaboration function. Because it's a web-based application, it's relatively easy to collaborate with others on group presentations.

We covered Google Docs' collaboration function in depth in Chapter 19, "Using Google Docs." That function works pretty much the same in Google Presentations as it does in the word-processing application; you find the sharing/collaboration functions on the Share tab, and the publishing functions on the Publish tab.

> **tip**
> You can also use Google Presentations offline, thanks to Google Gears. This lets you access your presentations even when you're not connected to the Internet. Learn more about this functionality in Chapter 19, as well.

Giving Live Presentations

Of course, the main reason to create a presentation is to present it to others. Google Presentations lets you give in-person presentations or Internet-based presentations that let other users at any location see your presentation in their web browsers.

Presenting Your Presentation

Google Presentations makes it easy to give presentations. After you've created and edited your presentation, you can connect your computer to a projector or large monitor and show it to any sized group of people. In fact, you can take your presentation anywhere you travel just by connecting your computer to the Internet—where your presentation is stored.

To give a live presentation in person, start by opening the presentation and selecting the first slide; then click the Start Presentation button. This opens your live presentation in a new browser window, as shown in Figure 21.9. Press the F11 key on your keyboard to display the presentation full-screen.

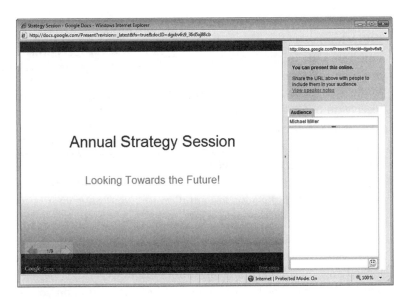

FIGURE 21.9
Giving a live presentation.

To advance to the next slide in the presentation, click the next slide (right) arrow or press the right-arrow key on your keyboard. If a slide includes objects formatted with incremental reveal, only the slide background and immediate reveal objects will appear when the slide first displays. To reveal the next object on the slide, click the next slide arrow or press the right-arrow key on your keyboard.

When the presentation is finished, you see an End of presentation dialog box. Click the Restart button to start the presentation over, or click the Exit button to close the presentation window.

Giving an Online Presentation

Another unique feature of Google Presentations is the capability of giving a presentation in multiple locations over the Internet. Invited attendees view the presentation in their own web browsers as you give it.

To invite viewers to your presentation, open the presentation and click the Share tab at the top-right corner of the window. When the Share This Document page appears, check the As Viewers option.

> **tip**
> To view your presentation notes in a separate window, click the View Speaker Notes link.

21

Enter the email addresses of the people with whom you want to share this presentation into the Invite people box; separate multiple addresses with commas. Click the Invite Viewers button, and your recipients receive an invitation via email that contains a link to the presentation.

> **tip** Even when you've taken control of the presentation, viewers still have control over the slide displayed in the main portion of their screens. To see the presenter's current slide in the main portion of their screens, each viewer must click the Follow the Presenter button.

At the appointed time for the presentation, make sure that you and all viewers are logged on and have the presentation open on your desktops. From your open presentation, click the Start Presentation link, and have your viewers do the same.

This opens your live presentation in a new browser window. At the right side of the window is a Google Chat pane, which lists each viewer who is currently logged on. You can exchange instant messages with other viewers by entering text into the message box and pressing the Enter button on your keyboard.

To synchronize the presentation for all viewers, click the Take Control of the Presentation button. Viewers will now see your current slide displayed above the Google Chat pane. To advance to the next slide in the presentation, click the next slide (right) arrow or press the right-arrow key on your keyboard. To return to the previous slide, click the previous slide arrow or press the left-arrow key on your keyboard.

The Bottom Line

Google Presentations is a great idea, and a long-overdue addition to the Google Docs suite. It's particularly well-suited for giving presentations on the road; you no longer have to worry about carrying big PowerPoint files with you (and getting them installed on whatever computer the host facility provides!).

That said, Google Presentations doesn't yet offer all the functionality you get from Microsoft PowerPoint. For example, Google Presentations doesn't offer slide-to-slide transitions or the ability to create charts and tables. Although Google continues to add functionality over time, if you need these particular features, you'll have to stick with Microsoft PowerPoint for the time being.

Using Google Calendar

Like most Google Docs, Google Calendar is a Web-based application accessible from any computer over the Internet, using any web browser. In the case of Google Calendar, that's a good thing, because you can keep track of your schedule and appointments wherever you are, even if you're away from home or the office. All you have to do is log onto the Google Calendar website from any web browser, and all your appointments and schedules are displayed.

Read on to learn more.

All About Google Calendar

Google Calendar (calendar.google.com), shown in Figure 22.1, looks like ever other Web-based calendar you've ever seen. (And like most software-based ca endars, too.) You enter your appointments (which Google calls "events") directly into the calendar, which you can display in either daily, weekly, or monthly view. You can also, if you like, view your weekly agenda on a single page.

FIGURE 22.1

Google Calendar—not just another calendar application.

Nothing unusual about any of that. So, compared to all the other calendar applications, what's unique about Google Calendar?

- Google Calendar is a Web-based calendar. This means that your calen dar information is stored on Google's servers, not on your own computer. The advantage of this is that you can access your calendar from any computer anywhere in the world. Just log onto the Google Calendar page, and your calendar and all events are there.

- Because Google Calendar is Web-based, you can use it to create not only a private calendar for yourself, but also public calendars for your company or organization. When you create a public calendar, all employees or attendees can access it via the Web. In addition, special event invitation features make it easy to invite others to an event— public or private.

- Google allows you to create several different—and different types of—calendars. You can create one calendar for home, another for work, and yet another for your son's soccer team. Then you can view all your calendars from the same Google Calendar page.

- Because Google Calendar is part of the Google empire, it integrates smoothly with Gmail. Google Calendar can scan your email messages for dates and times. With a few clicks of the mouse, you can create events based on the content of your Gmail messages.

- Google Calendar tries to be as universal as possible. That means relatively seamless integration with the information you created previously with any other calendar programs you may be using, such as Yahoo! Calendar or the Microsoft Outlook calendar.

The bottom line is that Google wants to make it both beneficial and easy to move from your current calendar program to Google Calendar. Give it a try and see what you think.

COMMENTARY

TARGETED ADS

Google Calendar offers yet another opportunity for Google to sell profitable advertising space. To be fair, though, Google Calendar is not yet littered with these pesky little things. But rest assured, that's why Google created Google Calendar—as yet another vehicle to deliver highly targeted ads.

Think through all the detailed information Google Calendar is collecting about you and your activities, and then imagine how that information can be used from an advertising perspective. For example, if you create an event to go to a movie on Saturday night, Google can theoretically parse that information and then sell targeted ad space to movie studios or theater chains—or maybe even restaurants in the nearby neighborhood. The more information you enter, the more targeted Google's ads can be.

It sounds cynical, I know, but why else would Google offer such a service with no supporting direct revenue stream? The rewards of such an investment come from future advertising—in this case, very targeted, and thus very profitable, advertising.

22

If you don't like the idea of Google keeping all this personal information on its company servers, don't use Google Calendar—or any other
Web-based calendar application, for that matter. The benefits of a Web-
based calendar are purchased at the cost of personal privacy. Even
though Google says your private information will stay private, it still
can use that information to send you event-specific ads. If the privacy
issue bothers you, switch to a software-based calendar and forgo the
ability to share events and calendars with your friends and colleagues.
That's the trade-off you have to consider.

Setting Up Your Google Calendar

Google Calendar is designed to be easy to use. To that end, Google succeeds.

Setting Up Your First Calendar

Setting up your first calendar is comically easy. In fact, there's nothing to set
up. When you first sign in to the Google Calendar page, your calendar is
already there, waiting for your input. There's nothing to create and nothing to
configure. Could it be any easier than that?

Setting Up Multiple Calendars

One of the key features of Google Calendar is the ability to create and manage multiple calendars. For example, you might want to create one calendar
with work events and another with social events.

To create a second (or third or fourth) calendar, follow these steps:

1. From the main Google Calendar page, click the Create link in the My
   Calendars pane.
2. When the Create New Calendar page appears, as shown in Figure 22.2,
   give the calendar a name and description, and then enter other appropriate information.

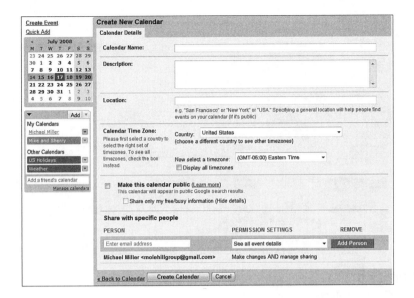

FIGURE 22.2

Creating a new calendar.

> **3.** Click the Create Calendar button.

All the calendars you create are listed in the My Calendars pane on the left side of the Google Calendars page.

Viewing Your Calendar

The main Google Calendar page (calendar.google.com) is where you view all your calendars—in any of several different views.

Using Different Views

Google Calendar lets you view your calendar in several different ways. You select each view by clicking the appropriate tab above the main calendar. You can view your calendar by day, week, month, next four days, or agenda. Figure 22.3 shows the Agenda view, which lists only your upcoming events.

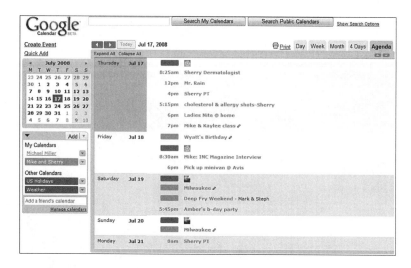

FIGURE 22.3
Google Calendar Agenda view.

For each view, you can move backward and forward in time by clicking the left and right arrow buttons at the top of the calendar. To center the calendar on the current day, click the Today button.

You can also create customized calendar views that include any number of days. For this, you use the mini-calendar on the left side of the Google Calendar page. Just click and drag the mouse cursor across the mini-calendar from the first to the last day you want to view; the main calendar changes to reflect the number of days you select.

Viewing Multiple Calendars

The main calendar on the Google Calendar page can display any single calendar individually, or multiple calendars simultaneously. It all depends on which—and how many—calendars you check in the Calendars box.

By default, every calendar is displayed in the main calendar. To display only a single calendar, click that calendar; the name changes from the normal shaded box to just a link. Click the link again to redisplay the events from that calendar in the main calendar, color-coded appropriately.

Viewing Your Calendar from Other Calendar Applications

Google Calendar can export its event information in XML, HTML, or iCal formats. (iCal is used on the Macintosh, XML is used by most Web-based calendar applications, and HTML calendars can be viewed in any web browser.) This lets you read your Google Calendar data in other calendar applications.

The key is to distribute your calendar's private address to another calendar application. To do this, follow these steps:

note Sharing your calendar's private address lets others read your calendar information, but not add to or change that information.

caution You use the private address to view your calendar within another calendar application that you are personally using. To share your calendar publicly with other users, use the calendar's *public* address.

1. In the Calendars box, click the down arrow next to the calendar you want to share, and then select Calendar Settings.

2. When the Details page appears, scroll down to the Private Address section.

3. Click either the XML, HTML, or iCal button in the Private Address section.

4. A pop-up window containing your calendar's address appears; copy this address into the other calendar application.

Working with Events

All the items scheduled on your calendar are called *events*. An event can include all sorts of information, some of which is augmented by information provided by the Google website.

Adding an Event to Your Calendar

Google provides several different ways to add events to your calendar. Let's look at each in turn.

First, you can simply click the hour or the day on your calendar on which you'd like to create a new event. If you add an event to a daily calendar, click and drag the cursor over the entire timeframe of the event. This opens a new event balloon, like the one shown in Figure 22.4. Enter the name of the event into the balloon, and select which calendar you want to add the event to.

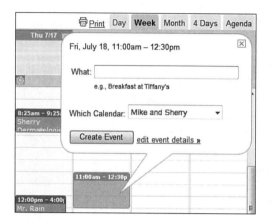

FIGURE 22.4

Adding information to a new event balloon.

If you use this approach on a monthly calendar, unfortunately you can't eas
ily determine the length of the event. To fine-tune these and other details of
the event, click the Edit Event Details link in the event balloon. This opens th
page shown in Figure 22.5, where you can enter the following information:

- What (name of the event)
- When (start and end times—or days)
- Repeats (use for repeating events)
- Where (the event's location)
- Calendar (which of your calendars the event should be added to)
- Description (a brief overview of the event)
- Reminder (how much in advance you want to be reminded of the
  event, and how)
- Show Me As (either available or busy, for anyone viewing a public cal
  endar)
- Privacy (determines whether the event is private, public, or your
  default setting)
- Add Guests (enter the email addresses of any guests you want include
  you're prompted to email them with notice of the event, if you like)
- Guests Can (either invite others to your event, see the guest list, or
  neither)

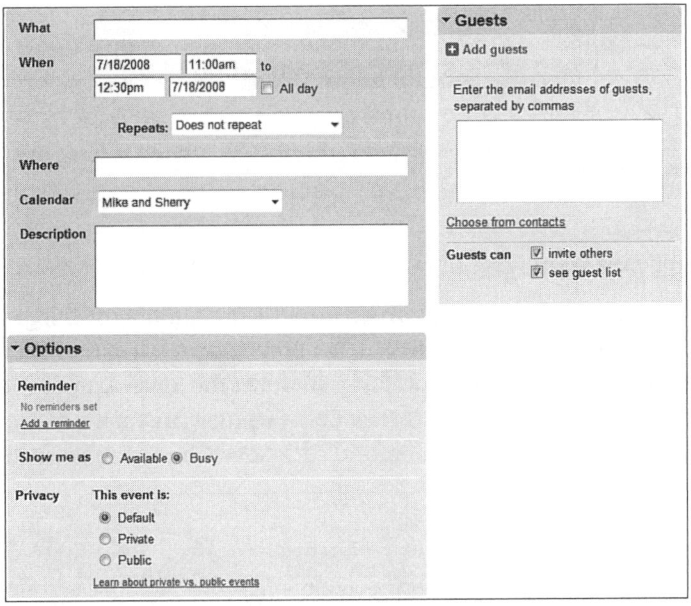

FIGURE 22.5

Entering more-detailed event information.

You can also add an event by clicking the Create Event link in the upper-left corner of the Google Calendar page. This opens the page shown in Figure 22.5; enter the appropriate information, and then click the Save button.

Adding an Event via Quick Add

Perhaps the easiest way to add an event is with Google Calendar's Quick Add feature. When you click the Quick Add link (or type the letter Q), the Quick Add entry box appears, as shown in Figure 22.6. Enter the name and time of the event, and then press Enter. This method is quite intelligent; if you enter **Lunch with George at noon Monday at Applebee's**, Quick Add translates the text and enters the appropriate event at the specified date and time.

> **tip** Another way to access the Create Event page is to click the down arrow next to a calendar in the Calendars box and then select Create Event on This Calendar.

FIGURE 22.6

Using Quick Add to add an event.

Adding an Event from Gmail

Here's a neat feature that arises from the integration of Google Calendar and Gmail. When you're reading a Gmail message that contains information pertaining to a possible event, just pull down the More Actions menu and select Create Event. This opens a New Event window, as shown in Figure 22.7; enter the appropriate information and click Save Changes. The event is added to your Google Calendar.

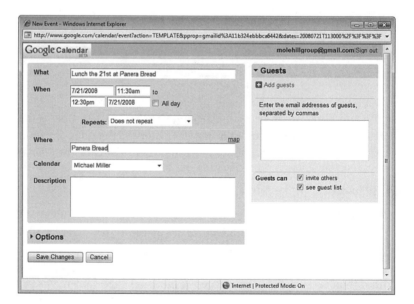

FIGURE 22.7

Adding an event from a Gmail message.

Synching Events with Microsoft Outlook

If you use Microsoft Outlook to manage your home or work schedules, you can import your Outlook events into Google Calendar—and export your Google Calendar events into Outlook. All you need is the Google Calendar Sync utility, which you can download for free at www.google.com/support/calendar/bin/answer.py?answer=89955.

> **tip** When you include location information about an event, Google Calendar includes a Map link in that event's information. Click the Map link to view a Google Map of that event's location.

When you install Google Calendar Sync, you see the configuration window shown in Figure 22.8. Enter your Google Account info, as well as how you want to sync:

- 2-way automatically syncs events from each application to one another.
- 1 way: Google Calendar to Microsoft Outlook calendar syncs your Google Calendar events to Outlook (Google Calendar is the master app).
- 1-way: Microsoft Outlook calendar to Google Calendar syncs your Outlook events to Google Calendar (Outlook is the master app).

You also have to determine how often you want to synchronize your events, in minutes. Make your choices, and then click the Save button. Now, whenever your computer is online, your events are synchronized between your two calendars; events you add in the one application are automatically added to the other.

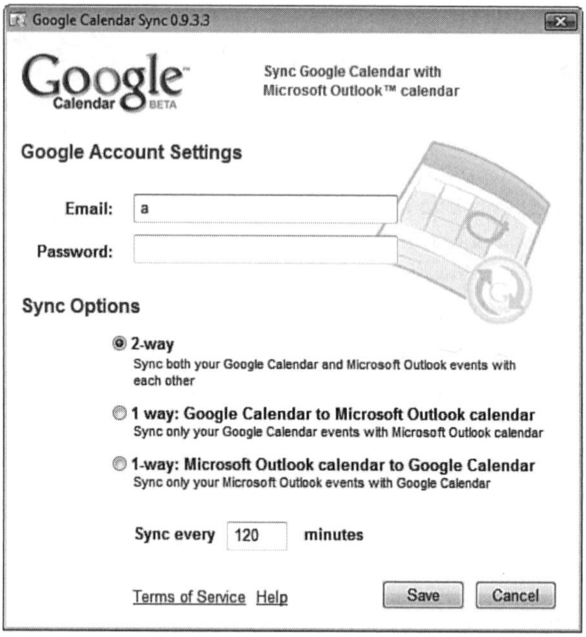

FIGURE 22.8
Configuring Google Calendar Sync.

Receiving Event Notifications on Your Mobile Phone

If you want to take your Google Calendar with you wherever you go, all you have to do is enable automatic phone notifications. Go to the Google Calendar home page and click the Settings link. When the Settings page appears, select the Mobile Setup tab.

The first time you access this page, you have to verify your mobile phone number, which you do by having Google send a verification number to your phone via text message. After this is done, enter the verification code into the appropriate box on the Settings page, and then click the Finish Setup button.

The Notifications tab changes to its final form, as shown in Figure 22.9. You can choose to be notified via SMS (text message), email, or pop-up (if you have a Web-enabled phone, like the Apple iPhone). Select how long before each event you want to be notified, as well as how you want to be notified for each type of item (new invitations, changed invitations, and the like). Click the Save button, and you're ready to go.

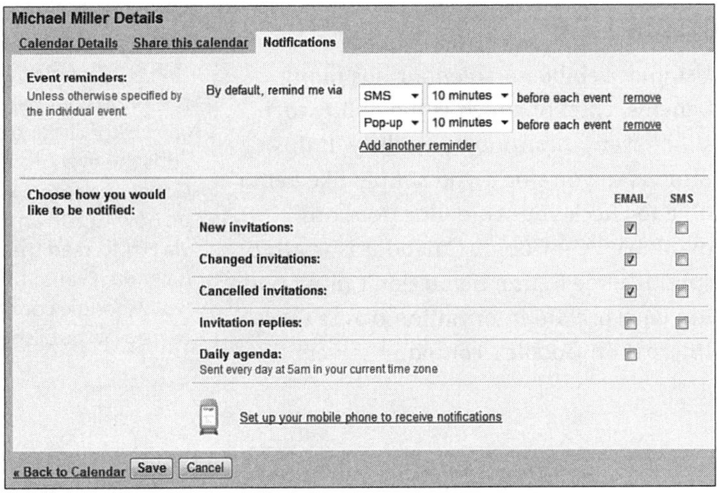

FIGURE 22.9
Enabling mobile notifications for Google Calendar.

Inviting Others to an Event

When you first created an event, you had the option of adding guests to this event's information. If you did so, you were prompted to send email invitations to those guests.

After you've created an event on your calendar, you can invite more guests at any time. Just follow these steps:

1. Edit the selected event to display the event page.

2. Click the Add Guests link, and then enter the email addresses of your guests into the text box. Separate multiple addresses with commas.

3. Click the Save button.

4. Google Calendar now displays the message "Would you like to send invitations to new guests?" Click the Send button to do so.

Google now sends invitations to all the guests you added. Each invitation includes links for the guest's response—Yes, No, or Maybe. When the guest clicks one of these links, he is taken to a Submit Response web page. His response is then automatically entered into the event in your Google Calendar, as shown in the Guests section of the event page.

22

The Bottom Line

Using a Web-based calendar has many benefits, chief of which is the ability to share event information publicly. If this matters to you—or if you simply like being able to check your calendar from any available PC—Google Calendar is worth a spin. It's free to use, if you don't mind posting your private information across the Internet on Google's company servers.

tip You can also add a Google Calendar event button to your personal website; any visitor clicking this button adds the event to his or her own Google Calendar. For instructions on how to add an event button via HTML, read the Google Calendar Event Publisher Guide (www.google.com/googlecalendar/event_publisher_guide.html)

Using Google Reader

When you want to read the postings from your favorite blogs or news sites, you need some sort of feed-reading mechanism. That can be a feed-reader software program, or a website that aggregates feeds from a variety of sources.

Google Reader is such a feed aggregator. Actually, it's more than that; Google Reader is a web-based reader that lets you subscribe to blog and news feeds and then read the latest postings from those feeds.

Reading Blog Postings

You access Google Reader at reader.google.com. Google Reader lets you read both blog feeds and news feeds. That means you can use Google Reader to display the latest news headlines from popular news sites, as well as catch the latest ponderings from your favorite bloggers. All you need to do is know which feed you want to subscribe to; Google Reader automatically displays th latest content, all in one place.

note To use Google Reader, you must have a Google Account—and be signed into that account.

As you can see in Figure 23.1, the blogs you've subscribed to are displayed in the left panel. To read the latest postings for a given blog, just click the blog name; the blog postings are displayed in the window on the right, as shown in Figure 23.2. Use the scroll bar or the Previous Item/Next Item buttons to move through the postings.

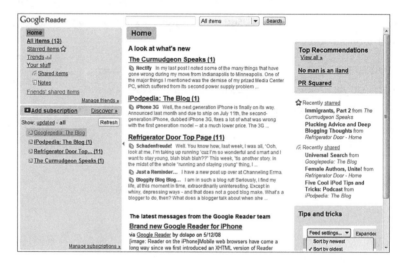

FIGURE 23.1

Reading blog and news feeds with Google Reader.

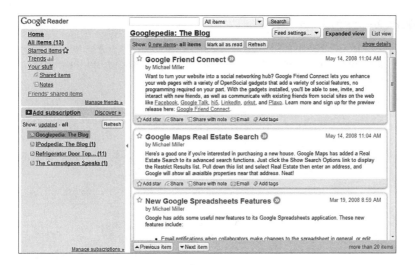

FIGURE 23.2

Reading posts for a selected blog.

If you'd prefer to view only the titles of the blog postings, select the List View tab. This displays a list of postings; click any title to expand the listing and read the complete posting.

By the way, if you'd prefer to read a posting on the original blog site itself, rather than in Google Reader, click the title of the blog entry. The selected post on the original blog site opens in a new browser window.

Categorizing with Tags

To help categorize your postings, Google lets you add tags. Just click the Add Tags link under any posting, and then enter one or more keywords to describe the posting.

Emailing Blog Postings

You can also send blog postings to your friends and family via email. Click the Email link under the posting to expand it, and then enter the recipient's email address, add a personal note, and click the Send button. The blog post is sent to the recipient via your Gmail account.

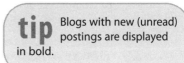

tip

Blogs with new (unread) postings are displayed in bold.

23

Sharing Blog Postings

You're not limited to sharing individual blog posts via email. Google Reader also lets you create a new feed composed of the individual blog feeds you want to share.

All you have to do is click the Share link under the blog entries you want to share. Then click the Shared Items link in the left panel. The Your Shared Items page displays a link to a web page that contains your shared items; you can email this link to anyone you like. Figure 23.3 shows a typical shared items page; it's like a blog of your favorite blog postings!

FIGURE 23.3
Your shared blog postings, on a new web page.

Subscribing to Feeds

There are several ways to add a blog feed to Google Reader. They're all relatively easy to do.

> **note** Learn more about blog feeds in Chapter 10, "Searching for Blogs and Blog Postings."

Searching for Blog Feeds

You start by clicking the Add Subscription link in the left panel; this displays an Add Subscription box. From here, you can do one of the following:

- Enter the URL for a blog
- Enter the URL for a blog's RSS or Atom feed
- Enter one or more keywords to search for blogs of a given type

Google Reader returns a list of matching blogs. Click the Subscribe button to add that blog subscription to Google Reader.

Browsing for Blog Feeds

Alternatively, you can browse for blogs to subscribe to. When you click the Discover link next to the Add Subscription link, you see the Discover and Search for Feeds page.

From here you can select from Google's recommended blogs (the Recommendations tab) or click the Browse tab. This tab, shown in Figure 23.4, presents three ways to find blog feeds:

- Subscribe to a preselected bundle of feeds, based on a particular topic. (Three bundles are shown on the main page; click the More Bundles link to view—well, more bundles.)
- Subscribe to feeds from friends and family—as long as their blogs are hosted by Blogger, Flickr, or MySpace. Just enter the username, select the blog host service, and click the Subscribe button.
- Search for blogs by keyword (the same as with the Add Subscription box).

23

FIGURE 23.4
Browsing blog feeds.

Importing Feeds from Other Readers

If you've already created a list of feed subscriptions in another feed aggregator or feed reader, you can import that list into Google Reader—which definitely beats reentering your feeds by hand. This assumes, of course, that your previous feed reader/aggregator saved its subscription list in industry-standard OMDP format and that you have that file stored on your computer's hard disk. All that assumed, here's what you need to do:

1. From the Google Reader home page, click the Settings link.

2. When the Settings page appears, click the Import/Export tab.

3. From the Import/Export tab, click the Browse button to find and select the OMDP file that holds your feed subscriptions.

4. Click the Upload button.

tip Google Reader isn't the only feed aggregator site on the Web. Some popular competing aggregators include Bloglines (www.bloglines.com) and NewsGator (www. newsgator.com). Alternatively, you can read your blog feeds in a freestanding feed-reader software program, such as FeedDemon (www.feeddemon.com).

That does the trick. All the feeds in your old subscription file now appear as subscriptions in Google Reader.

Managing Your Subscriptions

Want to change your subscription list—to delete a feed, or change information about a feed? It's easy enough to do. Just click the Settings link at the top of the Google Reader home page, and then select the Subscriptions tab. This tab, shown in Figure 23.5, lists all the feeds you're currently subscribed to.

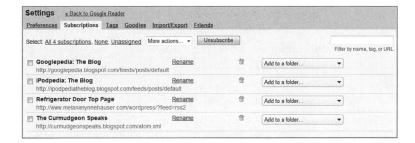

FIGURE 23.5

Editing your Google Reader subscriptions.

To delete a feed, all you have to do is click the trash can icon next to the feed name. To rename a feed (perhaps to something more meaningful to you), click the Rename link. To organize your feeds into folders, click the Add to a Folder button and either select an existing folder or create a new one. The tasks are relatively self-explanatory.

The Bottom Line

Whether you're an avid follower of a particular blog, or you just want to see the latest headlines from an online news site, you need some way to keep track of all the latest postings. That's where Google Reader shines: It organizes all your blog feeds and keeps you up to date on what's new.

Viewing Images and Videos

Searching for Pictures with Google Images

Among Google's many specialized searches, perhaps the most popular is Google Image Search, also known as Google Images. This is a subset of Google's basic Web search that lets you search for photos, drawings, logos, and other graphics files on the Web. It's perhaps the best way I know to find pictures online.

The fact that Google can find pictures that match your search criteria is something short of amazing. After all, pictures aren't like web pages; they don't have any text that Google can parse and index. Instead, Google analyzes the file extension, image caption, text on the host web page adjacent to the image, and other factors to try to determine what the image is a picture of. It's to Google's credit that most of the time it gets it right.

Searching for Images

There are two ways to access Google Image Search, shown in Figure 24.1. You can click the Images link on any Google search page, or you can go directly to images.google.com. (Google Image Search results also appear as part of Google's universal search results when you search from the main search box.)

FIGURE 24.1

The home page for Google Image Search.

Basic Searching

For most users, searching Google Image Search is as easy as entering your query into the search box and clicking the Search Images button. Nothing to it.

You can use any of Google's advanced search operators within your query. Of particular use is the **filetype:** operator, which you can use to limit your search to JPG or GIF image files.

Advanced Searching

If you want to fine-tune your image search, the best way to do so is to use the Advanced Search page. When you click the Advanced Image Search link on the main Image Search page, you see the form shown in Figure 24.2. From here you can fine-tune your search in a number of ways:

■ **Find results.** Narrow your search by searching for all the words, the exact phrase, any of the words, or pictures not related to the words.

note Learn more about advanced search operators in Chapter 6, "Getting the Most Out of Google Search."

- **Content types.** Search only for images that contain news content, faces, or any content.
- **Size.** Search only for images that are small, medium, large, or extra large.
- **Filetypes.** Search only for JPG, GIF, PNG, or BMP format files.
- **Coloration.** Search only for black-and-white, grayscale, or full-color images, or search for any color.
- **Domain.** Search only for images within a specified domain or website.
- **SafeSearch.** Apply moderate, strict, or no filtering to the image search results.

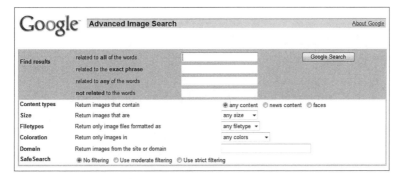

FIGURE 24.2

Fine-tuning your search from the Advanced Image Search page.

The Advanced Image Search page is great if you're looking for images of a particular file type—for example, if you're looking only for JPG images. It's also good if you want to look for portraits or other pictures of people by using the Content Types option. In addition, this page helps you find larger or higher-resolution pictures for print purposes (both of which are likely to be of a larger file size) or smaller or lower-resolution pictures for Web use (both of which are likely to be of a smaller file size).

This begs the question of how small is small. Or how large is large, for that matter. The answers to these questions are detailed in Table 24.1.

Table 24.1   Google Image Search Size Parameters

Size	Approximate Dimensions (in Pixels)
Small	50×50 or smaller
Medium	Larger than 50×50
	Smaller than 600×800
Large	Larger than 600×800
	Smaller than 1200×1600
Extra Large	Larger than 1200×1600

Viewing Image Search Results

When you click the Search Images button, Google returns the first page of results. As you can see in Figure 24.3, the matching images are displayed in a grid of thumbnail pictures, ranked in terms of relevance.

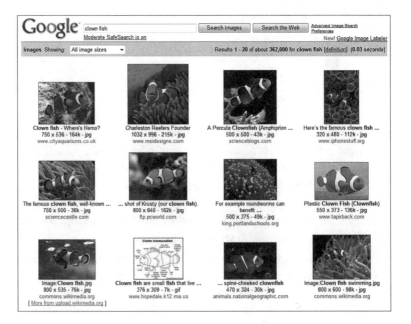

FIGURE 24.3

The results of a Google image search.

For each thumbnail image, Google lists an image caption, the size of the image (in both pixels and kilobytes), the file type, and the host website. To view any image, all you have to do is click the thumbnail.

When you click a thumbnail image, the original page is displayed in a frame at the bottom of the next page, as shown in Figure 24.4. At the top of the page is the Google Images frame, which includes the image thumbnail, information about the image, and a few important links:

tip If you'd rather limit the results to images of a particular size (small, medium, large, or extra large), pull down the Images Showing: list at the top of the page and make the appropriate selection.

- To view the host page without the Google frame, click the Remove Frame link.

- To view the picture full size, click the See Full-Size Image link. (Not available if you've selected to display small images only.)

- To return to your search results, click the Image Results link.

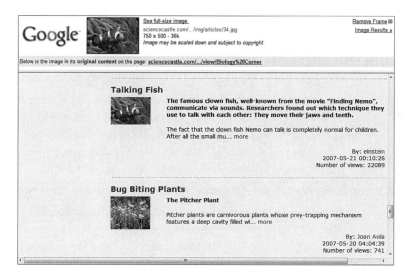

FIGURE 24.4

Viewing an image found with Google Image Search.

Saving and Printing Images

Almost any image you find on the Web can be saved to your hard disk or printed. (Unless the page designer has implemented some form of copy protection for the image, that is.) Saving and printing images is a function of your web browser, but here's how to do it in Internet Explorer.

To save an image to your hard disk, right-click the picture and select Save. When the Save As dialog box appears, select a location for the picture, and then click the Save button.

To print a picture (without printing the surrounding web page), right-click the image and select Print. When the Print dialog box appears, click the Print button.

note Some sites use special code to prevent users from downloading images. If you right-click the image and see a message to this effect, you can't save that particular image to your hard disk.

caution Commercial use of copyrighted images is prohibited, so be careful how you use the pictures you find with Google Image Search.

note Learn more about SafeSearch content filtering in Chapter 6.

Filtering Out Dirty Pictures

One of the bad things about searching the Web for pictures is that, depending on your query, you're likely to stumble across a few adult-oriented pictures in your search results. Assuming that you don't want (or don't want your kids) to see these dirty pictures, Google enables its moderate SafeSearch content filter by default when you use Google Image Search. (Moderate SafeSearch filtering blocks the display of questionable images only, not text.)

If you'd prefer to view your search results unfiltered, you have two options:

- From any search results page, click the Moderate SafeSearch Is On link. This takes you to the Preferences page; check the Do Not Filter My Search Results option, and then click the Save Preferences button.

- From the main Google Image Search page, click the Preferences link. When the Preferences page appears, check the Do Not Filter My Search Results option, and then click the Save Preferences button.

Removing Your Images from Image Search

If you're an artist or photographer, you might find that your copyrighted images appear in Google Image Search. This might be okay with you, or it might not. If you'd prefer that your images not be displayed in Google Image Search, you can request that Google remove them.

To remove a copyrighted image from Google Image Search, you have to add a special text file to the root directory of your website. This file should be labeled robots.txt, and it needs to include specific information about the images you want to protect.

> **tip** If you want to help Google improve the accuracy of its Image Search results, click the Google Image Labeler link at the top of any Image Search page. Google Image Labeler is a voluntary program where you and an automatically selected online partner view a set of images and enter as many labels as possible for each image. Your responses are used to categorize the images that Google shows you.

If you want to remove a specific image file from the Google search index, add the following lines to the robots.txt file:

```
User-agent: Googlebot-Image
Disallow: /subdirectory/file.jpg
```

You replace *subdirectory* with the name of the subdirectory where the image file is located, and you replace *file.jpg* with the name and extension of the file you want to protect.

Alternatively, you can instruct Google to remove all images on your site from the Google search index. In this instance, you want to add the following lines to the robots.txt file:

```
User-agent: Googlebot-Image<
Disallow: /
```

When the GoogleBot spider crawls your site, it automatically reads the contents of the robots.txt file for instructions. If your site includes a robots.txt file, the spider will follow the instructions you specify, and not add the image file(s) you noted.

24

COMMENTARY

FAIR USE

On May 16, 2007, the 9th U.S. Circuit Court of Appeals ruled that Google Image Search did not violate the copyrights held by an adult website by displaying thumbnail versions of copyrighted photos. This ruling overturned the previous ruling by a federal judge that said that Google did violate those copyrights; Google had appealed that ruling.

The legal battles started when the Perfect 10 website (www.perfect10.com) sued Google over use of the photos in Google's search results. The site claimed—and the original judge agreed—that the free availability of the photos on Google Image Search, even in thumbnail form, could harm Perfect 10's ability to sell small versions of its photos as downloads to cell phones.

The judge issued a preliminary injunction against Google, ruling that Google's creation and display of the Perfect 10 thumbnail images "likely do not fall within the fair use exemption." Fair use, if you're unschooled in copyright law, is the legal standard that allows for limited use of copyrighted works for specific purposes, such as news reporting, criticism, or comment.

Google, obviously, disagreed. The company pointed out that it doesn't display full-sized versions of the photos in question; when a user clicks a thumbnail image, he leaves Google and is taken to the Perfect 10 website. For these purposes, Google argued that display of thumbnail images is fair use.

The appeals process took about a year but then was settled in Google's favor. The appeals court ruled that the lower court erred in granting the preliminary injunction, saying that the display of a thumbnail could be considered "fair use" under copyright law.

"There is no dispute that Google substantially assists Web sites to distribute their infringing copies to a worldwide market and assists a worldwide audience of users to access infringing materials," the court said. And I agree.

While I'm all for artists' rights, it seems to me that the display of thumbnail images for navigational purposes doesn't do anyone any harm. If Google were displaying the full-sized images without permission, that would be one thing. But displaying thumbnails is what makes Google Image Search particularly useful, and I'd wager that having Perfect 10's photos listed in Google's search results drives a lot of traffic to the (paid) Perfect 10 site. If the original ruling had stood, forcing Google to remove thumbnails of their images, Perfect 10 would have likely seen a decrease in traffic—which is a "cut off your nose to spite your face" sort of scenario.

I'm pleased that the court finally ruled in Google's favor. If websites could force Google to remove their thumbnail images from its search results, it would negatively affect the usability of Google Image Search. The fewer images you can see, the less useful Image Search would be.

The Bottom Line

I like Google Image Search. It's easy to use, and it normally returns quite accurate results. I use it often; I particularly like the ability to filter results by image size. It is, in my mind, the best image search engine available today.

Using Picasa and Picasa Web Albums

Of all of Google's applications, I like Picasa the best. Why do I like Picasa so much? Because it does just about everything that a program like Adobe Photoshop Elements or Paint Shop Pro does, but with a much smaller footprint (very small file size—very quick to download) and for free. Whether you need to fix bad digital pictures or just organize all the photos on your hard drive, Picasa does it with ease.

Installing and Configuring the Program

As I just mentioned, Picasa isn't like Google's Web-based applications; it's a software program that you download (for free) from picasa.google.com. The program is actually quite small, so the download isn't time-consuming at all. Just click the download link (Try Picasa Now), and you'll be ready to go in no time.

The first time you launch the program, Picasa scans your computer for picture files. You can have Picasa scan your entire hard disk, or only the files in your My Documents, My Pictures, and Desktop folders. Obviously, it takes less time to scan these selected folders than it does to scan your entire hard disk; if you're well organized, select this second option. (If not, well, you might as well have Picasa search everywhere for files you might have haphazardly stored.)

note This chapter is based on Picasa version 2.7. As this book was going to press, Google announced the beta release of Picasa version 3, which might be available for general release by the time you read this. New features include a Retouch tool for touching up blemishes and the like, a movie editor, a computer screen-capture utility, watermarks, and improved file management.

note Picasa is available only for computers running Windows 2000, XP, or Vista. Picasa does not run on older versions of Windows or on Apple Macintosh computers—although a Linux version is being tested in Google Labs.

The picture files that Picasa finds are used to create an index within the Picasa program. This picture index is used to organize your photos into visual albums. Most users find that it's easier to locate pictures from within Picasa's albums than it is to use the My Pictures or Pictures folder in Windows.

The balance of this chapter is devoted to showing you how to use Picasa to organize and edit your photos. Picasa has so many features that one could write an entire book about it (is my editor reading this?). Page count constraints force me to limit coverage to common tasks that the typical user is likely to perform.

Getting to Know the Picasa Desktop

By default, Picasa shows all photos in its picture library, as shown in Figure 25.1. The individual folders in your library are displayed in the left folders pane; the photos within the selected folder are displayed in the main window. You can also use the scroll bars to scroll up and down through all the photos in Picasa's index.

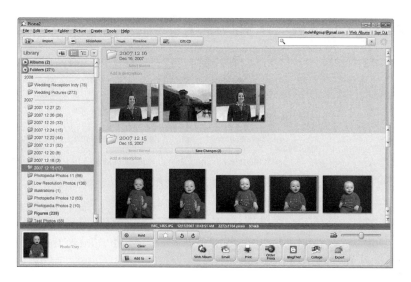

FIGURE 25.1

Picasa's picture library.

When you select a photo, it's surrounded by a blue border and displayed as a thumbnail in the Photo Tray at the bottom left of the screen. You can select more than one picture at a time; the thumbnails are then resized to all fit within the Photo Tray.

Also along the bottom of the screen are various function buttons. They are described in Table 25.1.

Table 25.1   Picasa's Function Buttons

Button	Description
Hold	Holds selected pictures in the Photo Tray.
Clear	Clears all pictures from the Photo Tray.
Add to	Adds the selected picture to the screensaver, your Starred Photos album, or a new album.
Add/Remove Star	"Stars" selected photos for future use—or removes previously applied stars.
Rotate counterclockwise	Rotates the picture 90 degrees to the left.
Rotate clockwise	Rotates the picture 90 degrees to the right.
Web Album	Uploads selected photos to a Web photo album.

Continues

Table 25.1 **Continued**

Button	Description
Email	Emails pictures (using either your default email program, Gmail, or Hello's Picasa Mail).
Print	Prints the selected pictures.
Order Prints	Orders prints of selected photos from an online photo-printing service.
Blog This!	Sends the selected photo to your Blogger blog (as a new photo posting).
Collage	Creates a collage of the selected photos.
Export	Saves a copy of any photo you've edited.

Just above all the function buttons, at the bottom right of the main display, is a zoom slider control. You use this slider to adjust the size of the photos that appear in the main display.

At the top of the Picasa window are four buttons and a search box. The buttons let you import new photos, display the pictures in the selected folder as a slide show, display your photos in an innovative timeline view, or burn selected photos to a "gift" CD. The search box lets you search your hard disk for photos that match specific criteria.

Organizing Your Photos

One of the neat things about Picasa is how easy it is to reorganize your photos. You can easily move photos from one folder to another or rename your photos, all from Picasa's library view.

Moving Photos

Picasa displays all your photos in their original folders, with the folders listed in the folder pane. To move a picture from one folder to another, simply drag it from the library window to a new folder in the folder pane. To move *all* the pictures in the folder to another folder, just drag and drop that folder in the folder pane.

Renaming Photos

It's equally easy to rename a photo. Just select the picture you want to rename, and then select File, Rename. When the Rename Files dialog box appears, enter a new name for the file, and click the Rename button. (Alternatively, you can check the options to automatically include the picture's date and/or image resolution in the filename.)

> **tip**
> You can also rename a photo by selecting it and pressing the F2 key on the keyboard.

To rename a group of photos, select all the photos you want to rename, and then select File, Rename. This time when the Rename Files dialog box appears, enter the common name you want all the photos to share. When you click Rename, the photos are renamed accordingly, with each photo having a "–1," "–2," and so on appended to the common name.

Fixing Common Photo Problems

If you're like me, not every photo you take is a keeper. Some of my photos are too dark, some are too light, some have a bad color balance, some aren't composed properly, some are shots of people with really bad red eye—you get the picture. (No pun intended.) The nice thing about taking photos digitally (as opposed to shooting on film) is that fixing bad pictures is a simple matter of moving around the appropriate digital bits and bytes—which is something that Picasa does with aplomb.

When you want to fix a picture, you start by double-clicking it in the photo library. This displays a large version of the photo in the main window, along with a new control pane on the left side of the window, as shown in Figure 25.2. The control pane has three different tabs: Basic Fixes, Tuning, and Effects. Each tab contains a variety of controls you can use to edit and manipulate the selected picture.

> **tip**
> You return to Picasa's photo library by clicking the Back To Library button.

25

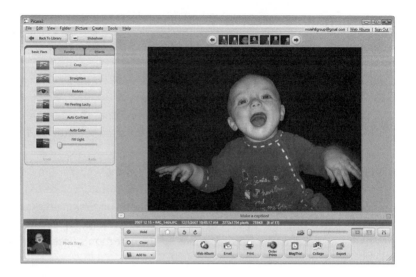

FIGURE 25.2

Editing a picture.

Read on to learn how to perform some of the more common fixes.

Fixing a Dark (or Light) Picture

If you shoot a lot of photos indoors, chances are you'll run across a few shots that are underlit—that is, the photos appear too dark. Conversely, shooting outdoors in bright sunlight can result in some photos being too light, or washed out. Fortunately, Picasa can fix both these problems.

Whether your picture is too dark or too light, you can use several different methods to fix the problem. The easiest method, and the first to try, is to select the Basic Fixes tab (shown in Figure 25.3) and click the Auto Contrast button. Nine times out of ten, this will do the trick.

If using Auto Contrast doesn't fix the problem, try adjusting the Fill Light slider (also on the Basic Fixes tab). Moving the slider to the right lightens the picture as if you shot it with additional fill light; moving the slider to the left removes the fill light and darkens the picture.

> **tip**
> You can undo any change you make by clicking the Undo button in the control pane. Reapply the change by clicking the Redo button.

FIGURE 25.3
Picasa's Basic Fixes tab.

You can make additional adjustments from the Tuning tab, shown in Figure 25.4. From here you can (once again) adjust the Fill Light, as well as Highlights (lightens or darkens only the brightest areas of the picture) and Shadows (lightens or darkens only the darkest areas of the picture). (Color Temperature and Neutral Color Picker are discussed in the next section.)

25

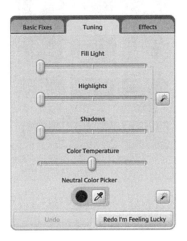

FIGURE 25.4
Picasa's Tuning tab.

Fixing an Off-Color Picture

Another problem with shooting indoors is that you don't always get the right colors. Shooting under fluorescent lights can turn everything a little green, and shooting under too low a light can give everything a warmish orange cast.

To fix tint problems (when the entire picture looks the wrong color), go to the Basic Fixes tab and click the Auto Color button. If this doesn't do the trick, go to the Tuning tab and adjust the Color Temperature control. Moving this slider to the left creates a "cooler" picture (more blue), and moving it to the right creates a "warmer" picture (more red).

You might also consider using the Neutral Color Picker on the Tuning tab. Click the eyedropper button, and then click an area in your picture that should be neutral white or black. This adjusts all the other colors to match.

If you need more control over the picture's tint, go to the Effects tab, shown in Figure 25.5, and click Tint; this displays the Tint control. Click within the Pick Color box, and then move the cursor around the resulting color box until you find the proper tint. Click to confirm your choice.

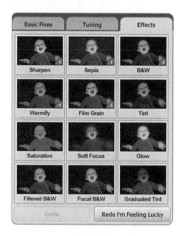

FIGURE 25.5

Picasa's Effects tab.

Finally, if a picture has too much (or too little) color, you need to adjust the photo's color saturation. You do this from the Effects tab. Click the Saturation control, and then adjust the Amount slider to the left (to remove color from the picture) or to the right (to increase the amount of color).

Fixing Red Eye

When you shoot indoors with a flash, you sometimes get what is called the "red eye" effect. (You know this one; it's when your subject looks like the red-eyed spawn of a devil.) Fortunately, Picasa makes removing red eye a snap. Here's what you do:

1. Select the Basic Fixes tab.

2. Click the Redeye button.

3. When the Redeye Repair control appears, click and drag the mouse cursor over the first eye you want to fix. Picasa automatically removes the red from the selected eye.

4. Repeat Step 3 for the other eye you want to fix.

5. Click the Apply button to confirm the fix.

Cropping a Picture

Sometimes, for whatever reason, you don't properly compose a picture. Maybe your subject isn't centered; maybe your subject is too far away. Whatever the case, you can crop the photo to put the subject front and center in the picture, using Picasa's Crop control.

To crop a picture, follow these steps:

1. Select the Basic Fixes tab.

2. Click the Crop button.

3. When the Crop Photo control appears, as shown in Figure 25.6, select what size you want the resulting picture to be: 4×6, 5×7, 8×10, or a custom size (Manual). This fixes the dimensions of the crop area.

4. Click at the top left of the photo, where you want to crop, and keep holding down the mouse button.

5. Drag the cursor diagonally (down and to the right) until you have selected the area you want to remain in the final picture.

6. Release the mouse button.

7. Click the Apply button to confirm the crop.

25

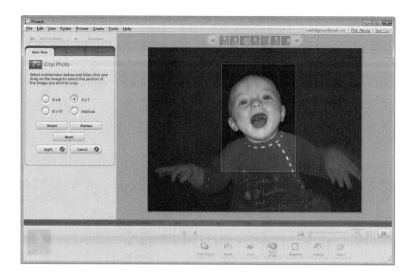

FIGURE 25.6

Cropping a photo.

Applying Special Effects

Picasa's Effects tab not only lets you adjust tint and color saturation, but it also lets you apply a bevy of special effects to your photos. Table 25.2 details the available special effects.

Table 25.2 Picasa's Special Effects

Special Effect	Description
Sharpen	Sharpens the photo's edges.
Sepia	Converts the photo to sepia tone, like old-time photos.
B&W	Removes all color from the photo.
Warmify	Boosts the warm tones in the photo (good for skin tones).
Film Grain	Adds a film-like grain to the photo.
Tint	Lets you adjust the photo's tint.
Saturation	Lets you adjust the photo's color saturation.
Soft Focus	Adds a soft-focus effect to the photo's edges while keeping the center of the photo in sharp focus.
Glow	Adds a gauzy glow to the photo.

Special Effect	Description
Filtered B&W	Creates the effect of a black-and-white photo taken with a color filter.
Focal B&W	Similar to the soft-focus effect, removes color from the photo's edges while keeping the center of the photo in full color.
Graduated Tint	Applies a gradated filter to the photo (useful for shooting skies and landscapes).

Saving Your Changes

After you're done editing and adding special effects to your photos, it's time to save your changes. Picasa always retains your original photo in its original state in case you want to return to it for different editing in the future. Your edited photo is exported (saved) under a new filename.

Saving an Edited File

To save an edited photo, follow these steps:

1. Click the Export button.
2. When the Export to Folder dialog box appears, as shown in Figure 25.7, check the Use Original Size option.
3. Click the OK button.

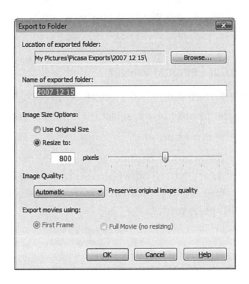

FIGURE 25.7

Exporting an edited photo.

Picasa saves your edited picture in the My Pictures/Picasa Exports folder on your hard disk. Note that Picasa only saves files in the JPG format.

tip Picasa can also export a folder full of pictures as a photo web page, which you can then upload to your website. Select Folder, Export As Web Page to begin the process.

Resizing a Photo for the Web

Here's something else you can do from the Export to Folder dialog box—resize your photos to use on a web page.

If you have a high megapixel camera, and you're shooting at the highest quality setting, you're creating some very large photos, too large to fit comfortably on a web page. You don't want photos any wider than 800 pixels on a web page—and probably a lot smaller than that. For this reason, you should resize your photos to make them small enough for Web use.

Picasa lets you resize any photo when you export it. All you have to do is check the Resize To option in the Export to Folder dialog box, and then adjust the slider to a new width (in pixels). You can also enter a custom width in the corresponding box. It's that easy.

Printing and Sharing Your Photos

There are many ways to share your digital photos. You can make photo prints (either on your own printer or using a photo printing service), email the photos, or burn them onto a picture CD. Picasa lets you do all these tasks, quite easily.

Printing Photos on Your Personal Printer

To print one or more photos on your photo printer, follow these steps:

1. From the photo library, select the photo(s) you want to print.
2. Click the Print button.
3. The Picasa window changes to the one shown in Figure 25.8. Select the print size or layout you want. You can select from 12 wallet-sized prints, four 3.5×5 prints, two 4×6 prints, two 5×7 prints, one 8×10 print, or a full-page print.

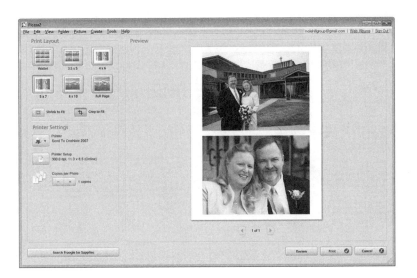

FIGURE 25.8

Printing a photo.

4. Select whether you want the photo shrunk or cropped to fit the print area.

5. If the correct printer isn't selected, click the Printer button and select a different printer.

6. If you need to configure your printer for printing, click the Printer Setup button and proceed from there.

7. Select how many copies you want to print.

8. Click the Print button.

Printing Photos via an Online Print Service

If you don't have a photo printer, or you prefer more-professional prints, Picasa lets you send your photos to an online photo-printing service. Your photos are sent over the Internet to the print service; your prints are mailed to you when completed.

To send one or more photos to a print service, select the photo(s) in the photo library and then click the Order Prints button. When the Picasa window changes to the one shown in Figure 25.9, click the button for the service you want to use, and then follow the specific onscreen instructions from there.

25

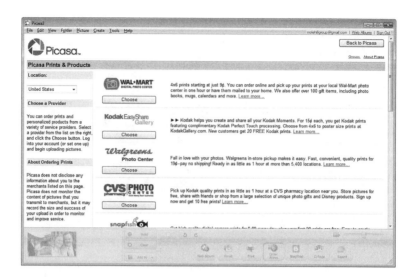

FIGURE 25.9
Choosing an online photo print service.

Emailing Photos

These days, many people share their photos via email. To that end, Picasa lets you quickly and easily email photos to your friends and family. Just follow these steps:

1. In Picasa's photo library, select the photo(s) you want to send.

2. Click the Email button.

3. When the Select Email dialog box appears, select which email service you want to use to send your photo(s).

4. If you select Gmail, you see the Gmail dialog box, shown in Figure 25.10. (If you select another option, you see that application's send email screen.) Enter the name of the recipient into the To: box, and then click the Send button.

> **tip**
>
> If you like, you can have Picasa automatically resize photos you send via email to make for faster uploading/ downloading. All you have to do is Select Tools, Options from the main Picasa window; when you see the Options dialog box, select the E-Mail tab. In the Output Options section, use the slider to select an output size (anything less than 800 pixels wide is safe), and then check the *xx* Pixels, As Above option for the When Sending Single Pictures selection.

FIGURE 25.10

Sending a photo via Gmail.

Burning Photos to a Picture CD or DVD

Another way to share your photos with others is to burn and distribute a CD or DVD containing those photos. Picasa makes this a relatively painless process, all things considered. Just follow these steps:

1. In Picasa's photo library, select the photos you want to burn to CD or DVD.

2. Click the Gift CD button (above the library window). The bottom of the window changes, as shown in Figure 25.11.

3. If you want to include an automatic slide show for your photos, check the Include Slideshow option.

4. To include the pictures at less than their original size, pull down the Photo Size list and select a new size.

5. Enter a name for the disc into the CD Name box.

6. If you want to include a copy of the Picasa program on the disc, check the Include Picasa option.

7. Insert a blank CD or DVD into your PC's CD/DVD drive, and then click the Burn Disc button.

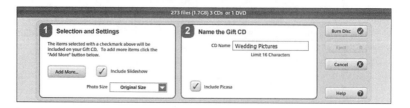

FIGURE 25.11
Getting ready to burn a picture CD.

Sharing Your Photos with Picasa Web Albums

When you want to share your photos with lots of different people, the easiest way to do that is online, via a photo-sharing site. Google has its own photo-sharing site, tied into the Picasa application; this site is called Picasa Web Albums (picasaweb.google.com).

Uploading Your Photos

To post a photo or group of photos online, select those photos within Picasa, and then click the Web Album button. If this is your first time to use this feature, you're prompted to sign in or create a new account. You can use your normal Google Account or create a separate account just for Picasa Web Albums.

Picasa connects to the Web Album website and displays the dialog box shown in Figure 25.12. You can add these photos to an existing album or create a new album. If you choose the latter option, give the album a title and description (optional). You should also choose an upload setting; in most instances, the Optimized setting works best. You should also select whether

> **note** Picasa Web Albums replaces Google's previous Web-based photo service, Hello, which is now defunct.

> **tip** You can also upload pictures directly from the Picasa Web Albums website. Just click the Upload Photos button on the main page, and fill in the blanks from there.

your album should be public (for all to see) or unlisted (viewable by invitation only). Click OK to upload the photos.

FIGURE 25.12

Uploading a photo to a Picasa Web Album.

When the upload is complete, you see a Completed dialog box. To view your uploaded photos, click the View Online button. This opens a new web browser window with your photo album displayed, like the one shown in Figure 25.13. From here you can click any photo to view it larger. You can also order prints of any photo; just select the photo and click the Order Prints button.

Mapping Your Photos

Picasa also lets you map your photos—that is, create a Google Maps mashup that pinpoints where each photo was taken. You do this after you use the Picasa program to upload your photos, from the Picasa Web Albums website. Just open a photo album and click the View Map button, and you're prompted to enter a location for your photos. After you do so, the website displays a map page with all of that album's photos thumbnailed on the left, as shown in Figure 25.14. To place a photo on the map, use the mouse to drag the thumbnail and drop it on a specific location. Click the Done button when you're done mapping your photos. (Visitors can view your photos on a map by clicking the View Map button when they visit your album.)

FIGURE 25.13

Viewing the photos in a photo album.

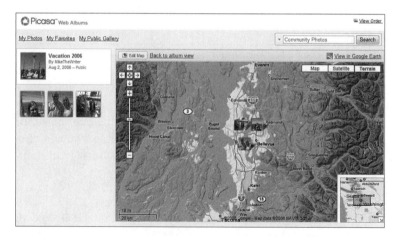

FIGURE 25.14

Adding your photos to a Google map.

Sharing Your Photos Online

To share an album with friends and family, open the album and click the Share Album button. This displays the page shown in Figure 25.15. Enter the recipients' email addresses, along with a personal message, and then click the Send Invitation button. The recipients receive an email inviting them to view the album, along with a link to the album.

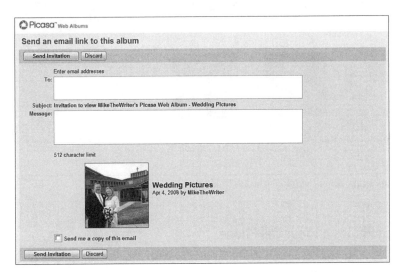

FIGURE 25.15

Inviting others to view your photo album.

To return to all your online photo albums, go to picasaweb.google.com. After you sign in, you see a page like the one shown in Figure 25.16; click an album to view the photos in that album.

note By default, Google gives you 1GB of photo storage for free, which should be enough to store close to 10,000 photos at the optimized setting.

FIGURE 25.16

The home page for all your Picasa Web Albums.

Viewing Photos on Your Cell Phone

Google also offers a version of Picasa Web Albums for mobile phone users, which lets you view your stored photos on your Web-enabled cellular phone. Point your phone's web browser to picasaweb.google.com/m/ and sign in, and you see your web albums displayed in a list, as shown in Figure 25.17. Click an album to view the photos within.

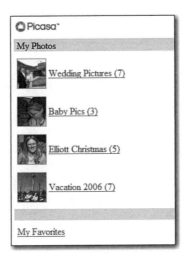

FIGURE 25.17

Viewing Picasa Web Albums on a mobile phone.

The Bottom Line

As I said at the beginning of this chapter, I really like Picasa. Practically anything I can do in Adobe Photoshop Elements and other low-priced photo-editing programs, I can do in Picasa—in many cases, faster and easier. And, unlike Elements and its competitors, Picasa is free. It's a great little program that all amateur photographers should use. Picasa makes it easy to fix those occasional bad photos that we all take.

> **note** Learn more about Picasa Mobile at www.google.com/intl/en_us/mobile/photos/.

25

Viewing and Uploading Videos with YouTube

Video is the hottest thing on the Web today. Google's a big part of that, thanks to YouTube, the largest video-sharing community on the web. It's a great place to watch videos—and to upload videos of your own!

Welcome to YouTube

YouTube is a video-sharing site that lets users upload and view all sorts of video clips online. The site is a repository for literally millions of movie clips, TV clips (both current and classic), music videos, and home videos. The most popular

note YouTube was founded in early 2005 by three former PayPal employees. The site had its official launch in December 2005 and was acquired by Google in October 2006.

YouTube videos quickly become "viral," getting passed around from email to email and linked to from other sites and blogs on the Web. If a YouTube video is particularly interesting, you'll see it pop up virtually everywhere, from TV's *The Daily Show* to the front page of your favorite website.

All of those videos and all of that sharing make YouTube one of the hottest sites on the Internet today. The YouTube site is one of the largest and fastest-growing on the Web. According to Nielsen/NetRatings, YouTube consistently ranks in the top 10 of all websites, with close to 20 million visitors per month. And those visitors are watching a lot of videos; *USA Today* reports that more than 100 million clips are viewed on the site each day, with more than 65,000 new videos uploaded every 24 hours.

What makes YouTube so appealing? It's the videos, of course, all uploaded by other YouTube users. (It's a video-*sharing* site, after all.) Whatever you want to watch, chances are you can find it on YouTube.

Many videos on YouTube are the Internet equivalent of *America's Funniest Home Videos*, amateur videos of everything from birthday parties to *Jackass*-style stunts. Anybody with a video camera can easily upload home movies to YouTube and make them available for the whole world to see.

Other videos on YouTube are decidedly more professional. Budding film professionals can post their work on YouTube, which essentially converts the site into a giant repository of filmmakers' resumes. Student films, independent videos, acting and directing tryouts—they're all there.

Then there is the category of "video blog," or *vlog*. These are video versions of the traditional text-based blog, a personal journal typically captured via webcam and posted to YouTube on a regular basis. Most video bloggers post new entries on a regular basis—or when they have something particularly interesting to say.

YouTube is also a repository for "historical" items. We're talking old television commercials, music videos, clips from classic television shows, you name it.

26

Want to revisit your childhood and watch an old Maypo commercial? Several are on YouTube. How about a clip of the Ronettes performing on *Hullabaloo*? Or the Beatles on the *Ed Sullivan Show*? Or your favorite episode from the old *Speed Racer* cartoon? They're all there, believe it or not. YouTube is a great site for nostalgia buffs, collectors, and the like.

note This chapter covers only a portion of what you can do with YouTube. For more in-depth coverage, check out my companion book, *YouTube 4 You* (Que, 2007). Or, if you're interested in using YouTube to promote your business, check out my other companion book, *YouTube for Business* (Que, 2008). It's ideal for all online marketers.

Speaking of music videos, there is no better site on the Web to find your favorite video clips. In fact, YouTube has announced that it hopes to offer every music video ever created and is in talks with Warner Music Group, EMI, Universal Music Group, Sony BMG Music Entertainment, and other record labels to make this happen. That makes YouTube a great place to promote hot new music and bands. If you're a music lover, you'll love YouTube.

A lot of current television content is also on the YouTube site. Although not every television network agrees that YouTube is a valid promotional medium (meaning that some networks have asked YouTube to pull their content), many clips from popular TV shows are still on the site—plus movie trailers, promotional videos, and similar items. YouTube is a TV and movie lover's dream.

So what's on YouTube tonight? As you can see, a little bit of everything!

Exploring—and Joining—the YouTube Site

When you first access YouTube (www.youtube.com), you see the home page, shown in Figure 26.1. This is your home base for the entire site; from here, you can browse videos, search for videos, access your favorite videos, and even upload your own videos.

To take full advantage of YouTube's features, you need to set up your own YouTube account. (You can also sign up with your normal Google account.) Naturally, you must have an account before you can upload any videos to the site. But you also need an account to save your favorite videos, create playlists, join groups and communities, and so on.

26

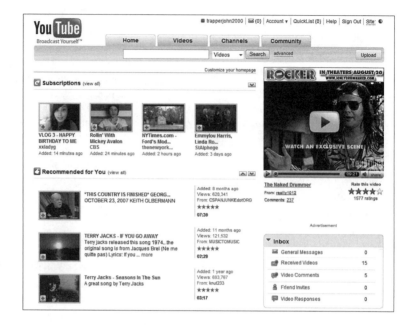

FIGURE 26.1

The YouTube home page.

Fortunately, it's both easy and free to create a YouTube account. Just go to the home page and click the Sign Up link at the top of the page. When the Join YouTube page appears, select an Account Type (for most users, a Standard account is the way to go). Then enter the appropriate personal information—email address, desired username, desired password, country where you live, postal code, gender, and date of birth—and click the Sign Up button. YouTube sends a confirmation message to your email address; click the link in that email message to confirm your subscription.

Finding Videos on YouTube

How do you find videos to watch on the YouTube site? Most new users start by browsing for interesting videos. Browsing is perhaps the best way to discover new videos; you can click through the categories until you find something you like.

caution YouTube has strict content policies and a self-policing community, but it has no parental controls.

Browsing for Videos

Browsing YouTube is a simple matter of clicking a link—and then another link, and another, and another. The more you click, the more you discover.

For example, when you choose to browse by category, you start by clicking the Videos tab on the YouTube home page. This takes you to the Videos page, shown in

> **note** Actually, many people are introduced to YouTube when they're sent a link to a particularly interesting video. If you receive such an email, just click the enclosed link; this will take you to the YouTube page for that video, and playback should start automatically.

Figure 26.2. On this page, you click a link for a particular category—Music, for example. This displays a page of featured videos in the selected category. To view an individual video on this page, just click the video.

FIGURE 26.2

Browsing YouTube via the Video page.

Searching for Videos

When you're not sure what you want to watch, browsing YouTube is probably the way to go. If you have a particular type of video in mind, however, searching is a better approach.

Searching YouTube is easy. A search box is located at the top and bottom of every YouTube page. (It's the same search box, just in different locations.) To search for a video, simply enter into this search box a keyword or two that describe what you're searching for, and then click the Search button.

YouTube returns a list of videos that best match your search criteria, as shown in Figure 26.3. If you see a video you want to watch, just click it.

caution The only problem with browsing is that you don't get to see everything that's available. That's right—you can't browse YouTube's complete video catalog. Instead, you browse a list of featured videos in that category, as selected by the YouTube staff. Still, it's a good way to explore what's available—and to see the best of the best.

tip You can also search YouTube from the main Google search site. Any Google video search you do returns primarily YouTube videos—another benefit of Google's owning YouTube!

FIGURE 26.3

The results of a YouTube search.

Each search result contains the following information:

- The opening frame from the video
- The title of the video
- The total length of the video, in minutes and seconds
- A short description of the video
- When the video was added to YouTube
- Which category the video resides in
- The user who uploaded the video (click the user's name to see all the videos in his or her channel)
- The number of times the video has been viewed
- The video's star rating (from one to five stars—more is better)

Watching YouTube Videos

The whole point of browsing or searching for videos on YouTube is to find a video to watch. Watching videos is what YouTube is all about, after all.

The nice thing about watching YouTube videos is that they play back in your web browser; no additional software is necessary, save for the flash plug-in for your browser. So get comfortable in front of your computer screen, and get ready to watch!

Exploring the Video Page

When you click the title or thumbnail of any video on a search or browse page, a page for that video is displayed, like the one shown in Figure 26.4. This page has several sections, including the following:

- **Video player.** Where you watch the videos.
- **Rating and views.** How high the video is rated and how many people have viewed it.
- **Share/Favorite/Playlists/Flag.** Tabs for sharing the video, saving it as a favorite, adding it to a playlist, or flagging it for inappropriate content.
- **Commentary/Statistics & Data.** What other users think about this video, plus detailed statistics on this video's viewership.
- **Options.** Information about the video, and a link to embed it on your own web page.

26

- **More From.** Other videos by this producer.
- **Related Videos.** A great way to explore similar videos.
- **Promoted Videos.** Videos that YouTube would like you to watch.

FIGURE 26.4

A YouTube video page.

Playing a Video

The most important part of the video page is the video player; this is where the video plays back. In fact, playback is automatic—the video starts playing almost immediately after you open the video's page.

The video itself displays in the main video player window. The playback controls are located directly under the main window. From left to right, you use these controls to

> **caution** Some large videos or videos played over a slow Internet connection may pause periodically after playback has started. This is because the playback gets ahead of the streaming video download. If you find a video stopping and starting, just click the Play/Pause button to pause playback until more of the video has downloaded.

- Pause playback by clicking the Play/Pause button; to resume playback, click the Play/Pause button again.
- Navigate anywhere within the video by using the slider control. (This control also indicates how much of the video has downloaded; the slider fills with red as the video stream downloads.)
- View the elapsed and total time for the video via the time display.
- Control the sound level by either clicking the mute button or hovering the cursor over the button to display a volume slider.
- Display the video full-screen.

Viewing Your Videos Full-Screen

By default, all YouTube videos display in the video player window in your web browser. If you'd rather watch your videos larger, however, you can display any video in its own full-screen window.

To view a video full-screen, click the Full-Screen button at the bottom right of the YouTube video player. When you view full-screen, you get the same transport controls under the video as you do on the standard video viewing page. To return to normal viewing mode, just press the Esc key.

Rating the Videos You Watch

Directly beneath the video window is the Rate box. The stars represent how high the video is rated by other viewers; 1 is lowest, and 5 is highest.

You can also use this box to add your own rating. Think a particular video is really hot? Give it a five-star rating. Think a video is really bad? Give it a one-star rating. Your voice will be heard.

To rate a video, all you have to do is drag the cursor across the stars in the Rate box; stop over the star rating you want to give, and click the mouse. After you've rated a video, your vote is added to the ratings given by other users to create an average rating.

> **caution** You may not want to watch all videos full-screen. Because most YouTube videos are optimized for the smaller video player, blowing them up to a larger size might make them too grainy or blocky to watch.

> **tip** To browse for the highest-rated videos, go to the Videos tab and click the Top Rated link at the top of the page.

26

Sharing and Saving a Video

Below the Rate box are four tabs that let you share and save the video in var‍ous ways:

- ■ **Share.** Click this tab to share this video via MySpace, Facebook, or Digg. Click the More Share Options link to post to other social sharing sites, post the video to your blog, or send the video to a friend or colleague via email.
- ■ **Favorite.** Click here to add this video to your YouTube favorites list.
- ■ **Playlists.** Click here to add this video to a video playlist.
- ■ **Flag.** Click here to tell YouTube that something about this video is unacceptable (sexually explicit, mature content, graphic violence, hat‍ speech, or other Terms of Use violation).

Reading and Posting Comments and Responses

On most video pages, the bottom left of the page is taken up by a series of viewer comments, under the Commentary tab. Users can post their comment‍ about any video; comments can be detailed or just exclamatory ("Cool video!"), depending on the person doing the posting. You can even reply to individual comments by clicking the Reply link.

To add your own text-based comment, simply scroll to the bottom of the Commentary section and use the Comment on This Video box. Enter your comments, and then click the Post Comment button.

You can also post another video as a response to a video. To do this, click the‍ Post a Video Response link. You can record a video response (using a webcam‍ and microphone), choose another video you've already uploaded to YouTube‍ as your response, or upload a new video as your response. Follow the onscree‍ instructions to choose/upload the video you want to respond with.

Viewing Statistics and Data

Want to know more about the viewership of the video? Click the Statistics & Data tab. This displays how many times the video has been viewed, rated, and chosen as a favorite; what honors the video has been awarded; which sites link to this video; and, if available, a map of where the video was recorded.

26

Viewing More Video Information

The primary information about the video is located in a box to the right of the video player. This box also includes a Subscribe button; click this button to subscribe to all videos posted by this particular user.

> **tip** When you click the Subscribe button, you're automatically notified of all new videos posted by this member.

Beneath these links is a short description of the video. When you click the More Info link, you see the full description, the category in which the video is listed, the tags used to describe the video, and the video's URL, which you can use to link to the video from your own web page.

> **tip** Click the user's name to view her YouTube channel, which includes other videos the user has uploaded.

Saving Your Favorite YouTube Videos

Watching videos on YouTube is great. But with so many videos to watch, how do you keep track of your favorites? And how do your share your favorite videos with others?

Actually, there are several ways to save your favorite videos for easier rewatching. And YouTube also makes it easy to share those videos with friends and family, via email. Read on to learn more.

Flagging Videos for Future Viewing

Here's a familiar situation. You're browsing the YouTube site, and you find a video that looks interesting, but you don't have the time or inclination to watch it right then. Fortunately, YouTube lets you save this video in a temporary QuickList, without having to open the video page and start playback. Then, when you're ready, you can go back to this video and watch it at your leisure.

To add a video to your QuickList, all you have to do is click the + button at the lower-left corner of any video thumbnail. Videos stay in your QuickList as long as your web browser is open; as soon as you close your browser window, the QuickList is flushed.

To see all the videos stored in your QuickList, click the QuickList link at the top of any YouTube page; this displays the Quicklist page, shown in Figure 26.5. Click any video to view it, or play all the videos in your Quicklist one after another by clicking the Play Quicklist link.

26

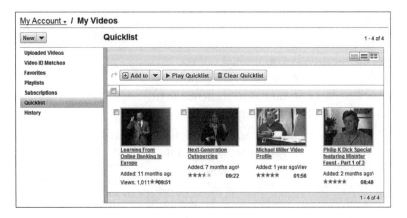

FIGURE 26.5

The Quicklist page.

Once you've added some videos to your QuickList, YouTube also places a QuickList panel on the right side of all the video pages you open. You can play videos directly from this panel, or click the QuickList title to go to the main QuickList page.

Saving Your Favorite Videos

When you view a video you really like, you don't want to forget about it. That's why YouTube lets you save your favorite videos in a Favorites list.

A YouTube Favorites list is kind of like the Favorites or Bookmarks list you have in your web browser. All your favorite videos are saved in a list that you can easily access for future viewing.

To save a video to your Favorites list, all you have to do is click the Favorite tab beneath the YouTube video player. The video is automatically added to your Favorites list.

When you want to revisit your favorite videos, hover the cursor over the My Account link at the top of any YouTube page, and then click Favorites on the drop-down menu. As you can see in Figure 26.6, this displays a list of all your favorite videos. Click any video to watch it again.

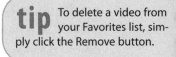

tip To delete a video from your Favorites list, simply click the Remove button.

FIGURE 26.6
The videos in your Favorites list.

Creating a Video Playlist

One of the challenges with YouTube is the sheer volume of videos available. Saving videos to your Favorites list is one way to manage this volume, but even your Favorites list can get too large to be easily manageable.

For that reason, you may want to create *playlists* separate from (or in addition to) your Favorites list. A YouTube playlist is simply a collection of videos, organized by whatever criteria you deem appropriate. You can play the videos in a playlist individually or as a group, just as you would the songs in a music playlist on your iPod. And, of course, YouTube lets you create multiple playlists, so you can have as many as you want.

There are several ways to create a playlist and add a video to that playlist. The most common method is to open the page for that video and click the Playlists tab. When the Add to Your Playlist panel appears, pull down the Select a Playlist list, select the playlist you want, and click OK.

If you haven't yet created a playlist, select [New Playlist] from the list and click OK. This displays the Create/Edit Playlist page, shown in Figure 26.7. From here, you have to enter some specific information about the new playlist:

- **Playlist Name.** The name you assign to the playlist.
- **Video Log.** Check this option if you want this playlist used as the Video Log in your channel profile page.
- **Description.** A short description of the contents of this playlist.
- **Tags.** Optional keywords you can use to describe this playlist.
- **Privacy.** Select whether this playlist should be public (for all YouTube users to view) or private (only you can view it).
- **Embedding.** Select whether this playlist can be embedded on other websites.

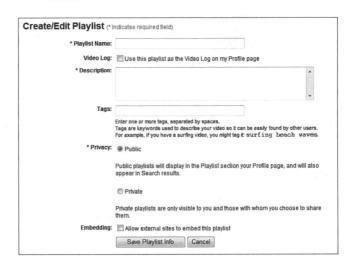

FIGURE 26.7

Creating a new playlist.

After you've filled in all the blanks, click the Save Playlist Info button. Your playlist is now saved.

Viewing Your Playlists

To view the playlists you've created, go to the YouTube home page, scroll to the bottom of the page, and click the Playlist link in the Your Account section. This displays the Playlists page, shown in Figure 26.8. All your playlists are listed on the left of the page; click a playlist name to see the videos in that playlist.

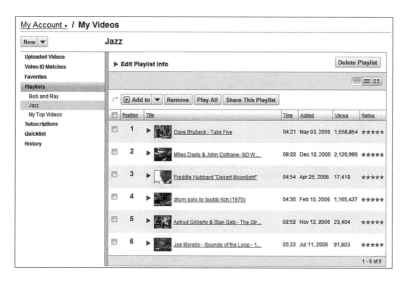

FIGURE 26.8

Viewing your YouTube playlists.

To play an individual video in a playlist, click that video. To play all the videos in a playlist one after another, click the Play All button.

Sharing YouTube Videos

If you like a YouTube video, chances are you have a friend or two who might like that video, too. That's why YouTube lets you share the videos you like. In fact, this type of video sharing is a defining feature of the whole YouTube experience.

You share YouTube videos via email. That is, YouTube lets you send an email that contains a link to the video you like to your friends. When a friend receives this email, he or she can click the link in the message to go to YouTube and play the video.

Sharing a Video Via Email

When you want to share a video, go to that video's page, click the Share tab under the YouTube video player, and then click the More Share Options link. When the Share tab expands, scroll to the Send This Video section, shown in Figure 26.9.

FIGURE 26.9

Sharing a video via email.

Enter the email addresses of the intended recipients in the To box (separate multiple addresses with commas), or select one or more recipients from your contacts list. Enter a personal message if you want, and then click the Send button. In a few minutes your recipients receive the message, complete with a link to the selected video.

To view the video, all a recipient has to do is click the video thumbnail in the message. This opens a web browser, accesses the YouTube site, and starts playing the video you shared.

Sharing a Playlist Via Email

YouTube also lets you share complete playlists with your friends. Just go to your Playlists page, select a playlist, and then click the Share This Playlist button. You now see an email window; fill in the necessary information, click the Send button, and the playlist invitation email is sent.

Downloading YouTube Videos

YouTube is a streaming video service. This means that it streams its videos from its site to your computer screen; you don't actually download and save the videos to your computer.

Even though YouTube doesn't let you download its videos, other sites and software programs step in to get the job done. There are many options for downloading YouTube videos to your computer's hard drive—and even to your iPod for portable viewing.

26

Downloading and Playing YouTube Videos with RealPlayer

Several websites and software programs let you do what YouTube doesn't—save YouTube videos to your computer's hard drive. After you've saved a YouTube video, you can watch it anytime you want, even if you're not connected to the Internet.

The best of these solutions is to use the latest version of RealPlayer (www.real.com/player/). Not only does RealPlayer enable one-button downloading of any video from the YouTube site, but it also functions as a player for .FLV-format videos (among others).

When you install RealPlayer, you also install a special add-in for Internet Explorer. This add-in automatically displays a Download This Video button above the top-right corner of any video you view on the YouTube site, as shown in Figure 26.10. (It displays the same button on any video-streaming site, so you can download videos from any website that offers streaming videos, such as CNN.com or ESPN.) To display the Download This Video button, simply hover the cursor over the video you want to download; the button should appear automatically.

FIGURE 26.10

Click the Download This Video button to download the video for RealPlayer playback.

Note that the RealPlayer program doesn't have to be running to display the Download This Video button in your web browser. The button is an add-in program that launches automatically whenever you launch your web browser.

To download a video, just click the Download This Video button. RealPlayer displays the Download & Recording Manager window and automatically saves the video to your hard drive. You don't have to do anything; the file is automatically named and saved.

To play back a saved video, launch the RealPlayer program and select the M Library tab. The videos you've downloaded in this fashion should be listed here; double-click a video to start playback. If you've downloaded a video using another download website, select File, Open to locate the file on your hard drive, and then load the video for playback.

Playback takes place within the RealPlayer window itself, as you can see in Figure 26.11. You use RealPlayer's transport controls to pause, stop, rewind, and fast-forward the video. You can even play back in slow motion by clickir Pause and then using the Slow Reverse and Slow Forward buttons.

FIGURE 26.11

Viewing a downloaded YouTube video in RealPlayer.

All in all, the new RealPlayer is an elegant solution for downloading and playing YouTube and other streaming videos. And the best thing is, it's free—which means that it's worth your consideration.

Downloading YouTube Videos to Your iPod or iPhone

If you have a video-enabled iPod or iPhone, you're always looking for new (and low-cost) videos to play on your iPod. YouTube videos are ideal for iPod playback—after they've been properly converted, that is.

Several programs available convert downloaded FLV-format YouTube videos to the MPEG-4 file format (with .MP4 or .MPV file extensions) used by the iPod. The most popular Windows-compatible programs include these:

- YouTube-to-iPod Converter (free, www.dvdvideosoft.com)
- iTube (free, www.benjaminstrahs.com/itube.php)
- Ivy Video Converter ($15, www.ipodsoft.com)

Online, the vixy.net Online FLV Converter (www.vixy.net) downloads and converts any YouTube video to iPod video format, with no software necessary. The service is free.

Viewing YouTube Videos on Your Cell Phone

If you have a Web-enabled mobile phone, such as the Apple iPhone, you can watch YouTube videos wherever you are. YouTube has gone mobile, with the new Mobile YouTube service. As you can see in Figure 26.12, the mobile interface lets you search for, download, and view videos on your Web-enabled mobile phone. (Just be sure you have a fast mobile Internet service—and a fully charged battery!) To try it, point your phone to m.youtube.com, and get ready to watch.

tip If you have one of Apple's new iPhones, you can access YouTube videos directly from the main screen. Just be sure you're connected to the Internet, and then click the YouTube button—and enjoy!

26

FIGURE 26.12
Mobile YouTube for your cellular phone.

Adding YouTube Videos to Your Website or Blog

One of the great things about YouTube is how easy it is to share YouTube videos. You've already learned how to share videos via email links; now it's time to learn how to share videos via your own web page or blog.

Linking to an Individual Video

The easiest way to reference a YouTube video from your web page is via a link to that video page on the YouTube site. Every YouTube video has its own unique URL; you can copy and paste this URL into email messages, newsgroup postings, or your own web page.

You find a video's link URL by clicking the More Info link in the description box to the right of the video. It's the bit in the URL box.

tip To insert a YouTube video link into an email message, simply copy the URL from the video page and paste it into the body of your email message.

To insert the link into a web page, copy it from the video page and insert it into your page's underlying HTML code, surrounded by the appropriate link tag. The resulting code should look something like this:

```
Click <a href="http//:www.youtube.com/watch?v=12345">here</a> to view my
YouTube video.
```

Naturally, you replace the href link with the URL from the video you're linking to. When visitors click the resulting link on your web page, they're taken to that video's YouTube page.

Embedding a YouTube Video in a Web Page

Linking to YouTube videos from your web page is one thing; embedding an actual video into your web page is quite another. That's right—YouTube lets you insert any of its public videos into your web page, complete with a video player window. And it's easy to do.

That's because YouTube automatically creates the embed code for every public video on its site (as well as your own private videos) and lists this code on the video page itself. The code is in the description box to the right of the video, in the Embed box. You need to copy this entire code (it's longer than the Embed box itself) and then paste it into the HTML code on your website.

Insert this code into your web page's HTML, where you want the video player window to appear. You get a special click-to-play YouTube video player window, inline on your web page. The video itself remains stored on and served from YouTube's servers; only the code resides on your website. When a site visitor clicks the video, it's served from YouTube's servers to your viewer's web browser, just as if it were served from your own server. (This means you don't waste any of your own storage space or bandwidth on the video.)

> **tip**
> To customize the video player that appears on your website, click the Customize link above the Embed code. This lets you change the color scheme and border for the embedded player. You also can choose not to include a list of related videos with the player.

Adding YouTube Videos to Your Blog

If you have a blog, YouTube makes it easy to send any public YouTube video to your blog as a blog posting. First, however, you have to tell YouTube about your blog so that it knows where to send the post.

> **note**
> Learn more about creating your own blog in Chapter 18, "Blogging with Blogger."

26

Start by clicking the Account link at the top of any YouTube page. When the My Account page appears, scroll down to the Account section, and click the Blog Posting Settings link. When the Blog Posting Settings page appears, click the Add a Blog/Site button.

> **note** YouTube supports automatic posting to the following blog hosts: Blogger, BlogSpot, Freewebs, Friendster, LiveJournal, Piczo, and WordPress.

YouTube displays the Add a Blog/Site page, shown in Figure 26.13. Pull down the Blog Service list and select your blog host; assuming you're using Blogger, it's in the list. Enter your blog username and password, click the Add Blog button, and you're finished with this preliminary setup.

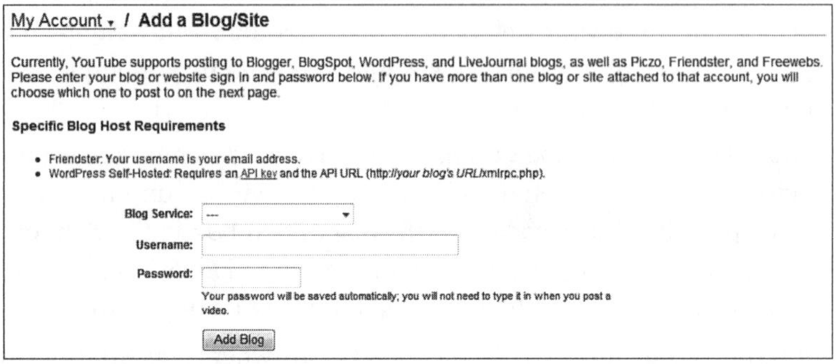

My Account ▾ / Add a Blog/Site

Currently, YouTube supports posting to Blogger, BlogSpot, WordPress, and LiveJournal blogs, as well as Piczo, Friendster, and Freewebs. Please enter your blog or website sign in and password below. If you have more than one blog or site attached to that account, you will choose which one to post to on the next page.

Specific Blog Host Requirements

- Friendster: Your username is your email address.
- WordPress Self-Hosted: Requires an API key and the API URL (http://your blog's URL/xmlrpc.php).

Blog Service: ---

Username:

Password:

Your password will be saved automatically; you will not need to type it in when you post a video.

Add Blog

FIGURE 26.13

Adding a blog to your YouTube configuration.

After the configuration, it's a snap to send any public YouTube video to your blog. Just open the video page, click the Share link, and then click the More Share Options link. When the Share panel expands, scroll down to the Post to a Blog section, shown in Figure 26.14. Pull down the Blog list and select your blog, enter a title for this post, and then enter any text you want to accompany the video. Click the Post to Blog button, and YouTube posts the video (and accompanying text) to your blog as a new post.

> **tip** If you have multiple blogs, you can configure YouTube accordingly. Just repeat this setup procedure for each blog you post to.

FIGURE 26.14

Adding a YouTube video as a blog post.

Uploading Videos to YouTube

As you know, YouTube isn't just for viewing; you can also upload your own videos to the YouTube site. How you do this depends on what type of video you're uploading.

Uploading Videos from Your PC

Most users upload videos that are stored on their PC's hard disk. YouTube makes this kind of PC-based upload easy.

First, however, you have to make sure that your video file meets YouTube's requirements, which are as follows:

- MPEG-4 format video with either DivX or XviD codecs
- MP3 format audio
- 640×480 resolution
- Frame rate of 30 frames per second (FPS)
- Length of 10 minutes or less
- File size of 100MB or less

Assuming that your video is in a YouTube-approved format, you're ready to upload. You start by clicking the Upload button in the top-right corner of any YouTube page. This displays the Video Upload page, shown in Figure 26.15. You now have a little paperwork to do.

26

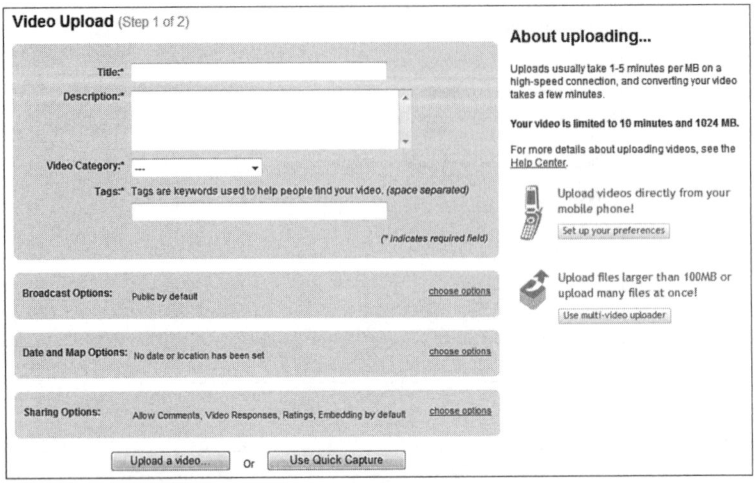

FIGURE 26.15

Getting ready to upload your video to YouTube.

First, enter a title for your video. Make sure it's descriptive without being overly long. Then enter a description for the video; this can (and should) be longer and more complete.

Next, pull down the Video Category list, and select a category for the video. Then enter one or more tags for the video, separating each tag with a space. Tags are keywords people use when searching; use as many tags as necessary to capture all possible search words.

The next three parameters typically are set in advance, although you can change any of the defaults by clicking the appropriate Choose Options link. These include Broadcast Options (whether the video is public or private), Date and Map Options (when and where the video was recorded), and Sharing Options (whether you want to allow comments, links, and embedding). Click the Upload a Video button when you're ready to proceed.

Step two of the video upload process is where you specify the file to upload. Click the Browse button to open the Choose File dialog box; navigate to and select the file you want, and then click Open.

This loads the filename into the Select a Video to Upload box on the Video Upload page.

When these steps are done, the final step is to click the Upload Video button. YouTube

> **tip**
> Use the private option when you're sharing home videos with friends and family.

finds the video on your hard disk and starts uploading it; the progress is shown on the Video Upload page.

After you click the button, you need to be patient; it can take several minutes to upload a large video, especially over a slow Internet connection. Additional processing time is needed after the upload is complete, while YouTube converts the uploaded video to its own format and adds it to the YouTube database.

When the video upload finishes, YouTube displays the Upload Complete page. To view your video, click the My Videos link on any YouTube page, and then click the thumbnail for your new video.

note Videos you upload are not immediately available for viewing on YouTube. They must first be processed and approved by the site, which can take anywhere from a few minutes to a few hours.

caution When you use Quick Capture to upload "live" webcam videos to YouTube, you can't edit those videos; whatever you record is what gets shown on YouTube, warts and all.

Uploading Videos from Your Webcam

If you have a webcam video camera connected to your PC, you have two ways of uploading webcam videos to YouTube.

caution If you see an Adobe Flash Player Settings window on the Quick Capture page, click the Allow button.

First, you can save your webcam videos as you normally do and then upload those videos via YouTube's normal video upload process. Or, if you like, you can upload videos as you shoot them, "live" from your webcam.

This second method of uploading webcam videos utilizes YouTube's Quick Capture feature. Here's how it works.

With your webcam connected and running, click the Upload button on any YouTube page. When the Video Upload page appears, enter the title, description, and other information as normal, but then click the Use Quick Capture button.

This displays the Quick Capture page, shown in Figure 26.16. Pull down the list boxes above the video window to select your webcam video and audio options. You should see the picture from your webcam in the video window; click the Record button to start recording.

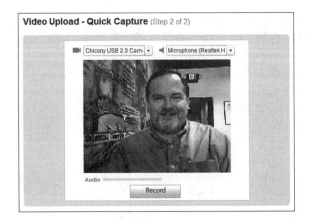

FIGURE 26.16
Getting ready to record a "live" webcam video with Quick Capture.

When you're finished with the recording, click the Stop button. At this point you can click Cancel to delete your recording, click Preview to view a preview of the video you just recorded, or click Save to save your video to the YouTube site. When you click Save, YouTube automatically uploads the video to the site and displays the Upload Complete page. Your video will be available for viewing in a few minutes.

Uploading Videos from Your Mobile Phone

Finally, if your mobile phone has a built-in video camera, you can upload videos directly from your cell phone without first copying them to your PC. All you have to do is set up YouTube's mobile upload options and then email your videos to the YouTube site.

To configure YouTube for your mobile phone, click the Account link at the top of any YouTube page. When your Account page appears, scroll down to the Account section and click the Mobile Video Upload Settings link. When the next page appears, supply the necessary information. This includes the profile name, video title, whether you want the filename or date appended to the video title, a short description of the profile, whether your mobile videos should be public or private, tags for your mobile videos, a category for your videos, whom you want to share them with, and how you want to be notified when the upload is complete. Click the Save Settings button, and your profile is created.

26

Your completed profile includes the email address to which you should send your mobile videos, typically a series of numbers @mms.youtube.com. To upload a video from your mobile phone, simply email the video to this address. You're notified via email or text message when YouTube has received the email and begun processing the video; you can then go to YouTube's website and edit specific information about the newly uploaded video.

COMMENTARY

GOOGLE'S OTHER VIDEO SITE: GOOGLE VIDEO

YouTube isn't the only video site in the mighty Google empire. Before there was YouTube, there was Google Video (video.google.com), which, unfortunately, was a flop.

Originally (pre-YouTube acquisition), Google Video was intended to be a competitor to YouTube and other Web video sites, offering a combination of user-uploaded videos and commercial videos for sale. Google Video never gained much traction, however, which is why Google purchased YouTube.

However, Google kept the Google Video site, which ultimately morphed into the site it is today. It is nothing more or nothing less than a video version of Google Images—that is, a site you can use to search the Web for specific types of videos. The only thing is, Google Video pretty much limits its search to YouTube videos (Google does own YouTube, after all), so it doesn't return too many results from other sites. Still, it's a nice interface for searching YouTube, if nothing else. Just don't expect to see a lot of non-YouTube videos in your search results!

26

The Bottom Line

YouTube is one of the shining stars of the Web, a top-ten site on its own before it was absorbed into the Google empire. It's a great place to find interesting videos to watch, and to upload your own videos for others to watch. It's easy to spend hours surfing the YouTube site, watching one video after another. There's lots of good stuff there!

Working with Google Maps

Finding Your Way with Google Maps

N ot sure how to get to a particular location? In the old, pre-Internet days, you had to try to find addresses on your AAA roadmap, or humble yourself by stopping and asking directions at the local gas station. Thanks to the Internet, however, you can now use Google Maps to generate online maps and driving directions.

You'll never stop for directions again.

Introducing Google Maps

Of all the cool Google features, I find Google Maps to be the absolute coolest. Not only does Google Maps compete head-to-head with other online mapping sites, such as MapQuest, Microsoft's Live Search Maps, and Yahoo! Maps, but it offers a raft of unique and, dare I say, *fun* features. It'll help you get to where you want to go, and show you a lot of neat and useful information on the way there.

> **tip** Google also offers many Google Maps services for use on your cell phone. Learn more in Chapter 35, "Using Google on Any Mobile Phone."

Google Maps (maps.google.com) offers a ton of useful mapping services, all packed into an easy-to-use interface. Yes, you can generate maps for any given address or location, but you can also click and drag the maps to view adjacent sections, overlay the map info on satellite images of the given area, view local traffic conditions, display nearby businesses as a series of pushpins on the map, and have Google Maps plot driving directions to and from this location to any other location.

And all this map and direction stuff is done from the familiar Google search box. Unlike other map sites, there are no forms to fill out; just enter what you want to see into the search box, and let Google Maps do the rest.

Searching for Maps

As the name implies, Google Maps is all about the maps. To display a map of a given location, all you have to do is enter information about that location into the top-of-page search box, shown in Figure 27.1. When you click the Search button, a map of that location is displayed on the page.

Searching by Address

The most obvious way to display a map of a given location is to enter the location's street address or general location. There are a number of ways you can enter an address or a location, as detailed in Table 27.1.

Table 27.1 Google Maps Address Formats

Address Format	Example
city, state	indianapolis, in
ZIP	46204
address, city, state	101 e washington street, indianapolis, in

Address Format	Example
address, city, ZIP	101 e washington street, indianapolis, 46204
street intersection, city, state	e washington and n Pennsylvania, indianapolis, in (can use the & sign instead of the word "and")
street intersection, ZIP	e washington and n Pennsylvania, indianapolis, 46204 (can use the & sign instead of the word "and")
latitude, longitude	39.767, -86.156
airport code	LAX
subway station, country (in UK and Japan only)	paddington, uk

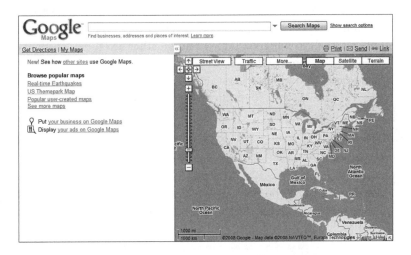

FIGURE 27.1
The Google Maps home page.

Remember to put a comma after each part of the address. In most instances, you don't need to spell out words like "east," "street," or "drive"; common abbreviations are okay, and you don't need to put a period after the abbreviation.

For many major cities, Google Maps also accepts just the city name. For example, entering **miami** gives you a map of Miami, Florida; entering **san francisco** displays a map of the California city. If, on the other hand, you enter a city name that's fairly common (such as **greentown**—which appears in Indiana, Ohio, and several other states), Google will either display a map of the largest city with that name, or provide a list of cities or matching businesses for you to choose from.

If you want to enter latitude and longitude, you have two options. First, you can enter latitude and longitude as decimal degrees, using the - sign to express west longitude or south latitude. Second, you can use N, S, E, and W designations. What you *can't* do is express latitude and longitude using degrees-minutes-seconds (such as 28 24' 23.4"); Google doesn't recognize the ' and " syntax.

If Google doesn't recognize an address you entered (such as when an address could either be on an "east" or a "west" street, or the same address for a "drive" and a "lane"), Google will display a list of possible addresses. Assuming you can identify the correct address from this list, click the link to display the map of that location.

Searching by Landmark

Sometimes you don't need to know the exact address to generate a Google map. Google has hard-coded many landmarks and institutions into its map database, so that you only have to enter the name of the landmark or location into the search box. For example, entering **hoover dam** generates the map shown in Figure 27.2.

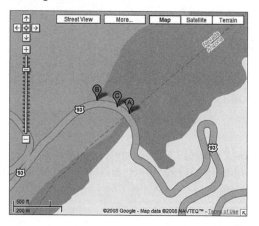

FIGURE 27.2

The Hoover Dam on a Google map.

Displaying Street Maps from a Google Web Search

Here's another tip. You don't have to go to the Google Maps page to display a Google map. When you enter a street address, city, and state (or ZIP code) into the standard Google web search box, the OneBox at the top of the search results page displays a small map of the address, shown in Figure 27.3. Click the link to see the full Google Maps page, or use the Start Address box to generate a page of driving directions to the address.

> **caution** What landmarks are and are not in the Google Maps database is somewhat arbitrary. It's always worth trying, but don't be disappointed if what you're looking for isn't so easily found.

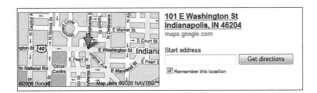

FIGURE 27.3

Map results from the standard Google search page.

Navigating a Google Map

When you map an address, Google displays a map of that address in the right side of the browser window, as shown in Figure 27.4. The address itself is listed in the Search Results tab on the left side of the window (along with pictures of that address, if available), and information about the address is displayed as a balloon overlaid on the main map. You can use the balloon info to set this address as your default location in Google Maps, to generate driving directions to or from this address, to initiate a search for nearby businesses, or to save this map in Google's My Maps. (More on all these features later in this chapter.)

Once you have a Google map displayed onscreen, there are many, many different ways to navigate around, into, and out of the map—both with your mouse and with your computer keyboard. Table 27.2 describes the ways.

> **tip** To display the map the full width of your browser window, click the little arrow on the top-left corner above the map. This hides the entire left-hand panel, and expands the map to fill the space.

27

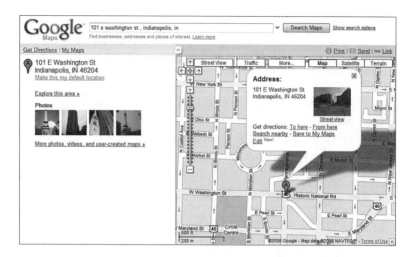

FIGURE 27.4

A typical Google Maps display; information about the mapped address is displayed in a text balloon.

Table 27.2   Google Map Navigation

Navigation	With Mouse	With Keyboard
Pan left (west)	Click the left arrow button.	Press the left-arrow key—or pan wider with the Home key.
Pan right (east)	Click the right arrow button.	Press the right-arrow key—or pan wider with the End key.
Pan up (north)	Click the top arrow button.	Press the up-arrow key—or pan wider with the Page Up key.
Pan down (south)	Click the bottom arrow button.	Press the down-arrow key—or pan wider wit the Page Down key.
Zoom out (wider area)	Click the - button *or* drag the zoom slider down.	Press the − key.
Zoom in (smaller area)	Click the + button *or* drag the zoom slider up.	Press the + key.

You can drag the map in any direction by positioning the cursor anywhere on the map, clicking and holding the mouse button, and then dragging the map around. You can also reposition the map by dragging the little blue rectangle in the inset map (located in the lower-right corner of the main map) to a new

27

location. And you can simply center the map on a new location by positioning the cursor over that location and then double-clicking the mouse.

tip To re-display the last map you viewed, click the Return to Last Result button in the middle of the arrow buttons on the map.

The closer you zoom in, the more detail displayed on the map. You won't see specific road information until you're fairly zoomed in; even then, major roads are displayed first, and then minor roads displayed on more extreme zoom levels. For example, Figures 27.5, 27.6, and 27.7 show different levels of zoom over Branson, Missouri; note the emergence of detailed road info at the closer zoom levels.

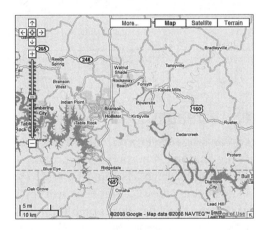

FIGURE 27.5

Branson, Missouri—not so close up.

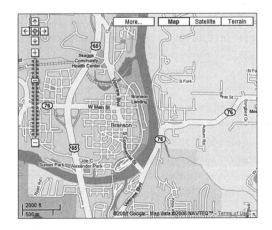

FIGURE 27.6

Branson, viewed a little closer—note the major highway labeling.

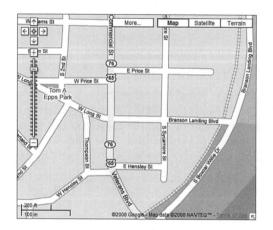

FIGURE 27.7

Branson at a more extreme zoom—even the smallest streets are labeled.

Displaying Satellite Images

By default, Google Maps displays a standard map of any location you enter. But that's not the only way you can view a location. Google Maps also incorporates satellite images, which lets you get a bird's eye view on the actual location. It's like having access to your very own spy satellite! Be warned, however, that Google's satellite images aren't always current, meaning that you could be looking at an image that was taken today or months ago! Google doesn't say how current any of its satellite images are.

The View from Above

To display the satellite image of a location, click the Satellite button at the top of the map. You can use the standard navigation and zoom controls to pan around and zoom into or out of the satellite image. Depending on the level of magnification, you may be able to see rooftops and trees. (Figure 27.8 shows a satellite map of Chicago's Wrigley Field—if it were game day, you could almost see the pitcher on the mound!)

note Google Maps sources its map from NAVTEQ and TeleAtlas. It sources its satellite images from DigitalGlobe and EarthSat. Note that the satellite images are apt to be less current than the map data.

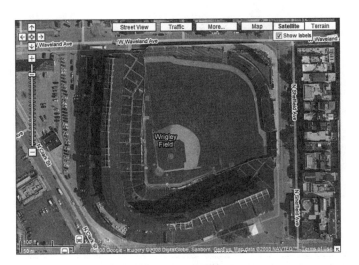

FIGURE 27.8

A satellite map of Wrigley Field.

And here's something kind of creepy. Some satellite images have been digitally altered, supposedly for "national security" reasons. For example, Figure 27.9 shows 1 Observatory Circle in Washington, D.C., the official residence of the Vice President. As you can see, the entire area on the left has been pixilated on the map to keep anyone (terrorists included, I suppose) from seeing what's going on there. (Interestingly, a similar view of the White House is completely unpixelated, which makes one wonder what it is about the VP's place that makes it more top secret than the President's house....)

caution If you zoom in too far on a satellite map, you may reach the limits of the satellite imagery. That is, not all locations have super-high-resolution satellite photos. When you zoom in too far, you'll see a screen with the repeated message "We are sorry, but we don't have imagery at this zoom level for this region." If you see this message, zoom out a little to see what you can see.

27

FIGURE 27.9

A digitally altered satellite image of the Vice President's residence.

Displaying Terrain Maps

Want to view the different types of terrain (woods, fields, lakes, and so on) in a given location? Your wish is Google's command; just click the Terrain button to view a color-coded terrain map, like the one shown in Figure 27.10.

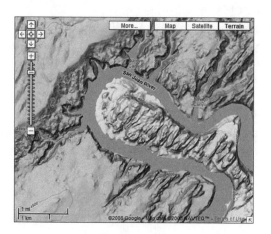

FIGURE 27.10

Viewing a terrain map of the San Juan River, near Monument Valley, Utah.

Displaying Street View Photos

Here's something else new and cool on Google Maps—for selected locations, anyway. If you're viewing a map of many cities and towns, you see a Street View button. Click this button, and certain streets on the map turn blue, as shown in Figure 27.11, and you see a little person icon standing on the street. Click the icon, and Google displays a panoramic photo of that location, as shown in Figure 27.12.

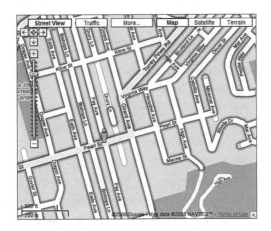

FIGURE 27.11

Blue-lined streets have Street View photos attached.

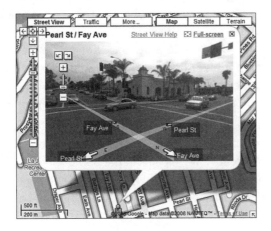

FIGURE 27.12

A Google Street View panoramic photo.

Use your mouse to pan left or right around the photo, or drag within the photo to move up or down the street. You can also use the navigation controls in the upper left of the photo to pan around and zoom in and out of the photo. To display the

> **note** If Street View is not available for a given location, the Street View button will not be present.

panoramic photo full-screen, click the Full-screen link in the photo window.

COMMENTARY

TOO MUCH EXPOSURE?

Google Street View photos are supplied by Immersive Media, a company that specializes in 360-degree photography. (Except for the San Francisco Bay area, where Google staff took their own photos.) The photos are taken with a special revolving camera fitted on the top of a car, snapping one photo each second. Multiple photos are sewn together digitally to give the panoramic view.

These Street View photos have generated a bit of controversy for their apparent invasion of privacy. For example, one photograph showed people playing hooky from work, another showed someone furtively going into an adult bookstore, and another showed a gentleman apparently scaling a privacy fence around a sealed building. All a bit embarrassing, if you're the one in the photo. Technically, there's nothing illegal about snapping a photo of someone in a public place. But what if you're sitting inside a restaurant, still visible to the Street View camera? Or you're inside your house but can be seen through your living room window? And do you really want your license plate viewable by everyone on the web, if you happen to be driving down the street when a photo is snapped? The situations become murkier.

If you find yourself in a Google Street View photo and don't want the attention, you can petition Google to remove your photo from the site. Click the Street View Help link in the photo window, and then click the Report Inappropriate Image link. The following page lets you request a photo removal based on the image infringing on your privacy, containing inappropriate content, or presenting personal security concerns. (An image of you breaking into a military installation while not wearing any pants might fit under all three categories.)

27

Viewing Live Traffic Conditions

How can Google make Google Maps even more useful? How about adding live traffic data?

That's right, Google Maps (in both its desktop and mobile versions) now displays live traffic conditions for over 30 major cities. To display this traffic data, just call up a map and then click the Traffic button.

> **tip** This live traffic data is especially useful when you're driving, which is why it's great that I can access it via Google Mobile on my cell phone. See Chapter 35 for more details.

As you can see in Figure 27.13, major roads appear as green (smoothly flowing traffic), yellow (busy), or red (congested). Road construction is indicated by a separate icon, as are road closures. And on interstate highways, you get the green/yellow/red separately for lanes in both directions!

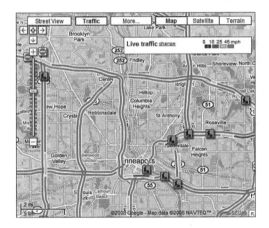

FIGURE 27.13
Minneapolis traffic conditions via Google Maps.

Sharing Maps

Once you've created a map of a given location, it would be great if you could save the map for use in the future—rather than re-entering the location and manipulating the navigation and zoom controls. Fortunately, there are several ways to save and share the maps you create. Read on to learn more.

27

Linking to a Specific Map

The key to saving or sharing any map you've created is that Google assigns every possible map its own unique URL. When you know the URL, you can share it with others—or save it to your computer desktop.

tip If you're running Google Desktop, Google offers a Maps gadget for the sidebar. Learn more in Chapter 4, "Creating a Custom Workspace with Google Desktop."

Here's how it works:

1. Create a map for the desired location.
2. Click the Link link.
3. Google now displays the URL for this map in a separate dialog box. Highlight this URL, right-click your mouse, and select Copy from the pop-up menu.
4. To paste this link into an email message or text document, position your cursor in the message, right-click your mouse, and select Paste from the pop-up menu.

Alternatively, you can save the map as a shortcut on your desktop. To do this, create the map, click the Link link, highlight the URL, and then drag it onto your desktop.

Emailing a Map

There's an even easier way to email a map to friends and family—or to yourself, so you'll have a link to the map as a message in your inbox. Just follow these steps:

1. Create a map for the desired location.
2. Click the Send link.
3. This opens a new email message in your default email program. As you can see in Figure 27.14, the link to the map is displayed in the text of the message; enter the recipient's email address, and then click the Send button.

Printing a Map

Of course, you can also just print a hard copy of the map. This is as easy as clicking the Print link above the map you've created; nothing more is necessary.

FIGURE 27.14
Emailing a link to a map you created.

Displaying Driving Directions

Google Maps does more than just display maps; it can also generate driving directions from one location to another. It's a simple matter of entering two locations, and letting Google get you from point A to point B (and even to points C and D).

Generating Turn-by-Turn Directions

To generate driving directions, follow these steps:

1. From the Google Maps main page, click the Get Directions link.

2. The left-hand pane now expands to include two search boxes, as shown in Figure 27.15. Enter your starting location into the first (A) box, and your ending location into the second (B) box.

3. Assuming that you're driving to your destination, select By Car from the pull-down list. (If you're walking to a destination within a major city, select Walking from the list instead.)

4. Click the Get Directions button.

tip
If Google mapping locations on this planet is too limiting for you, check out Google Moon (www.google.com/moon) and Google Mars (www.google.com/mars). As the names imply, these are Google Maps for extraterrestrial bodies, in the form of landing site images (for Google Moon) and shaded relief maps (for Google Mars). These are fun applications of Google Maps technology—and they're educational, too!

27

FIGURE 27.15

Entering starting and ending addresses.

You can also generate driving directions to or from any location you've previously mapped. When the location is pinpointed on the map, click either the To Here or From Here links in the info balloon. The balloon now changes to include a Start Address or End Address box; enter the second address, and then click the Go button.

Generating Multiple-Stop Directions

Initially, Google Maps only let you generate simple driving directions, from one point to another with no stops in-between. But that's seldom how we drive, especially on long trips and vacations.

That's why Google has finally added multiple-stop directions to Google Maps. This means you can plan a multi-stop trip (point A to point B to point C), instead of merely going from point A to point C with no stops in-between.

To create multiple-stop directions, start by generating directions from the starting point to your first stop. Then click the Add Destination link; this extends the Directions panel to include a third (C) address box. Enter your second stop into this box, then click the Add Destination button; directions from the first stop to the second stop will now be generated. Keep clicking the Add a Destination link to create more complex trips and directions.

Following Directions

However you enter your locations, Google now generates a page of driving instructions, as shown in Figure 27.16. The step-by-step directions are listed on the left side of the page; an overview map is displayed on the right.

> **tip** Google also lets you generate driving directions directly from the Google Maps search box. Just enter your first location, followed by the word **to**, followed by the second location. For example, to drive from San Francisco International Airport to the Transamerica Building in downtown San Francisco, enter **SFO to 505 sansome st, san Francisco, ca**.

27

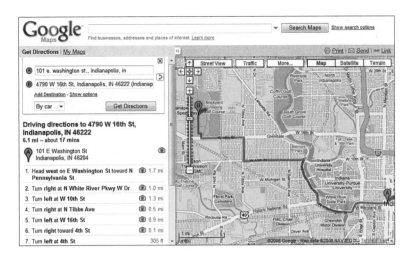

FIGURE 27.16

Driving directions and a map of your route.

It seems pretty straight ahead so far, but there's a neat little feature hidden on this page. When you click any of the numbered steps on the left, a Street View photo pops up on top of the overview map, as shown in Figure 27.17. This is a great way to see those detailed directions that are easy to misunderstand—as long as photos are available for that location, of course.

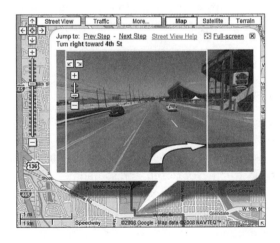

FIGURE 27.17

A pop-up Street View photo that zooms into a particular piece of your route.

Changing Your Route

Don't like the directions that Google suggested? Rather take a slightly different route to your destination? Well, fortunately for you, Google lets you change your driving directions—just by dragging the route on the map.

tip You can also fine-tune your directions to avoid highways and tolls. Just click the Show Options link in the Get Directions pane and make the appropriate selections.

Here's how it works. Generate your driving direction as normal, then locate that part of your route that you want to change. Click that part of the route, press and hold down your left mouse button, and then drag the route to a different location. The route readjusts to include the changes you've made.

For example, generate driving directions from Indianapolis to Minneapolis. (That's a long drive—which I can confirm from experience!) The default directions route you through Chicago, but that's not the only (or best) way to go. If you'd rather travel via central Illinois, click on the Chicago area of the route and drag it down to Bloomington, Illinois. The directions now change to reflect your preferred route.

Printing Your Directions

One last thing. Google Maps' driving directions are great, but they won't do you any good if they're displayed on your home PC screen while you're on the road. To take a copy of your directions with you, just click the Print link. This makes a hard copy printout of the directions page, map and all.

COMMENTARY

BAD DIRECTIONS

I've learned from experience that Google's driving directions aren't always perfect. Sometimes they provide a longer or more circuitous route than you might prefer; sometimes they include roads that are under construction or closed; and sometimes they're just plain wrong. As an example, Google recently directed my wife to turn the wrong way into a one-way street—not an ideal route!

Google recognizes this, and provides the following caution in the Google Maps help system:

> **Google Maps may occasionally display incorrect locations or direc-
> tions. You may also find that the icon for a location you've mapped
> on a satellite image is off by a house or two. Please be assured that
> we're continually working to improve the accuracy of this service.**
>
> Like that really helps when you've just turned into a road that isn't
> there. Although it's good to know they admit they have occasional
> problems, I'd rather not have to deal with bad directions from the start.
>
> If you're served up bad directions or a faulty map, you can let Google
> know about it by going to maps.google.com/support/bin/request.py.
> This page leads to a series of web forms that let you input your com-
> plaints and criticisms—including specific errors you encounter. Use it,
> but be polite.
>
> I've also found that Google Maps sometimes offers different routes
> than served up by MapQuest, Yahoo! Maps, and other competing map
> sites. I'm not sure why this is; perhaps the different services use differ-
> ent algorithms to determine the shortest or most direct route. In any
> case, I recommend inputting your coordinates into several map sites
> when you're planning a longer trip; you might find a better route than
> the one Google Maps provides.

Finding Nearby Businesses

One of the most useful features of any online mapping service is being able to
find and map nearby businesses. That's also one of the key features of Google
Maps, as you'll soon learn.

Searching for Businesses

As part of its Google Maps service, Google hosts a large database of local
retailers. This lets you use Google Maps to search for retailers within any area
or neighborhood, or near any address.

The easiest way to find a local business is to start with a map of your location.
Now enter the name or type of business into the top-of-page search box, then
click the Search Maps button.

27

Viewing Local Businesses

Google now displays a map of the specified location with matching businesses pinpointed on the map and listed on the left side of the page, as shown in Figure 27.18.

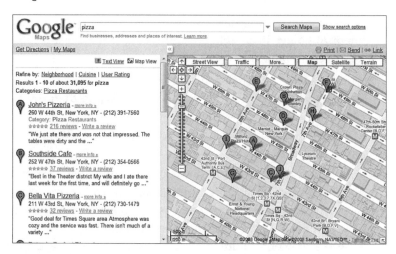

FIGURE 27.18

The results of a Google Maps business search.

When you click a business name or pinpoint, an information balloon appears, as shown in Figure 27.19. To display more information about a business, click the More Info link in the Search results page; this displays a new box of information and links.

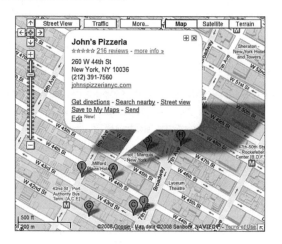

FIGURE 27.19

Displaying general information about a business.

Note that Google Maps only lists 10 businesses per page. To display the next page of results, you have to scroll down the left side of the page and then click the Next link. The map will change (zoom in or out) to display this next batch of businesses; Google Maps typically lists the closest businesses first, and then expands its results, geographically.

> **tip** Google Maps gathers the bulk of its local retailer information from various Yellow Pages directories. If your business isn't automatically included, you can add your business to the Google Maps database from Google's Local Business Center (www.google.com/local/add/). Follow the onscreen instructions to submit your business info; you can also use this page to correct or delete existing business information.

The Bottom Line

Google Maps is a worthy competitor to more established map sites such as MapQuest and Yahoo! Maps. What sets Google Maps apart is its interactive zoomable and movable maps, and its capability to display satellite imagery and hybrid maps in addition to traditional maps. You also get a great search function you can use to find local businesses, as well as live traffic data for many major cities. I used to use MapQuest in years past, but I've long switched all my map-based activities to Google Maps; it's that much better.

Google Maps also lets anybody access its map database to create a Google map "mashup"—that is, a specialized application that adds new data to a standard Google map. You learn how to create your own custom Google maps in Chapter 28, "Creating Google Map Mashups;" read ahead to learn more.

Creating Google Map Mashups

O ne of the coolest things about Google Maps is that Google lets anyone can create his or her own custom Google map, overlaid with his or her own personal data. These maps can be accessed from your Google Maps page, or posted on your own website.

This overlaying of third-party data points on a Google map is called a Google map *mashup*. That's because you're mashing together a Google map with your own personal data. That data might simply be a set of coordinates so that you map a specific location, or it might be a collection of locations that you want to display on a map.

You don't have to be a programmer to create your own map mashups. Read on to learn the various ways to create your own custom Google maps.

Creating Simple Mashups with My Maps

If you want to create a custom map for your own personal use, the easiest way to do this is with Google's new My Maps feature. As you can see in Figure 28.1, My Maps is located on its own tab on the Google Maps page; you use this tab to create new maps and to access previously created ones.

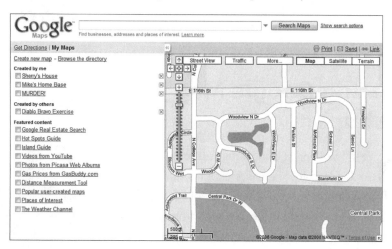

FIGURE 28.1
The My Maps tab on the Google Maps page.

Creating a Custom Map

To create a My Maps mashup, go to the Google Maps page and enter the location you want to map. Once the map is onscreen, click the My Maps link (in the left-hand pane) and then click the Create New Map link. As you can see in Figure 28.2, four new buttons now appear on your map, and the My Maps tab changes to allow data input.

tip The My Maps tab includes all your saved map mashups, as well as selected mashups from other users, as selected by Google.

28

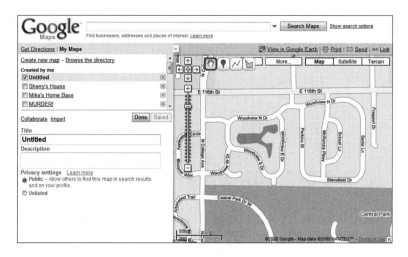

FIGURE 28.2

Getting ready to create a new custom map with My Maps.

To highlight a location on the map:

1. Click the Add a Placemark button and then click the location on the map. This places a placemark on the map and opens an information balloon for editing, as shown in Figure 28.3.

2. Enter a title and description for the placemark; you can enter either plain text, rich text, or HTML code.

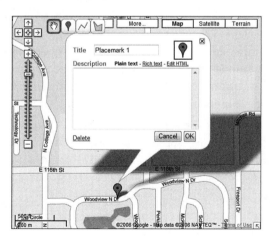

FIGURE 28.3

Adding a placemark to your map.

28

3. To change the color or shape of the placemark, click the Placemark icon (in the placemark balloon); this displays a menu of choices, as shown in Figure 28.4. Click a new icon to select it.

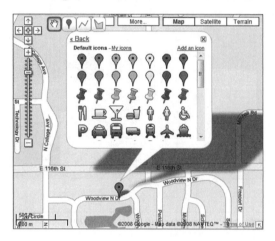

FIGURE 28.4

Changing the placemark icon.

4. To add a picture to a placemark, click the Rich Text link in the place-mark balloon. The balloon now changes to include a variety of editing options. Click the Photo icon (last icon on the right); when the input dialog box appears, enter the URL of the photo and click OK.

5. You can also insert YouTube videos into your placemarks. For this, open the placemark balloon for editing and click the Edit HTML link. Next, open a second browser window, go to the YouTube site, and copy the snippet of code displayed for embedding the video on other web pages. Now return to your My Maps placemark balloon and copy that code snippet into the Description box.

6. You can also draw lines and areas on the map. Just use the Draw a Line and Draw a Shape buttons; click once on the map to start draw-ing, click again to draw a second segment, and then double-click to stop drawing.

7. When you've finished creating your map, enter a title and description into the My Maps pane on the left.

> **note** Any picture you add to a placemark must be hosted on another website.

28

8. If you want the map to be accessible only to you, check the Unlisted option; if you want to share your map with others, click the Public option.

9. Click the Save button when done, and the map will now appear in your My Maps list.

Of course, you can add more than one placemark to any map. Just repeat the preceding steps to create as content-rich a mapping experience as you want.

Sharing Your My Maps Mashups

One of the nice things about My Maps is that you can share them with others. For example, if you're an apartment owner, you might want to create a map of all your properties, and then share it with potential renters.

To share a map you've created, go to My Maps and display the map. Click the Link link above the map; this displays the map's URL in a new dialog box. You can then copy this URL onto your website or your blog for public use.

Even easier, if you want to email your custom map to others, display the map and then click the Send link. This opens a new email message with the link to the map already embedded. Enter the normal To: and Subject: information; then send the message to interested parties.

Embedding a Map on Your Website

Once you've created your mashup, you can embed the resulting map in your own website. All you need is a bit of HTML editing knowledge, and you're ready to go.

Start by creating your map; then click the Link link above the map. The second box in the resulting dialog box includes the HTML code you use to embed the map. Highlight and copy this code; then paste the code into the appropriate spot in your web page's HTML. The map will now be displayed on your web page.

If you want more control over how the map looks on your page, click the Customize and Preview Embedded Map link. This opens a new browser window that lets you choose the size of the embedded map (Small, Medium, Large, or Custom). Select the size you want; then copy the resulting HTML code into your web page's HTML.

28

Collaborating on Group Mashups

A Google Maps mashup doesn't have to be a solitary affair. Because these ar
web-based maps, Google lets you collaborate with others on your mashups.

All you have to do is click the Collaborate link in the My Maps pane. This
opens the dialog box shown in Figure 28.5. Enter your collaborators' email
addresses into the Invite Collaborators box, add a message, and select
whether you want collaborators to invite others. Click the OK button, and
your collaborators will be emailed the URL of the mashup to edit at their
pleasure.

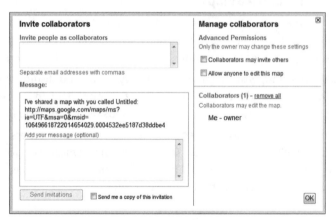

FIGURE 28.5
Inviting collaborators to a group mashup.

Creating Complex Mashups with the Google Maps API

For more sophisticated map mashups, you have to use the Google Maps API.
This API lets you embed advanced Google
Maps in your own web pages. You need to
know a little HTML and JavaScript, but it's
not that hard to create a basic map.

To create more advanced map mashups,
you just add more sophisticated code. For
example, the Google maps API lets you
add custom markers, info windows, and
overlays to your maps. Each element is
added via a distinct line of code, which

> **note** *API* stands for
> *Application
> Programming Interface.* You use
> APIs to interface one application
> with another, or with a web data-
> base such as that offered by
> Google Maps. Learn more about
> Google's APIs in Chapter 43,
> "Using Google's APIs and
> Developer's Tools."

then uses the Google Maps API to retrieve the appropriate map from Google. Like all of Google's other development tools, the Google Maps API is free for your noncommercial use.

Using the Google Maps API

To use the Google Maps API, you have to obtain a license key. This key can be used only on the web domain you specify—so if you plan on using a practice board or another website for development, you'll want to get a key for that site in addition to your main site.

You obtain your Google Maps API key at www.google.com/apis/maps. This is also where you download the API's documentation, access online help files, and link to the official Google Maps API blog. (You can also access the blog directly at googlemapsapi.blogspot.com.)

To obtain a license key, you'll need to have a Google account, and then enter the domain of your website. Google will then email you the key, which you'll include in all your Google Maps code.

Creating a Basic Map

To create a static map focused on a specific location, you need to create three blocks of JavaScript code. One block goes in the **<HEAD>** section of your document, the next augments the **<BODY>** tag, and the final block goes into the body of your document where you want the map to appear.

Let's start with the opening code. Insert the following lines of code between the **<HEAD>** and **</HEAD>** lines of your document:

```
<script src="http://maps.google.com/maps?file=api&amp;v=2&amp;key=APIKEY"
type="text/javascript">
</script>
<script type="text/javascript">
//<![CDATA[


function load() {
if (GBrowserIsCompatible()) {
var map = new GMap2(document.getElementById("map"));
map.setCenter(new GLatLng(LATITUDE, LONGITUDE), ZOOM);
}
}


//]]>
</script>
```

28

In this code, replace *APIKEY* with the license key Google supplied to you. I stated this in the previous section, but it bears repeating: The key is specific to the web domain you specified when you applied for the key; if you use this code on another website, you'll need to edit the code to use a separate license key for that site.

You'll also need to replace *LATITUDE* and *LONGITUDE* with the precise latitude and longitude coordinates of the location you want to map. You can obtain these coordinates by generating a map on the Google Maps site, clicking the Link to This Page link, and then copying the coordinates from the resulting URL. (Latitude and longitude are listed in the URL following the &ll parameter.) For example, I generated a map for St. Catherine College in St. Paul, Minnesota; the latitude and longitude coordinates for this location are **44.928835, -93.185177**.

In addition, you want to replace *ZOOM* with a number from 0 to 17. The smaller the number, the wider the view; to zoom into street level, try a zoom of 13 or larger.

Next, you need to edit the **<BODY>** tag to include the following parameters:

```
<BODY onload="load()" onunload="GUnload()">
```

Finally, insert the following line of code into the body of your document, where you want the map to display:

```
<div id="map" style="width: 500px; height: 300px"></div>
```

You can play around with this last line of code a bit. For example, you can make the map larger or smaller by using different width and height parameters, or center the map on the page by surrounding it with **<CENTER>** and **</CENTER>** tags. It's your choice in terms of formatting.

Adding Map Controls

You may have noticed that the map you created is just a map—it doesn't include any controls that let users zoom around or into or out of the default location. That's fine if you want a static map (of your company's headquarters, let's say), but if you want to make the map interactive, you have to add the appropriate map controls. You do this by adding the following lines of code between the **var map** and **map.setCenter** lines in the **<HEAD>** of your document:

```
map.addControl(new GSmallMapControl());
map.addControl(new GMapTypeControl());
```

The resulting map now includes the expected right, left, up, down, and zoom in/zoom out controls—as well as the Map/Satellite/Hybrid display controls.

Adding an Info Balloon

Another neat thing is to display an info balloon centered on the location you selected. The info window can display whatever text you specify.

To create an info window, enter the following lines of code directly after the **map.setCenter** line in the <HEAD> of your document:

```
map.openInfoWindow(map.getCenter(),
document.createTextNode("YOURTEXT"));
```

Naturally, you replace *YOURTEXT* with the text you want to appear in the info window.

Creating an Animated Map

Here's an example of a neat effect you can add to your map. By inputting two locations into the code, you can make your map pan from one location to another. This is a good effect to add when you're showing how to get from one location to another.

All you have to do is insert the following lines of code after the **map.setCenter** line in the <HEAD> of your document:

```
window.setTimeout(function() {
  map.panTo(new GLatLng(LATITUDE2, LONGITUDE2));
}, 1000);
```

Naturally, replace *LATITUDE2* and *LONGITUDE2* with the coordinates for the second location on the map. Increase the **1000** parameter if you want to slow down the speed of the pan.

Adding a Marker to Your Map

What's a map mashup without an icon to mark a specific location? All you have to do is insert the following lines of code after the **map.setCenter** line in the <HEAD> of your document:

```
var point = new GLatLng(LATITUDE,LONGITUDE)
map.addOverlay(new GMarker(point));
```

Replace *LATITUDE* and *LONGITUDE* with the precise latitude and longitude of the marker's location, of course.

28

Adding Multiple Markers from Your Own Database

A first-class map mashup plots multiple markers on a map, based on a data-base of individual locations. Each location in the database has to be express as a latitude/longitude coordinate, of course; the database of coordinates can then be easily plotted as an overlay on the base Google map.

Let's start with the database of locations. You need to create an XML file named **data.xml**. The contents of the file should be in the following format:

```
<markers>
   <marker lat="LATITUDE1" lng="LONGITUDE1" />
   <marker lat="LATITUDE2" lng="LONGITUDE2" />
   <marker lat="LATITUDE3" lng="LONGITUDE3" />
   <marker lat="LATITUDE4" lng="LONGITUDE4" />
</markers>
```

Add as many **<marker>** lines as you like, each with its own coordinates.

You then call this file into your Google Maps code, using the **GDownloadUrl** command. You do this by adding the following lines of code after the **map.setCenter** line in the **<HEAD>** of your document:

```
GDownloadUrl("data.xml", function(data, responseCode) {
   var xml = GXml.parse(data);
   var markers = xml.documentElement.getElementsByTagName("marker");
   for (var i = 0; i < markers.length; i++) {
     var point = new GLatLng(parseFloat(markers[i].getAttribute("lat")),
                             parseFloat(markers[i].getAttribute("lng")));
     map.addOverlay(new GMarker(point));
```

This adds a new overlay to your map, with each point from the **data.xml** file translated into its own marker on the map. Cool!

And Even More...

This gives you a pretty good idea of how to add a simple Google map to your web page. To create more sophisticated mashups, you need to get more famil-iar with the Google Maps API and the use of overlays. That's more detail than we have space for here, but you can find all the documentation you need on the Google Maps API site. It's not that hard, especially if you know your way around a little JavaScript. And the results are worth it!

FINDING GOOGLE MAP MASHUPS ON THE WEB

Now that you know how easy it is to create your own custom Google map mashups, it should come as no surprise that there are a lot of these mashups on the web. There are mashups that display everything from community statistics to local bus stops to available housing to who knows what.

Where, pray tell, does one find all these Google map mashups? One can search Google with the query **google map mashup**, of course, or one can just go to the Google Maps Mania blog (googlemapsmania.blogspot.com). This blog lists the best and the latest map mashups; it's "unofficial," but it's the de facto directory to the world of Google map mashups.

Another good source of map mashups is CommunityWalk (www.communitywalk.com). This is a site that lets you create your own mashups, based on simple web-form entry; it's also host to a ton of user-created mashups. It's worth a look.

The Bottom Line

Unlike some other types of Google application development (which we'll cover later in this book), creating your own custom Google Maps mashup is relatively easy. Whether you use My Maps or do your own HTML scripting, creating a map mashup is a great way to display specific information or add map data to your own web page.

28

Getting the Big Picture with Google Earth

If you like the maps you get with Google Maps, you're going to love Google Earth. Google Earth is a software program that lets you create, view, and save high-resolution, three-dimensional fly-bys of any location on the planet. This might sound like a high-end, expensive piece of software, and you'd be half-right; Google Earth (the basic version, anyway) is available free of charge for all users.

Read on to learn more.

29

Which Version Is for You?

Before you use Google Earth, you have to download the software to your PC, which you do from earth.google.com. Google offers four different versions of Google Earth:

- Google Earth (basic), the version for most users that lets you perform a variety of general mapping functions. This version is a free download.

- Google Earth Plus, which can be purchased for $20. This version includes all the features of the basic version, and adds support for GPS devices (Magellan and Garmin units only), the ability to import spreadsheet data, a variety of drawing tools for annotation purposes, and high-resolution printing.

- Google Earth Pro, designed for professional and commercial use. This version, which costs $400, includes all the features of Google Earth Plus, augmented with multiple terabytes of detailed aerial and satellite images from cities around the world, the ability to import custom data and blueprints, and use a variety of add-on modules. The add-on modules (which cost $200 apiece) include a Movie Making Module (for creating WMV-format movies of zooms and tours), a Premium Printing Module, a GIS Data Importing Module, a CDT Traffic Counts Module, and an NRB Shopping Center Data Module.

- Google Earth Enterprise, which offers a variety of on-site deployment solutions for large organizations, including Google Earth Fusion (integrates custom data), Google Earth Server, and Google Earth EC (Enterprise Client). Contact Google for custom pricing.

Which version should you use? For most individuals, the basic (free) version is more than adequate. If you want to interface Google Earth with a GPS unit, spend the twenty bucks for Google Earth Plus. And if you intend to use Google Earth for professional use (commercial real estate, construction and engineering, insurance, intelligence and homeland security, and so on), investigate the much more robust Google Earth Pro or Google Earth Enterprise versions.

For the purposes of this chapter, however, we'll focus on the basic version of Google Earth.

Introducing Google Earth

When you first launch Google Earth, you see a large view of the planet Earth, as well as surrounding navigation and display controls, as shown in Figure 29.1. The major parts of the screen include three panes (Search, Places, and Layers), the main view display, and the navigation controls. You can hide or display certain parts of the interface by checking them on or off in the View menu.

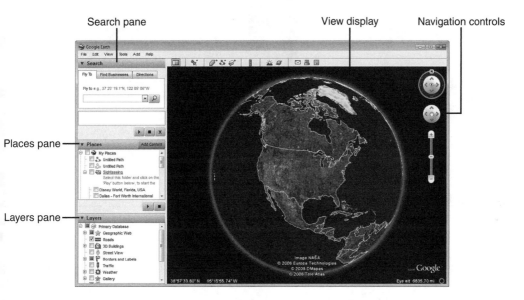

FIGURE 29.1

The Google Earth interface.

Navigating Google Earth

You start your journey through Google Earth from the 3D view of the globe. You can zoom in on any location on the planet, and navigate from place to place around the planet. All it takes is a mastery of Google Earth's navigation controls.

Of course, since you're doing three-dimensional navigation, complete with panning, tilting, and rotating, the navigation is a bit more complicated than what you have with a flat web-based Google map. With Google Earth, you can navigate around the 3D globe by using the navigation controls along the right side of the screen, by using your mouse, or by using select keyboard commands. We'll look at each method in turn.

Navigating with the Onscreen Navigation Controls

Perhaps the easiest way to navigate Google Earth is with the onscreen navigation controls, shown in Figure 29.2. Just click the appropriate control with your mouse, and you can do the following:

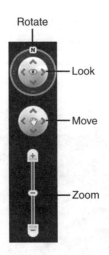

FIGURE 29.2

Google Earth navigation controls.

- Click the Zoom In and Zoom Out buttons (or use the corresponding slider control) to zoom into or out of the map. Clicking Zoom In (+) displays a closer, more detailed view; clicking Zoom Out (-) displays a further away, less-detailed view.

- Click and drag the Look control to move around from a single vantage point, as if you're turning your head.

- Drag the Rotate control (the outer ring of the Look control) to rotate the view. (Rotating clockwise moves north to the right; rotating counterclockwise moves north to the left.)

- Double-click the North button (the N at the "top" of the Rotate control) to return north to the straight-up position.

- Click or click and drag the Move control to move your position from one point to another.

Both the Look and Move controls work like a joystick—that is, you can use your mouse to click and hold each control, and then drag your mouse to move or look in the designated direction. It sounds more complicated than it is; these controls are really quite easy to use.

Navigating with the Mouse

If you're handy with your mouse, you can use it alone (without the onscreen navigation controls) to zoom around Google Earth.

Here's what you can do:

- To zoom in to a specific point, double-click on that point in the viewing pane.

- To generally zoom in, use your mouse's scroll wheel (if it has one) to scroll toward you. You can zoom in smaller increments by holding down the Alt key on your keyboard while scrolling.

- You can also generally zoom in by clicking and holding the *right* mouse button, and then moving your mouse up (away from you).

- To generally zoom out, use your mouse's scroll wheel to scroll away from you. You can also click and hold the right mouse button, and then move your mouse down (toward you).

- To zoom continuously in or out, hold down the right mouse button, briefly move the mouse up (to zoom in) or down (to zoom out), and then quickly release the mouse button. To stop the zoom, click once in the viewer.

- To move the map in any direction, click and hold the left mouse button, and then drag your mouse in the desired direction.

- To "drift" continuously in any direction, hold down the left mouse button, briefly move the mouse in the desired direction, and then quickly release the mouse button. To stop the drift, click once in the viewer.

- To tilt the view, hold down the Shift key on your keyboard and then move the mouse's scroll wheel up or down. Alternatively, if your mouse has a depressible scroll wheel or middle button, depress the scroll wheel or middle button and then move the scroll wheel up or down.

- To rotate the view, hold down the Ctrl key on your keyboard and then move the mouse either left or right. Alternatively, if your mouse has a depressible scroll wheel or middle button, depress the scroll wheel or middle button and then move the mouse either left or right.

Navigating with the Keyboard

You can also navigate through any Google Earth view by using your computer keyboard. Table 29.1 details the keyboard navigation commands.

Table 29.1 Google Earth Keyboard Navigation Commands

Navigation	Keyboard Command
Move left	Left arrow
Move right	Right arrow
Move up	Up arrow
Move down	Down arrow
Zoom in	Ctrl+Up arrow *or* +
Zoom out	Ctrl+Down arrow *or* -
Tilt up	Shift+Up arrow *or* PgUp
Tilt down	Shift+Down arrow *or* PgDn
Rotate clockwise	Shift+Right arrow
Rotate counterclockwise	Shift+Left arrow
Stop current motion	Spacebar
Reset tilt	u
Reset view to "north-up"	n
Reset both tilt and compass view	r

Taking a Quick Tour of Google Earth

Now that you know how to get around in Google Earth, let's take a quick tour

Anytime you start Google Earth, the view defaults to the extended zoom of the planet Earth, focused on the continent of North America. This is a great place to start because you can get just about any place you want from here.

Let's start by panning east (to the right) until we focus on Europe. Double-click the N button on the Rotate control to put North back at the top, and then click the up-arrow button until Europe is centered onscreen, as shown in Figure 29.3.

tip You can make more refined movements (that is, move more slowly) by holding down the Alt key in combination with most of these keyboard commands.

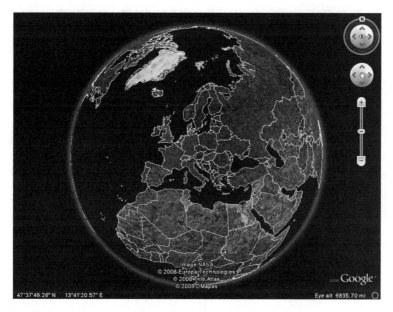

FIGURE 29.3

The Google Earth globe panned east and north, to focus on Europe.

Next, we want to zoom into the map. Click the Zoom In button (or use the zoom slider control) until France fills up the screen; then use a combination of zooming and panning until you see the city of Paris, as shown in Figure 29.4.

Now zoom further into the city, following the river Seine to the west (left). You'll notice a grouping placemarks on the map; each placemark denotes a specific location or attraction. When you hover your cursor over a placemark, the name of that location appears. Look for the swirly placemark shown in Figure 29.5; this is the Eiffel tower. Zoom into the Eiffel tower placemark until you get the view shown in Figure 29.6.

FIGURE 29.4
Zooming in on Paris.

FIGURE 29.5
The placemark for the Eiffel tower.

Next, rotate around and zoom in a little more until you're looking down the bridge beside the tower. As you can see in Figure 29.7, you can make out individual cars on the bridge—pretty neat!

FIGURE 29.6
Zooming in on the Eiffel tower.

FIGURE 29.7
An even closer view, looking down the bridge.

And, to demonstrate how easy it is to navigate directly to placemarked locations, go to the Places pane, open the Sightseeing folder, check the Google Campus placemark, and then click the Play button. After a dizzying spin-and-turn around the globe, you'll see the Googleplex appear, as shown in Figure 29.8. Feel free to zoom in and see exactly what Google's world headquarters looks like—up close and personal!

FIGURE 29.8
A Google Earth view of Google's worldwide headquarters.

Making Google Earth More Three-Dimensional

Google Earth offers two options to make its three-dimensional views look even more realistic—by displaying 3D buildings and terrain.

Let's look at the 3D buildings option first. Start by opening the Places pane and going to the London Eye placemark. Zoom in and tilt the map a little, until you see the view shown in Figure 29.9. That's the big Ferris wheel by the Thames, although it's hard to tell from this view. Now check the 3D Buildings option in the Layers pane, and Google Earth will add the blocky 3D structures shown in Figure 29.10—a much more realistic perspective of what this area of London really looks like.

FIGURE 29.9

A non-3D view of the London Eye.

FIGURE 29.10

The same view of the London Eye, with 3D structures added.

The 3D terrain option is a good one when you're viewing an area of hilly terrain. You turn this on by checking the Terrain option in the Layers pane. You can see this option at work by going to the Grand Canyon placemark. The view without the 3D ter-

rain function enabled is shown in Figure 29.11; Figure 29.12 shows the much more realistic look with the 3D terrain.

FIGURE 29.11

A non-3D view of the Grand Canyon.

FIGURE 29.12
The same view of the Grand Canyon, with 3D terrain.

Configuring View Options

Google Earth is quite versatile in terms of what you see onscreen. There are a lot of viewing options, more than we can cover here, but we'll try to address some of the most popular and useful ones.

Setting View Preferences

Most of Google Earth's view options are set from within the Options dialog box, shown in Figure 29.13. You open this dialog box by selecting Tools, Options.

> **tip** The Terrain option should be enabled by default; the 3D Buildings option isn't.

FIGURE 29.13

The Options dialog box.

Within the Options dialog box, you want to select the 3D View tab. From here you can adjust the settings detailed in Table 29.2.

Table 29.2   Google Earth View Settings

Setting	Description
Texture Colors	Sets the color depth of the display; True Color (32 bit) displays a more realistic view.
Anistropic Filtering	This is a texture mapping technology that produces a smoother-looking image, especially around the horizon (when viewing a tilted angle). You should turn this on only if your graphics card has at least 32MB memory.
Labels/Icon Size	Determines the default size for labels and icons in the viewer.
Graphics Mode	Google Earth is a graphics-intensive application. If your PC has a high-powered graphics card, it can run in the better-looking Direct X mode. If, however, your PC has a less-powerful graphics card (as do many notebook PCs), you can run Google Earth in the less-demanding OpenGL mode. (Safe mode is used only when you're experiencing display problems.)

Setting	Description
Show Lat/Lon	Displays latitude and longitude in either degrees, minutes, and seconds; degrees only; or using the universal transverse Mercator (for professional mapsters).
Show Elevation	Displays elevations in either feet and miles or meters and kilometers.
Fonts	Determines which fonts are used to display labels in the viewer.
Terrain Quality	Enables you to select a higher-quality terrain display (takes longer to draw) or a lower-quality one (runs faster on most PCs).
Elevation Exaggeration	Choosing a higher number exaggerates the height of tall objects (terrain and buildings) in the viewer.
Overview Map	Selects the size of the overview map, as well as the degree of zoom relation.

Using Full-Screen Mode

By default, the Google Earth viewer appears in a window within the Google Earth window. To display the viewer full-screen, press the F11 key (or select View, Full Screen). To return to the standard mode, press F11 again.

Displaying a Latitude/Longitude Grid

To overlay a latitude/longitude grid on any Google Earth view, press Ctrl+L (or select View, Grid). This grid tilts along with the overall view tilt.

Displaying the Overview Map

There's one more view setting that can help you navigate Google Earth. This is the Overview map, which you switch on by pressing Ctrl+M (or by selecting View, Overview Map). As you can see in Figure 29.14, this shows you where you are in the viewer in relation to the rest of the world. You can double-click anywhere in the Overview map to navigate to that location.

FIGURE 29.14
The Overview map displayed in the Google Earth viewer.

Saving and Printing a View

You can save any image displayed in the Google Earth viewer by selecting
File, Save, Save Image. You can also print the current image in the viewer by
selecting File, Print. Note, however, that the free version of Google Earth prints
images only at screen resolution; the $20 Google Earth Plus prints images at a
much higher resolution—about 2400 pixels, according to Google.

Searching for Locations to View

You know how to zoom and pan around the Google Earth globe—but this isn't
always the easiest way to zoom into a specific location. Fortunately, Google
Earth lets you search for places just as you do in Google Maps, and then zoom
directly into the desired location.

To search for a location, make sure the Fly To tab is selected in the Search
pane and then enter the location into the search box. When you click the
Search button, Google Earth zooms into the location you entered.

As with Google Maps, Google Earth lets you search using a variety of entry
formats. Table 29.3 details the different ways to search for a location:

Table 29.3   Google Earth Search Formats

Format	Example
location	Disney World
country	France
city country	paris france
city, state	minneapolis, mn
ZIP	60515
number street, city, state	1500 opus place, downers grove, il
number street, city, ZIP	1500 opus place, downers grove, 60515
cross street, city, state	42nd and broadway, new york, ny
latitude, longitude (in decimal)	37.7, -122.2
latitude, longitude (in DMS format)	37 25'19.07"N, 122 05'06.24"W

By the way, Google Earth also lets you search for businesses by using the Find Businesses tab in the Search pane. You can search within the current view, or within any city, state, or country you enter. Items that match your query are pinpointed in the view pane.

Displaying Driving Directions

You can also use Google Earth to map driving directions, just as you can with Google Maps. The big difference in using Google Earth for this purpose is that your directions are mapped in a 3D view, so you can get more of a bird's-eye view of where you'll be driving.

Getting Directions

The easiest way to generate driving directions is to select the Directions tab in the Search pane, and then enter your starting (From) and ending (To) addresses. When you click the Search button, your route is mapped onscreen, with each turn placemarked on the map, as shown in Figure 29.15. You can zoom into, rotate, pan, and tilt the map as you like, as well as zoom into any specific

note Street-level searching is limited to locations in selected countries only.

direction by double-clicking that placemark. As you can see in Figure 29.16, zooming into a placemark like this gives you a very good idea of what you'll encounter when you make your trip.

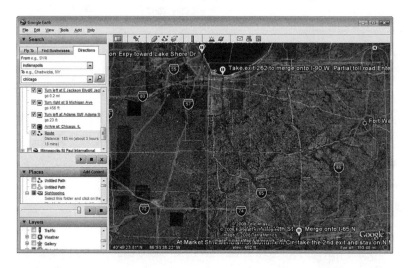

FIGURE 29.15
Using Google Earth to generate driving directions.

FIGURE 29.16
Zooming into a specific turn-by-turn instruction—it's almost like you're there!

Touring Your Route

And here's an even neater feature. Once you have your route displayed onscreen, you can use Google Earth's tour feature to "fly" the complete route in the viewer. Just select the Route item at the end of the directions listing, click the Play button, and get ready for a wild ride!

Printing and Saving Directions

To print step-by-step directions for your route, all you have to do is click the Printable View link in the directions listing. This will open a Google Maps web page in a new browser window, with the directions displayed in that window. From this window, click the Print link to print the directions.

To save your route for future use, select File, Save, Save Place As. Confirm or enter a new filename for your trip, and then click the Save button.

Displaying and Using Layers

One of the things that makes Google Earth so useful is its capability to overlay other data on top of its maps. This data is added in the form of *layers*; available layers can be enabled via the Layers pane.

You've already seen several different types of layers in use. When you enabled the 3D buildings and terrain features, you added these layers to the underlying map. Disable the feature, and the layer is taken away.

There are many other kinds of layers you can add to most Google Earth maps, from roads and geographic features to dining, lodging, and other attractions. See for yourself what's available—check an option to display that layer, and uncheck the option to hide it.

> **tip**
> In the Layers pane, layers are organized in folders. Double-click a folder to see and activate specific layers within the major layer category.

Displaying Places of Interest

Many of the layers available in Google Earth contain what are known as places of interest (POI). These are specific locations overlaid on a map, such as ATMs, restaurants, gas stations, and the like.

When you click a POI, Google Earth displays an information box for that item,

> **caution**
> Not all layers contain information for all locales. For example, you won't find 3D building data for the middle of the Nevada desert.

like the one shown in Figure 29.17. Within this info box is information about this location, as well as links to additional information.

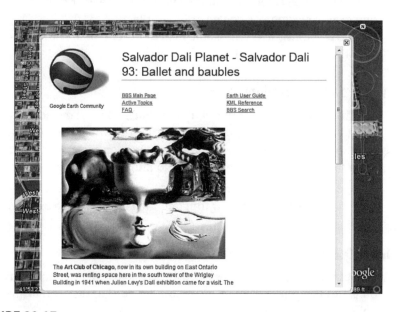

FIGURE 29.17
Viewing information about a place of interest.

Right-click a POI, and you get a pop-up menu that lets you copy or save this location, as well as generate driving directions. Saving the POI puts it in your My Places folder in the Places pane, so you can return to it at any future time. Alternatively, you can copy the POI and then paste it into a specific subfolder in the My Places folder.

Creating Custom Placemarks

About that My Places folder.... This is a folder where you can store any item for future use. You can store pre-existing POIs, as we just discussed, or store custom placemarks that you create yourself.

To mark any place on any Google Earth map as a placemark, follow these steps:

1. Zoom into the location you want to placemark.

2. Click the Add Placemark button on the toolbar navigation panel (or select Add, Placemark).

3. A new, blank placemark is now placed on the map. If the placemark is not in the correct location, use your mouse to drag it around the map as necessary.

4. Also appearing at this time is a New Placemark dialog box, like the one shown in Figure 29.18. Enter a new name for the placemark, along with any descriptive text you'd like. You can also click the appropriate tabs to change the style or color of the placemark, as well as additional attributes. When you're done making your selections, click the OK button.

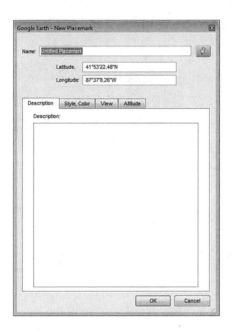

FIGURE 29.18

Entering information about the new placemark.

The placemark is now set on the map, with the name you provided. The placemark is also stored in the My Places folder.

Flying Google Earth's Flight Simulator

As if using Google Earth normally wasn't cool enough, the program also includes a built-in flight simulator! That's right, you can "fly" through Google Earth locations just as you would with a commercial flight simulator game.

29

To enter Google Earth's Flight Simulator mode, select Tools, Enter Flight Simulator. This displays the Flight Simulator dialog box shown in Figure 29.19. You can select from two different aircraft, a high-tech F16 fighter jet or an SR22 prop plane. You can also select your starting position, and whether you're using a joystick or not. Make your selections and then click the Start button.

This launches you on your flight, as shown in Figure 29.20. The best way to control your plane is with a joystick, but you can also use your computer keyboard. Good flying!

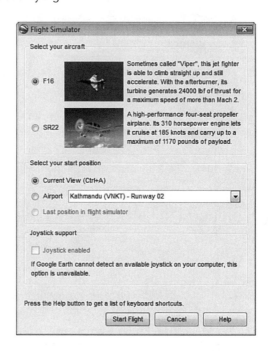

FIGURE 29.19

Configuring Google Earth's Flight Simulator.

FIGURE 29.20
Flying Google Earth's Flight Simulator.

Stargazing with Google Sky

And here's something else new and cool about Google Earth—it doesn't just show you the Earth, it also shows you the sky! That's right, Google Earth now includes Google Sky, a collection of stellar maps and pictures as seen by the Hubble Space Telescope.

> **tip** For a list of Flight Simulator keyboard commands and other instructions, go to earth.google.com /intl/en/userguide/v4/ ug_flightsim.html.

You enter Google Sky by clicking the Sky button on Google Earth's toolbar or by selecting View, Switch to Sky. As you can see in Figure 29.21, you navigate Google Sky the same way you navigate Google Earth. Sky also has its own layers, and you can search for objects using the normal search box. Click on any interstellar object to learn more about it—or, if you're well-versed in astronomical science, search for specific objects you want to view. Google Sky makes astronomy fun!

> **tip** You can also access a web-based Google Maps version of Google Sky, available at www.google.com/ sky.

29

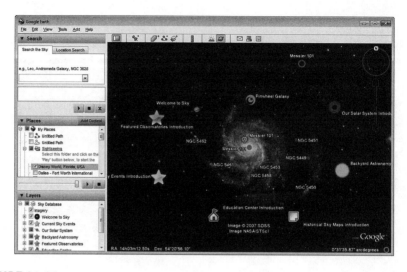

FIGURE 29.21

Space, the final frontier—as seen via Google Sky.

The Bottom Line

Google Earth is an incredibly feature-rich application. Even if you're just a casual user, you can have lots of fun zooming into specific locations, doing route fly-bys, and the like. The program's 3D capabilities take basic mapping to a new level—and provide added functionality. And that's not even mentioning the Flight Simulator or Google Sky, both of which are a lot of fun (and, in the case of Sky, educational!).

Bottom line? I like Google Earth a lot. I don't use it for all my mapping needs (Google Maps is just fine for most things, to be honest), but when I want an added bit of realism, it's the way to go. It's certainly worth your time and money (it's free, remember) to give it a look.

VII

Using Other Google Services

Keeping Up-to-Date with Google News

S ure, Google's main gig is the super search engine we all know and love (and its main source of revenue is selling ads on all those search results pages), but Google has also become one of the primary online resources for newshounds worldwide. Not that you have to search the Google index for old news stories (although you can, if you want to); no, Google does all the hard work for you with its Google News service.

Google News is a news-gathering service that identifies, assembles, and displays the latest news headlines from more than 4,500 different news organizations. It also offers a comprehensive news archive search, with more than 200 years' worth of historical newspaper articles available. So, whether you want the latest news or the oldest news, Google has it.

Viewing the Latest Headlines and Stories

You get to Google News directly at news.google.com, or by clicking the News link on any Google page. As you can see in Figure 30.1, Google News organizes its stories by category and lists a number of related stories under each lead headline. More headlines are displayed when you click the All Stories link under each story.

FIGURE 30.1
The default Google News page.

By the way, if you don't like the default headline+photos view, you can click the Text Version link to view an all-text version of the Google News page. As you can see in Figure 30.2, this version of Google News looks more like a standard Google search results page.

And there's even a new all-photo version, great for those who prefer a more visual approach to news gathering. Click the Image Version link to see the page shown in Figure 30.3.

FIGURE 30.2

Google News in all-text view.

FIGURE 30.3

Google News in all-image view.

Google News organizes its stories into nine sections that roughly correlate with the topic-oriented sections you find in a major daily newspaper. If you're using the standard view, you can see all the headlines in each section by clicking the section link in the left navigation box. The sections include the following:

- Top Stories
- World
- U.S.
- Business
- Elections (during major election years)
- Sci/Tech
- Entertainment
- Sports
- Health
- Most Popular

note Google doesn't write any of its own news stories; it has no reporters or editors on staff. Instead, it uses its search technology to search major news sites on the Web and collate the most relevant, most up-to-date news headlines on a single web page. (Google News headlines are updated every 15 minutes.)

To read any story, just click the headline link. This takes you from Google to the story on its originating website, with the selected story displayed.

Viewing International News

Not surprisingly, Google News isn't just for American users. Google offers more than 40 country- or language-specific versions of Google News, with each version customized with news of interest to that country. For example, Figure 30. shows the Italian version of Google News.

FIGURE 30.4
Google News for Italy.

To switch to a different country's news site, you can pull down the country list at the top of the Google News page, or click on a country link at the bottom of the page.

Personalizing Google News

The default Google News page is good, but you can also create a version of Google News customized for your own personal tastes and interests. That is, you can personalize Google News to display only those types of stories that you want to see.

To personalize Google News, click the Personalize This Page link. This displays a Personalize This Page box, as shown in Figure 30.5.

FIGURE 30.5

Personalizing Google News.

From here, you can rearrange any of the standard modules by simply dragging and dropping them into new positions. To change the number of stories displayed within each module, or to delete a module from the page, click the link within any section module.

You can also click the Add a Standard Section link to add a module from any of the U.S. or international versions of Google News. Or, if you like, you can create your own custom news modules by clicking the Add a Custom Section link. This displays the Add a Custom Section box, shown in Figure 30.6. Custom modules are essentially custom Google news searches; enter your query into the Keywords box, select how many stories you want to display in the module, and then click the Add Section button.

FIGURE 30.6

Creating a custom news module.

Once you have your personalized page configured the way you like it, you can display this page by clicking the Personalized News link at the top of the Google News page.

> **tip** To add a label or change the language for your custom section, click the Advanced link.

Searching for News Articles

Although reading Google News' current headlines is nice, if you're searching for specific stories or older stories, you need to use Google's Advanced News Search. You access this advanced search from the Google News page by clicking the Advanced News Search link.

As you can see in Figure 30.7, you can use the Advanced News Search to search by a variety of parameters, as detailed in Table 30.1.

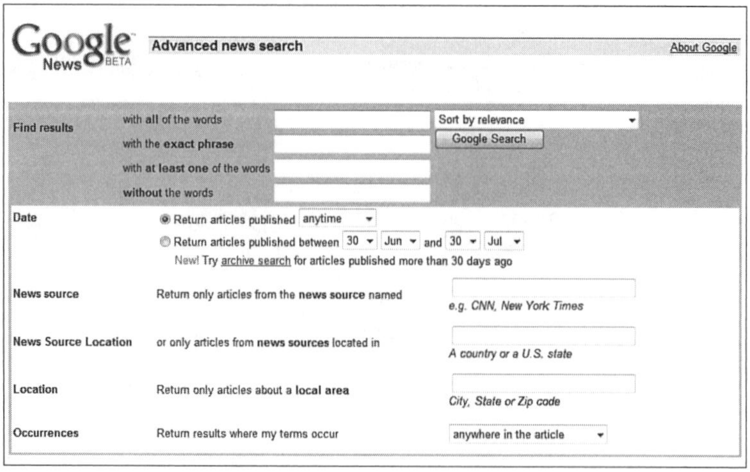

FIGURE 30.7

The Advanced News Search page.

Table 30.1 Advanced News Search Options	
Option	**Description**
Sort by	Specifies in what order results are displayed—by relevance or by date.
Find results with all of the words	Default search mode.
Find results with the exact phrase	Searches for the exact phrase entered.
Find results with at least one of the words	Searches for either one word or another.
Find results without the words	Excludes pages that contain the specified word(s).
Date	Returns articles published between two specific dates, or within the last hour, day, week, or month.
News source	Searches for articles from a specified newspaper or news site.
News source location	Searches for articles from news sources located in a specific country or state.
Location	Searches for articles about a local area
Occurrences	Returns articles where the keywords occur in the article's headline, body, URL, or anywhere in the article.

Searching the News Archive

By default, Google News keeps 30 days' worth of articles in its database. If you want to find news older than 30 days—up to 200 years old, in fact—you can use Google's News Archive Search. In addition to finding recent-but-not-too-recent news headlines, it's also a great tool for learning about historical events.

> **tip** Once you create a query for a specific topic, you can bookmark the search results page in your web browser. Every time you access this bookmark, you'll display an updated search results page containing the latest news stories on the specified topic. You can even put a shortcut to this bookmark on your desktop and double-click it when you want up-to-date news on the topic at hand.

You access News Archive Search by clicking the News Archive Search link on the Google News main page, or by going directly to news.google.com/archivesearch. As you can see in Figure 30.8, the News Archive Search includes a standard search box, but with two buttons instead of one.

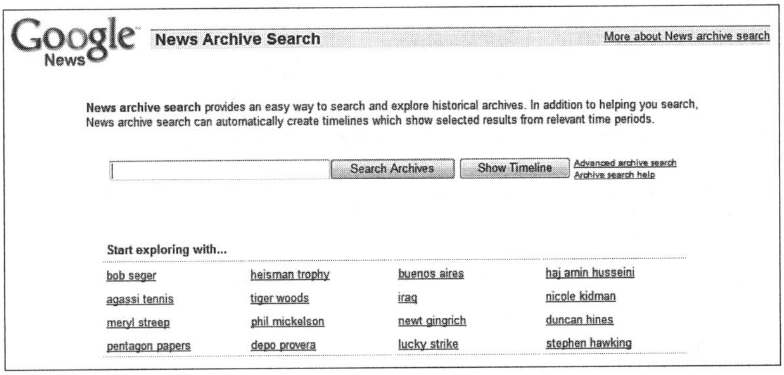

FIGURE 30.8

The Google News Archive page.

To conduct a normal archive search, enter your query into the search box and then click the Search Archives button. The search results page, shown in Figure 30.9, includes a list of matching newspaper articles from the archive. You can filter this list by selecting a date range or publication from the left-hand column.

FIGURE 30.9

The results of a Google News Archive search.

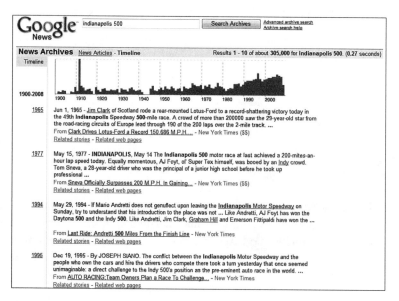

FIGURE 30.10

Viewing a Google News Archive timeline.

The Google News Archive also has a nifty timeline feature, which lets you view articles by date. (Figure 30.10 shows a typical timeline.) You can display the timeline by clicking the Show Timeline button on the main News Archive page or the View Timeline link on any search results page.

note Some news archive results are free to read; others require a one-time payment or subscription to read. You'll see viewing/payment options underneath the article title.

Reading Google News Feeds

I've discussed blog feeds and news feeds several times in this book, so there's no need to go into what a feed is at this point. Suffice to say, you can sign up for RSS or Atom feeds from any Google News section or custom search, and then read the latest headlines for that section or search as a feed in your favorite feed reader or aggregator.

tip Google also offers an advanced archive search, accessible from the Advanced Archive Search link on the main Google News Archive page. This page lets you filter your results in the normal Google fashion; there are also options to display articles at various price ranges.

Google lets you sign up for three types of news feeds, as follows:

note Learn more about feeds and the Google Reader feed aggregator in Chapter 23, "Using Google Reader."

- ■ **News section feeds.** These contain headlines from a given Google News section. Click any section link to go to that section page, and then use the RSS or Atom link in the left column.

- ■ **News search results feeds.** These contain headlines that match any news search you initiate. Conduct your search, and then use the RSS or Atom link in the left column of the search results page.

- ■ **Customized news feeds.** These contain all the headlines from your personalized version of Google News. After you've personalized your Google News page, use the RSS or Atom link in the left column of your personalized page.

Signing Up for News Alerts

Back in Chapter 7, "Saving Your Searches—and Signing Up for Google Alerts," you learned all about Google Alerts. As you recall, you can use Google Alerts to notify you via email when news articles appear online that match the topics you specify. This way, you can monitor breaking news stories, keep tabs on industries or competitors, or just stay up-to-date on specific types of events.

To sign up for a Google News Alert, follow these steps:

1. From the Google News page, click the News Alerts link.

2. When the Google Alerts page appears, go to the Create a Google Alert box, shown in Figure 30.11, and enter your query into the Search Terms box.

3. Pull down the type list and select News.

4. Pull down the How Often list and select how often you want to receive alerts—Once a Day, Once a Week, or As-It-Happens.

5. Enter your email address into Your Email box.

6. Click the Create Alert button.

FIGURE 30.11
Setting up a Google News Alert.

You'll now receive email messages, on the schedule you specified, containing the latest news headlines on that specific subject.

Getting News on the Go

There's one more way to get the latest Google News headlines, and it doesn't

> **tip** As-It-Happens is the best option for receiving alerts about breaking news stories.

involve your computer. That's right—you can receive Google News headlines on your cellular phone or other mobile device. It's a great way to keep up-to-date when you're on the go.

note Learn more about all of Google's mobile services in Chapter 35, "Using Google on Any Mobile Phone."

You access Google Mobile News by going to mobile.google.com on your mobile phone and clicking News. You can then browse the top headlines by section, or search for news stories as you would on the Google News web page. Learn more by clicking the Mobile News link on the main Google News page.

30

The Bottom Line

I find Google News to be one of the best sources of news available online. By assembling stories from literally hundreds of different newspapers, magazines, and websites, it provides a depth of coverage that simply isn't possible from single-source sites like CNN.com. Granted, Google News focuses on the top stories only, but where else can you go to read coverage from the *New York Times*, the *Melbourne Herald Sun*, and the *Arabic News*—all on the same page?

Searching for Financial Information

L ooking to see how your stock portfolio is performing? Then check out Google Finance, a full-featured financial information site.

Like other financial information sites, Google Finance offers a combination of general market news plus in-depth financial information on specific stocks, mutual funds, and public and private companies. The information offered by Google Finance comes from a variety of financial data providers, as well as content obtained by the GoogleBot crawler and stored in Google's main search database.

Accessing General Financial Information

The main Google Finance page (finance.google.com), shown in Figure 31.1, offers a variety of general financial news and information. Here's what you'l find:

FIGURE 31.1

The main Google Finance page.

- **Market summary.** This section displays the latest Dow, Nasdaq, and S&P 500, as well as an intra-day graph of all three indexes. Click any exchange link to view detailed trading data and news.

- **Top stories.** The top financial headlines, as reported from a variety o news sites; click any headline to read the entire story. Stories are orga ized by tab in three categories: Market, Portfolio Related, and Video. view additional headlines, scroll down to the bottom of the section ar click the View All of Today's News link.

- **Sector summary.** A table of price movement by sector.

- **Portfolios.** Stock prices for those securities in your personal portfolios

- **Recent quotes.** This is a list of stocks/companies you've recently searched for, accompanied by the current stock price.

- **Trends.** A list of today's trend-setting stocks—in terms of popularity, price, market cap, and volume.

Then, of course, there's the ubiquitous Google search box at the top of the page. This isn't a standard Google search box, however; you use this search box to search Google Finance for specific company and stock information. Just enter a stock symbol or company name, and the matching company page will be displayed.

Accessing Specific Stock and Company Information

General financial information is good; more detailed information on specific companies, stocks, or mutual funds is even better. To that end, Google Finance offers dedicated pages for companies and securities, complete with all sorts of useful news and data.

To view a company/security-specific page, you can click the security's name anywhere it's displayed on the Google Finance site or in general Google search results. Alternatively, you can search for that company or security using the search box at the top of the Google Finance main page; instead of a list of search results, Google will display the dedicated company/security page.

> **tip** You can also display basic stock information from the main Google search page. The easiest way is to simply enter the stock or fund symbol into Google's search box, without any additional keywords, although you can preface the symbol with the **stocks:** operator. Using the operator is recommended if you're looking up multiple stocks at one time. This displays a OneBox section on the search results page, which includes a graph of the current day's stock performance; the current stock price; opening, high, and low prices; volume and average volume; and market capitalization (market cap).

> **tip** Stock quotes from Google Finance can also be delivered to your cell phone or PDA via SMS text messaging. Learn more in Chapter 35, "Using Google on Any Mobile Phone."

As you can see in Figure 31.2, a dedicated company/security page includes a plethora of financial information. Here are the major sections you'll find:

- **Key metrics.** Located in the top-left corner of the page, these include the company/fund name, ticker symbol, current price, dollar/percentage change, open/high/low prices, trading volume and average volume, market cap, 52-week high and low prices, price/earnings (P/E) ratio, forward price/earnings (F P/E) ratio), beta, and earnings per share (EPS). In addition, you can view and download (in spreadsheet format) historical end-of-day prices by clicking the Historical Prices link in this section.

FIGURE 31.2

View detailed information about a company, stock, or mutual fund.

■ **Stock chart.** This chart tracks the price of the stock over any period from 1 day to 10 years (or more). Key events are noted on the chart by letters; each letter corresponds to one of the news stories displayed to the right of the chart. (Read more about how to use these interactive charts later in this chapter.)

■ **Recent stories.** These numbered headlines correspond to the numbered events on the 1-week stock chart. Click any headline to read the complete story.

■ **Related companies.** A list of market sectors and companies that are similar to the company in question. Click any company link to view that company's dedicated Google Finance page.

■ **Discussions.** A list of posts discussing the company in the Google Finance Groups. (Learn more about Google Finance Groups later in this chapter.)

■ **Blog posts.** From Google Blog Search, blog postings from around the blogosphere that discuss the company and its stock. Click a

> **note** Learn more about Google Blog Search in Chapter 10, "Searching for Blogs and Blog Postings."

posting title to read more, or click the More Blogs link to view more related posts.

tip To add any upcoming company event to your Google Calendar, click the Add to Calendar link. Learn more about Google Calendar in Chapter 22, "Using Google Calendar."

- **Financials.** Key financial data from the company's most recent annual report, including income statement, balance sheet, and cash flow numbers.

- **Events.** Recent and upcoming financial events for the company.

- **Summary.** A brief description of what the company is and what it does.

- **Key Stats & Ratios.** More data about the company, including net profit margin, operating margin, return on average assets, return on average equity, number of employees, and such.

- **Officers and directors.** The names and titles of the company's key officers and senior management.

- **More Resources.** Links to additional information about the company, in the form of SEC filings, analyst estimates, research reports, and the like. Click any link to learn more.

COMMENTARY

FINANCIAL METRICS

To the uninitiated, the various financial metrics displayed by Google Finance amount to nothing more than acronym soup. To the savvy investor, however, these metrics are key to evaluating the risk and potential reward for any investment.

So, what do these metrics mean? Here's a short primer:

Trading volume. The number of shares traded on the most recent trading day. Important only when compared to the average volume.

Average volume. The total number of shares traded for the previous three months, divided by the number of total trading days in that period. Compare this number to the daily trading volume to see if investor interest in the stock has increased or decreased. For example, if the daily trading volume is higher than the average volume for the past three months, this means that more shares are being traded now than is usual for that stock; the increased investor interest, however, could mean almost anything.

Market capitalization (market cap). The company's market capitalization, calculated by multiplying the current stock price with the number of shares outstanding. For example, if a company's stock is trading at $10 per share, and there are 1 million shares outstanding, then the company's market cap is $10 million.

52-week high. The highest price that this security has traded over the past year.

52-week low. The lowest price that this security has traded over the past year.

Revenue. The total sales generated by the company. Typically reported quarterly and yearly.

Operating income. The company's revenue minus all day-to-day operating expenses. It excludes financial-related items, such as interest income, dividend income, and interest expense, as well as taxes.

Operating margin. The company's operating income divided by revenue, expressed as a percentage.

Net income (profit, earnings). The amount of money left over after the company subtracts *all* its costs and expenses (including interest income, dividend income, and the like) from its revenue.

Net profit margin. The company's total net income divided by revenue, expressed as a percentage.

Earnings per share. The company's profits divided by the number of shares outstanding—in other words, the amount of profit earned by each share of stock.

Price/earnings ratio (P/E). The current stock price divided by the company's most recent earnings per share. You use P/E to compare the earnings power of different companies.

Forward price/earnings ratio (F P/E). The current stock price divided by the company's estimated future earnings per share. Some investors think this is a more accurate way to compare the future earnings potential of different companies than standard P/E analysis.

Return on average assets. The ratio of net income divided by average total assets. This is a financial measurement of the efficiency with which a company uses its assets.

Return on average equity (return on equity). The ratio of net income divided by average equity. This is a financial measurement of how effective a business has been in investing its net worth.

Beta. For mutual funds, this is a measure of the fund's volatility relative to the market, typically compared to the performance of the S&P 500. A beta of 1.0 indicates that the fund is more volatile than the market; a beta of less than 1.0 indicates that the fund is less volatile than the market.

Viewing Interactive Financial Charts

The stock chart displayed on the company/stock Google Finance page is more informative than it might first appear. That's because this is an interactive chart that you can manipulate to display a variety of different information. You can click the chart to display more or different information.

First of all, you can change the date range displayed on the chart—in several different ways. Quick view zooming is accomplished by clicking the 1d (1-day), 5d (5-day), 1m (1-month), 6m (6-month), 1y (1-year), or Max (life-to-date) links. You can also click and drag the chart to the left or right to display a different range of dates; just hover your cursor anywhere on the chart, hold down the left mouse button, and drag.

In addition, the overview graph just above the main graph displays the stock's price over the life of the stock, with the currently selected range for the main chart displayed as a small slice of the life-to-date chart. To enlarge or shrink the time span displayed in the main chart, click and drag the left positioning handle in this "window" on the subsidiary chart. Alternatively, you can drag the positioning button below this "window" to display a different date range.

note To fully display Google Finance charts, your computer needs to be running Microsoft Windows 2000, Windows XP, Windows Vista, Mac OS, or Linux. You also need to be using a current version of the Internet Explorer, Firefox, Opera, or Safari web browsers, and have Macromedia Flash Player 7.0 or higher installed. (The charts themselves are displayed using Flash technology.)

31

Another fun thing about these interactive charts is the ability to display price information at a specific time. All you have to do is hover your cursor over a specific spot on the trend line, which highlights a specific date and time of day. The price and volume information for that point in time is displayed at the top of the chart.

And, as discussed previously, key news stories about the company are pinpointed on the chart by a series of letter buttons (A, B, C, and so on). Click a letter and the corresponding news story is highlighted in the section to the right of the graph. Click the headline to read the full story.

Tracking Your Portfolio

There's one other section on the Google Finance site that you might find useful: the Portfolios page, shown in Figure 31.3. You access your portfolio by clicking the Portfolios link at the top of the main Google Finance page. (This feature is visible only if you have a Google account and if you're signed in at

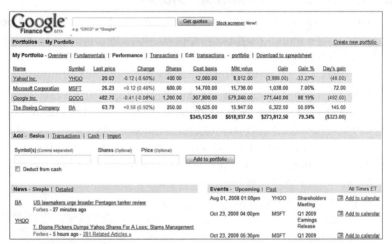

the time.)

FIGURE 31.3

Tracking your personal portfolio with Google Finance.

Your Google Finance portfolio is how you track the performance of a selected group of stocks and mutual funds, right from the main Google Finance page. This list can be those stocks in your actual portfolio, or simply a group of stocks in which you have interest. In any case, it's a good way to put the financial information you're most interested in front and center on the Google Finance page.

What information is included on the Google Finance Portfolio page? For each stock, you'll see the following:

- Company or fund name (click either the symbol or name link to view the detailed Google Finance page for that security)
- Symbol
- Last price (current trading price)
- Change (dollar and percentage change from previous day price)
- Shares (the number of shares you own, if entered)
- Cost basis (your total investment in this security, if you entered price and share information)
- Mkt value (the current value of your investment in this security, based on the current share price, if you entered price and share information)
- Gain/loss (your current gain or loss on this security, if you entered price and share information)
- Gain/loss % (your current gain or loss, as a percent of your purchase price)
- Day's gain/loss (the amount of money you've gained or lost on that stock today)

To create your portfolio, make sure you have a Google account and that you're signed in before you access the Google Finance page. (Alternatively, you can click the Sign In link at the top of the Google Finance page.) Once you're signed in, you can then create your Google Finance Portfolio. Just follow these steps:

1. Click the Portfolio link at the top of the Google Finance page.
2. When the Portfolios page appears, enter the stock symbol you want to track into the Add section.
3. If you want to track performance versus cost, you should also enter the price you paid and how many shares you own (both optional).
4. Click the Add to Portfolio button.
5. Repeat steps 2–4 to add additional stocks to your portfolio.
6. When you're done adding stocks, click the Google Finance logo to return to the main Google Finance page.

You can add new stocks to your portfolio at any time by entering the Symbol, Price, and Shares information and clicking the Add to Portfolio button. You can also change your portfolio information by clicking the Edit Portfolio button, and then changing the Buy Price and Shares information for any listed security. To delete any security from your portfolio, click the Delete link next to the security.

> **tip** To track a security with multiple shares purchased at different prices, you'll need to enter each purchase of the security separately.

> **tip** You can also add a security to your portfolio by clicking Add to Portfolio on any dedicated company/security page.

Using Google's Stock Screener

When you're looking for good stocks to invest in, use Google's Stock Screener feature. The Stock Screener lets you specify various performance parameters, and then generates a list of stocks that match those parameters.

To access the Stock Screener, click the Stock Screener link next to the Google Finance search box. This displays the screener page shown in Figure 31.4. You now enter the desired minimum and maximum values for the following parameters:

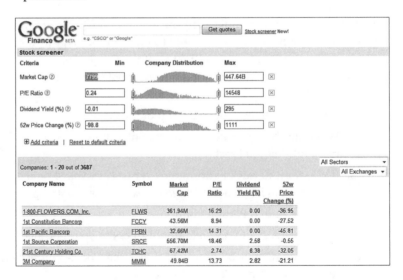

FIGURE 31.4

Searching for stocks with Google's Stock Screener.

- Market cap
- P/E (price/earnings) ratio
- Dividend yield (%)
- 52-week price change

You can add more parameters by clicking the Add Criteria link. The stocks that meet these parameters are listed below the screener section.

Discussing Finances in Google Finance Groups

Savvy investors know that dry financial data can only tell you so much. Often, it helps to get opinions and tips from other investors—to test the waters, so to speak, by talking to people who might have a little more information (or a few more opinions) about the company in question.

One of the best places to find like-minded investors is on the Google Finance Discussion Groups. This is a subset of the overall Google Groups discussion forums, tailor-made for financial discussions.

The Google Finance Discussion Groups differ from standard Google Groups in that the Google Finance discussions are moderated by Google staffers. The intent is to keep the junk off the boards; postings are monitored to find and delete spam, pornography, hateful or harassing content, and offers to buy or sell any security. It's kind of a sanitized version of the discussions you find at other financial information sites—sanitized for your protection, or so Google says.

Finding Google Finance Discussions

Google Finance discussions are organized by company. You access the discussions for a given company by going to the company's dedicated Google Finance page, scrolling down to the Discussions section, and clicking the More Discussions link. This displays a Discussions page, like the one shown in Figure 31.5.

note Learn more about Google Groups in Chapter 16, "Forming Communities with Google Groups."

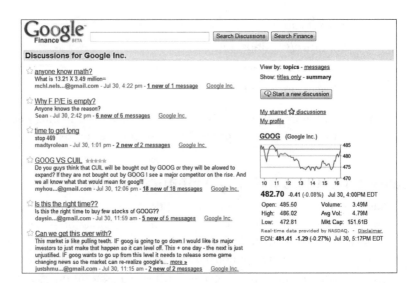

FIGURE 31.5

Viewing Google Finance discussions about a specific company.

Messages are listed in reverse chronological order, with the newest messages a the top of the left column. To view older messages, scroll to the bottom of the page and click the Older link.

Reading and Rating Messages

To read a complete message, all you have to do is click the message header. This displays a page like the one shown in Figure 31.6, where the message you clicked and all other messages in the same thread are displayed, in chronological order. For each message, you see the poster's Google account ID a link to the poster's profile, the date posted, a rating for this message, and then the message text.

The message rating is an interesting feature. Readers are encouraged to vote on the messages they read, assigning each message a rating on a scale of 0 to 5 stars. It's an attempt to highlight those messages that other users find the most useful.

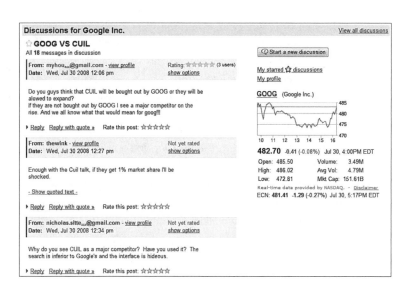

FIGURE 31.6
Reading Google Finance messages.

Replying to Messages

To reply to a message, click the Reply link below the message text. This opens a Reply text box; enter your reply into this box, and then click the Post button. Your reply will now be added to the thread in progress.

Starting a New Discussion

You're not limited to replying to existing messages, of course. You should feel free to start your own discussions, about topics that interest you.

To start a new discussion about a particular company, follow these steps:

1. Go to the company's main Discussions page.

2. Click the Start a New Discussion button.

tip Before you can rate a message or start a new discussion, you have to create a Google Finance profile aside from your normal Google account. To create a profile, go to any company's Discussions page and click the My Profile link in the right column. When the My Profile page appears, click the Edit link; when the Edit My Profile page appears, enter the required information; then click the Save button.

3. The first time you post, you'll see the Finance Posting Application page. Assuming you agree with the terms, check the I've Read and Accepted... option, and then click the Next Step button. You'll now see your Google Finance profile; if

caution If your message is *not* approved, Google will notify you via email. If you don't receive an email, your message was approved and posted as normal.

you've not yet filled in the blanks, do so now, and then click the Next Step button.

4. When the Start a New Discussion page appears, enter a subject for the message, and then enter your message text. (You can preview your in-progress message by clicking the Preview button.)

5. If you want a copy of the message emailed to you, check the Send Me a Copy of This Message option.

6. When you're done composing your message, click the Post Message button.

Your message will now be reviewed by Google staff. If you pass muster, the message will be posted to the discussion group.

The Bottom Line

Although not quite as robust as some other online finance sites, Google Finance is a good one-stop-shop for basic company and stock information. The easy incorporation of Google Groups discussions and blog searches make Google Finance even more useful; I also like the interactive stock charts.

Of course, for quick financial information, you can't beat Google's simple search box search. When you want stock quotes fast, just enter the company's ticker symbol into the ever-present Google search box. It's the fast way to get basic info!

Organizing Patient Records with Google Health

A t its heart, Google's search index is nothing more than a giant database. Well, if Google can create a database of web pages, why not databases of other types of information?

This leads us to Google Health, a giant database of personal health records. Google Health is meant to be a technological solution to the problem of a healthcare system that still keeps its massive number of patient records using 1970s-era technology. Instead of using physical filing cabinets, Google Health provides a cloud-based electronic storehouse for millions of medical records—the better to help patients share their medical histories with doctors, insurance companies, and other health care providers.

What Is Google Health?

Google Health is nothing more than a big database of medical records. These are *your* medical records, provided by you; other individuals submit their own personal records. Your Google Health account can include physician's records, hospital reports, and pharmacy histories. The result is a giant repository of medical information, usable by patients and providers alike.

Storing all your health-related information in one place has numerous benefits, including the ability to do the following:

- Generate reports on your medical and prescription history.
- Check for unanticipated drug interactions.
- Keep your doctor and other medical professionals up-to-date with your health status.
- Keep you informed about important health issues.

All your medical information is submitted by you online at the Google Health website (www.google.com/health). This is also where you access your medical history and generate a variety of useful reports.

Creating Your Health Profile

To use Google Health, you have to create a health profile. You can enter as little or as much information as you want or know. Of course, the more data you enter about your medical conditions, allergies, surgeries, medications, and the like, the more use you can get out of the site.

To create your health profile, go to the Google Health home page and log on with your Google account. You then have to agree to share your health information; this is important, and you really should read through the agreement to make sure you're comfortable with it. Assuming you are comfortable, check "I agree," and you're taken to the Google Health gateway, shown in Figure 32.1.

32

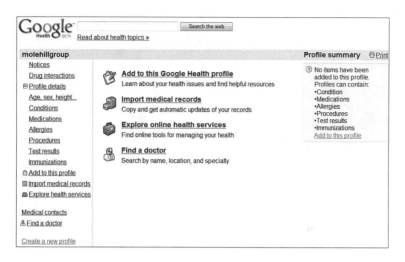

FIGURE 32.1

The Google Health gateway page—where it all starts.

Add Your Medical Information

The first thing you need to do is add some information to your health profile. Start by clicking the Add to This Google Health Profile link; this displays the Add to This Profile page, shown in Figure 32.2.

From here, you can add Conditions, Medications, Allergies, Procedures, Test Results, and Immunizations, just by clicking the appropriate tab. You can add an item by browsing the long list provided, or by entering it directly into the provided box.

As you add conditions, medications, and the like to your profile, they're listed in the Profile Summary at the top-right corner of the page. You can add additional details, such as your age and weight, by clicking the links in the navigation pane on the left.

32

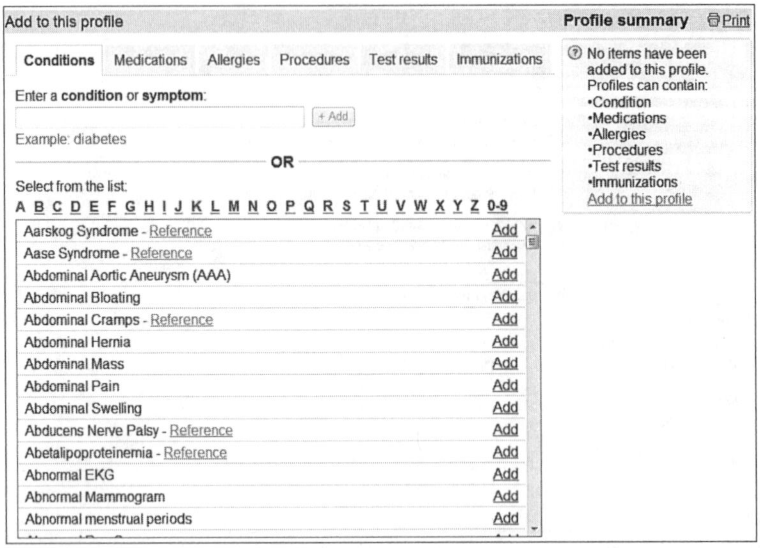

FIGURE 32.2
Adding information to your Google Health profile.

32

Import Your Medical Records

An even easier way to add your medical history to your profile is to import your existing medical records. Click the Import Medical Records link, and you see a list of participating health organizations—clinics, hospitals, pharmacies, and the like. If your doctor or pharmacy is listed, you can click through to import the records they have stored.

Viewing Your Medical History

After you've entered or imported your medical information, you can view your medical history from the Google Health site. The Profile Summary presents a good overview of your current conditions and medications, but you can display more information about any given topic by clicking the link in the left-hand navigation pane. For example, Figure 32.3 shows the details of a typical Medications profile.

> **tip** Google Health automatically checks for potentially dangerous interactions between the medications that you enter. Click the Drug Interactions link to see any potential interactions.

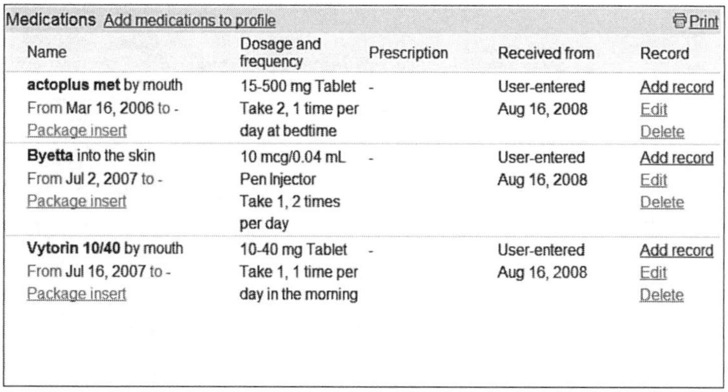

Medications Add medications to profile				🖶Print
Name	Dosage and frequency	Prescription	Received from	Record
actoplus met by mouth From Mar 16, 2006 to - Package insert	15-500 mg Tablet Take 2, 1 time per day at bedtime	-	User-entered Aug 16, 2008	Add record Edit Delete
Byetta into the skin From Jul 2, 2007 to - Package insert	10 mcg/0.04 mL Pen Injector Take 1, 2 times per day	-	User-entered Aug 16, 2008	Add record Edit Delete
Vytorin 10/40 by mouth From Jul 16, 2007 to - Package insert	10-40 mg Tablet Take 1, 1 time per day in the morning	-	User-entered Aug 16, 2008	Add record Edit Delete

FIGURE 32.3

Viewing personal medical information.

Learn More About Health Topics

Want to learn more about a particular disease or medical condition? In addition to its tracking of your personal medical records, Google Health also offers a wealth of information about a variety of health-related topics.

To view Google's database of health-related articles, click the Read About Health Topics link at the top of the Google Health gateway page. This displays a huge list of health topics; click any given topic to view the page devoted to that topic. As you can see in Figure 32.4, a typical topic page includes information on symptoms, causes, treatment, tests and diagnosis, prognosis, prevention, and complications, as well as links to related news articles, news groups, and search trends.

note Google's medical articles are courtesy of A.D.A.M. (www.adam.com), an Atlanta-based provider of medical and health-related information.

FIGURE 32.4

Reading a Google Health article.

Search for Doctors and Hospitals

Looking for a new doctor? Then check the database of medical professionals offered by Google Health.

Click the Find a Doctor link on the left side to display the Find a Doctor page, shown in Figure 32.5. Select a specialty and enter your location; then click the Search button. Google now returns a list of appropriate physicians in your area; click a doctor's name to view more information or a map to his or her office.

note Google Health partners with a variety of health-related companies and organizations to provide additional resources to users. These providers link to your Google Health profile to customize their services to your needs. Click the Explore Online Health Services link to learn more.

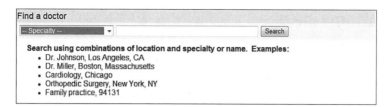

FIGURE 32.5
Searching for local physicians.

GOOGLE HEALTH AND PRIVACY

The concept of centralizing all your medical records in one place sounds admirable, but is it really a good idea? What if your medical records fall into the wrong hands?

First off, Google says they keep your records secure. But, as we all know, security is only good until it's breached—and the breach doesn't have to come from Google's end. Anyone who breaks into your Google account (and how secure is your Google password, anyway?) has access to your medical records. That's not a good thing.

Beyond that, Google's definition of "security" might not be the same as yours. In its privacy policy, Google openly says it may share your personal health records with a number of different groups, including information processors and the U.S. government. In other words, Google could sell off or give away your private medical information—which might not be something you want future employers, insurers, or other individuals to see. Not to say that will happen, but it *could*.

It's a dilemma. Centralizing your medical information can be beneficial, but if an unauthorized entity gets hold of that information, it could be disastrous. Do you want to risk the possibility of someone or some business finding out more about you, medically, than you'd like to share? I'm not sure I personally want to take that risk, at least until Google has a longer history of security. Until then, there are things I'd rather keep private between my doctor and myself.

32

The Bottom Line

Google Health attempts to serve the admirable purpose of making patient medical information more accessible and useful. It's actually easy to enter all your medical information, and having it all in one place is of tremendous potential value. No doubt Google Health will become even more useful as more physicians and organizations sign up as partners; I can envision a future where you can automatically transfer your medical history from Google Health directly to your physician's office or to a local hospital. It's not there yet, unfortunately, but it's still a relatively new service. Expect increased functionality as time goes by.

32

Selling Products and Services with Google Checkout

I f you've ever purchased anything online, chances are you've used PayPal or a similar online payment service. These services let small retailers and individuals accept credit card payments for the items they sell. The buyer pays the online payment service directly, typically via credit card; the service then processes the credit card payment and passes the funds on to the seller, typically via an electronic deposit in the seller's bank account.

For small sellers, online payment services are a necessary part of doing business online. For buyers, they're simply the way to pay for goods and services offered at many websites and via online auction.

Although the most popular online payment service today is PayPal (owned by eBay, and used in millions of eBay auctions), there's a new competitor in the market: Google Checkout. That's right, Google is now in the online payment business, and promises to give PayPal a run for the (electronic) money.

Buying and Selling Electronically: How Online Payment Services Work

Put simply, an online payment service such as Google Checkout or PayPal functions as a "middle man" between buyers and sellers, handling the details of the payment process. The need for such a service exists because, for most sellers below a certain size, it's both impractical and unprofitable to handle their own electronic payments.

If you're a big merchant, like Best Buy or L.L. Bean, you can afford to design and invest in your own electronic payment systems. Even medium-sized retailers can contract with banks and other financial institutions for merchant checking accounts and online checkout services. But small retailers and individuals selling online don't have the time or money to invest in custom-built payment systems, and aren't big enough to qualify for merchant credit card accounts and similar services.

For these small merchants and individuals, the only way they can accept electronic payments online is to let someone else do it for them—hence the creation of PayPal, Google Checkout, and similar online payment services. These services are big enough to build their own electronic payment and checkout services; they provide these services to smaller merchants and individuals, so that they can accept credit card payments from their customers.

Tracking a Typical Transaction

How exactly does Google Checkout do what it does? To answer that question, let's take a look at a typical online transaction:

1. The transaction starts when a customer (let's call him "Bob") goes to the website of a small online retailer that sells collectible sports cards. Bob finds a card he wants to purchase and clicks the "buy" button.

2. At this point, Google Checkout kicks in. The website has previously contracted with Google Checkout to handle all its checkout and payment processes. As such, the retailer has followed Google's instructions to insert the proper HTML code onto the site's web pages. The "buy" button is part of Google's HTML code.

3. When Bob clicks the "buy" button, an electronic command is sent over the Web to Google Checkout. The service now takes over the rest of the purchasing process, directing Bob's web browser to the payment service's website.

4. Google Checkout now displays for Bob a shopping cart page. This page shows the item that Bob wants to purchase, as well as other information regarding the purchase. Bob can, if he wants, return to the retailer's website to resume shopping, or he can click the "checkout" button to finalize his purchase.

5. Bob, his shopping finished, clicks the "checkout" button. This displays another page on the Google Checkout website, this one showing all the items in Bob's shopping cart, along with shipping/handling charges and sales tax (if any). This information is inserted by Google Checkout based on the retailer's pre-arranged instructions. (That is, the retailer specifies ahead of time how much shipping and handling to charge per order, as well as whether or not to charge sales tax.)

6. If Bob concurs with the total amount listed on the checkout page, he clicks a "pay now" button. This directs him to a payment page, again hosted by Google Checkout. Bob will now be asked if he's already signed up for Google Checkout. If he has, Bob can simply enter his user name and password, and the rest of his personal information—address, phone number, and so on—are retrieved from Google's database and automatically entered onto the payment form.

7. Next, Bob has to specify how he's going to pay for his purchase. Google Checkout accepts payment via MasterCard, Visa, American Express, and Discover card. So Bob enters his credit card number and expiration date (unless it's already stored with Google Checkout), and then clicks the "pay" button to authorize payment.

8. Bob's credit card information is now transmitted to Google Checkout. The service contacts the issuing bank for Bob's credit card, ensures that Bob has enough left on his credit line to cover the purchase, and charges the purchase.

9. At this point, several things start to happen. First, Bob is notified by Google Checkout that his purchase has been completed, in the form of a confirmation web page. Second, the retailer is notified by Google Checkout of the purchase, via an email message that includes information about what was purchased, as well as Bob's shipping information. Third, an electronic transfer of funds is initiated from Bob's credit card company to Google Checkout; the funds don't arrive immediately, but the transfer process is started.

Note what *doesn't* happen at this point: The retailer does not receive specifics about how Bob paid. Bob's credit card information is retained

33

by Google Checkout, but not transmitted to the retailer. This keeps Bob's financial information secure, and helps to protect Bob's credit card from theft.

10. Once notified of the purchase, the retailer puts the purchase into process, so that the item can be pulled from inventory, packed, and sent to the designated shipping carrier. Depending on the retailer, this might happen immediately, or it may take several days to pack and ship the item. Note that the inventorying, packing, and shipping of the item are all handled by the retailer, not Google Checkout.

11. For its part, Google Checkout now waits for the funds to be transferred from Bob's credit card account to its bank account. This might take a few minutes or it might take a few days; two days is the norm. Once the funds are transferred from the credit card company, Google Checkout initiates an electronic transfer of those funds to the retailer's bank account—minus any fees charged, of course.

Note that the retailer ships out the purchase before it physically receives the funds for that purchase. That's because the retailer trusts Google Checkout to transfer the funds owed; since the actual payment has been made (by Bob to the online payment service), the retailer knows the funds are in the system.

And that ends the transaction. Here's what happened, from each entity's point of view:

■ Bob shops at the retailer, places his order with Google Checkout, pays Google Checkout, and receives his item from the retailer.

■ The retailer offers the item for sale to Bob, receives notice of the sale from Google Checkout, ships the item to Bob, and then receives payment for the item from Google Checkout.

■ Google Checkout receives the order from Bob, transmits the order to the retailer, receives payment from Bob (actually, from Bob's credit card company), and then pays the retailer.

> **note** Although the buyer has to create an account with Google Checkout, this account is free; the account exists only to facilitate future transactions, since the buyer's address and payment information doesn't have to be re-entered for each new transaction. The seller also needs to create an account with Google Checkout, and this account is also free—although the seller probably has to supply banking information, so the service can electronically deposit funds due.

So, Google Checkout serves as the "middle man" for the transaction, both processing the order (using its own checkout system) and accepting Bob's credit card payment. The retailer receives both notice of the sale and processed payment for the sale from the online payment service.

HOW GOOGLE CHECKOUT MAKES MONEY

It goes without saying that all online payment services are in business to make money. Just how that money is made might surprise you, however.

You might think that Google Checkout and other online payment services generate their profits from the fees they collect from sellers. Although it's true that these fees generate revenue, they don't always generate a lot of profit. That's because the online payment service has to pay fees of its own to the credit card companies (MasterCard, Visa, American Express, and Discover) to use their networks. In most instances, the fees charged by the credit card companies are very close to the fees that the online payment service charges its sellers. There's a little margin for profit there, but it's slight; the payment service's fees just cover the credit card companies' fees.

Instead, Google Checkout, PayPal, and the like make most of their profits from interest. You see, there's a lag between when funds are received from the credit card companies and when those funds are withdrawn by retailers. That time lag might only be a day or two, but during that time, the funds reside in the payment service's bank accounts, where interest is earned on the money. You might think that the interest earned for a day on a $25 transaction would be so slight as to be unnoticeable, and you'd be right. But multiply that single transaction by a few million, and you can see how quickly the pennies add up.

In other words, Google Checkout and other online payment services make their money by handling your money—even if just for a few days.

In addition, Google uses Google Checkout to drive business to its AdSense advertising division, which is a big revenue generator. This is one reason Google charges lower fees than does PayPal; it has an additional profit driver in the form of increased advertising sales.

33

Getting to Know Google Checkout

On June 29, 2006, Google announced its entry into the online payment services market, via the new Google Checkout service. Google Checkout functions in much the same manner as PayPal, offering checkout and payment services for Internet retailers of all shapes and sizes.

> **note** The Google Checkout home page is located at checkout.google.com.

For buyers, Google Checkout lets you store your shipping and credit card information in a single Google Account, and then have that information entered automatically when you make a purchase from any retailer using the Google Checkout system. In this regard, Google Checkout is almost identical to PayPal.

Like PayPal, Google Checkout lets buyers pay via Visa, MasterCard, American Express, and Discover cards. Unlike PayPal, Google Checkout doesn't offer payment via e-check or electronic bank withdrawal. And, at present, Google Checkout is only available to United States and United Kingdom merchants; it doesn't offer PayPal's international payment options.

For sellers, Google Checkout offers the same type of checkout and payment services offered by PayPal. That said, Google Checkout offers two big advantages to sellers—lower transaction fees (2.0% vs. PayPal's 2.9% for most merchants) and big discounts if you also advertise via Google's AdWords service. For every $1 a merchant spends on AdWords, that merchant can process $10 in sales through Google Checkout, at no charge.

This last bit reveals Google's real goal with Google Checkout—to increase its advertising revenues. In fact, Google looks to use Google Checkout to enhance the value of its AdWords advertisements; interested users can now click on a link in an AdWords ad and be offered an instant purchase option via Google Checkout. This should appeal to advertisers who can now realize a true click-to-purchase experience, and perhaps even to those buyers who want to purchase the items advertised.

The one thing Google Checkout doesn't offer, at this point in time, is the ability to be used in eBay auctions. Shortly after the launch of Google Checkout, eBay announced that Google Checkout was banned from use in eBay auctions. Although that might change sometime in the future, eBay's ban for now ensures that Google Checkouts is not the PayPal killer some thought it might be.

> **note** Learn more about AdWords in Chapter 39, "Advertising with Google AdWords."

Buying Items with Google Checkout

Google Checkout is used by many online merchants, large and small. For example, most individuals selling via Google Base use Google Checkout for payments, as do many large retailers, including Blue Nile, Buy.com, CompUSA, Dick's Sporting Goods, Linens 'N Things, RitzCamera, Toys "R" Us, and Zales.

> **tip** For a full list of Google Checkout merchants, go to www.google.com/checkout/m.html.

Creating a Google Account

To pay via Google Checkout, you'll first want to create a Google account. This is free and relatively easy to do; once you create your account, paying via Google Checkout is as easy as entering your email address and password.

To create a Google account, follow these steps:

1. Go to the Google Checkout page (checkout.google.com).
2. Click the Sign Up Now button.
3. When the next page appears, enter the necessary information—name, address, email address, password, and credit card number.
4. Click the Create My Account button to finalize your account.

Using Google Checkout to Make a Purchase

When you encounter a merchant that accepts Google Checkout payments, you'll proceed through the item-ordering process as expected. Find an item you want to buy, click the Add to Cart button, and then keep on shopping.

When you're ready to check out, go to the shopping cart or checkout page; then click the Google Checkout button, like the one shown in Figure 33.1. You'll now see a checkout page, like the one in Figure 33.2, with all the shipping and billing information already filled out for you. If everything is copasetic, click the Place Your Order Now button, and your order will be processed.

> **caution** If you have concerns about your online privacy, know that when you create a Google account, your personal information (including credit card number) is stored on Google's servers. Although Google says it will not share this information with others, it's still out there—and could be stolen or used for nefarious purposes.

33

FIGURE 33.1

This merchant offers payment via Google Checkout.

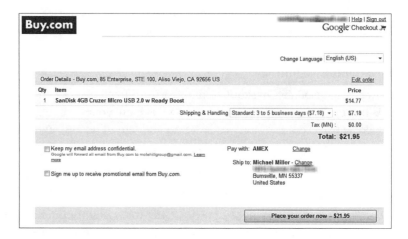

FIGURE 33.2

A typical Google Checkout page—all the information is already entered for you.

Reviewing Your Google Checkout Purchases— and Managing Your Account

One other nice thing about Google Checkout is that it lets you review all your recent purchases on a single page, even if you purchased from multiple retailers. Just go to the Google Checkout page and click the My Account link at the top of the page. When the next page appears, click the Purchase History link, and you'll be taken to the Purchase History page. As you can see in Figure 33.3, all your purchases are listed here.

note If you don't yet have a Google account, the Checkout page prompts you to create one. It's nice that you can create your account from the merchant's website, without having to exit out to Google.

note Purchases made via Google Checkout typically appear on your credit card bill as **GOOGLE * seller's name**.

33

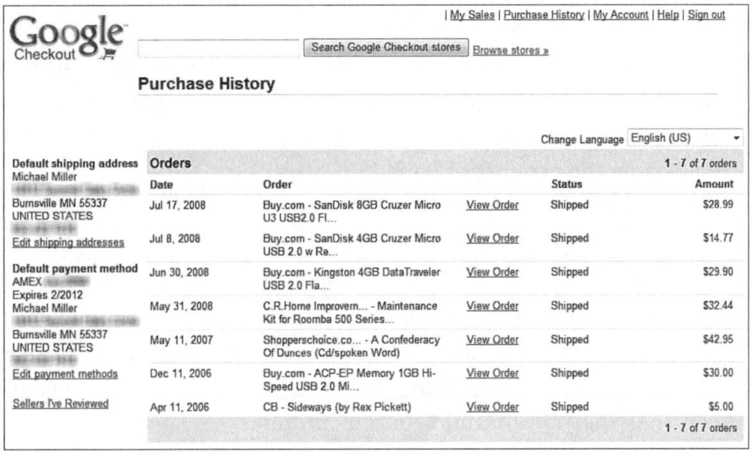

FIGURE 33.3

Reviewing past purchases on the Purchase History page.

Selling Items with Google Checkout

Google Checkout is an attractive alternative to PayPal for anyone selling items on their website. Your customers get a similar checkout and payment experience, while you end up paying less in transaction fees than you would if using PayPal.

There are drawbacks to using Google Checkout, of course. First, you can only use Google Checkout for U.S. and U.K. orders; at this point in time, you can't sell to Europe or Asia. Second, you can only use Google Checkout for sales on your own website; it's not available for eBay auctions. And third, you can only accept credit card payments; Google Checkout has no provision for customers who want to pay via e-check or bank account withdrawal.

That said, Google Checkout for sellers is very similar to the PayPal service, and quite easy to get up and running on your site.

> **tip** To protect your privacy, Google Checkout offers the option of keeping your email address private from the merchants you buy from, unless you explicitly consent otherwise. When you reach a merchant checkout page, check the option for Keep My Email Address Confidential. When you do this, the merchant won't get your email address, thus keeping you out of their system and off their mailing lists.

Setting Up a Google Checkout Account

To use Google Checkout for website payments, you first need to sign up for the service. You start this process by going to the Google Checkout for Merchants page (checkout.google.com/sell/) and signing in with your Google account ID and password.

> **note** If you've already provided some or all of this information for your Google account or AdWords account, you won't be prompted for all this information.

(If you don't yet have a Google account, now's the time to sign up for one.)

When you first sign up, you'll see a page that lets you know what you'll need to create your Google Checkout account. You'll also be asked to describe your business; check the option that best categorizes the type of business you run; then click the Sign In and Continue button.

You're now taken to the Contact Information page. You'll need to enter your primary contact name (that's you), your business name, address, and phone number.

When you click Next, you see the Financial Information page. Now you get to enter even more information about your business, including current sales volume, estimated average order, and Federal tax ID (EIN) or your social security number and credit card information.

Click the Next button, and you see the Public Business Information page. Here you enter as much information about your business as you like, including your website URL, the types of products you sell, the business name you want to appear on customers' credit card statements, your email address and other information for customer support, and your return/cancellation and shipping policies.

Click the Finish button, and you're signed up—and ready to integrate Google Checkout with your website.

> **note** You can edit any of this information at any time by selecting the Settings tab on the Google Checkout Merchants page.

Paying for Google Checkout

How much does it cost you, as a merchant, to use Google Checkout? The fee structure is simple. You pay 2% of the total sale price (that's the price of the item, plus shipping, handling, and sales tax), plus 20 cents per transaction. For small and medium-sized merchants, that's significantly lower priced than PayPal's 2.9% (for volumes under $3,000/month) + 30 cents per transaction fee. These charges, of course, are deducted from your funds due in your Google Checkout account.

33

Integrating Google Checkout with Google AdWords

Here's something that makes Google Checkout even more attractive—and, perhaps, free. If you advertise with Google AdWords, you get a discount on your Google Checkout fees. For every $1 you spend on the AdWords program, you can process $10 in Google Checkout sales for free.

For example, if you spent $100 on AdWords in the previous month, you can process $1,000 in sales through Google Checkout at no cost. Obviously, this is an incentive for you to use AdWords to advertise your website, but it's a useful incentive—one that can save you big money over time.

And once you sign up for Google Checkout, a shopping cart icon will appear next to all your AdWords text ads. This provides a fast track for customers to click your ad and purchase your item, using the Google Checkout system.

Evaluating Google Checkout's Payment Services

Google offers three different ways to integrate Google Checkout with your website. Which service you use depends on the number of items you're selling, and how sophisticated your site is:

- **Buy Now buttons**, designed for smaller merchants and individuals selling a limited number of items. This service lets you use the checkout function on Google's website, and requires only a basic knowledge of HTML to implement.

- **Shopping cart integration**, which is useful if you're using a shopping cart application supplied by one of Google Checkout's partners.

- **Google Checkout API**, which lets you program your own shopping cart and checkout and then tie your site into the Google Checkout Application Programming Interface (API). This option is for larger merchants only.

33

Table 33.1 details the Interface (API). This features of these different services.

Table 33.1 Google Checkout's Online Payment Services

	Buy Now Buttons	Shopping Cart Integration	Google Checkout API
Designed for...	Individuals and small businesses	Medium-sized and larger businesses	Large businesses
Where customers check out	Google Checkout	Third-party checkout service	Your website
Internet merchant account	Not needed	Not needed	Not needed
Technical skills	HTML needed	None	HTML and API programming
Setup fee	Free	Free	Free
Monthly fee	Free	Free	Free
Per-transaction fees	2% + $0.20	2% + $0.20	2% + $0.20

Which option should you choose? If you're a small merchant or individual selling a limited number of items, the choice is simple—go with the Buy Now buttons. If you're a larger merchant with a pre-existing checkout system, the choice is also simple—use the Google Checkout API. And if you happen to already use a checkout system provided by one of Google's merchant services partners, go with the e-commerce partner integration option.

For larger merchants, the Google Checkout API is the way to go. This assumes that you already have a shopping cart application installed on your website; you then use the Google Checkout API to tie your system into the Google Checkout payment system. This requires programming expertise, of course, but provides a seamless

note Google Checkout also offers the option of invoicing customers via email, which is useful if you do the majority of your business via phone or fax. Just go to the Tools tab, select Send an Invoice through Email, and fill out the resulting form to email your invoice.

note Google Checkout has more than 40 shopping cart partners, including ChannelAdvisor, eCRATER, Mercantec, Miva, and MonsterCommerce. See the full list at checkout.google.com/seller/integrate_cart.html.

integration between your site and the Google Checkout system. Learn more at code.google.com/apis/checkout/.

Adding a Google Checkout Buy Now Button to Your Website

For most smaller sellers, the easiest route is to add Google Checkout Buy Now buttons to your website. When a customer clicks on the Buy Now button, he's taken to the checkout system hosted by Google Checkout, where he can pay via credit card.

To add a Buy Now button to your website, sign into Google Checkout, select the Tools tab, and then click the Buy Now Buttons link. This takes you to the Create a Buy Now Button page, shown in Figure 33.4.

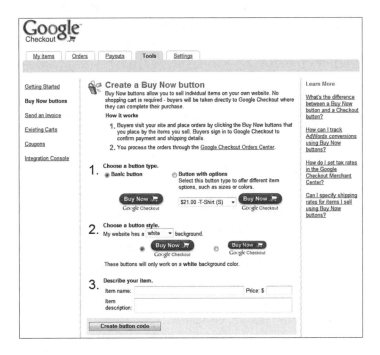

FIGURE 33.4

Creating a Buy Now button for your website.

From here, you select a button type (basic button or button with pull-down options list) and button style, and enter your item's name, price, and description. Click the Create Button Code button, and Google generates the HTML code for the button. Copy the code from this page into your web page's basic HTML code, where you want the button to appear, and you're ready to go.

Collecting Google Checkout Payments

What happens when someone clicks the Google Checkout Buy Now button on your website? If you've configured Google Checkout appropriately, Google will email you whenever a new order is received. Otherwise, you can manually check the Orders tab of the Google Checkout Merchant Center. All recent orders will be displayed here.

> **tip** If you want to be notified via email of all new purchases, go to the Google Checkout Settings tab and click the Preferences link. On the Order Processing page, check the option for Email Me Each Time I Receive an Order, Cancellation, or Other Transaction, and then click the Save Preferences button.

To view information about a specific order, simply click the order number. You'll now see the order details, and have the option of choosing a shipping carrier and entering a tracking number. You'll also need to okay the order and charge the customer's credit card; you do this by clicking the Charge button beside the order.

When you're ready to ship the order, return to the Orders tab and click the Ship button beside the order. This will mark the item as shipped, and send an automatic email message to the customer, informing him that the package is on the way.

Withdrawing Google Checkout Funds

Google Checkout automatically deposits all funds due into your bank account, electronically. For this to happen, you have to supply your bank account information to Google Checkout. You do this by going to the Settings tab and clicking the Financials link. This displays the Bank Information page; click the Set Up Account button.

When the Bank Account Setup page appears, enter the type of account (checking or savings), bank name, routing number, and account number; then click the Save Account button. Google will now deposit a small amount (a few pennies) into this account; when you see this deposit in your account, return to the Account Verification page and enter the amount deposited. This will verify that the system is working, and activate your account for direct deposit.

On an ongoing basis, Google Checkout will initiate payment to your account within two business days of a transaction. Know, however, that it might take up to three additional days for your bank to process the funds transfer. So, expect payment from a purchase to show up in your bank account within five days of the original purchase.

Google Checkout's Seller Protection Policy

To protect sellers from online fraud, Google Checkout offers both Chargeback Resolution and Payment Guarantee policies.

Under these policies, Google evaluates all chargebacks filed against your account for potential fraud, and reimburses you from claims of unauthorized purchases and non-receipt of goods. Provided your claim is accepted, Google will reimburse you within a week.

Of course, the transaction in question has to meet certain qualifications for you to be protected. In particular:

- You have to ship to the buyer's stated shipping address, using the shipping method specified when the order was placed.

- You have to provide a tracking number or other proof of shipping (for transactions less than $250).

    or

    You have to provide the customer's signature for proof of delivery (for transactions greater than $250).

- You have to display a clear return policy on your website.

- You provide all requested documentation to Google within ten business days of the request.

Google promises to reimburse you from fraudulent chargebacks up to $10,000 per year. If your gross Google Checkout sales exceed $1 million per year (lucky you!), Google will protect you for 1% of those sales.

The Bottom Line

For online merchants, Google Checkout is a viable alternative to PayPal. It lets you accept most major credit cards, and you'll pay less in transaction fees than you do to PayPal.

The main thing you can't do with Google Checkout is use it in your eBay auctions. At this point in time, it's strictly a merchant tool, not an auction tool. That said, Google Checkout will save you money over PayPal and similar alternatives, which is a good reason to check out Checkout.

33

Creating Web Pages with Google Sites

Here's one more Google service you might find useful, especially if you don't have your own page on the Web yet. That's right, Google can help you create your own web page—and share it with others. It's all possible via Google Sites, a combination page-creation and web-hosting service. via the Google Sites service…for free!

Understanding Google Sites

Google Sites (sites.google.com) is a way to create both personal and group web pages and sites. You can use Google Sites to create a single personal web page or a website

note Google Sites replaces Google Page Creator, Google's previous web page creation/hosting service.

for your business, community group, or family. In fact, Google Sites shines in its collaborative features; it's a great way to work on group projects online.

It all starts with web page creation, which Google Sites lets you do with a simple "fill in the form" interface. Enter some basic information, make a few choices, and you've created your first Google Sites page.

After you've created one page, it's equally easy to create more—and thus generate an entire website. It's also easy to open that website to authorized collaborators, who can then edit the site's pages, add their own content, and share web-based assets.

Your Google Site pages are hosted free by Google. You get 100MB of file storage; your site can hold an unlimited number of pages.

Creating Your First Web Page

To create your first Google Sites web page, go to sites.google.com and click the Create a Site button. You now see the Create New Site page, shown in Figure 34.1. As you can see, this page is nothing more than a short form, in which you enter the following information:

- Site name—the title that will show in your visitors' web browsers.
- Desired URL—enter the last part of the URL you want in the Your Site Will Be Located At box, or accept the URL that Google enters for you based on your site name.
- Site description—an optional description of your site's content.
- Mature content—check only if your site contains adult content not suitable for minors.
- Share with—decide whether you want your site to be public (Everyone in the world can view this site) or private (Only people I specify can view this site).

note Google Sites pages have URLs that follow the general form http://sites.google.com/sites/ *yourURL*. You get to choose the *yourURL* part of the address.

34

■ Site theme—choose from one of the proffered color and graphics schemes, or click the More Themes link to view additional themes.

After you've filled in the blanks and made your selections, click the Create Site button. Google now displays your page, as shown in Figure 34.2.

FIGURE 34.1

Your new Google Sites web page.

FIGURE 34.2

The Google Sites dashboard.

34

Adding Content to Your Web Page

To add content to your web page, click the Edit Page button above your page. (Only you, the site creator, sees this and other management buttons; regular users see only the page itself.) This opens the page for editing, as shown in Figure 34.3.

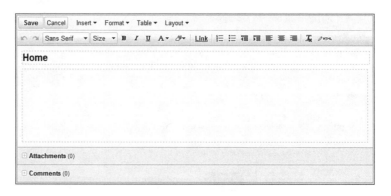

FIGURE 34.3

Editing a web page.

As you can see, what you have here is an "empty" page with two main sections, the title and the body. You add content to the page by clicking within each section and typing in your own text. For example, to add a title, replace the "Home" placeholder text with your own title.

To add a link to another web page, highlight the anchor text for the link, then click the Link link. When the Create Link dialog box appears, click Web Address and then enter the URL for that page. (Alternatively, you can link to other pages on your Google site by clicking Existing Page and selecting the page from those listed.)

To add an image to your web page, select Insert, Image. When the Add an Image dialog box appears, click the Browse button and select the image on your computer's hard drive. When you click the Add Image button, the image is inserted into your web page at the current cursor position.

Google also lets you insert various gadgets and Google elements to your page. The gadgets are similar to those you can add to your iGoogle page or to the Google Desktop; the Google elements include calendars (from Google Calendar), spreadsheets (from Google Docs), videos (from YouTube), and photo slideshows (from Picasa Web Albums). Just position your cursor where

34

you want the gadget or element to appear, select Insert, then select the item you want. You'll then be prompted with instructions specific to the type of element you added.

For example, to insert a photo slideshow, select Insert, Picasa Web Slideshow. When the Picasa Web Slideshow dialog box appears, as shown in Figure 34.4, enter the URL of your Picasa Web Album, choose a slideshow size, select other necessary options, then click the Save button. The slideshow is then automatically inserted into your web page.

FIGURE 34.4
Adding a Picasa slideshow to your web page.

When you're done editing your page, click the Save button. The changes you made will now display when you select that page in the Google Sites dashboard.

Adding New Web Pages

You probably don't want to create a site with just a single web page. To add more pages to your site, click the Create New Page button above your web page. This opens the Create New Page page, shown in Figure 34.5. Enter a name for this page, select what type of page it should be (a normal web page, a dashboard for group projects, an announcement page for group projects, a file cabinet to hold group files, or a list page for group to-do lists), and choose where you want the page in your site's hierarchy (to be the top-level home page or somewhere below that). Click the Create Page button, and the new page is added.

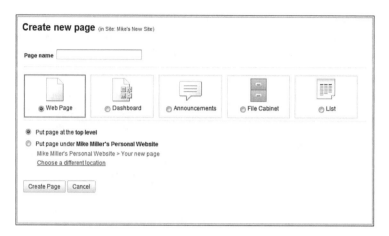

FIGURE 34.5

Adding a new page to your site.

You can then add content to that page the same way you added content to your original page. Just select that page in the dashboard and start typing!

Formatting Your Pages

When you create the pages of your site, Google applies the theme you originally selected for that first page. If you decide you don't like this theme, you can change it—as well as other elements of your web pages.

To change your site's theme, click the Site Settings link at the top of the page. When the next page appears, select the Appearance tab. This displays the Appearance page, shown in Figure 34.6. From here you can choose a new theme (click the Themes tab), customize your site layout (click the Site Elements tab), or change the color and font scheme (click the Colors and Fonts tab). Make your selection then click the Save Changes button.

> **tip**
>
> Google doesn't limit you to a single site. You can add more sites to your portfolio by clicking the My Sites link at the top of any Google Sites page. Your current sites are listed on the page that follows; to create a new site, click the Create New Site button and work your way through the familiar site creation process.

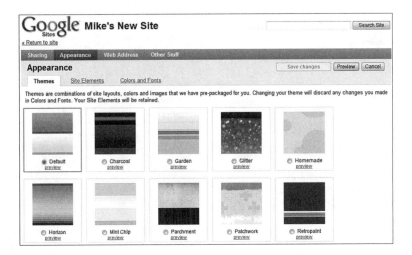

FIGURE 34.6
Choosing a new template.

Collaborating with Google Sites

If you want others to collaborate on your website, you have to invite them. You can invite other users with three different levels of access:

- **Viewers** can only view the site, not make any changes.
- **Collaborators** can create, edit, and delete pages; add attachments and comments to pages; and subscribe to be notified of site changes.
- **Owners** can do everything collaborators can, plus they can change the site theme and layout; change the site name; invite other owners, collaborators, and viewers; and delete the site.

To share your site with others, click the Site Settings link at the top of the page and then select the Sharing tab, shown in Figure 34.7. Check what level of access you want, then enter the users' email addresses into the Invite People box. Click the Invite These People button and the users you specified will receive an invitation via email. After a user has accepted your invitation, he'll be listed in the right side of the Sharing page.

34

FIGURE 34.7

Inviting others to share your page.

The Bottom Line

There's a lot more you can do with Google Sites than we have space for here, including adding specialized pages to better manage your group projects. I encourage you to check out Google Sites and explore all its features and capabilities. It's a great tool for both individuals and groups—and best of all, you get completely free web hosting!

34

Using Google on the Go

Using Google on Any Mobile Phone

As you've learned throughout this book, Google offers a wealth of features above and beyond basic web searching—maps, news, email, and the like. Wouldn't it be great if you could access all these features when you're out and about, away from your computer?

Well, you can—thanks to Google Mobile. This service lets you use almost any mobile phone to get the best of Google wherever you are. Now you can use your cell phone to get driving directions, avoid traffic congestion, compare product prices, check the weather forecast, send and receive email, and more—all from the convenience of your cell phone.

Signing Up for Google Mobile

To use most Google Mobile services, you must have a Java-enabled (J2ME) phone or mobile device and be subscribed to your cellular provider's data plan. The service itself from Google is free, although you may have to pay your cellular service provider for airtime or data download fees (which may be a good reason to look into your carrier's flat-rate data plans...).

note Google offers several mobile applications specifically for the Apple iPhone. Learn more in Chapter 36, "Using Google on the iPhone and iPod Touch."

To learn more about and sign up for Google Mobile, point the web browser of your desktop PC to www.google.com/mobile/. From there, enter the number your mobile phone, and Google sends an invitation text message to your phone. Click the link in the text message, and you'll see the Google Mobile home page on your cell phone's display. As you can see in Figure 35.1, this is the place to start using all the Google Mobile features.

FIGURE 35.1
The main Google Mobile screen on your mobile phone.

The Google Mobile home page on your mobile phone includes a web search box and the following menu items:

- Image Search
- iGoogle
- More

note Alternatively, you can point the web browser in your mobile phone to www.google.com/m; this also takes you to the Google Mobile start page.

35

- Settings
- Feedback
- Help

Select a menu item to start that service.

note All mobile phone screens and services are unique. The screens you see on your mobile device might look slightly different from those shown in this chapter.

Searching Google on the Go

Let's start with the service that Google is known for—searching the web. Thanks to Google Mobile, searching Google on your phone is every bit as easy as it is searching on your desktop PC.

To search Google on a web-enabled phone, all you have to do is go to the Google Mobile home page, enter your query into the search box, and then click the onscreen Search button. Google now returns a list of matching web pages, like the one shown in Figure 35.2. Click any link to view that page on your phone's web browser.

Google
Results: **birds**

Web pages
Bird - Wikipedia, the free encyclopedia **Birds** range in size from the 5 cm (2 in) Bee Hummingbird to the 2.7 m (9 ft) ...
en.wikipedia.org/wiki/Bird

WhatBird | identify birds | bird identification guide | north america Identify **birds** in North America for **bird** watching or as a **bird** guide. www.whatbird.com/

FIGURE 35.2
Search results displayed on a mobile phone.

Using Google Maps on Your Mobile Phone

Beyond basic search, the most useful Google Mobile service for many users is Google Maps. It's great to be able to access

tip If you've entered your location into Google Mobile, Google will automatically return local results based on your location. This makes it easier to search for local businesses, such as restaurants, hotels, and the like.

35

street maps, satellite maps, driving directions, and real-time traffic information
from the convenience of your mobile
phone—especially when you're driving in
your car!

> **note** You can also down-
> load the Google
> Maps application from
> www.google.com/gmm.

To access Google Maps for the first time, go to
the Google Mobile home page on your cell phone, select More, and then sele
Maps. This accesses and downloads the Google Maps application. Once dow
loaded, you can access Google Maps from the web application menu on you
phone.

Displaying a Location Map

Using Google Maps on your mobile phone is a snap. The first screen you see
a map of North America. To access all the Google Maps features, press the
Menu button on your phone's keypad. This displays an onscreen menu; you
can select an option from the menu, or press the keypad button correspondi
to that option.

To load a map of a specific location, display the Google Maps menu and
select Find Location. You're now prompted to enter an address, or to select a
recent or favorite address. You can use your phone's keypad to enter a specif
street address, a city, a state, or a ZIP code; when you press OK, Google displays a map of the selected location, like the one shown in Figure 35.3.

FIGURE 35.3

A Google map displayed on your cell phone screen.

Once the map is displayed, you scroll the map up or sideways by using the
direction buttons on your phone's keypad. To zoom closer, press the OK or ce
ter select button on your keypad; to zoom out, press the Zoom - softkey.

35

Displaying a Satellite Map

Alternatively, you can opt to display a satellite image of the selected area. Just press the menu key and select Satellite View; the map now switches from a street map to a satellite map, as shown in Figure 35.4.

> **tip**
>
> Once you've entered a location, you can save that location as a favorite for future use, so you don't have to type in the location's name each time. Just press 1 on your phone's keypad and select Save as a Favorite from the pop-up menu.

FIGURE 35.4

A Google map displayed in satellite view.

Displaying Traffic Information

One of my favorite Google Maps features is the ability to check for traffic congestion; this is especially useful during rush hour. Google displays this information for more than 30 major metropolitan areas.

To display real-time traffic info, select a location, display the menu, and then select Show Traffic. As you can see in Figure 35.5, clear traffic is displayed as a green route; moderately busy streets are displayed in yellow; congested routes are displayed in red.

FIGURE 35.5

Real-time traffic information on your mobile phone.

35

Displaying Driving Directions

Google Maps also lets you generate driving directions to or from your current location. This is a real boon when you're traveling and can't find a specific location—or just need help getting from point A to point B.

You start by displaying the Google Maps menu; then select Directions. You are now prompted to select a start point and an end point; these can either be points on the current map, or you can enter new addresses.

Google now calculates the route and displays step-by-step driving directions, as shown in Figure 35.6. To view a map of the currently selected step, press the # key on your phone; press the # key again to return to the text directions.

FIGURE 35.6

Viewing step-by-step directions on your mobile phone.

Finding Local Businesses

You can also use Google Maps to find local business in your current area. Just generate a map for the area and then click the Search soft key on your phone. When prompted, enter the type or name of the business you're looking for. Google will now display a list of matching businesses; select any individual business to view more information, or press the # key to view that business on a map. It's a great way to find the nearest gas station or restaurant while you're on a road trip!

tip

You don't have to use Google Maps to find local businesses. Google offers a local search service that can be accessed from Google's search function. Go to the Google Mobile home page on your phone and conduct a search for a particular type of business. When the search results screen appears, scroll to the bottom of the screen and enter your location (city, state, or ZIP code) into the Search Nearby box. Google will now return a list of businesses in the selected area.

Reading Google News on Your Mobile Phone

If you want to keep in touch with the outside world while you're on the go, you can browse Google News on your mobile phone. Just select News from the Google Mobile More menu, and you'll see a screen like the one in Figure 35.7. There's a search box at the top, with a list of today's top headlines below. Click any headline to read the full story.

FIGURE 35.7
News headlines on your mobile phone.

Scroll down the screen and, beneath the list of top stories, you'll see a list of major news categories—U.S., World, Entertainment, Sports, Sci/Tech, Business, and Health. Click any category to view the latest headlines within that category.

You can also search for specific news stories from this same page. Enter one or more keywords into the search box; then click the onscreen Search News button. Google will display a list of matching stories for you to read.

Sending and Receiving Gmail on Your Mobile Phone

Sometimes even an hour away from your computer can be a bad thing, particularly if you're expecting to receive an important email message. Fortunately, Google Mobile lets you access your Gmail account while you're on the go, using your mobile phone.

Of course, to use this feature, you first must have a Google Gmail account. Assuming you have a Gmail account, it's a snap to access your Gmail inbox from your mobile phone. Just go to the Google Mobile home

> **note** Learn more about Gmail in Chapter 14, "Sending and Receiving Email with Gmail."

35

page on your phone, select More, and then
select Gmail. You'll now be prompted to
download and install the separate Gmail
application; do so. Once downloaded, you
can access Gmail from the web application
menu on your phone.

note You can also download the Gmail application from www.gmail.com/app.

The first time you use the Gmail application, you'll be prompted for your
Gmail username and password. Your phone now displays your Gmail inbox,
as shown in Figure 35.8, with all read and unread messages listed.

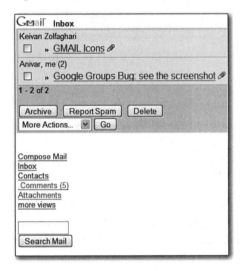

FIGURE 35.8

Viewing all the messages in your Gmail inbox.

Click a message header to read the full message. If a message has an attach
ment, click the attachment to view it onscreen. To reply to this message, pres
the Menu button and then select Reply. To delete this message, press the Men
button and then select More Actions, Delete.

To create a new message, go to the inbox and then select Compose Mail. En
the recipient's email address in the To box, the message subject in the Subj:
box, and the text of your message in the main text box. To send the email,
press the Actions button and select Send.

35

Viewing Google Calendars on Your Mobile Phone

note You can also access your Google Calendar by going directly to calendar.google.com from your mobile phone.

Want to keep track of your schedule and appointments while you're on the go? It's easy to do, now that Google Calendar is available for your mobile phone.

Assuming that you've already created a Google Calendar on the Web, it's simple to access that calendar from your mobile phone. Just go to the Google Mobile home page, select More, and then select Calendar. All upcoming events are displayed on your phone's screen, as shown in Figure 35.9. Select an event to view more details.

FIGURE 35.9

Viewing scheduled events on your mobile phone.

You can even add new appointments from your mobile phone. Just enter the name of the event into Quick Add box; then click the Add Now button. Any events you add from your phone are automatically synched to your web-based calendar.

Creating Mobile Blog Posts

If you're a blogger and you use Blogger to host your blog, Google Mobile lets you blog from anywhere at any time, using your mobile phone. All you have to do is create a blog post with your phone, as either a text message or email message. Send the message to go@blogger.com, and your message is automatically posted to your Blogger blog.

35

The same thing goes if you want to post a photo to your blog. Assuming tha[t] you have a camera phone, use your phone to snap a photo and then email that photo to go@blogger.com. The photo now appears as a new blog post.

Personalizing Your Google Mobile Search Page

If you like Google Mobile on your cell phone, you can customize your own Google personal home page—and then use this page as your starting page for your phone's web browser. In effect, your Google Mobile personalized home page uses the same content selected for your iGoogle personalized home page on the Web.

note Learn how to create a personalized iGoogle home page in Chapter 3, "Creating a Personalized Home Page with iGoogle."

On your mobile phone, you access your personalized home page by selecting iGoogle from the main screen. You'll be prompted to log onto your Google account, and then you'll see the mobile version of the personal home page you created on the Web.

If you like what you see, you can tell your cell phone to save this page as a favorite, or (when allowed) set this page as your phone's home page. Know, however, that many cellular service providers don't let you change home pages; they like you to lock into their home page, whether you like it or not.

Additional Google Mobile Features

We've discussed only the most popular features offered by Google Mobile. If you have a web-enabled cell phone, you can also access the following Googl[e] Mobile services (from the More menu):

- Google Docs (view word processing and spreadsheet documents—but not, as yet, presentations).
- Google Notebook (view and create notes and to-do lists).
- Google Reader (view blog posts and newsfeeds).
- Photos (from your Picasa Web Albums).
- YouTube (view videos).

Learn more about all of these features at mobile.google.com.

Search for More Information via Google Text Messaging

Google Mobile requires the use of a web-enabled cell phone. But even if your phone doesn't have Internet capability, you can still use it for Google searches—using text messages.

Here's how it works. Just create a new text message with your query as the message text; then send that message to number **46645** (that's "GOOGL" in numbers). Google will immediately text message back the matching results.

You can use this text-messaging approach to search for all sorts of information on Google—weather conditions, driving directions, sports scores, stock quotes, you name it. All you have to do is include the appropriate keywords in your query, and Google will know what type of search to conduct.

Here's just a sampling of information you can search for using Google's text messaging:

- **Weather conditions and forecast**—Enter the keyword **weather**, followed by the ZIP code or city name.

- **Real-time flight info**—Enter your flight number.

- **Stock quotes**—Enter the ticker symbol for the stock.

- **Sports scores**—Enter the name of the team (available only for sports in season).

- **Driving directions**—Enter the starting location, followed by the keyword **to**, followed by the ending location, like this: **minneapolis mn to hudson wi**.

- **Local businesses**—Enter the type of business, followed by the ZIP code, city, or state name.

- **Movie showtimes**—Enter the name of the movie, followed by the ZIP code or city name.

- **Product prices**—Enter the keyword **price**, followed by the product name or details; comparative prices are returned from the Google Product Search shopping search engine.

- **Word definitions**—Enter the keyword **define**, followed by the word you want to look up.

- **Foreign-language translations**—Enter the keyword **translate**, followed by the word to be translated, followed by the keyword **in**, followed by the language, like this: **translate toilet in german**.

35

■ **Conversions**—Enter the first number, followed by the keyword **in**, followed by the second number, like this: **20 dollars in yen**.

■ **Mathematical calculations**—Enter the appropriate formula, like this **5*5** or **10/3** or **2+2** or **7-5**.

Using Google for Directory Service

Here's a Google service that's not web-based. Google now offers voice-based directory service. GOOG-411, as it's called, is a voice-activated service that taps the same database used in Google Maps. It's just like the directory information you normally have to pay for when you dial 411; Google's service is free.

To access GOOG-411, dial 1-800-GOOG-411 (1-800-466-4411) from your phone and speak your request. You'll hear a voice menu of matching numbers; speak your selection, or press the corresponding key on your phone keypad. You'll be automatically connected to the selected business.

If you want a text version of your results, just speak "map it" into the phone Google will now send you a text message with details of your search, along with a link to a map of the location you asked about. Click the link to view the map on your phone's screen.

And remember—the service is completely free!

The Bottom Line

It's amazing everything Google can do, even when you're not around a PC. With Google Mobile and Google text messaging, a world of information is at your fingertips—all you need is your cell phone!

And if you happen to be a proud owner of an Apple iPhone, these applications are even snazzier—which you'll discover in the next chapter. Turn the page to learn more.

35

Using Google on the iPhone and iPod Touch

I f you like the way Google Mobile works on a normal cellular phone, you're going to love how Google apps work on Apple's iPhone. If you have a second-generation iPhone 3G (or a first-generation model or iPod Touch upgraded with the 2.0 version of the operating software), you get an entire suite of Google applications custom-designed for Apple's sweet little touchscreen.

Downloading Google's iPhone Apps

Google offers nearly a dozen applications designed for the iPhone and iPod touch. Two of these apps are built into the iPhone software, sort of, while the others have to be downloaded manually. All these applications are available free of charge.

iPhone's Native Google Apps

Two Google apps are part of the default iPhone interface and can be accessed from the home screen.

The first default application is Google Maps, which is what you get when you press the iPhone's Maps icon. That's right, the iPhone's Maps application is actually Google Maps, configured especially for iPhone use. We'll discuss this application separately in the "Google Maps" section later in this chapter.

The second default application is Gmail, which is one of the choices you get when you first access the iPhone's email application. Actually, you can configure the iPhone's email for any one of the major web-based email services—AOL Mail, Yahoo! Mail, Apple's MobileMe mail, and Gmail. (You can also configure the iPhone to work with Microsoft Exchange on corporate email servers.) If you choose to configure the iPhone for Gmail, you access your Gmail inbox every time you press the Mail icon. We'll cover this feature in more depth in the "Gmail" section later in this chapter.

Downloading Other Google Apps

Google's other applications have to be downloaded manually to your iPhone from the iPhone App Store. You can do this by pressing the App Store icon on the iPhone screen, or by accessing the Web via your host computer at www.apple.com/iphone/appstore/. If you use the former method, you download the applications directly to your phone; if you use the latter method, you download the applications to the iTunes software on your computer, and then transfer them to your phone the next time you sync your iPhone.

In any instance, search for Google Mobile App and make your download. It's completely free, and a relatively small download at that.

Evaluating Google's iPhone Apps

Google offers a full suite of applications custom designed for the iPhone and iPod Touch. Many of these applications use the iPhone's built-in GPS functionality to pinpoint your exact location; this is particularly useful when searching for local information or drawing a map.

The available applications include the following:

- Gmail
- Google Maps
- Google Web Search
- Google Calendar
- Google Docs
- Google Talk
- Google News
- Google Notebook
- Google Photos
- Google Reader
- iGoogle
- Blogger
- YouTube
- Goog411

We'll discuss each of these applications separately.

Gmail

As noted previously, Gmail can be configured as your default iPhone email service. Once configured, pressing the Mail icon on the iPhone's home screen brings up the Gmail folder list shown in Figure 36.1. Press the Inbox folder, and you see a list of your email messages, as shown in Figure 36.2.

36

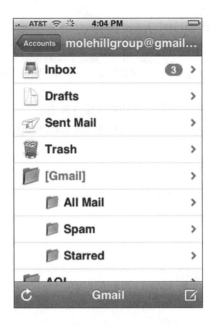

FIGURE 36.1

Viewing Gmail folders on your iPhone.

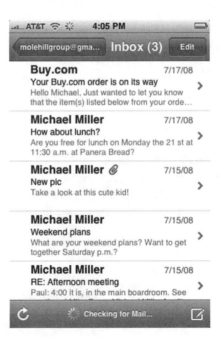

FIGURE 36.2

The contents of the iPhone's Gmail inbox.

To view an individual message onscreen, as shown in Figure 36.3, all you have to do is press the message in your inbox. You can reply to existing messages and create new ones, using the iPhone's onscreen keyboard to tap out your text.

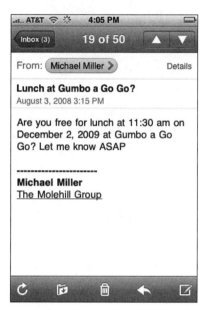

FIGURE 36.3

Reading a Gmail message onscreen.

Google Maps

The second Google application built into the iPhone is Google Maps. Press the Maps icon and Google Maps appears onscreen, as shown in Figure 36.4.

The neat thing about using Google Maps on an iPhone is that you can quickly locate your current location on the map. The iPhone 3G includes built-in GPS functionality, which means it uses satellite technology to pinpoint your exact location. Press the button at the lower-left corner of the screen and Google Maps centers on your current location. To display other locations, just enter the new location into the search box at the top of the Google Maps screen.

tip By default, the iPhone displays the standard map view. To switch to Satellite view or to display live traffic conditions, click the icon at the lower-right corner of the screen.

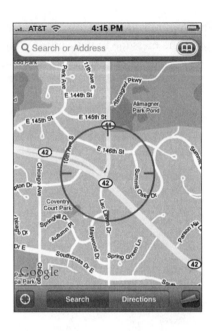

FIGURE 36.4

Mapping your current location with Google Maps.

You can also use Google Maps to display driving directions. Press the Directions button at the bottom of the screen; then click the Start button. The screen changes to display Start and End boxes at the top of the screen. Your current location is the default start location, although you can change this. Enter the desired destination into the End box; then click the Route button. Google now displays your route onscreen, as shown in Figure 36.5. Click the Start button to view turn-by-turn driving directions, one screen at a time.

Google Web Search

When you download Google Mobile Apps, a Google icon now appears on the iPhone home screen. (It's the big lowercase "g.") Press this icon, and you launch Google Web Search, as shown in Figure 36.6. This is what you use to search the web from your iPhone. Use the onscreen keyboard to enter your query into the search box; then press the Search button. Your search results are now displayed onscreen; press any link to access a given web page.

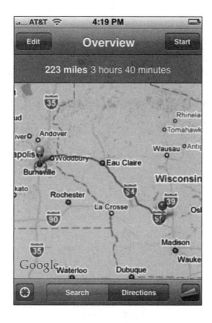

FIGURE 36.5
Generating driving directions.

FIGURE 36.6
Searching the web from your iPhone.

There's one other important item on the Google Web Search page—a link to all the other Google applications. Press the Explore More Google Products button and you see the list of apps shown in Figure 36.7. From here, you can press any icon to access that particular application.

FIGURE 36.7

Accessing all of Google's iPhone applications.

Google Calendar

Next on our tour of Google applications is Google Calendar. Press the Calendar icon on the Google apps screen, and you see a list of your upcoming Google Calendar events, like the one shown in Figure 36.8. Press any specific event to view more details.

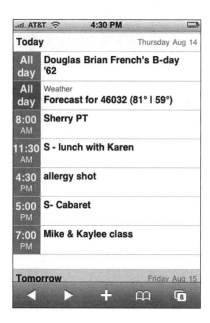

FIGURE 36.8

Viewing Google Calendar events.

This event list is downloaded from your web-based Google Calendar, of course. Unfortunately, you can't add new events from your iPhone; you have to do this from a computer connected to the Internet.

Google Docs

Did you know you can you use iPhone to view word-processing documents, spreadsheets, and presentations? That's right—all your favorite Google Docs applications are accessible via your iPhone and iPod Touch, from any location. Just press the Docs icon, and you're taken to the Google Docs home page, shown in Figure 36.9. Press any document title to view the document onscreen, as illustrated in Figure 36.10.

caution Don't confuse the Google Calendar application with the default Calendar application on the iPhone home screen. They're totally separate applications.

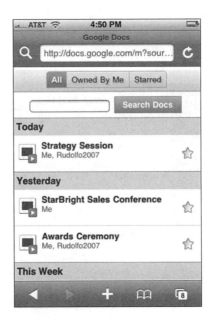

FIGURE 36.9

The Google Docs home page on the iPhone.

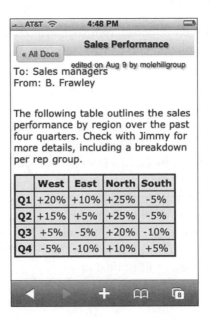

FIGURE 36.10

Viewing a word-processing document on the iPhone.

Google Talk

Want to stay in touch with your instant messaging buddies? Then use your iPhone to access the Google Talk network. When you press the Talk icon, your iPhone displays a list of your Google Talk contacts, as shown in Figure 36.11. Press the name of a contact to initiate a chat session, using the onscreen keyboard to type your messages.

> **caution** Google Docs is read-only on the iPhone; you can't edit your documents, only view them.

> **tip** Want to make your road presentations *really* portable? Give them from wherever you're at via Google Presentations on your iPhone; just connect your iPhone to an external monitor or projector via a third-party adapter cable and you're good to go!

FIGURE 36.11
Google Talk contacts on the iPhone.

Google News

With its dual WiFi/3G data access and included Safari web browser, you'd expect the iPhone to be a good way to keep abreast of the latest news events. Even easier than using the browser to go to a dedicated news site, however, is using Google News to deliver up-to-the-minute news headlines from a variety of sources. Press the News icon and you see a version of the normal Google News site customized for viewing on the iPhone. As you can see in Figure 36.12, you can scroll through the selected headlines on the front page, click the Sections button to view headlines on other topics, or search for specific news topics.

FIGURE 36.12
Viewing news headlines with Google News.

Google Notebook

As you recall from Chapter 7, "Saving Your Searches—and Signing Up for Google Alerts," Google Notebook lets you clip text and images from the web into your own notebooks, the easier to catalog the information you find online. You can access your Google notebooks from your iPhone by pressing the Notebook icon. This displays a list of your stored notebooks; you can

search through your notebooks or view a
given notebook in its entirety. You can
even add new notes to existing notebooks,
by pressing the Add Note to *Notebook* button within the notebook.

Google Photos

If you store your photos online in Picasa
Web Albums, you can view them with your
iPhone. Press the Photos icon, and you see a list of all your albums; open an
album and you see your pictures as thumbnails, as shown in Figure 36.13.
Press any photo to view it full screen.

> **tip** To save new notes while
> browsing the web with
> your iPhone, open Google
> Notebook and press the Add
> Note to Mobile Notes button.
> Mobile Notes is a special note-
> book you use to store all the
> notes you snip while browsing
> on the go.

FIGURE 36.13
Viewing photos in a Picasa Web Album.

Google Reader

If you follow a lot of blog feeds, you can read the latest posts on your iPhone
via Google Reader. Press the Reader icon, and you see a list of the most recent
posts for the feeds to which you've subscribed. Press a post title to read the
entire post, or press the Feeds button to see a list of your subscribed-to feeds.

iGoogle

If you like your iGoogle home page on your computer, you'll probably like the iPhone version, as well. Press the iGoogle icon, and you see a text-based version of the iGoogle page, like the one shown in Figure 36.14.

This iPhone iGoogle page isn't the same as your web-based iGoogle page, so you'll have to customize it from scratch. To add items to the page, press the Add Stuff link; to delete items from the page, press the Delete link; and to rearrange the order of items on the page, press the Delete link.

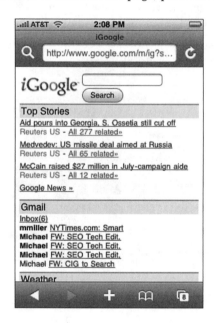

FIGURE 36.14

An iGoogle page for the iPhone.

Blogger

If you have one or more blogs hosted on Blogger, you can manage those blogs from your iPhone. Press the Blogger icon and you see a version of the Blogger Dashboard page. Press the appropriate links to create new posts, change your blog's layout and settings, or view your blog onscreen.

tip To add the iGoogle page or any other page to your iPhone favorites, press the + icon and then press the Add Bookmark button. Likewise, you can add an icon for this page to your iPhone's home screen by pressing the Add to Home Screen button.

YouTube

Here's a neat feature—and one accessible from the iPhone's home screen. With the iPhone's fast 3G connection, it's relatively painless to watch YouTube videos in the palm of your hand. Press the YouTube icon (from either the home screen or the Google Apps screen), and you're taken to a mobile version of the YouTube site. From here, you can search for videos, display a list of featured videos, and (of course) view videos. Videos are displayed in widescreen mode, which means you have to turn your iPhone sideways to view them. As you can see in Figure 36.15, transport controls are overlaid on the screen; touch the screen to display or touch again to hide the controls.

FIGURE 36.15
Watching a YouTube video on the iPhone.

Goog411

Finally, Google's voice-assisted phone directory service, Goog411, is accessible just by pressing a button on the iPhone. Press the Goog411 icon and your iPhone switches to cellular phone mode and dials the Goog411 service; from there, it's a simple matter of voicing your request into the phone.

The Bottom Line

If the iPhone is your mobile phone of choice, or if you're an iPhone Touch user, you have access to a world of customized Google applications. Google has truly embraced Apple's iPhone platform, the result being some of the best-working and most useful apps for the iPhone. Because they're all available free of charge, there's no reason at all not to download them and give them a try!

The Google Phone: Understanding Android

I n 2007, Apple introduced the iPhone, a revolutionary take on the traditional smartphone. This led to rumors of a "Google phone" to compete with the iPhone, especially in the realm of web-based applications and services.

But Google isn't a hardware company, as Apple is, and had no interest in manufacturing or selling a phone itself. Google did, however, see tremendous profit potential in the mobile market, but from selling advertising tied to mobile services, not from selling phone hardware. This, then, was to be the "Google phone"—not a mobile phone but rather a mobile platform on which Google could port its many web-based services and break into the mobile advertising market.

This new mobile platform was dubbed *Android*—and is the basis for a new generation of smart web-based phones from a variety of global manufacturers.

37

What Is Android?

Android is not a mobile phone; it's software, not hardware. Specifically, Android is a software platform and operating system for a variety of mobile devices. It was developed jointly by Google and the Open Handset Alliance, a consortium of 34 hardware, software, and telecom companies.

> **note** Learn more about Android, the Android SDK (software development kit), and Android applications at code.google.com/android.

The Android project was unveiled on November 5, 2007, shortly after Apple's release of the first-generation iPhone. Android is based on the Linux operating system; software developers write programs for Android using a Java-like scripting language.

The Android platform supports a wide variety of connectivity technologies, including GSM/EDGE, CDMA, Bluetooth, and WiFi. It supports both text (SMS) and multimedia (MMS) messaging, and includes an open-source web browser. Android also supports a variety of audio/video/photo formats, including JPG, PNG, GIF, MP3, AAC, MPEG-4, and H.264. It can also accommodate touch-screen input, video/still cameras, and GPS technologies.

Examining the HTC Dream: The First Google Phone

Several manufacturers, including Samsung and LG Electronics, are said to be developing phones based on the Android platform, and numerous carriers, including T-Mobile and Sprint, are supporting the platform for their cellular networks. That said, the first Android phone on the market is likely to be the Dream, manufactured by HTC and offered for sale by T-Mobile.

What is the HTC Dream? It's an iPhone-like smartphone, complete with touchscreen input and the capability to run a variety of custom applications. Look for these features on the final shipping unit:

- Large touchscreen with haptic feedback—that is, a tactile response when you touch a control on the screen.
- Slide-out design that reveals a full QWERTY keyboard under the touch-screen.
- Icon-based interface, like the one shown in Figure 37.1.

- Capability to enhance functionality by downloading custom applications.

- Internet connectivity with built-in web browser.

- 3G data network support.

- 3 megapixel digital camera.

- iPhone-like dimensions of 3" wide by 5" long.

FIGURE 37.1

A preview of the Android phone home screen.

In other words, the HTC Dream, powered by the Android platform, will be a head-to-head competitor with Apple's iPhone 3G. And you can expect it to come pre-loaded with a suite of Google's web-based applications, including Gmail, Google Maps, Google Calendar, and Google Docs.

note I'm writing about the Dream in September 2008, and details are predictably scarce. By the time you read this chapter, however, the Dream will be on sale and you'll know exactly what it is and what it does.

37

COMMENTARY

WHY ANDROID?

Given Google's history of Internet-based services for computer users, why is it diving head-first into the mobile phone market? After all, unlike Apple, Google has no intentions of making money from selling phones or sharing the revenue from cellular phone service.

No, Google isn't interested in hardware or service plans. It's interested, as always, in advertising. And Google believes that the market for mobile phone advertising will be even bigger than the market for Internet advertising in which it currently competes.

Remember, Google gives away its applications, both on the computer and for mobile phones. What it makes money on is selling the advertising that surrounds these applications, whether we're talking ads on search results pages, email messages, maps, or whatever. If Google can serve up the screen, it can serve up an advertisement on that screen.

And we're talking about a lot of mobile phone screens. The global mobile phone market consists of more than 2 billion users, which presents a lot of opportunities to serve up ads on those users' phones. *That* is why Google is aggressively pursuing the Android platform; it wants to ensure an open platform for its mobile apps and services—and its very profitable advertising.

As Google CEO Eric Schmidt said in an interview, "We can make more money on mobile than we do on the desktop, eventually." That's what it's all about.

The Bottom Line

Get this straight: Google isn't selling a "Google phone" to compete with Apple's iPhone. Instead, it's addressing the software/operating system end of things by helping develop the Android platform, all the better to propagate its applications and services to billions of mobile phone users around the globe. Phones based on the Android platform are open to all developers but will be especially Google-friendly; expect to see a variety of Android-powered phones from many major cell phone manufacturers and service providers throughout the coming months and years.

Making Money with Google

Optimizing Your Site for Google Search

I f you have your own personal website or manage a commercial website, making sure your site appears in Google's search results is a very important issue. Not only do you want to ensure that your site appears when someone searches Google for the appropriate subject, but you also want your site to rank as high as possible in those results. Appearing as the 99,999th result in a list of 100,000 isn't a good thing.

Although submitting your site to Google is a relatively easy process, increasing your site's ranking is a more involved process—so much so that an entire industry has risen around the topic of search engine optimization. So, if you want to improve your Google search ranking, roll up your sleeves and get ready for a little hard work!

How to Submit Your Site to the Google Index—The Easy Way

Although you could wait for the GoogleBot crawler to find your site on the Web, a more proactive approach is to manually submit your site for inclusion in the Google web index. It's an easy process—in fact, the easiest thing we'll discuss in this chapter.

All you have to do is go to www.google.com/addurl/, shown in Figure 38.1. Enter the URL for your home page into the appropriate box (including the http://), add any comments you might have, and then click the Add URL button. That's it; Google will now add your site to the GoogleBot crawl list, and your site will appear in the appropriate search results.

FIGURE 38.1

Submitting your site to the Google index.

Note that you only have to add the top-level URL for your site; you don't have to add URLs for any subsidiary pages. (For example, if your home page is http://www.homepage.com/index.html, enter only http://www.homepage. com.) GoogleBot will crawl the rest of your site once it finds the main URL.

How to Remove Your Site from the Google Index

If, for some reason, you want to remove your website from the Google index, the process is slightly more involved. What you need to do is place a special text file in the root directory of your website's server. This file should be named **robots.txt**, and should include the following text:

```
User-agent: Googlebot
Disallow: /
```

This code tells the GoogleBot crawler not to crawl your site. If you want to remove your site from *all* search engines (by preventing all robots from crawling the site), include the following text instead:

```
User-agent: *
Disallow: /
```

If you only want to remove certain pages on your site from the Google index, insert the following text into the **robots.txt** file, replacing *page.html* with the filename of the specific page:

```
User-agent: Googlebot
Disallow: /page.html
```

Finally, you can use the **robots.txt** file to exclude all pages within a specific directory. To do this, insert the following text, replacing *directory* with the name of the directory:

```
User-agent: Googlebot
Disallow: /directory
```

How to Submit a Complete Sitemap

There's another, better way to get your site listed in the Google index. This method lets you submit the URLs for every page on your website, manage the status of your pages, and receive reports about the visibility of your pages on Google. You do this by submitting a *sitemap*—literally, a map of the URLs of your entire site—to Google Sitemaps.

Google Sitemaps serves two general purposes. First, it helps to keep Google informed of all the new and updated pages on your site—in other words, to improve the freshness of the Google index. Second, the program should help to increase the

> **tip** To disallow other specific crawlers and spiders, see the (long) list at www.robotstxt.org/db.html.

coverage of all your web pages in the Google index. The first goal benefits Google; the second benefits you; and both goals should benefit Google's search users. Participation in Google Sitemaps is free.

Note that the Google Sitemaps program supplements, rather than replaces, the usual methods of adding pages to the Google index. If you don't participate in Google Sitemaps, your pages may still be discovered by the GoogleBot crawler, and you may still manually submit your site for inclusion in the Google index.

> **note** Google also has a separate Mobile Sitemaps program to add pages to its Mobile Web Index. Learn more information at www.google.com/webmasters/sitemaps/docs/en/mobile.html.

Creating a Map of Your Site

At first glance, creating a sitemap might seem daunting. Do you have to write down every URL on your site by hand?

Well, of course you don't; the whole sitemap process can be automated. To that end, many third-party sitemap generator tools exist for just that purpose.

For most of these tools, generating a sitemap is as simple as entering your home page URL and then pressing a button. The tool then crawls your website and automatically generates a sitemap file; this typically takes just a few minutes. Once the sitemap file is generated, you can then submit it to Google Sitemaps, as we'll discuss in short order.

Some of these sitemap tools are web-based, some are software programs, and most are free. The most popular of these tools include the following:

- AutoMapIt (www.automapit.com)
- AutoSitemap (www.autositemap.com)
- G-Mapper (www.dbnetsolutions.co.uk/gmapper/)
- GSiteCrawler (www.gsitecrawler.com)
- Gsitemap (www.vigos.com/products/gsitemap/)
- Site Magellan (www.sitemagellan.com)
- SitemapsPal (www.sitemapspal.com)
- SitemapDoc (www.sitemapdoc.com)
- XML-Sitemaps.com (www.xml-sitemaps.com)

In most instances, you should name your sitemaps file **sitemaps.xml** and place it in the uppermost (root) directory of your website—although you can name and locate it differently, if you like.

note Google also offers its own free sitemap generator (www.google.com/ webmasters/tools/docs/en/ sitemap-generator.html)— although, to be honest, it's not quite as user-friendly as some of the third-party tools available.

Submitting Your Sitemap—the Hard Way

After you've created your sitemap, you have to let Google know about it. There are two ways to do this—the easy way and the hard way.

The hard way (which isn't all that hard) is to reference your sitemap within your site's **robots.txt** file, which should be located in the root directory of your website.

What you need to do is add the following line to your **robots.txt** file:

```
SITEMAP: www.sitename.com/sitemaps.xml
```

Naturally, you need to include the actual location of your sitemaps file. The preceding example works only if you have the file in your site's root directory; if it's in another directory, include that full path. Also, if you've named your sitemaps file something other than **sitemaps.xml**, use the actual name, instead.

The next time the GoogleBot spider crawls your site, it will read your **robots.txt** file, learn the location of your sitemaps file, and then read the information in that file. It will then crawl all the pages listed in the file, and submit information about each page to the search engine for indexing.

Submitting Your Sitemap—the Easy Way

If all you're interested in is Google reading your sitemap (fie on you, Yahoo!), then you can submit your sitemap directly to Google Sitemaps. This ensures that Google will know about your sitemap—and its contents.

tip The advantage of referencing your sitemap via the **robots.txt** file is that it makes your sitemap visible to searchbots from all the major search engines, not just Google. Every searchbot reads the **robots.txt** file and thus is directed to your sitemap.

38

To upload your sitemap to Google, follow these steps:

1. Upload your sitemap file to the highest-level directory (typically the root directory) on your web server.

2. Go to your Webmaster Tools Dashboard (www.google.com/webmasters/tools/dashboard).

3. If your site is not yet added to your Dashboard, do so now.

4. Click the Add a Sitemap link beside your site.

5. When prompted, select which type of sitemap you're adding—for most web pages, that's a general web sitemap.

6. The Add Sitemap page now expands, as shown in Figure 38.2. Check that you've created the sitemap in a supported format and uploaded your sitemap to your website's highest-level directory.

7. Enter the URL for the sitemap file.

8. Click the Add General Web Sitemap button.

note Even when you submit a complete sitemap, Google doesn't guarantee that it will crawl or index all the URLs on your website. However, since Google uses the data in your sitemap to learn more about your site's structure, it should improve the crawler schedule for your site, and ultimately improve the inclusion of your site's page in Google's search results.

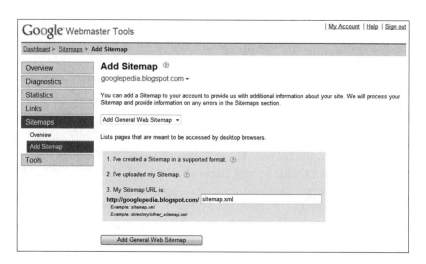

FIGURE 38.2

Adding a sitemap for your website.

How to Optimize Your Site's Ranking

Making sure your web pages are included in the Google search index is one thing; working to ensure a high PageRank within those results is something else. The process of tweaking your website to achieve higher search results on Google and other search sites is called *search engine optimization (SEO)*, and it's a major consideration for all big-time webmasters.

> **tip** To learn more about search engine optimization in general, check out my companion book, *The Complete Idiot's Guide to Search Engine Optimization* (Alpha Books, 2008).

To increase your site's ranking in Google's search results, you have to increase your site's PageRank. There are a number of ways to do this, almost all of which involve manipulating the content and HTML code of your site. Read on to learn some of the most effective techniques.

Increase the Number of Inbound Links to Your Site

Probably the biggest impact you can have on your site's PageRank is to increase the number of sites that link to the pages on your site. (These are called *inbound links*.) As you learned back in Chapter 1, "Inside Google," the PageRank rating is based on a complex and proprietary algorithm, which is heavily weighted in favor of inbound links to your site. The more sites that link to your site—and the higher the PageRank of those links sited—the higher your site's PageRank will be.

To increase your PageRank, then, you want to get more higher-quality sites to link back to your site. And it's not enough for those sites to have a high PageRank; they should also have content that is relative to your site. For example, if you have a site about NASCAR racing, you'll get more oomph with a link from another NASCAR-related site than you would with a link from a site about Barbie dolls. Relevance matters.

Create a Clear Organization and Hierarchy

The GoogleBot crawler can find more content on a web page and more web pages on a website if that content and those pages are in a clear hierarchical organization.

Let's look at page organization first. You want to think of each web page as a mini-outline. The most important information should be in major headings,

38

with lesser information in subheadings beneath the major headings. One way to do this is via standard HTML heading tags, like this:

```
<h1>Most important information
    <h2>Less important information
        <h3>Least important information
```

This approach is also appropriate for your entire site layout. Your home page should contain the most important information, with subsidiary pages branching out from that containing less important information—and even more subpages branching out from those. The most important info should be visible when a site is first accessed via the home page; additional info should be no more than a click or two away.

This hierarchical organization is easily seen when you create a sitemap for your users. (This is distinct from the sitemap you create for and submit to Google Sitemaps.) A visible sitemap, looking for all the world like a big outline, not only makes it easier for visitors to find information on your site, it also gives the GoogleBot crawler some very meaty information to process.

Include Appropriate Keywords

Just as important as a page's layout is the page's content. You want to make sure that each and every page on your site contains the keywords that users might use to search for your pages. If your site is all about drums, make sure your pages include words like **drums**, **percussion**, **sticks**, **heads**, **drumset**, **cymbals**, **snare**, and the like. Try to think through how *you* would search for this information, and work those keywords into your content.

Put the Most Important Information First

Think about hierarchy and think about keywords, and then think about how these two concepts work together. That's right, you want to place the most important keywords higher up on your page. The GoogleBot will only crawl so far, and you don't want it to give up before key information is found. In addition, PageRank is partially determined by content; the more important the content looks to be on a page (as determined by placement on the page), the higher the PageRank will be.

Make the Most Important Information Look Important

Google also looks to highlighted text to determine what's important on a page. It follows, then, that you should make an effort to format keywords on your page as bold or italic.

38

Use Text Instead of Images

Here's something you might not think about. At present, Google parses only text content; it can't figure out what a picture or graphic is about, unless you describe it in the text. So, if you use graphic buttons or banners (instead of plain text) to convey important information, Google simply won't see it. You need to put every piece of important information somewhere in the text of the page—even if it's duplicated in a banner or graphic.

> **caution** Similarly, don't hide important information in Flash animations, JavaScript applets, video files, and the like. Remember, Google can only find text on your page—all those non-text elements are invisible to the GoogleBot.

If you do use images on your site, make sure you use the <ALT> tag for each image, and assign meaningful keywords to the image via this tag. GoogleBot will read the <ALT> tag text; it can't figure out what an image is without it.

Link via Text

Following on the previous tip, make sure that you link from one page to another on your site via text links—not via graphics or fancy JavaScript menus. Google will find and use the text links to crawl other pages on your site; if the links are non-text, GoogleBot might not be able to find the rest of your site.

Incorporate <META> Tags

When calculating PageRank, Google not only considers the visible content on a page; it also evaluates the content of key HTML tags—in particular, your site's <META> tags. You want to make sure that you use <META> tags in your page's code, and assign important keywords to each of those tags.

The <META> tag, which (along with the <TITLE> tag) is placed in the head of your HTML document, can be used to supply all sorts of information about your document. You can insert multiple <META> tags into the head of your document, and each tag can contain a number of different attributes. The two most important <META> attributes, when it comes to search index ranking, are **DESCRIPTION** and **KEYWORDS**. You use the first to provide a brief description of the page's content; you use the second to list all the important keywords that might be used to search this page.

38

You use separate <META> tags to define different attributes, using the following format:

```
<META name="attribute" content="items">
```

Replace *attribute* with the name of the particular attribute, and *items* with the keywords or description of that attribute.

note There are many more <META> attributes than the ones listed here (such as **CHANNEL**, **DATE**, and so on), but neither Google nor most other search engines read them.

For example, to include a description of your web page, you'd enter this line of code:

```
<META name="DESCRIPTION" content="All about stamp collecting">
```

To add keywords that GoogleBot can index, enter this line of code:

```
<META name="KEYWORDS" content="stamps, stamp collecting, collectable
stamps, stamp history, stamp prices">
```

Note that you separate each keyword by a comma, and that a "keyword" can actually be a multiple-word phrase. You can include up to 10 keywords with this attribute.

You can include all three of these <META> attributes in the head of your HTML document, each in separate lines of code, one after another, like this:

```
<META name="DESCRIPTION" content="All about stamp collecting">
<META name="KEYWORDS" content="stamps, stamp collecting, collectable
stamps, stamp history, stamp prices">
```

Make Good Use of the <TITLE> Tag

Your page's title is important because it's one of the first places that Google's searchbot looks to determine the content of your page. GoogleBot figures, hopefully rightly so, that the title accurately reflects what the page is about; for example, if you have a page titled "The Dutch Apple Pie Page," that the page is about Dutch apple pies. Unless you mistakenly or purposefully mistitle your page, the searchbot will skim off keywords and phrases from the title to use in its search engine index.

In addition, when your page appears on Google's search results page, the title is the search engine uses as the listing name. The title is also what appears in the favorites list when a visitor adds your site as a favorite.

For all these reasons, you need to get your most important keywords and phrases into your page's title—which you do via the HTML <TITLE> tag. In fact, <TITLE> tag is just as important as the <META> tag—which is why you shouldn't fall into the trap of assigning only your site name to the tag. Instead, the <TITLE> tag should contain two to three important keywords, followed by the site name.

For example, if your stamp collecting site is called The Stamp Shop, you might use the following <TITLE> tag:

```
<TITLE>The Stamp Shop - Collecting,
Prices, and History</TITLE>
```

> **tip** What's the ideal length of a title? There's a 64-character limit (anything beyond that gets truncated), and you should probably pace your title to include anywhere from 3 to 10 words total. This makes the title both readable for users (short enough to scan) and useful for Google and other search engines (long enough to include a handful of keywords).

Use Heading Tags Instead of CSS

This is a tough one. Most cutting-edge web designers have switched from standard heading tags (<H1>, <H2>, and so on) to Cascading Style Sheet (CSS) <DIV> and <SPAN> codes. That's unfortunate, as Google looks for the old-fashioned heading tags to determine the content (and thus the PageRank) of your site. If you want to optimize your ranking in the Google index, you'll switch back to the <H1> and <H2> tags for your page headings—and make sure you use the content of those tags wisely.

Update Your Code Frequently

GoogleBot crawls the Web with some frequency, looking for pages that have changed or updated content. If your site hasn't changed in awhile, this can affect your PageRank. So you'll want to make sure you change your content on a regular basis; in particular, changing the content of your heading tags can have a big impact on how "fresh" Google thinks your site is.

Use RSS Feeds for Dynamic Content

Contrary to the previous advice, Google actually has a problem tracking some frequently updated content—in particular, the type of dynamic content generated by blogs, news sites, and the like. Put simply, GoogleBot doesn't crawl dynamic pages as well as it does static pages. (It has to do with how long it takes some dynamic pages to load; spiders only allocate a certain amount of time per page before they move on to the next site to index.)

There are two solutions to this problem. One is to use a content management system (CMS) that loads fast enough to appease the GoogleBot crawler. The second solution is to publish your dynamic content as an RSS feed. This second solution is probably the best one, as Google does a really good job digesting RSS feeds to populate its search index. When in doubt, make sure that you generate an RSS feed for all your dynamic content.

Provide Authoritative Content

I've saved the best SEO tip to the last. If you want to increase your Google PageRank, increase the quality of your site's content. It's simple: The better your site is, content-wise, the higher it will rank.

That's right, when it comes to search rank, content is king. Google's goal is to figure out what your site is all about so it can better answer its users search queries. The higher quality and more relevant your site's content to a particular search, the more likely it is that Google will rank your site higher in its results.

So forget all about keywords and <META> tags for the time being, and focus on what it is your site does and says. If your site is about quilting, work to make it the most content-rich site about quilting you can. Don't skimp on the content; the more and better content you have, the better.

How *Not* to Optimize Your Site's Ranking

Now that you know the things you can do to increase your site's ranking, let's take a quick look at the things you *shouldn't* do—that is, things that can actually *decrease* your site's PageRank.

Avoiding Things Google Doesn't Like

There are some things you can do to your site that Google absolutely, positively won't like. And when Google doesn't like something, your PageRank suffers—or, worst-case scenario, you don't show up in the search index at all.

What are some of these ill-considered techniques? Here's a short list:

- **Long and complicated URLs.** The shorter and more straightforward a page's URL, the better. Google doesn't like long URLs, nor does it like URLs that contain special characters. To that end, don't use &id= as a parameter in your URLs; similarly, avoid the use of dynamic URLs. Google indexes only static URLs, not those that are dynamically generated. If your site does include dynamic pages, use a URL rewrite tool to turn your dynamic URLs into static ones.

note When done deliberately, including too many keywords is known as *keyword stuffing*, which we'll discuss later in this chapter.

■ **Splash pages.** Here's the thing about splash pages (those introductory pages that appear before users can advance to your site's true home page): Nobody likes 'em. Visitors don't like them, because they make it longer to get into your site. And Google doesn't like them, because they don't include the types of internal links and menus found on a true home page; nor do they include much, if any, text content. (If there are no links to other pages from the first page that GoogleBot encounters, it won't know about the other pages on your site.) So, you should make your site's first page a traditional home page, not a splash page; both your visitors and the searchbots will be much happier.

■ **High keyword density.** Although keywords are good, too many of them are bad. (Google assumes that you're including keywords just to get a high PageRank, instead of creating unique content for your users.) So don't include too many keywords (especially repeated keywords) in your content or <META> code. If a page has too high a keyword density, Google will categorize your page as a doorway page—and penalize you accordingly.

■ **Hidden text.** This is when you disguise keywords or links by making them the same or similar color as the page background, using a tiny font size, or hiding them within the HTML code itself. Many webmasters think this is a clever way to stuff lots of keywords onto a page without looking as if they're doing so. Unfortunately, you can't trick a searchbot; GoogleBot sees hidden text just as easily as it does the regular text on your page—which means they'll see all those keywords you're trying to stuff. And, as you know, searchbots don't like keyword stuffing.

■ **Duplicate content.** Here's another false trick that too-savvy webmasters sometimes employ, to their own detriment—duplicating content on a site, in the hopes of increasing the number of hits in search engine results. This may be done by putting the same content on multiple pages, or via the use of multiple domains or subdomains. Unfortunately, duplicating content is a bad idea, as Google utilizes

38

duplicate content filters that will identify and remove duplicate sites from their search results. When you duplicate your content, you run the risk that your main site or page will be filtered out—while the sub sidiary content remains!

■ **Bad outbound links.** You know that the quality of your inbound link matters; did you know that the quality of your *outbound* links can als affect your search rankings? That's right, Google considers the sites yc link to as part of its page-ranking process—at least when it comes to overtly low-quality sites. For that reason, you don't want to link to a site that's been dropped or banned from a search engine's index; you could get tarred by relation.

■ **Images, videos, and animations.** It's a simple concept—searchbots read text (including HTML code); they can't view images, videos, or Flash animations. Which means, of course, that creating an image- o animation-heavy page renders that page virtually invisible to Google spider. Your page might look great to visitors, but if GoogleBot can't s it, it won't get indexed. When in doubt, go with a text-based approac

■ **Big pages.** Here's another reason to go easy on web page images: GoogleBot doesn't like big pages. More specifically, it doesn't like long load times. If it takes too much time for all the elements on a page to load, GoogleBot will give up and move on to the next page in its queue—bad for you.

■ **JavaScript code.** As you've learned, Google's spider reads text and HTML code—well, *some* HTML code. GoogleBot will ignore JavaScript code in your HTML, which means anything you have in a script won' be indexed. This is particularly vexing if you use a JavaScript menu system; searchbots may not see all the internal links you have in you menus.

■ **Too much code.** Speaking of HTML code, don't overdo it. Having mor code than you do actual text on your page will cause GoogleBot to giv up before your entire page is crawled. You should avoid employing to many code-heavy effects, such as nested tables or JavaScript effects. If your important text is buried under hundreds of lines of code, you'll b at a disadvantage compared to a well-optimized site.

■ **Messy code.** One last thing when it comes to the coding of your site: Don't create messy code. This is one instance where neatness counts; messy HTML can confuse Google's searchbot and cause it to miss important content.

Deliberate Practices to Avoid

The previous section talked about things you might accidentally do that can adversely affect your PageRank rating. There are also some practices that sneaky web designers deliberately do to increase their page rank; Google takes issue with these practices, and can ban you from their index if you're caught.

> **note** Any attempt to influence search engine rank via misleading methods is referred to as *search engine spamming* or *spamdexing*. The practice of creating a website solely for the purpose of achieving a high PageRank is called *Googleating* (pronounced "Google-ating," not "Google-eating").

To that end, here are some of the more nefarious outlawed optimization practices:

- **Google bombing.** Sometimes called *Google washing* or *link bombing*, this is an attempt to increase your PageRank by having a large number of sites link to a page by using identical anchor text. For example, you might register several domains and have them all link to a single site using the same anchor text for the links. Searching for the term used in the link anchor text will return the linked-to site high in the search results. (Google bombing often occurs in blogs, where a site owner will "bomb" multiple blog postings with replies linking to the owner's site.)

- **Keyword stuffing.** This is when you insert hidden, random text on a page to increase the keyword density, and thus increase the apparent relevancy of a page. For example, if your page is about trains, you might insert several lines of invisible text at the bottom of the page repeating the keyword **train**, over and over, or include multiple instances of the word **train** in a <META> tag. In the past, some search engines simply counted how often a keyword appeared on a page to determine relevance; today, Google employs algorithms to detect keyword stuffing. (A related technique is *meta tag stuffing*, where keywords are stuffed into HTML meta tags.)

- **Doorway pages.** This is a web page that is low in actual content, instead stuffed with repeating keywords and phrases designed to increase the page's search rank. Doorway pages typically require visitors to click a "click here to enter" link to enter the main website; in other instances, visitors to a doorway page are quickly redirected to another page.

38

- **Link farms.** This is a group of web pages that all link to one another. The purpose of a link farm is to increase the number of links to a given site; since PageRank is at least partially driven by the number of linked-to pages, using a link farm can make it appear as though a large number of sites are linking to given site.

note Doorway pages are also known as gateway pages, landing pages, bridge pages, portal pages, zebra pages, jump pages, and entry pages.

- **Mirror websites.** This is the hosting of multiple websites, all with the same content, but using different URLs. The goal is to increase the likelihood that any one (or more) of the mirror sites will appear on Google's search results pages.

- **Cloaking.** This is an attempt to mislead Google by serving up a different page to the GoogleBot crawler than will be seen by human visitor. This is sometimes used for *code swapping*, where one page is optimized to get a high ranking, and then swapped out for another page with different content.

- **Scraper sites.** This is a site that "scrapes" results pages from Google and other search engines to create phony content for a website. A scraper site is typically full of clickable ads.

PROFESSIONAL SEARCH ENGINE OPTIMIZATION

When it comes to optimizing your site for search, should you try to do everything in-house or should you hire an outside SEO firm to do at least part of the work for you? The answer to this question depends on your own particular situation.

For many companies, doing their own search engine optimization is the only financially viable alternative. It costs money to hire a professional SEO consultant, and most SEO techniques can be implemented by in-house marketing and technical staff. In other words, it's cheaper to do it yourself.

That said, hiring a professional to optimize your site makes sense if you want the best possible optimization done as quickly as possible. That's because SEO professionals have done it all before; they know exactly what has to be done, and know how to do it. You'll pay for their expertise, of course, but it might be worth it.

When you're looking for an SEO professional, consult one of the several SEO directories on the web. These include SEOfinders.net (www.seofinders.net) and the SEO Services Marketplace (www.seomoz.com/marketplace/). You can also search Google for SEO professionals; you can expect the firms with the best optimized sites to appear high in the search results.

Know, however, that search engine optimization is an area that attracts a number of scam artists. And, given that the topic of SEO is confusing even to experienced web designers, it's easy to be taken in by false claims and unrealistic promises.

When you're evaluating an SEO firm, beware those that promise you specific results, or that claim a "special relationship" with Google (or Microsoft or Yahoo!). There is no way to guarantee a number-one ranking in any search engine's search results; all anyone can do is follow good design practices.

So, how can you tell a legitimate SEO firm from a fraudulent one? No legitimate SEO firm will attempt to falsify results, generate phony results or traffic, or use deceptive spamdexing methods. Nor will any legitimate firm guarantee a particular Google ranking. When it comes to improving your search engine ranking, there is no magic formula; success is directly related to the amount of hard work involved.

38

The Bottom Line

Google makes it easy to get listed in its web index, but getting listed is just the start. Making sure that your listing appears high in Google's search results requires a lot of hard work, a bit of technical savvy, and—oh, yeah—useful and relevant content. In fact, too many webmasters get hung up on arcane search engine optimization techniques, when they should be focusing on creating sites that more visitors actually want to visit. If you spend your time creating a compelling and well-designed website, a high Google ranking will, more often than not, naturally follow.

Advertising with Google AdWords

"Sponsored links." You've seen them; they're the text ads that pop up on Google's search results pages, as well as similar text ads that appear on other pages across the Web. If you're a consumer, you might have even clicked a few. And if you're an advertiser—well, if you're a web advertiser—these little ads are probably a big component of your online marketing program.

Where do these "sponsored links" come from? It's all part of a Google program called Google AdWords. AdWords is nothing more and nothing less than an advertising network; it's where Google sells all the ads it places, both on users' sites and on its own search results pages.

AdWords is the web's largest proponent of what is called *pay-per-click* advertising. And if you or your business wants to place an ad (excuse me, a "sponsored link") on selected Google search results pages, you need to sign up for the AdWords program.

How Pay-Per-Click Advertising Works

Pay-per-click advertising isn't like traditional display advertising. PPC advertising doesn't buy discrete space on a given web page, nor does it allow for graphics-intensive advertisements. Instead, it's all about getting a text ad onto a specific search results page.

Purchasing Keywords

A PPC advertiser purchases a particular keyword or phrase from the AdWords ad network. More precisely, the advertiser purchases ad space that appears on Google's search results pages and other websites that relate to the keywords in question. The advertiser's text ad is linked to that keyword in two different ways.

First, when a user enters a query on Google's search site, the advertiser's ad is displayed on the first page of the search results, in the "sponsored links" section that appears at the top or side of the page. As you can see in Figure 39.1, the ad is designed to look kind of like an organic search result.

FIGURE 39.1
PPC ads on Google's search results page.

The second place the ad appears is on third-party sites that belong to the AdWords ad network. The ad is placed on specific pages that have content that relates to the purchased keyword. These ads, also text-only (as you can see in Figure 39.2), can appear anywhere on the given page; the ad placement is up to the owner of the web page.

FIGURE 39.2

PPC ads on a third-party web page.

So, for example, if you sold printer ink cartridges, you might purchase the words "printer," "ink," and "cartridges." When a consumer searches Google for any of these keywords, your ad appears. Your ad also appears when a consumer goes to a third-party website that features content containing these keywords.

Placing Ads in Context

The neat thing about PPC ads is that they use advanced search technology to serve content-focused ads—that is, an ad that relates to the underlying content of the host web page. And an ad that is somehow related to the content of a web page reaches a more targeted audience than a more broadly focused display ad.

You see, Google uses the same sophisticated algorithms that it uses to create its search index to determine the content of pages for sites that participate in its advertising program. It analyzes the keywords on the page, word frequency, font size, and the overall link structure to figure out, as closely as possible, what a page is about. Then it finds ads that closely match that page's content, and feeds those ads to the page.

For example, my personal website (www.molehillgroup.com) is all about the books I've written. On the page for my book *iPodpedia*, Google AdWords serves up ads titled "iPod Copying Software" and "Rescue Your iPod Music;" on the page for *The Complete Idiot's Guide to Playing Drums*, there are ads for "1,684 Video Drum Lessons" and "Yamaha DTX Drums 40% Off." The right ads for the right content—which greatly benefits the advertisers.

Paying by the Click (PPC Advertising)

The reason it's called pay-per-click advertising is that an advertiser pays the ad network only when customers click on the link in the ad. (The link typically points to the advertiser's website—or, most commonly, a special landing page on the website.) If no one clicks, the advertiser doesn't pay anyone anything. The more clicks that are registered, the more the advertiser pays.

39

Ad rates are calculated on a cost-per-click (CPC) basis. That is, the advertiser is charged a particular fee for each click—anywhere from a few pennies to tens of dollars. The actual CPC rate is determined by the popularity of and competition for the keyword purchased, as well as the quality and quantity of traffic going to the site hosting the ad. As you can imagine, popular keywords have a higher CPC, while less popular keywords can be had for less.

Advertisers typically bid on the most popular keywords. That is, you might say you'll pay up to $5 for a given keyword. If you're the high bidder among several advertisers, your ads will appear more frequently on pages that contain that keyword. If you're not the high bidder, you won't get as much visibility—if your ad appears at all.

> **note** Pay-per-click advertising is in contrast to traditional cost-per-thousand-impressions (CPM) advertising, where rates are based on the number of potential viewers of the ad—whether they click through or not.

> **note** A given PPC ad probably won't appear on every search engine results page for the keyword purchased. That's because page inventory for a given keyword is limited, while advertisers are theoretically unlimited. That's why AdWords rotates ads from multiple advertisers on its search results and third-party pages.

Sharing Ad Revenue

Here's something interesting about PPC advertising; it's not just Google that gets paid. Typically, any third-party site where the ad appears gets a cut of the ad revenues paid by the advertiser—which is why sites agree to put PPC ads on their web pages.

So, here's the way it works:

1. An advertiser creates an advertisement and contracts with Google AdWords to place that ad on the Internet.
2. Google serves the ad in question to a number of appropriate websites.
3. An interested customer sees the ad on a third-party site and clicks the link in the ad to receive more information.
4. The advertiser pays Google, based on the CPC advertising rate.
5. Google pays the host site a small percentage of the advertising fee paid.

> **note** The Google Network includes all of Google's sites (Google Maps, Gmail, YouTube, and the rest), the hundreds of thousands of small and medium-sized sites that participate in the Google AdSense program, and a number of major websites, including Amazon.com, AOL, and About.com.

If you're interested in placing AdWords ads on your website or blog, you need to sign up for Google's companion AdSense program. We'll talk more about AdSense in Chapter 40, "Profiting from Google AdSense;" turn there for more information.

Determining Your AdWords Costs—And Choosing a Payment Option

Advertising with Google AdWords isn't like a traditional advertising buy; there are no contracts and deadlines and such. You pay a one-time $5.00 activation fee, and then are charged either on a cost-per-click (CPC) or cost-per-thousand-impressions (CPM) basis. (You can choose either payment method.) You control your costs by specifying how much you're willing to pay (per click or per impression) and by setting a daily spending budget. Google will never exceed the costs you specify.

How much does AdWords cost? It's your choice. If you go with the cost-per-click method, you can choose a maximum CPC click price from $0.01 to $100. If you go with the CPM method, there is a minimum cost of $0.25 per 1,000 impressions. Your daily budget can be as low as a penny, up to whatever you're willing to pay.

If you go the CPC route, Google uses AdWords Discounter technology to match the price you pay with the price offered by competing advertisers for a given keyword. The AdWords Discounter automatically monitors your competition and lowers your CPC to one cent above what they're willing to pay.

You can opt to prepay your advertising costs, or to pay after your ads start running. With this last option, Google charges you after 30 days or when you reach your initial credit limit of $50, whichever comes first. Even small advertisers can participate, as Google accepts payment via credit card, debit card, direct debit, or bank transfer.

> **note** Just as Google is the largest search engine, Google AdWords is far and away the largest PPC ad network. Google sells ads on its own search results pages, throughout its entire network of sites, and on participating third-party sites. Google claims that its AdWords program reaches more than 80% of all Internet users; most advertisers confirm that AdWords generates the overwhelming majority of PPC traffic to their sites.

Creating an AdWords Ad

It's surprisingly easy to create and activate an AdWords ad. You need to determine which keywords you want to buy upfront, of course, but from there, it's a simple matter of filling in the appropriate web forms.

Here's how it works:

1. From the Google AdWords home page (adwords.google.com), click the Start Now button.

2. When the next page appears, choose either the Starter Edition or Standard Edition option; then click Continue. (If this is your first time listing, I recommend going the Starter Edition route—which is what I'll discuss throughout the rest of these numbered steps.)

3. If you select the Starter Edition, select whether you do or don't already have a web page.

4. When the next page appears, enter your location and language.

5. On the same page, scroll down to the Write Your Ad section, shown in Figure 39.3. Enter the following information: the URL of the website you want the add to link to, your ad's title (25 characters max), and two lines of text (35 characters max each).

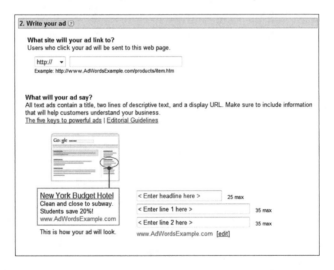

FIGURE 39.3
Writing an AdWords ad.

6. Scroll to the Choose Keywords section and enter up to 20 keywords that you want your ad linked to. (Enter one keyword or phrase per line; a "keyword" can actually be a multiple-word phrase.)

7. Scroll to the Choose Your Currency section and enter the currency you'll be paying in.

8. Scroll to the Set Your Budget section and select your monthly AdWords budget—$50, $100, $250, or a custom amount.

9. When you're done entering information on this page, click the Continue button.

10. Google now prompts you to sign in to your Google account, or to create a new AdWords-specific account. Follow the onscreen instructions to proceed.

11. Google will now email you with instructions on how to set up billing information for your account. Follow the instructions in this email to activate your account and launch your ads.

If you chose a Standard Edition campaign, you have a few more options to consider. In contrast to the Starter Edition, the Standard Edition lets you do the following:

- Create multiple ads (instead of the Starter Edition's single ad).

- Choose from a variety of pricing options, including keyword-specific bidding, content bidding, ad position preference, and so on.

- Control how much you're willing to pay per day, as well as the maximum you're willing to pay when someone clicks your ad (the cost-per-click).

- Target specific websites for ad placement.

- Utilize a variety of advanced planning and reporting tools, including conversion tracking, the AdWords traffic estimator, and a variety of sophisticated statistics and reports.

As I said earlier, the Starter Edition is probably the best way to get started. Once you get a few ad campaigns under your belt, then you can graduate to the advanced options available with the Standard Edition.

Monitoring Your Ads' Performance

Once your ad campaign is started, you can monitor performance from the main AdWords page. After you sign into this page, select the Campaign Management tab and then click Campaign Summary. As you can see in Figure 39.4, you can view the performance of each campaign you've created, in terms of impressions, clicks, cost per click (CPC), and total cost to-date.

To change the parameters of your campaign, click the Edit Settings button and proceed from there. Google also offers a variety of other tools you can use to enhance your ad's performance; click the Tools link to see what's available. Various reports and analyses are also available, by selecting the Reports and Analytics tabs. In short, Google offers a full range of services that help you create more effective online advertisements, and they're all available free-of-charge to AdWords advertisers.

note AdWords is just the start of the Google advertising empire. Google has also acquired and incorporated a well-known Internet advertising firm, and offers all sorts of advertising services—including services that let you place radio, television, and traditional print ads. It's all about the ads, baby!

The Bottom Line

If you want to drive more traffic to your site, you can tap into the power of Google search via the AdWords program. AdWords lets any website—no matter how small—advertise on Google's search results pages. It's a sure-fire way to get your site noticed by Google's millions of users!

39

Profiting from Google AdSense

As you recall from Chapter 1, "Inside Google," Google only appears to be a search technology company. Although it does develop and distribute all manner of search-based services, Google makes its money—and lots of it—by selling advertising.

In the previous chapter, you learned how Google's AdWords ad network works. Through the AdWords network, Google sells ads on its own search results pages, as well as throughout its entire network of sites (Gmail, Google Maps, you name it). It also sells ads on other sites, both big and small. As I said, that's where the money comes from.

And here's the good news: If you run your own website or blog, you can share in some of Google's advertising revenues. Google's AdSense program lets you add Google advertising to your own site, and take a cut of all moneys generated.

Adding Advertising to Your Website with Google AdSense

Any website, no matter how small, can generate revenue. On the Web, one of the primary ways of generating revenue is from advertising; you sell ad space on your site, and whenever a visitor clicks through the ad to the advertiser's website, you collect a small fee.

The problem with this scenario, of course, is that you're not in the advertising business; you have no sales force to sell advertising on your site, nor do you have the technology required to place the ads, track click-throughs, and then collect funds due from advertisers. You might be able to generate a bit of revenue, if only you could get the ads placed and managed.

This is where Google AdSense comes in. The AdSense program places content targeted ads on your site, sells those ads to appropriate advertisers, monitors visitor click-throughs, tracks how much money is owed you, and then pays you what you've earned. Granted, a typical personal website or blog isn't going to generate a lot of click-throughs on its ads, but even a few click-throughs a week will generate a bit of spare cash that you didn't have otherwise. All you have to do is sign up for the program, insert a few lines of code into your web page's underlying HTML code, and then sit back and let Google do the rest of the work.

Google AdSense is actually three primary programs in one. Google AdSense for Content is that part of the program that places targeted ads on your web pages; Google AdSense for Search lets you add Google search to your website, and thus generate even more traffic and advertising revenue; and Google AdSense for Feeds lets you add AdSense ads to your blog's RSS feed.

Understanding Google AdSense for Content

The main part of the AdSense program is dubbed Google AdSense for Content. This is the part of the program that puts ads on your web pages, and then generates revenue whenever visitors click on the ad links.

AdSense ads aren't just random advertisements; Google utilizes the same technology it uses to analyze web pages for its search index to determine the content of a page and place a content-appropriate ad on that page. For example, if your web page is about teeth, Google might place an ad for dentists; if your web page is about books, it might place an ad for book clubs. And so on and so forth.

> **note** In addition to AdSense for Content, Search, and Feeds, Google also lets you make money by adding YouTube content to your website, as well as by placing ads on websites designed for mobile phone users.

40

The nice thing about ads that actually relate to your page's content is that they're more appealing to your site's visitors. One can assume that if you have a page about teeth, your visitors are interested in all things teeth-related, and thus are likely to respond positively to ads selling teeth-related merchandise and services. At the very least, the ads Google places should be more relevant to your toothsome visitors than, say, ads for motor oil or Viagra. And the more relevant the ad, the higher the click-through rate will be—which means more profits, for both Google and you.

note Google calls this "contextual target-ing," and it works—more often than not. Google's content parser can only determine which words are used on your page, not how those words are used. So if you have a page that's critical of the dentistry profession, it will still generate ads for dentists and dental hygienists.

Even better, AdSense ad selection is automatic; you don't have to do a thing. Google automatically crawls your page to determine its content, and places ads appropriately. Your involvement is to activate the AdSense service, insert the appropriate HTML code (just once), and then sit back and let Google do everything else. You don't even have to notify Google if you change your site's content; AdSense automatically monitors your site for changes, and places new ads accordingly.

Understanding Google AdSense for Search

Then there's AdSense for Search, to which you get access when you sign up for AdSense for Content. The Search component lets you add a Google search box to your website. This is a good thing, as it keeps users on your site longer; they don't have to leave your site to conduct a web search.

Keeping visitors on your site longer increases the chances of them clicking through any ad placed on your site. In addition, you now collect a small per-centage of the ad revenue when a visitor clicks through an ad on the search results page. It's only pennies (or fractions of a penny) per click, but it can add up fast.

You can actually put two different Google search boxes on your web pages. You can utilize the standard Google web search box, of course, or you can cre-ate a box that lets visitors search within your own website. Either option is free; you can choose either or both.

As to how you get the ads onto your site, it's a simple matter of feeding some key information to Google, having Google generate the appropriate HTML code, and then you pasting that code into the code for your web page. After the code is inserted, the AdSense ads automatically appear. And every time a visitor clicks one of the ads on your site, you receive a percentage of the fee that the advertiser paid to Google. It's that simple.

Understanding Google AdSense for Feeds

If you run your own blog, you know all about RSS feeds; regular blog readers subscribe to a feed to be alerted when new postings are made. Google AdSense for Feeds lets you place targeted advertisements in your blog's feeds. As with the other AdSense programs, you control the appearance, positioning, and frequency of these text-based ads.

How Much Money Can You Make?

If you're like me, one of the first questions you have about AdSense concerns the money—just how much money can you make from the AdSense program? There's no easy answer to that question, unfortunately.

First, you have to know that Google simply doesn't disclose how much money you can make; it doesn't tell you how much it charges its advertisers, nor what percentage of the take you receive. That's right—when you sign up for the AdSense program, you're doing so with absolutely no idea what your earnings will be. It doesn't really sound like a fully informed contractual agreement to me, but that's the way it is.

That said, we do know in general how the AdSense program works. The ads you display on your pages can be placed on either a cost-per-click (CPC) or cost-per-thousand-impressions (CPM) basis. That is, the advertiser pays either when someone clicks an ad, or when someone simply views the ad. You have no choice on whether you get CPC or CPM ads on your site.

Whenever an advertiser pays Google (for either a click or an impression), you receive a cut of that payment, in the form of a commission. How much of a commission you make depends on how much the advertiser is paying Google for that particular ad. The payment varies by advertiser and by quality of content; competition for the most popular content and keywords causes advertisers to bid up the price accordingly.

What does that mean in terms of dollars? It all depends; I've heard of payments running anywhere from 2 cents to $15 per click, depending on the type of content you have on your site. You get a percentage of that. (And what percentage that is, Google doesn't disclose.)

note AdSense for Search ads are sold exclusively on a cost-per-click basis.

So, the amount you earn is dependent on the price that advertisers are paying, the amount of targeted traffic your site receives, and the number of visitors who view or click the ads on your site. To that last point, there are things you can do to improve your ads' visibility and click-through rate; I'll impart some tips in the "Ten Tips for Improving Your AdSense Earnings" section, later in this chapter.

Making AdSense Work for You

To add AdSense ads to your website, you first have to sign up for the AdSense program. After you've signed up, you then add the AdSense code to your site's HTML—and wait for the money to roll in.

Joining the AdSense Program

Signing up for the Google AdSense program is easy enough to do. You start at the main AdSense page (www.google.com/adsense/), and then click the Sign Up Now button. On the next page, shown in Figure 40.1, you get to fill out an application form. On this form, you need to supply the following information and make the following choices:

FIGURE 40.1

Applying to the Google AdSense program.

■ Website URL (Google needs this to generate the HTML ad code; enter the top-level URL of your site only)

■ Website language (English or otherwise)

■ Account type (individual or business)

■ Country or territory (U.S. or otherwise)

■ Contact information (your name, address, and so on)

Google will now verify your email address by sending you a confirmation email. Follow the instructions in the email message, and then Google will review your application. The review period typically runs two to three days, and then Google will notify you of your acceptance and you'll be ready to log into your AdSense account and get started with the rest of the process.

Adding AdSense Ads to Your Website

Once your AdSense application has been accepted, you can log into your account from the main AdSense page (www.google.com/adsense/). To add an ad to your website, follow these steps:

1. Select the AdSense Setup tab, shown in Figure 40.2.

FIGURE 40.2
Getting ready to set up an AdSense ad.

2. Click the AdSense for Content link.

3. When the AdSense for Content page appears, as shown in Figure 40.3, select whether you want to display an ad unit (a block advertisement) or a link unit (a list of linked topics). If you choose to display an ad unit, you also need to pull down the list and select the type of ads you want—text only, image only, or text and image (default). Click the Continue button to continue.

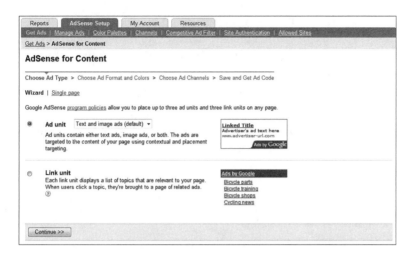

FIGURE 40.3

Choosing the type of ad to display—an ad unit or link unit.

4. When the next page appears, as shown in Figure 40.4, select the ad format and color scheme you want. Available ad formats include three sizes of horizontal ads, three sizes of vertical ads, and six sizes of square ads. Click the Continue button to continue.

FIGURE 40.4

Choosing the ad format and color scheme.

5. The next page lets you specify up to five custom channels for your ads (You can create different channels for different pages on your site.) Do so if you want (you don't have to); then click the Continue button.

6. You're now prompted to name the ad unit you've created. Do so, and then click the Submit and Get Code button.

7. The final page, shown in Figure 40.5, displays the code that Google generated for your ad. Copy the code from this page and then paste it into the HTML code for your web page.

FIGURE 40.5
The final ad code—copy it into your web page's HTML.

If you want to include the same type of ad (format and color) on every page of your site, you'll need to copy the final code into each page's HTML. If you want to generate different types of ads on different pages, you'll need to repeat this entire process for each different ad type on your site.

Note that Google generates different ads for the unique content on each page of your site. You only need to create new ad code if the format of the ad (size, type, color, and so on) changes from page to page.

tip Google makes it even easier to add AdSense ads to your Blogger blog, via pre-designed content modules. See Chapter 18, "Blogging with Blogger," for details.

Adding a Google Search Box to Your Site

If you want to add a Google search box to your pages, follow these steps from the main AdSense page:

1. Select the AdSense Setup tab.

2. Click the AdSense for Search link.

3. When the next page appears, click the Get Started button.

4. When the AdSense for Search page appears, as shown in Figure 40.6, select whether you want to search only the sites you select or search the entire web. If you select the first option, you'll need to enter URLS for those sites.

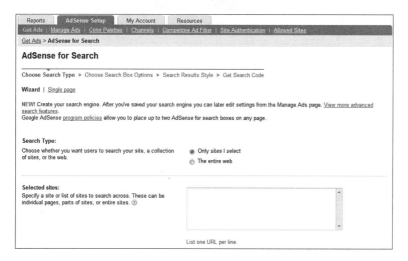

FIGURE 40.6
Adding Google search to your site.

5. In the Optional Keywords section, add one or more keywords that describe the subject and content of your site. (This helps Google fine-tune the ads it places on your site.)

6. Click the Continue button.

7. The next page, shown in Figure 40.7, lets you determine how the Google search box will appear on your site. Make the appropriate selections and then click the Continue button.

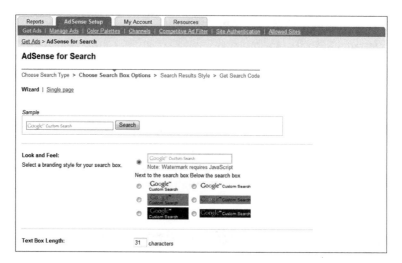

FIGURE 40.7

Configuring the look and feel of your Google search box.

8. On the next page, shown in Figure 40.8, you determine how you want the search results page to display (in the original browser or in a new window) and how you want the ads on this page to appear. Make your choices; then click the Continue button.

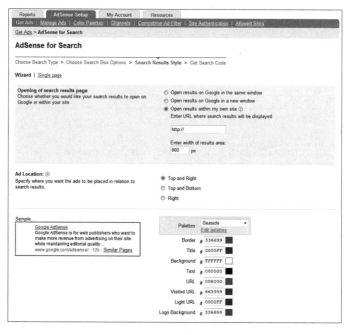

FIGURE 40.8

Configuring how the search results page—and the AdSense ads—will appear.

9. On the next page, agree to Google's terms and conditions and then click the Submit and Get Code button.

10. The final page, shown in Figure 40.9, displays the code that Google generated for the search box. Copy the code from this page and then paste it into the HTML code for your web page.

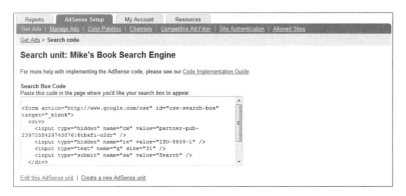

FIGURE 40.9
The final search box code—copy it into your web page's HTML.

Again, you'll need to copy this code into each page on your site where you want a search box to appear.

Adding AdSense Ads to Your Site Feeds

Google's newest way to make money is by selling ad space on site feeds. This is a great option if you have your own blog and offer RSS feeds of your new posts.

To add advertising to your site feed, follow these steps:

1. Select the AdSense Setup tab.

2. Click the AdSense for Feeds link.

3. When the next page appears, as shown in Figure 40.10, determine the type of ad you want; how frequently you want the ads to appear; the position of the ads; the ads' color scheme; and other requested information.

4. Select which of your feeds you want active.

5. Click the Save button, and Google will now display ads on the selected feeds.

FIGURE 40.10
Activating Google AdSense for Feeds.

Monitoring Your AdSense Performance

Once you have AdSense ads active on your website, you can monitor the performance of those ads—how many clicks you're generating, and how much that means in terms of earnings. Just go to the AdSense site, select the Reports tab, and click Overview. This report, shown in Figure 40.11, details your page impressions, clicks, click through rate (CTR), the effective cost per 1,000 impressions (eCPM), and total earnings; you can show this information for today, yesterday, the last seven days, this month, last month, and since your last payment.

AdSense also lets you generate additional custom reports. Select the Advanced Reports tab to view what's available.

> **note** If you or your company submit a Form W-9 to Google, you'll receive a Form 1099 at the end of the tax year—assuming you had AdSense revenues, of course.

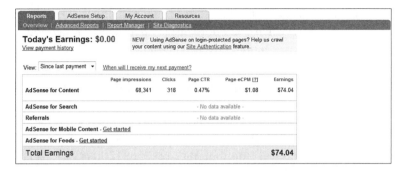

FIGURE 40.11
Viewing your AdSense performance.

Ten Tips for Improving Your AdSense Earnings

Just putting an AdSense ad on your website doesn't guarantee that you'll make a lot of money from it. The key to generating significant earnings is to get a lot of visitors to view or click-through the ads; that means both increasing your site traffic and the visibility and appeal of the ads themselves.

To that end, here are ten things you can do to improve the earnings potential of your AdSense ads:

Tip #1: Give your ads prominent position. If you hide your AdSense ads, no one will see them—and if no one sees them (or clicks them), you won't generate any earnings. Place the ads in a prominent position on your web pages, and your earnings will increase. The best position is one that a visitor can see without scrolling, which means near the top of your page, either centered above your main content or in the top-left corner. It's also important to place your ads near important content; you want visitors to see the ads when they view must-read content. (A good position is directly below the end of an article or other editorial content.) Also good is placement near navigational elements, such as menus and back/up buttons.

Tip #2: Display text and image ads. When you create your AdSense ad, you have a choice of a text ad, image ad, or both. You should choose the option to display both types of ads. That's because some advertisers choose the text format only and others choose the image format only; when you opt to display both types of ads, you have a wider pool of potential advertisers who can display their ads on your page.

Tip #3: Choose a large ad format. When it comes to advertising effectiveness, bigger is better. It should come as no surprise that wider ad formats tend to outperform narrower formats—even if the narrower ad is also taller. It's all about readability; visitors can read more text at a glance with a wider ad than they can with a taller one. Google says that the most effective formats are the 336×280 large rectangle, the 300×250 medium rectangle, and (contrary to the previous advice) the 160×600 wide skyscraper; I've also had good luck with the 728×90 leaderboard and 468×60 banner.

Tip #4: Format your ads to look like they're part of the regular page. Here's a test: What type of ad performs best—one that stands out from your regular page template or one that blends in? Contrary to what you might initially think, it's the ad that blends in that performs best; visitors tend to view such an ad as part of the page content, rather than as an ad. So, when it comes to choosing ad colors, go with a color scheme that is similar to your page's color scheme. Avoid colors that contrast too much with your page's colors.

Tip #5: Surround your ad with images. You can draw more attention to your AdSense ad if you surround it with images—attractive images that your visitors would want to look at, anyway. This probably means putting an image above or below (or both above and below) the AdSense module. It's even better if the images have something to do with the ad content. For example, if you have a page about notebook PCs, and you're fairly sure that AdSense will serve up an ad related to notebook PCs, then surround that ad with pictures of notebook PCs. This approach not only draws attention to the ad, but it actually makes the ad appear to be more integrated into your page's content.

Tip #6: Put multiple ads on your page. If you have a large web page (one with a lot of scrolling content), you have room to put more than one ad on the page. Google lets you put up to three ad units on each page, in addition to one link unit and one

caution Just because you can put multiple ads on your page doesn't mean you should. If you make your page too ad-heavy, you'll turn off visitors who might think your site is nothing but ads—and not enough content.

referral button. The more ads you include, the more earnings you can generate.

Tip #7: Add link units to your pages. You're not limited to placing just ads on your page. AdSense also lets you place *link units*, like the one in Figure 40.12, anywhere on your page. A link unit is a list of topics relevant to your site's content; when a visitor clicks one of these links, he's shown a page of ads related to that topic. You'll earn more money when the visitor clicks one of these topic-related ads.

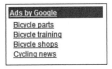

FIGURE 40.12

An AdSense link unit.

Tip #8: Add AdSense for Search to your pages. You're missing out on potential earnings if you don't add AdSense for search to your site. There's certainly no harm to be done by including a Google web search or site search box to your site; if and when visitors use the search box, you'll earn money. It's as simple as that.

Tip #9: Configure AdSense to display alternative ads. There's no guarantee that Google will always have advertisers interested in purchasing space on your site. For those times when ads aren't ready to serve, let AdSense display alternative ads instead. It's better to have *something* filling that ad space, rather than have open space on your page; plus, running a public service ad is a good thing to do.

Tip #10: Improve your site's content—and increase your traffic. Here's the most valuable tip of all. The better and more timely your site's content, the more visitors you'll attract. And the more visitors, the more click-throughs your ads will receive. To increase your ad revenue, improve your site; it's as simple as that.

The Bottom Line

If you run a website, there is no reason not to sign up for the Google AdSense program. Instead of being a drain on your finances, AdSense lets any website generate some amount of revenue. Even if it's just a few dollars per month, it might be enough to let your site pay for itself!

Google for Web Developers

Adding Google to Any Website

Wouldn't it be great to have a Google search box on your own website—so that your visitors can either search the Web from your site, or use Google search technology to search your site itself? Not surprisingly, Google makes it easy to add a search box to your site—in fact, Google offers several ways to add a Google search box, and they're all free.

Adding Google Free WebSearch

Lots of webmasters add Google search boxes to their sites, because Google makes it easy to do so. Google's main program is called Google Free, and it comes in several different flavors—basic web search, web search with SafeSearch filtering, and web search with site search added.

Adding a Basic Search Box for Web Searches

The first of these options is Google Free WebSearch. It's easy to add; all you have to do is insert the following HTML code into your web page's code, where you want the search box to appear.

Here's the code:

```
<!-- Search Google -->
<center>
<FORM method=GET action="http://www.google.com/search">
<input type=hidden name=ie value=UTF-8>
<input type=hidden name=oe value=UTF-8>
<TABLE bgcolor="#FFFFFF"><tr><td>
<A HREF="http://www.google.com/">
<IMG SRC="http://www.google.com/logos/Logo_40wht.gif"
border="0" ALT="Google" align="absmiddle"></A>
<INPUT TYPE=text name=q size=25 maxlength=255 value="">
<INPUT type=submit name=btnG VALUE="Google Search">
</td></tr></TABLE>
</FORM>
</center>
<!-- Search Google -->
```

The result is a standard Google search box, like the one shown in Figure 41.1

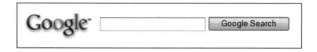

FIGURE 41.1
Adding a Google search box to your web page.

Adding a SafeSearch Search Box

If you want your visitors to be protected against unwanted adult content when they search Google from your site, you can add a Google search box with the SafeSearch content filter enabled. To add a Google Free SafeSearch box to your site, use the following HTML code:

```
<!-- Google SafeSearch  -->
<center>
<FORM method=GET action="http://www.google.com/search">
<input type=hidden name=ie value=UTF-8>
<input type=hidden name=oe value=UTF-8>
<TABLE bgcolor="#FFFFFF"><tr><td>
<A HREF="http://www.google.com/search?safe=vss">
<IMG SRC="http://www.google.com/logos/Google_Safe.gif"
 border="0" ALT="Google" width="115" height="45" align="absmiddle"></A>
<INPUT TYPE=text name=q size=25 maxlength=255 value="">
<INPUT type=hidden name=safe value=strict>
<INPUT type=submit name=sa value="Google Search">
</td></tr></TABLE>
</FORM>
</center>
<!-- Google SafeSearch -->
```

This adds the search box shown in Figure 41.2 to your page, where you inserted the code. (Notice the "SafeSearch" logo is added to the Google logo.)

FIGURE 41.2

Adding a Google search box with SafeSearch to your web page.

Adding a Box to Search Your Own Site

Google also lets you search your own website using Google's search technology. This option is dubbed Google Free WebSearch with SiteSearch; just insert the following HTML code:

```
<!-- SiteSearch Google -->
<FORM method=GET action="http://www.google.com/search">
<input type=hidden name=ie value=UTF-8>
<input type=hidden name=oe value=UTF-8>
<TABLE bgcolor="#FFFFFF"><tr><td>
<A HREF="http://www.google.com/">
<IMG SRC="http://www.google.com/logos/Logo_40wht.gif"
```

41

```
border="0" ALT="Google"></A>
</td>
<td>
<INPUT TYPE=text name=q size=31 maxlength=255 value="">
<INPUT type=submit name=btnG VALUE="Google Search">
<font size=-1>
<input type=hidden name=domains value="YOURDOMAIN"><br><input type=radic
name=sitesearch value=""> Web <input type=radio name=sitesearch
value="YOURDOMAIN" checked> This Site <br>
</font>
</td></tr></TABLE>
</FORM>
<!-- SiteSearch Google -->
```

For this option, you need to replace the two instances of *YOURDOMAIN* with your own domain name (either with or without the leading www). As you ca see in Figure 41.3, this inserts a search box with the option of searching the Web or your own website.

FIGURE 41.3

Adding a Google search box with both web and site search to your web page.

Adding a Custom Search Engine to Your Site

Here's another cool option for adding search to your site. Google Custom Search Engine, as the name implies, is a custom search engine you can add your site. With Google Custom Search Engine, you can specify which sites yo want to include in your searches, customize the look and feel of the search and results pages to match your website, invite your site visitors to contribut to your search engine, and make money from ads placed on the search resul page. And it's all a matter of filling in some simple web forms.

Creating Your Custom Search Engine

Google lets you create as many custom search engines as you like. To create new one, go to www.google.com/coop/cse/ and click the Create a Custom Search Engine button. When the next page appears, as shown in Figure 41.4 make the following choices:

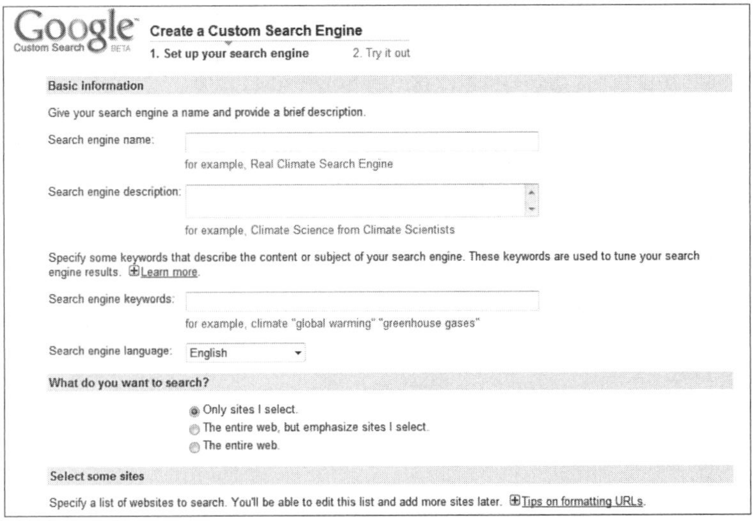

FIGURE 41.4

Creating a custom search engine.

- **Search engine name.** This is the name that appears on your search engine page.

- **Search engine description.** This is a short description of what your search engine is searching for.

- **Search engine keywords.** These are primary queries that help to define the focus of your search engine.

- **Search engine language.** Choose from available Google languages for your search and results pages.

- **What do you want to search?** This is important; you can choose to search the entire Web, only sites you select, or the entire Web emphasizing the sites you select.

- **Select some sites.** This refers to websites that you want your search engine to always search. (You can include your own site in this list.)

- **Select an edition.** Select the Standard edition (free, but displays ads on the results pages) or Business edition (doesn't display ads on results pages, but costs $100/year).

Agree to the Terms of Service; then click the Next button, where you can try out your new search engine. If you like the results, click the Finish button. This displays your Custom Search Engine console.

To customize the look and feel of your search engine, click the Control Panel link for that search engine. When the next page appears, click the Look and Feel link. This displays the page shown in Figure 41.5; from here, you can add a logo or other image, as well as customize the page colors. After you've saved your changes, you can view how your search engine looks by returning to the main control panel and clicking the Homepage link for that search engine.

FIGURE 41.5
Customizing the look and feel of your search engine.

Adding the Search Engine to Your Website

To add your new search engine to your website, click the Control Panel link for that search engine and select the Code link. When the next page appears, select your hosting options (on Google's website or your own site); then copy the HTML code displayed on this page into the HTML code for your web page. (You'll need to copy the code into each page where you want the search box to appear.) After the code is inserted (and you've saved your HTML page), a search box is displayed on your page.

When a visitor enters a query into your custom search box, Google serves up a page of custom results. By default, this page is hosted on the Google site but conforms to the look and feel (and the custom results) you specified.

tip To generate some cash from the AdSense ads placed on your custom search results page, click the Make Money link and follow the onscreen instructions.

The Bottom Line

I like the ability to add various types of Google searches to my website. The simplest method, of course, is the Google Free WebSearch. But if you don't mind putting in a little upfront work, Google Custom Search Engine is a great tool that lets you create truly custom searches for whatever topic you specify. And whichever type of search you use, it's totally free; all you have to do is copy the proper code into your page's underlying HTML.

41

Analyzing Your Website Traffic

Y ou might be surprised to know that Google offers a comprehensive set of tools for webmasters. In addition to tools that help you create and submit a sitemap of your site (for more probable inclusion in the Google search index), Google also offers several tools you can use to analyze the performance of your site—and find out which pages are attracting the most traffic.

Using Google's Webmaster Tools

Google's Webmaster Tools is a free service that analyzes the traffic coming into any registered website. Unlike some analytic tools (such as Google's own Google Analytics, which we'll discuss later in this chapter), you don't have to insert any code into your web pages to generate Webmaster Tools data. (It does help, however, if you've submitted a sitemap of your website to Google beforehand.)

Accessing Webmaster Tools

To access Webmaster Tools, start at Google Webmaster Central (www.google.com/webmasters/) and click the Sign In to Google Webmaster Tools link. This displays the Dashboard shown in Figure 42.1.

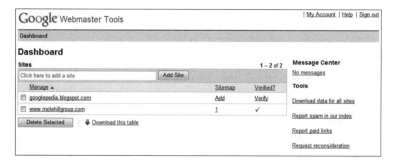

FIGURE 42.1
The Webmaster Tools Dashboard.

The Webmaster Tools Dashboard lists all the websites you've registered with Google to date. You can add websites to the Dashboard via the Add Site box at the top of the page.

Once added, Google performs all available analysis.

Viewing Overview Information

To view details about a website, click the site's name in the Dashboard. This displays the Webmaster Tools Overview page, shown in Figure 42.2. This page conveys the following information about your site:

tip You can access the Google Webmaster Tools Dashboard directly at www.google.com/webmasters/tools/.

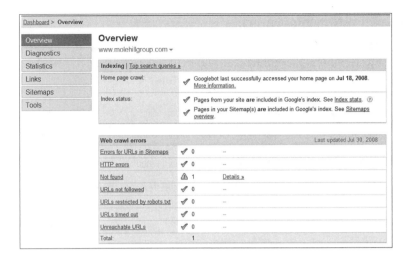

FIGURE 42.2
Google's Webmaster Tools Overview page.

- When Google last crawled your site.
- Whether or not pages from your site are included in the Google index.
- What type of errors, if any, Google found when crawling your site.

Additional information is available by clicking the links along the left side of this page, which we'll discuss next.

Viewing Diagnostic Information

When you click the Diagnostics link, you have access to various types of diagnostic information. Table 42.1 details the available reports.

Table 42.1   Google Webmaster Tools: Diagnostics

Report	Contents
Web Crawl	URLs from your site that Google had trouble crawling.
Content Analysis	Problems encountered with your site's <META> and <TITLE> tags.
Mobile Web	Mobile crawl errors.

42

Viewing Statistical Information

Although Google's diagnostic information is useful, I find its statistical information much more interesting. Here is where you'll get the most information about your site traffic, as detailed in Table 42.2.

Table 42.2   Webmaster Tools: Statistics

Report	Contents
Top Search Queries	Displays the top search queries and search query clicks.
Crawl Stats	Displays your site's PageRank data.
What Googlebot Sees	Phrases used by other sites in the anchor text that links to your site.
Index Stats	Links to standard Google site linkage and cache info, such as pages that link to your site, related pages, and the like.
Subscriber Stats	For sites with site feeds, the number of users who subscribe to those feeds through various services.

For example, the Top Search Queries page, shown in Figure 42.3, lists the top search queries that visitors used to find your site, as well as which of those search queries generated the most clicks. (Click any link to view the Google search for that phrase.)

Viewing Link Information

Google offers three reports that help you analyze your site's internal and external (inbound) links. These reports are detailed in Table 42.3.

Table 42.3   Webmaster Tools: Links

Report	Contents
Pages with External Links	Lists those pages on your site that have inbound links to them, along with the number of those external links.
Pages with Internal Links	Lists all the pages on your site that are linked to from other pages on your site.
Sitelinks	Displays additional links that Google sometimes generates, based on your site content, to help visitors better navigate your site.

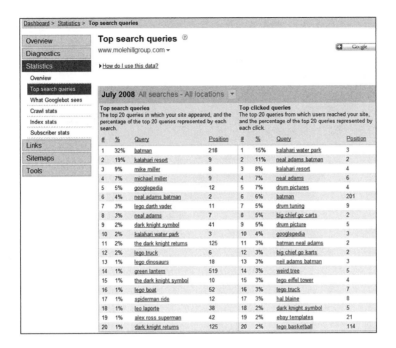

FIGURE 42.3

Google's Query Stats page.

For example, Figure 42.4 shows the Pages with External Links report. Click the link number to view all the sites that link to that page.

Viewing Sitemap Information

When you click the Sitemaps link, Google displays a page that lists some brief statistics about the sitemaps you've submitted. This information includes the sitemap status and how many pages were included in the sitemap.

Using Other Webmaster Tools

Google offers additional tools for webmasters, found by clicking the Tools link in the Webmaster Tools Dashboard. Table 42.4 details the available tools.

note Learn more about sitemaps in Chapter 38, "Optimizing Your Site for Google Search."

42

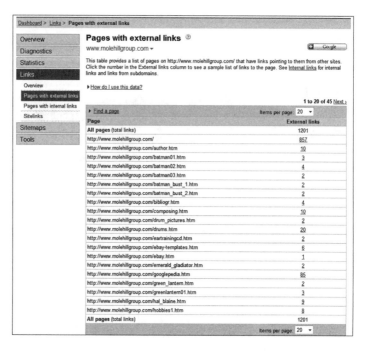

FIGURE 42.4

Viewing all the pages on your site that have external links, in alphabetical order.

Table 42.4   Webmaster Tools: Additional Tools

Tool	Description
Analyze **robots.txt**	Determines whether the **robots.txt** file blocks specific URLs.
Generate **robots.txt**	Helps you create a **robots.txt** file for your site.
Set Geographic Target	Identifies your site to a specific geographic location; great for enhancing mobile search.
Enhanced Image Search	Enables Google's Image Search for images on your site; adds advanced labels to your site's images.
Manage Site Verification	Displays and reverifies site owners.
Set Crawl Rate	Displays how often Google crawls your site—and lets you change the crawl rate.
Set Preferred Domain	Associates a preferred domain with this site.
Remove URLs	Deletes site pages from the Google Index.

42

You shouldn't gloss over these tools; a few are extremely useful for optimizing your site's performance.

In particular, the Generate **robots.txt** tool is a great way to create a **robots.txt** file for your site. As you learned in Chapter 38, you use the **robots.txt** file to tell the GoogleBot spider software where your sitemap file is, which pages you don't want crawled, and the like. Google's tool lets you create a **robots.txt** file just by selecting options from a series of pull-down lists. It's much easier than trying to create such a file by hand.

Using Google Analytics

Although Google's Webmaster Tools are useful, they're a little Spartan in their approach. If you want more in-depth and more colorful analysis, turn to Google's other set of tools for webmasters—Google Analytics.

What Google Analytics Analyzes

Google Analytics (www.google.com/analytics/) generates a variety of detailed statistics about your website's visitors. You can use Google Analytics to determine the following:

- The number of visitors to your site and how much time they spend there
- How fast an Internet connection is used by your visitors
- The types of web browsers and screen resolution used by your site's visitors
- Which sites are sending you the most traffic
- Where, geographically, visitors are coming from (on a city level)
- What keywords your visitors searched for to find your site
- Which pages on your site were most popular
- The most popular entrance (landing) and exit pages on your site
- Visitor trending over time

note If you use Google's AdWords pay-per-click advertising program, Google Analytics also helps you optimize your AdWords campaigns. The tool lets you define and track various goals, including sales, lead generation, page views, and file downloads.

42

Activating Google Analytics

To use Google Analytics, you have to first sign in with your Google account, and then sign up for the GA program. Participation is free.

The first time you log onto Google Analytics, you're prompted to provide some key information about your website—the site's URL, your name and contact info, and so forth. When you're done with this, Google creates your GA account and displays a block of HTML code. This code block *must* be inserted into the underlying HTML of each page you want to track; the code goes in the body text section of your page, immediately before the final **</body>** tag. The code looks something like this:

```
<script type="text/javascript">
var gaJsHost = (("https:" == document.location.protocol) ? "https://ssl
: "http://www.");
document.write(unescape("%3Cscript src='" + gaJsHost +
"google-analytics.com/ga.js' type='text/javascript'%3E%3C/script%3E"));
</script>
<script type="text/javascript">
var pageTracker = _gat._getTracker("trackingID");
pageTracker._initData();
pageTracker._trackPageview();
</script>
```

After the code has been inserted, Google Analytics can start tracking the pages on your site.

Using the Dashboard

Once you've set up your site with the Google Analytics code, and given Analytics time to crawl your site and assembled the requested data, you can then view the reports that Analytics generates about your site. Just go to the main Google Analytics page and click the View Reports link next to your site. This displays the Dashboard page, shown in Figure 42.5. Think of the Dashboard as a summary of the data gathered, as well as a gateway to more detailed reports.

note You can configure Google Analytics to track the performance of multiple websites under a single Google account.

FIGURE 42.5
The Google Analytics Dashboard.

The Dashboard displays the following information:

- Daily site traffic over the past 30 days
- Site usage statistics: number of visits, pageviews, pages viewed per visit, bounce rate, average time on site, and percentage of new visitors
- A Traffic Sources Overview pie chart that shows what types of sites (referring or linking sites, search engines, direct URL entry, and other) generated traffic to your site
- The most popular pages on your site, ranked by number of pageviews
- A world map that displays where your site visitors are located

At the top of the dashboard is an interactive graph that can display a variety of different data—visits, pageviews, pages per visit, average time on site, bounce rate, and percent new visitors. Select the data to

> **note** The *bounce rate* is the percentage of users who arrive at your site but then leave without going deeper than the landing page. Obviously, a smaller number is better.

42

display from the pull-down list; then click anywhere on the resulting chart t display more information in a pop-up window.

Additional Reports

Google Analytics includes 80 different reports and variations that analyze v ious aspects of your site traffic. These reports are available by selecting the appropriate links on the left side of the Dashboard.

What kinds of reports can you generate? Table 42.5 provides an overview of what's available.

Table 42.5   Google Analytics Reports

Report Type	Individual Reports
Visitors	Overview, Benchmarking, Map Overlay, New vs. Returning, Languages, Visitor Trending, Visitor Loyalty, Browser Capabilities, Network Properties, and various user-defined reports
Traffic Sources	Overview, Direct Traffic, Referring Sites, Search Engines, All Traffic Sources, Keywords, AdWords, Campaigns, and Ad Versions
Content	Overview, Top Content, Content by Title, Content Drilldown, Top Landing Pages, Top Ex Pages, Site Overlay, and various Site Search reports—Overview, Usage, Search Terms, Start Pages, Destination Pages, Categories, and Trending
Goals	Overview, Total Conversions, Conversion Rate, Abandoned Funnels, Goal Value, and Funnel Visualization

The reports generated by Google Analytics are quite useful and often visual, which makes the data easier to grasp. For example, the Search Engines repo shown in Figure 42.6, shows you which search engines are driving the most traffic to your site. (Not surprisingly, it's Google that drives the majority of traffic to my own site!)

There's a lot beneath the surface of Google Analytics—more than can be discussed in this chapter—including the ability to create custom dashboards and reports. I recommend you visit the site, click around the various reports, and check out the help files. I know you'll find information about your site that will surprise you—and help you increase your site traffic.

tip For more good advice on improving the performance of your website, check out the Official Google Webmaster Help group (groups.google.com/group/Google_Webmaster_Help) and the Official Google Webmaster Central Blog (googlewebmastercentral.blogspot.com).

FIGURE 42.6

The Search Engines report.

The Bottom Line

Analyzing your website's performance just got a lot easier, thanks to Google's free analytical tools. The original Webmaster Tools are good for basic information, but for detailed analysis, I definitely prefer Google Analytics. It requires a little bit of code manipulation on your website, but then the reports just keep coming. (And they're fun to look at!)

Using Google's APIs and Developer's Tools

You can use Google to search the Web. You can use Google to search for data stored on your own computer. You can use Google to search for data stored on a corporate network. But did you know you can use Google within custom-developed software and web-based applications?

That's right. If you're a software developer, you can incorporate Google search into the programs you write. That's because Google makes its Application Programming Interfaces (APIs) available for public use. Developers can use the Google APIs when they're writing their own program code, and thus tie their programs into all types of Google data.

The reality is that Google is very open about sharing its data and services with the developer community. Google publishes APIs for virtually all of its services, so that you can develop your own Google Desktop sidebar gadgets, or publish your own custom Google maps, or display your own custom interface to create Google Calendar events on your website.

Google's support of third-party developers is a very good thing, and it makes Google's services that much more usable. Read on to learn more.

Understanding Google's APIs

As noted, API is a synonym for Application Programming Interface. As the name implies, this is an interface used in the programming of applications. More precisely, a Google API is an interface between the application you develop and a specific Google service.

note To use any of Google's APIs, you must first register on the Google Code site (code.google.com). When you create your Google API account, Google issues you a personal license key; this license key must be integrated into your code so that every time your application queries a Google database, the license key is part of the query string.

For example, the Google Custom Search API lets you tie into Google's main search index. That lets you add web search capability to a software program, web-based application, or dynamic website. You develop the content around the search engine, and then use the Custom Search API to let your users query the Google search index.

By making its APIs publicly available, Google becomes a major web services provider. All the services that Google offers can now be incorporated in the applications you write; you provide the interface and subtext, while Google serves the "live" data.

To use a Google API, you have to remotely connect to the API within your program code. All such communications are executed via the Simple Object Access Protocol (SOAP), which is an XML-based technology used for web services.

Types of Google-Based Applications

You can use Google's various APIs to add all sorts of functionality to your applications. You can enable a program to automatically issue search requests to Google's web index (or have users search manually), and then receive results as structured data in whatever format you specify. You can have an application access historical data in the Google cache. You can even use the Google Gears API to transform your web-based applications so that they work when your users aren't connected to the Internet. The bottom line is, Google's developer tools let you do anything you can do from the Google website from within your applications.

What types of applications can you write using Google's developer tools? Here are just a few ideas:

> **note** Obviously, this chapter can only cover the bare basics of Google application programming. To learn more, check out the book *Google Web Toolkit Applications* (Ryan Dewsbury, Addison-Wesley Professional, 2007), available at a bookstore near you.

- **Market research.** Create a program that regularly monitors the Web to display new information about a given subject.

- **Data analysis.** Create a program that lets users analyze real-time information retrieved from the Web, such as stock market quotes, news headlines, and the like.

- **Trend analysis.** Create a program that retrieves and analyzes the amount of information available on a subject over time.

- **Search interface.** Create a program that lets the user search for information using a non-HTML interface.

- **Map mashup.** Add a customized map or driving directions to your website or application.

- **Event calendar.** Add a calendar of upcoming events to a website or application.

- **Video player.** Play selected YouTube videos in your application or on your website.

- **Spell checking.** Incorporate Google's spell-checking function into any application.

That's just the tip of the iceberg, of course. Recognizing the vast amounts of data that Google puts at your fingertips, how you incorporate that information into your applications is up to you.

Developing Your Own Google-Based Applications

If you're a software developer or web designer, here's a URL you need to know: code.google.com. This is the address of Google Code, the home base for all of Google's developer services.

As you can see in Figure 43.1, the Google Code home page links to all the developer resources that Google makes available for its various services. It's also home to the Google Code Blog, which keeps you up to date on all of Google's developer developments.

FIGURE 43.1
Google Code—the home page for third-party Google developers.

And just what tools are available? There's a ton; click the APIs & Developer Tools link, and you see the list detailed in Table 43.1.

Table 43.1 Google Developer Tools

Tool	URL	Description
Android API	code.google.com/android	Facilitates development of mobile applications for the Android-powered "Google phone."
Blogger Data API	code.google.com/apis/blogger	Enables your applications to view and update Blogger content.
FeedBurner API	code.google.com/feedburner	Offers the capability to interact with RSS feed management.

Tool	URL	Description
Gmail Atom Feeds	gmail.google.com/support/bin/answer.py?answer=13465	Provides a mechanism to read your Gmail inbox via an Atom news feed.
Google Account Authentication	code.google.com/apis/accounts	Incorporates Google account login into desktop or mobile applications.
Google AdSense API	code.google.com/apis/adsense	Places ads on your website.
Google AdSense for Audio API	code.google.com/apis/adsenseforaudio	Enables you to integrate AdSense for audio into a broadcast automation system.
Google AdWords API	www.google.com/apis/adwords	Helps you develop applications that interact directly with the AdWords server to manage large AdWords accounts and campaigns.
Google AJAX API	code.google.com/apis/ajax	Lets you implement dynamic websites in JavaScript and HTML.
Google AJAX Feed API	code.google.com/apis/ajaxfeeds	Lets you mash up public feeds using JavaScript.
Google AJAX Language API	code.google.com/apis/ajaxlanguage	Translates multiple languages in JavaScript applications.
Google AJAX Search API	code.google.com/apis/ajaxsearch	Puts a Google search box and results on your website.
Google Analytics API	code.google.com/apis/analytics	Enables the sending of information from your website to Google Analytics.
Google Apps APIs	code.google.com/apis/apps	Provides domain administration for customers of Google Apps Premier and Education editions.
Google Base Data API	code.google.com/apis/base	Manages Google Base content.
Google Book Search API	code.google.com/apis/books	Integrates your website or application with Google's book search database.
Google Calendar APIs and Tools	code.google.com/apis/calendar	Views and updates Google Calendar events from third-party applications and web pages; also lets you create a web front-end for your own calendars, generate public calendars, create Calendar Gadgets, and more.
Google Chart API	code.google.com/apis/chart	Lets you dynamically create and embe charts in any web page.
Google Checkout API	code.google.com/apis/checkout	Lets you incorporate Google Checkout forsales on your website.

Continues

43

Table 43.1 Continued

Tool	URL	Description
Google Code Search Data API	code.google.com/apis/codesearch	Enables your applications to view data from Google Code Search.
Google Contacts Data API	code.google.com/apis/contacts	Enables applications to view and update Google Contacts data via feeds.
Google Coupon Feeds	code.google.com/apis/coupons/	Provides coupon listings that are included in Google search results.
Google Custom Search API	code.google.com/apis/customsearch	Lets you create a custom search engine for your website or blog.
Google Data APIs	code.google.com/apis/gdata	Lets your applications read and write data on the Web using XML-based syndication tools.
Google Desktop Gadget API	code.google.com/apis/desktop	Creates gadgets for the Google Desktop and iGoogle.
Google Desktop Search APIs	code.google.com/apis/desktop	Inserts searches for any type file into your gadgets and applications.
Google Document List Data API	code.google.com/apis/documents	Enables client applications to view and search through Google Docs documents.
Google Gadgets API	code.google.com/apis/gadgets	Creates gadgets for various Google applications and personal web pages.
Google Earth API	code.google.com/apis/earth	Embeds Google Earth into your web pages.
Google Finance Data API	code.google.com/apis/finance	Enables client applications to view and update Google Finance content.
Google Friend Connect	www.google.com/friendconnect	Enhances your website with community features.
Google Gears	code.google.com/apis/gears/	Enables web-based applications to function offline.
Google Health API	code.google.com/apis/health	Enables client applications to view and send Google Health content.
Google KML	code.google.com/apis/kml	Lets you create and share content with Google Earth, Google Maps, and Google Maps for Mobile.
Google Mapplets	code.google.com/apis/ maps/documentation/mapplets	Lets you create mini-applications that can be embedded into the Google Maps site.

Tool	URL	Description
Google Maps API	code.google.com/apis/maps	Lets you embed Google Maps in your ownweb pages.
Google Maps API for Flash	code.google.com/apis/maps/ documentation/flash	Lets you add maps to Flash applications.
Google Mashup Editor	code.google.com/gme	Helps you write code for simple web applications and mashups.
Google News Feeds	news.google.com/intl/ en_us/news_feed_terms.html	Enables Atom and RSS feeds for topic and news searches.
Google Notebook Data API	code.google.com/apis/notebook	Enables your applications to view store data as Google data API feeds.
Google Safe Browsing APIs	code.google.com/apis/safebrowsing	Enables client applications to check URLs against suspected phishing and malware sites.
Google Search Appliance APIs	code.google.com/enterprise/	Helps you develop connectors to feed source data into the GoogleSearch Appliance (for large enterprises).
Google Sitemaps	www.google.com/webmasters/ sitemaps/docs/en/about.html	Enables Google to quickly crawl your website.
Google SketchUp Ruby API	code.google.com/apis/sketchup	Lets you manipulate SketchUp models.
Google Spreadsheets Data API	code.google.com/apis/spreadsheets	Enables your applications to view and update Google Spreadsheets data.
Google Static Maps API	code.google.com/apis/maps/ documentation/staticmaps	Lets you embed a Google Maps image on a web page without JavaScript or dynamic page loading.
Google Talk for Developers	code.google.com/apis/talk	Lets you hook your applications into or connect your IM service to Google Talk.
Google Themes API	code.google.com/apis/themes	Lets you personalize the iGoogle home page with custom themes.
Google Toolbar API	www.google.com/tools/ toolbar/buttons/apis/	Helps you create custom buttons for the Google Toolbar.
Google Transit Feed Specification	code.google.com/transit/spec/ transit_feed_specification.html	Helps make public transit information available through Google Maps, Google Earth, and other tools.

Continues

43

Table 43.1   Continued

Tool	URL	Description
Google Visualization API	code.google.com/apis/visualization	Helps you create visualization and reporting applications, as well as Google Spreadsheet Gadgets.
Google Web History Feeds	www.google.com/support/bin/answer.py?answer=54464	Enables an RSS feed of search history (for personalized search users).
Google Web Toolkit	code.google.com/webtoolkit	Helps you build AJAX applications in the Java language.
Google Webmaster Tools Data API	code.google.com/apis/webmastertools	Enables client applications to view and update site information and sitemaps vi data feeds.
OpenSocial	code.google.com/apis/opensocial	Lets you create applications that access a social network's friends and feeds.
Orkut Developer Home	code.google.com/apis/orkut	Enables you to create social applications for Orkut users.
Picasa APIs	code.google.com/apis/picasa	Lets you create buttons for the Picasa interface.
Picasa Web Albums	code.google.com/apis/Data API	Lets you include Picasa Web Albums in your picasaweb application or website.
Protocol Buffers	code.google.com/apis/protocolbuffers	Lets you serialize structured data.
Social Graph API	code.google.com/apis/socialgraph	Makes available information about publ connections between people on the Web.
Subscribed Links API	www.google.com/coop/subscribedlinks	Lets you create custom search results that users can add to their Google search pages.
YouTube Data API	code.google.com/apis/youtube	Enables integration of YouTube videos into your application or website.
YouTube Player Tools	code.google.com/apis/youtube/player_parameters.html	Lets you customize the YouTube video player on your website.

If you're developing any application that involves web search or other service that Google offers, you should make Google Code your starting point. From here, you can download all the APIs, tools, and documentation you need to incorporate Google technology into the applications you develop.

Developing with the Google App Engine

The quick way to start developing applications using Google's APIs is to utilize the Google App Engine (code.google.com/appengine). The App Engine lets you create and run your web-based applications using Google's infrastructure. You don't have to acquire or maintain your own web servers; applications housed on Google App Engine use Google's servers, instead.

The advantages of using Google to host your applications are many. Most notable is the fact that you don't have to scale your hardware as you get more users and your storage and bandwidth needs grow. You just upload your application to the Google App Engine servers, and Google does all the rest; as your user numbers increase, Google automatically assigns the necessary bandwidth and storage space.

The App Engine is more than just an application-hosting service, however; it's a fully integrated application environment. In addition to the dynamic web hosting, you get a development environment based on the App Engine software development kit (SDK). The SDK includes a web server application that lets you simulate the App Engine environment on your local computer, so you can develop offline as well as online. It runs on any computer using the Python 2.5 programming language; versions are available for Windows, Mac OS X, and Linux.

> **note** The Google App Engine is an example of cloud computing, where applications and data are housed in a web-based server "cloud" and accessible to any authorized user with an Internet connection. Learn more about cloud computing in my related book, *Cloud Computing: Web-Based Applications That Change the Way You Work and Collaborate Online* (Michael Miller, Que, 2008).

> **tip** If you're still not sure how to integrate Google APIs into your own applications, check out the applications featured in the Google Applications Gallery (appgallery.appspot.com). These are all applications developed within and hosted by the Google App Engine; there's a lot of exciting stuff here!

And here's the best thing, especially for developers on a budget: Google App Engine is completely free. That's right, after you sign up and download the SDK, you can develop and publish your application at no charge. At present, Google provides 500MB of persistent storage and enough bandwidth for approximately 5 million page views a month. (Of course, if you need more space or bandwidth, Google will be glad to sell it to you.)

COMMENTARY

WEB 2.0

By making its APIs public, Google is facilitating a ton of third-party development. All of this development essentially customizes existing Google information and services for specific purposes—by filtering search results, hiding Google access behind a different interface, or overlaying proprietary information on top of a Google map. In essence, an application built using a Google API isn't a freestanding application; it's a cooperative venture with Google, merging Google's public data with the application's interface or operation.

These Google-enabled applications are as good an example as any of what some people are calling Web 2.0. What is Web 2.0? Here's how tech pundit (and fellow publisher) Tim O'Reilly defined it:

"Web 2.0 is the network as platform, spanning all connected devices; Web 2.0 applications are those that make the most of the intrinsic advantages of that platform: delivering software as a continually updated service that gets better the more people use it, consuming and remixing data from multiple sources, including individual users, while providing their own data and services in a form that allows remixing by others, creating network effects through an 'architecture of participation,' and going beyond the page metaphor of Web 1.0 to deliver rich user experiences."

That's a lot of technospeak, but I think Tim's onto something. In essence, Web 2.0 is a more collaborative web, where applications are virtual (not solely housed on a single computer or website); where data is freely shared between applications, users, and websites; and where operating systems are irrelevant and the Web itself becomes the platform.

In this aspect, Google-based applications and mashups demonstrate a first step toward Web 2.0. The applications built around the Google

APIs aren't solely housed on a single computer or website; they require access to and coordination with Google's servers and databases. The data served by one of these applications isn't solely the developer's data; it's either mostly or partly Google's data, as shaped for the developer's needs. And these applications aren't Windows- or Mac-based apps; they're OS-independent, truly using the Web (or, more accurately, the Google API) as the platform.

When you encounter a Google map mashup or a custom Google search application, you're experiencing a little bit of the Web 2.0 future. In this Web 2.0 world, application developers depend on Google (and other companies that offer open access to their APIs and data) to complete their programs; users get as much value from Google's data as they do from the application itself. It's a cooperative effort, one in which the end user benefits tremendously.

The Bottom Line

If you're an application developer, Google makes it fairly easy to add Google search and other services into your code. We'll examine some specific examples of Google applications in the final chapters of this book. In Chapter 44, "Creating Google Gadgets," you'll learn how to add your own applications to the Google Desktop and iGoogle home page. In Chapter 45, "Creating Social Applications with OpenSocial," you'll learn how to add Google applications to MySpace, Orkut, and other social networks. And in Chapter 46, "Using Google Gears," you'll learn how to make your web-based applications work offline. And remember—it's all possible thanks to Google's publicly available APIs!

Creating Google Gadgets

O ne of the most popular types of applications to develop is the so-called *gadget*. Gadgets are relatively simple to conceive and relatively easy to create.

Google uses gadgets in many of its own services, including the Google Desktop, the iGoogle custom home page, Google Maps, Google Calendar, and Blogger blogs. You can use Google's developer tools to create your own gadgets, and share those gadgets with others.

Understanding Google Gadgets

What is a gadget? Put simply, a gadget is a small, simple, typically single-purpose application that can be embedded in web pages and other applications. For example, Figure 44.1 shows a time and date gadget—neat and compact.

FIGURE 44.1

A simple time and date gadget.

Gadgets are written in HTML and JavaScript, and don't necessarily require advanced programming skills to develop. You can, however, use Google's JavaScript libraries to create gadgets that contain Flash content, dynamic resizing, persistent storage, and more.

Where can you use Google Gadgets? The list of gadget-friendly sites is large and growing, and includes the following:

- Blogger blogs
- iGoogle personalized web pages
- Google Apps start pages
- Google Calendar
- Google Desktop
- Google Maps
- Google Spreadsheets
- Google Toolbar
- Orkut profile pages

In addition, you can add Google gadgets to many third-party websites and products, including MyAOL, IBM's websphere portal, RedHat's JBoss portal, the SUN portal, and the BEA weblogic portal. You can also add Google gadgets to your own web pages and blogs; all you have to do is insert the gadget code into your page's underlying HTML code.

tip

To view a variety of gadgets available for iGoogle and the Google Desktop, check out Google's Gadget Directory (www.google.com/ig/directory).

Getting to Know Google's Gadgets APIs

Gadgets are capable of interfacing with the host Google applications, thanks to Google's Gadgets Application Programming Interfaces (APIs). There's one core Gadgets API, two Desktop Gadgets APIs, and extensions to the core API for specific Google applications.

Core Gadgets API

The Core Gadgets API (code.google.com/apis/gadgets) is the basic API that enables the creation of all types of gadgets. The other gadget-related APIs are extensions of this core Gadgets API.

Desktop Gadgets APIs

If you're developing gadgets for the Google Desktop or iGoogle home page, you use Google's two Desktop APIs (code.google.com/apis/desktop). These include the following:

- Desktop Gadget API, used for creating rich desktop experiences.
- Desktop Search API, used to add Google Desktop search to gadgets and other applications.

Gadgets API Extensions

In addition to the core Google Gadget API and desktop gadgets APIs, Google also offers a number of Gadgets API extensions for use with other Google applications. These include the following:

- Google AdSense API (code.google.com/apis/adsense), used to place dynamic AdSense ads in gadgets and on websites.
- Google Calendar API (code.google.com/apis/calendar), used to build Calendar gadgets and display time-based information in gadgets and on websites.
- Google Finance Data API (code.google.com/apis/finance), used to retrieve and display Google Finance data in gadgets.
- Google Maps API (code.google.com/apis/maps), used to add customized maps to gadgets and websites.
- Google Spreadsheets Data API (code.google.com/apis/spreadsheets), used to add gadgets to Google Spreadsheets or add spreadsheet data to other gadgets.
- OpenSocial API (code.google.com/apis/opensocial), used to create gadgets for social networking websites.

Creating a Google Gadget: Basic Steps

note Learn more about OpenSocial gadgets in Chapter 45, "Creating Social Applications with OpenSocial."

If you know a little bit about HTML or JavaScript coding, it's easy to create a Google gadget. Here are the basic steps you need to follow:

1. Use any text or HTML editor or the Google Gadgets Editor to write the gadget code.

2. Host the gadget code on a public web server, or on Google's servers via the Google Gadgets Editor.

3. Use the Google Gadgets Editor to publish your gadget. Select File, Publish; then choose Add to My iGoogle Page.

4. Go to iGoogle (www.google.com/ig) to access your newly published gadget.

Using the Google Gadget Editor

By now you're probably curious about this Google Gadget Editor thing. The Google Gadget Editor, or GGE for short, is perhaps the easiest way to get started writing gadgets. It also serves as a public web host to the gadgets you create.

Navigating the Google Gadget Editor

You access the GGE at code.google.com/apis/gadgets/docs/legacy/gs.html#GGE. As you can see in Figure 44.2, the GGE is comprised of two tabs and a single pull-down menu. The Editor tab is where you enter your gadget code; the Preview tab displays the output of your code. The URL for your gadget is displayed in the upper-right corner of GGE.

When you first access the GGE, it is preloaded with the code for the Hello, World! gadget. Leave all the code as-is except for line 5 ("Hello, world!"); insert your own gadget code where the line 5 code is.

You use the File menu to start new projects (File, New), open existing projects (File, Open), save current projects (File, Save As or File, Save), and publish your projects to iGoogle (File, Publish).

tip For easier editing, you can add the Google Gadget Editor to your iGoogle page. Just click the +Google button below the GGC window.

FIGURE 44.2
Creating a gadget with the Google Gadget Editor.

Publishing Your Gadget

Let's talk a bit about publishing your gadget. When you select File, Publish, the GGE displays the Publish Your Gadget dialog box, shown in Figure 44.3. You have three publishing options:

- **Add to My iGoogle Page.** Adds your gadget to your iGoogle page.

- **Publish to iGoogle Directory.** Submits your gadget to the iGoogle Gadget Directory. If you choose this option, your gadget becomes public for anyone to use.

- **Add to a Webpage.** Takes you to the Add This Gadget to Your Webpage page, shown in Figure 44.4. This page helps you generate code that lets you add your gadget to any web page.

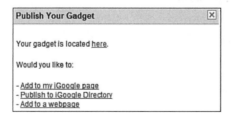

FIGURE 44.3
Google publishing options.

FIGURE 44.4
Adding a gadget to your own web page.

Writing Gadget Code

To write the code for a gadget, you need to know a little HTML, JavaScript, and XML. Your final code is saved in an XML file; it's this XML file that is referenced in your iGoogle, Google Desktop, or other application.

Understanding Gadget Code

Here's what a typical gadget code looks like:

```
<?xml version="1.0" encoding="UTF-8" ?>
<Module>
  <ModulePrefs title="title" />
  <Content type="html">
    <![CDATA[
        // Your code here...
    ]]>
  </Content>
</Module>
```

> **note** Google originally used the term "module" for what it now calls a gadget—so don't be surprised when you see the word "module" throughout the Gadgets API.

There are five main sections of any gadget code, with an optional sixth section, as detailed in Table 44.1.

Table 44.1   Google Gadget Code

Code	Explanation
<?xml version="1.0" encoding="UTF=9"?>	Declares XML version number.
<Module>	Indicates that this XML file contains a gadget.
<ModulePrefs>	Contains information about the gadget, such as its title.
<Content>	Contains the content of the gadget, including the type of gadget (HTML is the preferred type).
<! [CDATA[...]]>	Indicates the start of the gadget's HTML, CSS, or JavaScript code; insert the code after the second left bracket and before the closing right brackets.

The optional section, not shown in the previous example, is the <**UserPrefs**> section. This is where you define controls that enable users to specify their own personal settings for the gadget. For example, a map gadget might include an input field for the user's ZIP code or city.

Creating a Simple Gadget

Let's look at the code for a very simple gadget—the Hello, World! gadget included by default in the GGE. The Hello, World! code looks like this:

```
<?xml version="1.0" encoding="UTF-8" ?>
<Module>
  <ModulePrefs title="hello world example" />
  <Content type="html">
    <![CDATA[
      Hello, world!
    ]]>
  </Content>
</Module>
```

As described, this code starts with the declaration line, followed by the <**Module**> line. Then the <**Module Prefs**> line defines the title of this gadget ("hello world example").

The <**Content**> line declares the start of the module content, and defines the content type as HTML. Then we have the content container (the <**!CDATA[** line), followed by the actual programming code. In this example, the programming code is a single line: "Hello, world!"

The code ends up with the closing brackets for the CDATA, Content, and Module codes.

The result of this code is a very simple gadget. As you can see in Figure 44.5, this gadget does nothing more than display the words "Hello, world!" onscreen. If you want to display other words, just edit the "Hello, world!" line in the code.

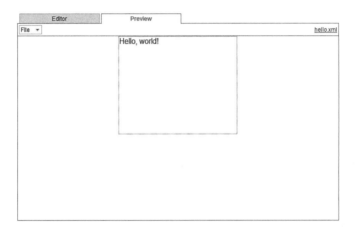

FIGURE 44.5
The Hello, World! gadget displayed in the GGE Preview tab.

Obviously, you can create gadgets that are much more complex than this. Instead of displaying a simple line of text, you can insert dynamic content via JavaScript code, for example. The type of gadget you can create is limited only by your programming skills—and your imagination!

The Bottom Line

A more in-depth discussion of gadget programming is beyond the scope of this book. Suffice to say, you can create just about any type of application you can imagine and include that application in your iGoogle, Google Desktop, or personal web page. You can even use Google's various APIs and API extensions to include Google applications and data in your gadgets. And it's all open source, which means Google provides the APIs free of charge. Whether you're a hobbyist, student, or professional application developer, it's a great resource.

Creating Social Applications with OpenSocial

O ne of Google's most recent and most interesting forays into open source development concerns social networks—sites like MySpace and Google's own Orkut. In conjunction with several of these social networking sites, Google has developed the OpenSocial API, a means of developing applications that work across multiple social networks. Use OpenSocial to develop a gadget for MySpace, and it's easy to port to Friendster and LinkedIn.

In this chapter, we examine what OpenSocial is and what it does, and walk you through developing your own OpenSocial gadgets.

Understanding the OpenSocial API

What is OpenSocial? Simply put, OpenSocial defines a common Application Programming Interface (API) for social applications across multiple social networking websites. In essence, you use the OpenSocial API to build hosted XML applications/documents written in HTML and JavaScript. The API lets your applications access the network's friends and update feeds.

OpenSocial applications can be written in any HTML or text editor, or using the Google Gadgets framework. In fact, creating an OpenSocial application is a lot like creating a Google gadget.

note Learn more about developing Google gadgets in Chapter 44, "Creating Google Gadgets."

note Learn more about OpenSocial at the OpenSocial Foundation website (www.opensocial.org). The OpenSocial Foundation is a not-for-profit entity jointly proposed by Google, MySpace, and Yahoo!

The nice thing about the OpenSocial API is that you no longer have to develop separate applications for each social network. The API is cross-network compatible, so the apps you develop for one network should easily port to other OpenSocial networks.

There are actually four different APIs within the general OpenSocial API:

- Activities API, used for publishing and accessing information about user activities.
- JavaScript API, used to interface with JavaScript-based social data.
- People and Friends API, used to access people and relationship data.
- Persistence API, used for server-free stateful applications.

Examining OpenSocial Compatibility

OpenSocial was developed by Google, Yahoo!, MySpace, and other popular social networks. The OpenSocial API was released on November 1, 2007, and already hundreds of OpenSocial applications are available.

OpenSocial Sites

Which sites currently or plan to support OpenSocial apps? Here's the list as of Fall 2008:

- Bebo (www.bebo.com)
- CityIN (www.cityin.com)
- Engage (www.engage.com)
- Freebar (www.freebar.it)
- Friendster (www.friendster.com)
- hi5 (www.hi5.com)
- Hyves (www.hyves.net)
- IDtail (www.idtail.com)
- iGoogle (www.google.com/ig)
- imeem (www.imeem.com)
- LinkedIn (www.linkedin.com)
- mixi (www.mixi.jp)
- MySpace (www.myspace.com)
- Netlog (www.netlog.com)
- NetModular (www.netmodular.com)
- Ning (www.ning.com)
- Orkut (www.orkut.com)
- Plaxo (www.plaxo.com)
- Sonico (www.sonico.com)
- Tianji (www.tianji.com)
- Tianya (www.tianya.cn)
- Viadeo (www.viadeo.com)
- Webon (www.webon.com)
- XING (www.xing.com)
- YiQi (www.yiqi.com)

Notice any social networking sites missing from this list? The big one, of course, is Facebook, which is defiantly not part of the OpenSocial alliance. In fact, OpenSocial is regarded in part as a

note Oracle, Salesforce.com, and Six Apart also support OpenSocial on their respective web platforms. In addition, Yahoo! is also part of the OpenSocial alliance, and is likely to support OpenSocial when its Mash social network moves out of the testing phase.

45

cross-platform alternative to the Facebook platform. So, if you develop OpenSocial apps, you'll won't be able to port them to Facebook; your Facebook apps will have to continue to be built from scratch, using that site's native developer tools.

OpenSocial Applications

What types of OpenSocial applications are available? Companies currently offering OpenSocial applications include the following:

- Flixster (www.flixter.com); movie reviews and ratings, shown in Figure 45.1.
- FotoFlexer (www.fotoflexer.com); online photo editor.
- iLike (www.ilike.com); music discovery and playlist sharing.
- Last.fm My Favorite Music (www.last.fm); music playlists.
- NewsGator (www.newsgator.com); RSS feed reader.
- RockYou (www.rockyou.com); photo sharing and slideshows, shown in Figure 45.2.
- Slide (www.slide.com); photo slideshows.
- TooStep BizX (www.toostep.com); virtual business card exchange.
- VirtualTourist (www.virtualtourist.com); travel guides and maps.

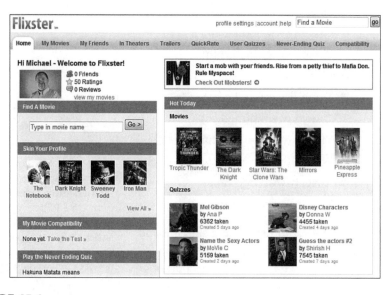

FIGURE 45.1

The Flixter application on MySpace.

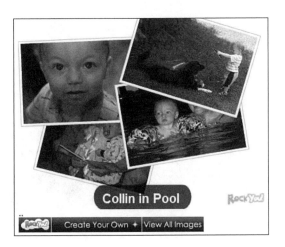

FIGURE 45.2

The RockYou slideshow on MySpace.

Developing with the OpenSocial API

If you want to develop your own OpenSocial applications, the place to start is the Google Code OpenSocial gateway (code.google.com/apis/opensocial), shown in Figure 45.3. From here, you can read the OpenSocial documentation, download the OpenSocial API, converse with other developers on the OpenSocial blog, and start developing your own OpenSocial apps.

> **tip** Find more OpenSocial applications at the OpenSocial Directory (www.opensocialdirectory.org) .

As noted previously, OpenSocial applications are built on the Google gadget model. This means that you can develop your social apps with little or no serving costs, using the Google Gadget Editor. Naturally, you first have to register and obtain your API key/value, which then goes in all your app code. This is all explained on the Google Code site.

Before you start developing your application, you have to pick one of the compatible social networks as your code/testing base. This will be the main network for your application; this base code can then be ported to other OpenSocial sites.

FIGURE 45.3

The Google Code OpenSocial gateway.

At its core, a social application is an XML gadget file. The code is actually quite straightforward, as you can see in this simple example:

```
<?xml version="1.0" encoding="UTF-8" ?>
<Module>
  <ModulePrefs title="title">
    <Require feature="opensocial-0.7" />
  </ModulePrefs>
  <Content type="html">
    <![CDATA[
        // Your code here...
    ]]>
  </Content>
</Module>
```

There are six main sections to the OpenSocial application code, as detailed in Table 45.1.

Table 45.1   OpenSocial Gadget Code

Code	Explanation
<?xml version="1.0" encoding="UTF=9" ?>	Declares XML version number.
<Module>	Indicates that this XML file contains a gadget.
<ModulePrefs>	Contains information about the gadget, such as its title.
<Require>	Denotes a required feature of the gadget, such as a particular version of the OpenSocial API.
<Content>	Contains the content of the gadget, including the type of gadget (HTML is the preferred type).
<! [CDATA[…]]>	Indicates the start of the gadget's HTML, CSS, or JavaScript code; insert the code after the second left bracket and before the closing right brackets.

You can use any text editor or HTML editor to create this code. Alternatively, you can develop the code using the Google Gadget Editor. To run, the code must be uploaded to a website host; again, you can use the Google Gadget Editor for this.

You'll also need an account at the social network site for which you're writing. You can then use that site's developer's sandbox. Within the sandbox, you'll need to supply the URL where the application is stored; you're then prompted to authorize the application to access your profile, friends, activity stream, and the like. This installs the application on your page on that social networking site.

note Learn more about the Google Gadget Editor in Chapter 43, "Using Google's APIs and Developer's Tools."

45

OPENSOCIAL VERSUS FACEBOOK

As noted previously in this chapter, OpenSocial was created as an alternative and competitor to the Facebook platform. Facebook is the Web's largest social networking site, and so far it's operated pretty much as a closed platform. It's also a big competitor to Google, Yahoo!, and so on, in terms of both users and advertising dollars.

That's why OpenSocial was developed—to harness multiple smaller guns to better compete with the big gun. Google could have tried to attack Facebook directly with its own social network, Orkut, but that would likely have failed. (In the U.S., at least; Orkut has a larger market share in other countries, such as Brazil and India.) Instead, Google recognized that there is strength in numbers, and sought to build a "coalition of the willing" to compete with Facebook in an open source environment.

For developers, it's a boon; instead of developing multiple applications for multiple sites, they develop one OpenSocial version and it works on all the OpenSocial sites. (They still have to develop a separate Facebook version, of course.) It's also a good deal for the smaller social network sites, which otherwise might have had fewer applications developed for their proprietary platforms.

Don't underestimate the importance or the profit potential of these web-based gadgets. Third-party developers stand to make big bucks by either selling their gadgets outright to users or selling advertising space surrounding the gadgets. And anything that can increase traffic to a social networking site also increases its advertising revenues.

So, it's no surprise that Google was able to line up such impressive support behind the OpenSocial initiative. Now, if it could only get Facebook on board…but that's probably wishful thinking.

The Bottom Line

OpenSocial is an initiative to help develop gadgets or web-based applications for many of the Internet's most popular social networking sites—Facebook excluded. If you're an application developer, OpenSocial lets you develop one gadget and easily port it to all the other sites that support the OpenSocial platform. It's a far sight better than developing separate apps for each site—which should save both time and money.

Using Google Gears

Most applications and gadgets that you develop using the various Google APIs are web-based applications. That is, they function by pulling data or services over the Web, which means they need you to be connected to the Internet to work.

But what do you do when you're not connected to the Internet?

Despite a very obvious web-based cloud computing bias, Google recognizes that not all users will always be connected to the Internet. As such, they've developed a way to run their web-based applications offline, without an Internet connection.

Welcome to Google Gears.

Why Do You Need Gears?

Google Gears (officially called just Gears) is Google's open source software that enables offline access to normally web-based services. When you incorporate Gears into your application or gadget code, that application can function when the user is not connected to the Internet—effectively turning your web-based application into traditional desktop software.

Why is that important?

Imagine, for example, that you're working on a big report using Google Docs Google's web-based word processor. All is well and good until you head off to your in-laws' house for the weekend. The in-laws, unfortunately, don't have an Internet connection in the house, and you can't sneak away to use the WiFi service in the local Starbucks. So, while you could be working on your report during your downtime, you're instead stuck with a computer that can access either your application or your document because it isn't connected to the Internet.

In this instance, if you could run your application offline and if your document was stored on your own computer, you could keep working and get your report done on schedule. Well, that's what Google Gears does—lets you run web-based applications locally, with no Internet connection necessary.

As you might recall from Chapter 19, "Using Google Docs," Google does offer offline workability for its web-based applications. This offline mode is facilitated by—you guessed it—Google Gears.

Now any application developer can utilize Gears to enable their own web-based applications to run locally without an Internet connection. If your application can benefit from this offline functionality, you need to incorporate Gears into your development plans.

How Does Google Gears Work?

A traditional web-based application works as shown in Figure 46.1. The application's user interface, displayed within the user's web browser, constantly accesses the Internet, where the application itself is stored. Separately, the application's data—via the browser-based data layer—also has to access the Internet to store the data online.

note Not all web browsers support Google Gears. At present, Gears runs only on Internet Explorer 6 or higher and Firefox 1.5 or higher. Google Gears is also built into the new Google Chrome web browser.

46

FIGURE 46.1

The flowchart for a traditional web-based application. (Illustration courtesy Google.)

Google Gears works in a slightly different manner. Key to its operation is the installation of a database engine on the user's computer. This database locally caches the user's data, which was previously stored exclusively on the Web.

This is accomplished via means of a data switch, as shown in Figure 46.2. This switch directs the data information to the local database when the user is offline, or to the web-based storage when the user is online. Gears also adds a Sync Engine that synchronizes the offline data with the online data.

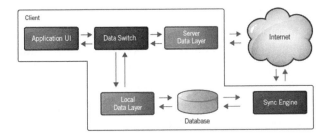

FIGURE 46.2

The flowchart for a Gears-enabled application. (Illustration courtesy Google.)

When the user is offline, then, Gears-enabled applications use data from the local cache instead of from the web-based service. Thus, a user can run your application in offline mode, using the locally cached data; when he goes back online, the local data is synchronized with the version stored on the web.

To make this all work, Gears utilizes three core modules, each of which has its own API:

- **LocalServer**, which caches and serves the application itself on the user's computer, without needing to contact a web-based server.

- **Database**, which stores and accesses the application's data on the user's computer.

- **WorkerPool**, which makes the application more responsive by performing long-running tasks in the background—such as the code that synchronizes data between the web-based server and users' computers.

note Gears uses the open source SQLite database system for its database.

Like all of Google's developers tools, Google Gears is open source and free for all developers to use.

Developing Gears-Enabled Applications

To use Google Gears with your application, you have to add explicit Gears code into your application's source code. In addition, all of your application users must have Gears installed on their computers.

Installing Gears on the Host Machine

It's best if your application's users already have Gears installed on their computers. One installation of Gears works with all Gears-enabled applications, if they've already installed Gears to use Google Docs offline, for example, the installation of Gears is available for you to use with your application.

To install Gears, users should go to gears.google.com. When they click the install link on this page and follow the resulting instructions, the Gears application is installed on their computer.

Initializing Google Gears

When you integrate Gears into your own application, the first thing you want to do is determine whether the user has Gears installed. You do this by initializing Gears with the **gears_init.js** source file.

This file detects whether Gears is installed. If it is, it defines Gears for your application. If Gears isn't installed, it directs the user to the Gears installation page.

You can download the **gears_init.js** source file from
code.google.com/apis/gears/tools.html#gears_init. Then reference the file with
the following code:

```
<script src="gears_init.js"></script>
<script>
  if (!window.google || !google.gears) {
    location.href =
    "http://gears.google.com/?action=install&message=<your welcome
message>"
    + "&return=<your website url>";
  }
</script>
```

Replace *your welcome message* with your own welcome message, such as
"Please install Gears to enable offline operation of this application." Replace
your website url with the URL for your application's website.

Developing for Gears

Now you have to add Gears functionality to your application's source code. In
particular, you need to add code for the following functions:

- Use the LocalServer Module API to enable your application to cache
  and serve its HTTP resources locally, on the client computer.
- Use the Database Module API to add local data storage to your application.
- Use the WorkerPool Module API to run your application's JavaScript
  code in the background.

With the appropriate code in place, your application will:

- Sense the Internet connection and run in offline mode when no connection to the Internet is present.
- Automatically store copies of the application's data/documents locally,
  on the client computer's hard drive.
- When the offline application reconnects to the Internet, automatically
  synchronize any changes made in the local database with the web-
  based server.

46

To download the Gears APIs and learn more about developing for Gears, go code.google.com/apis/gears.

WHO USES GOOGLE GEARS?

Gears is a relatively new developer's tool—so new, in fact, that it's still in beta development as this text is written. (The current version, as of August 2008, is version 0.4.) To that end, developers are still getting to know how Gears works and what Gears can do.

For new and interested developers, it helps to take a look at what other developers are doing with Gears. There are already several applications that have enabled Gears functionality, including the following:

- Google applications, including Google Docs, Google Reader, and Picasa
- Buxfer (www.buxfer.com)
- MySpace Mail Search (www.myspace.com)
- Remember the Milk (www.rememberthemilk.com)
- WordPress (www.wordpress.com)
- Zoho Writer (writer.zoho.com)

The Bottom Line

The concept of a web-based application is appealing; a user can access the application and his documents from any computer located anywhere—as long as he has an Internet connection. The concept loses appeal when a user doesn't have an Internet connection handy and thus can't access his application or documents.

Google Gears, then, turns an exclusively web-based application into a full-time online/offline application. Not only does the application work without an Internet connection, all the user's offline work is stored in a local database and then synched to the web-based versions when the user goes back online. It's a perfect solution to the online/offline dilemma.

As a developer, it's worth your time to add Gears functionality to your web-based applications. It doesn't cost you anything but time and a little learning; you supply the time, and Google will supply the documentation and tutorials on their Google Code Gears website.

Appendixes

Google's Site Directory

Google Site	URL
Android	code.google.com/android
Blogger	www.blogger.com
Gmail	mail.google.com
Google Accounts	www.google.com/accounts
Google Add Your URL	www.google.com/addurl
Google AdSense	www.google.com/adsense
Google AdWords	adwords.google.com
Google Alerts	www.google.com/alerts
Google Analytics	www.google.com/analytics
Google Apps	www.google.com/a
Google Apple Macintosh Search	www.google.com/mac
Google Base	base.google.com
Google Blog Search	blogsearch.google.com
Google Book Search	books.google.com
Google BSD Unix Search	www.google.com/bsd
Google Business Solutions	www.google.com/services
Google Calendar	calendar.google.com
Google Catalogs	catalogs.google.com
Google Checkout	checkout.google.com
Google Chrome	www.google.com/chrome

Continues

Google Site	URL
Google Code	code.google.com
Google Dashboard Widgets for Mac	www.google.com/macwidgets
Google Desktop	desktop.google.com
Google Directory	directory.google.com
Google Docs	docs.google.com
Google Earth	earth.google.com
Google Enterprise Solutions	www.google.com/enterprise
Google Extensions for Firefox	www.google.com/tools/firefox
Google Finance	finance.google.com
Google Gears	gears.google.com
Google Groups	groups.google.com
Google Health	www.google.com/health
Google Hot Trends	www.google.com/trends/hottrends
Google Image Search	images.google.com
Google Labs	labs.google.com
Google Language Tools	www.google.com/language_tools
Google Links	www.google.com/relatedlinks
Google Linux Search	www.google.com/linux
Google Maps	maps.google.com
Google Mars	www.google.com/mars
Google Microsoft Search	www.google.com/microsoft
Google Mobile (information)	www.google.com/mobile
Google Mobile (from your cell phone)	www.google.com/m
Google Moon	www.google.com/moon
Google News	news.google.com
Google News Archive Search	news.google.com/archivesearch
Google Notebook	www.google.com/notebook
Google Pack	pack.google.com
Google Patent Search	www.google.com/patents
Google Product Search	www.google.com/products
Google Reader	reader.google.com

A

Google Site	URL
Google Ride Finder	labs.google.com/ridefinder
Google Scholar	scholar.google.com
Google Sets	labs.google.com/sets
Google Sites	sites.google.com
Google SketchUp	sketchup.google.com
Google Sky	www.google.com/sky
Google Talk	talk.google.com
Google Toolbar	toolbar.google.com
Google Transit	www.google.com/transit
Google Translate	translate.google.com
Google Trends	www.google.com/trends
Google U.S. Government Search	www.google.com/unclesam
Google University Search	www.google.com/options/universities.html
Google Video	video.google.com
Google Video Blog	www.googlevideo.blogspot.com
Google Web Accelerator	webaccelerator.google.com
Google Web Search	www.google.com
Google Webmaster Tools	www.google.com/webmasters/tools
iGoogle	www.google.com/ig
Knol	knol.google.com
Lively	www.lively.com
Official Google Blog	googleblog.blogspot.com
OpenSocial	code.google.com/apis/opensocial
Orkut	www.orkut.com
Picasa	picasa.google.com
Picasa Web Albums	picasaweb.google.com
YouTube	www.youtube.com

A

Google's Advanced Search Operators

Operator	Description[1]
..	Searches within a range of numbers in the form *number..number*.
-	Excludes pages that contain the specified word from the search results.
""	Searches for the complete phrase in the form *word1 word2*.
( )	Used to group keywords in a query.
*	Whole-word wildcard; searches for missing words in a phrase ("") search.
~	Searches for synonyms of the specified keyword.
+	Includes the specified "stop" word in the query.
after:	GMAIL—Restricts search to emails sent after a specified date.
allinanchor:	Restricts search to the anchor text (link text) of web pages; used with multiple keywords.
allintext:	Restricts search to the body text of web pages; used with multiple keywords.
allintitle:	Restricts search to the titles of web pages; used with multiple keywords.
allinurl:	Restricts search to the URLs of web pages; used with multiple keywords.

Continues

Operator	Description[1]
author:	GOOGLE GROUPS and GOOGLE SCHOLAR—Searches for messages or articles by a particular author.
bcc:	GMAIL and GOOGLE DESKTOP—Restricts search to the Bcc: lines of email messages.
before:	GMAIL—Restricts search to emails sent before a specified date.
blogurl:	GOOGLE BLOG SEARCH—Restricts search to the specified blog.
book	Initiates a Google full-text book search.
bphonebook:	Displays business phonebook listings.
cache:	Displays the cached version of the specified URL page as stored in the Google database.
cc:	GMAIL and GOOGLE DESKTOP—Restricts search to the Cc: lines of email messages.
define: *or* define	Displays definitions of the specified word or phrase.
filename:	GMAIL—Searches for file attachments with the specified filename.
filetype:	Finds documents with the specified extension.
from:	GMAIL and GOOGLE DESKTOP—Restricts search to the From: lines of email messages.
groups:	GOOGLE GROUPS—Searches for messages in the specified group(s).
has:attachment	GMAIL—Restricts search to emails with file attachments.
in:	GMAIL—Restricts search to emails stored in a specific location: **anywhere**, **inbox**, **trash**, or **spam**
info:	Displays information that Google knows about the web page in question.
inanchor:	Restricts search to the anchor text (link text) of web pages; used with a single keyword.
inblogtitle:	GOOGLE BLOG SEARCH—Restricts search to blog titles.
info:	Displays information about the specified URL.
inpostauthor:	GOOGLE BLOG SEARCH—Restricts search to blog postings by the specified author.
inposttitle:	GOOGLE BLOG SEARCH—Restricts search to the titles of individual blog posts.
insubject:	GOOGLE GROUPS—Restricts search to the subject line of messages.
intext:	Restricts search to the body text of web pages; used with a single keyword.
intitle:	Restricts search to the titles of web pages; used with a single keyword.
inurl:	Restricts search to the URLs of web pages; used with a single keyword.
is:	GMAIL—Restricts search to emails that are **starred**, **read**, or **unread**.
label:	GMAIL—Restricts search to emails with the specified label.
link:	Finds pages that link to the specified URL.
location:	GOOGLE NEWS—Finds news articles from sources in the specified location.

B

Operator	Description[1]
machine:	GOOGLE DESKTOP—When the Search Across Computers feature is enabled, restricts search to the specified computer.
movie:	Searches for information about the specified movie, including show times.
OR	Searches for pages that contain one or another keyword, but not necessarily both.
phonebook:	Displays phonebook listings.
related:	Displays web pages that are similar to the specified URL.
rphonebook:	Displays residential phonebook listings.
safesearch:	Enables SafeSearch content filtering.
site:	Restricts search to a particular domain or website.
source:	GOOGLE NEWS—Finds news articles from the specified source(s).
stocks:	Displays current stock price for the specified stock symbol.
store:	GOOGLE PRODUCT SEARCH—Searches for products offered by the specified online store.
subject:	GMAIL and GOOGLE DESKTOP—Restricts search to the Subject lines of email messages.
to:	GMAIL and GOOGLE DESKTOP—Restricts search to the To: lines of email messages.
under:	GOOGLE DESKTOP—Restricts search to subfolders located under the specified folder.
weather	Displays the current weather conditions and forecast for the specified location.
what is *or* what are	Same as **define**; displays definitions of the specified word or phrase.

[1] Search operators that only work on a specific search service are so noted in the description.

B

Introducing Google Chrome

I've said it before, but it's worth noting again: Writing a book about Google is like shooting at a moving target. Just when you think you have everything nailed down, the folks in Mountain View come up with something new that needs to be covered.

In this instance, that something new is Google Chrome, a brand spanking new web browser that was announced as this book was getting ready to go to print. Chrome is so important, however, that it had to be covered in this book, so we've added this appendix to present the basics about this exciting new product.

Understanding Google Chrome

Google Chrome is, first and foremost, a web browser, similar to Internet Explorer, Firefox, Opera, and Safari. That said, Chrome is actually more than a web browser; some have compared it to a web-based operating system, or at the very least an operating container for web-based applications. I'll explain why in a few paragraphs.

First, let's examine Chrome as a web browser. As you can see in Figure C.1, the Chrome interface resembles that of Internet Explorer and other modern web browsers, complete with tabs for different web pages. Chrome is a bit sleeker than the other browsers, however, with no menu bar, search bar, status bar, or other extraneous bits and pieces. This makes the web page bigger in the window, which isn't a bad thing. In essence, it moves the business of the browser out of the way so that you can pay more attention to the web page itself.

FIGURE C.1
Google Chrome—Google's web browser.

Where Chrome really shines, however, becomes apparent when you use it to run a web-based application, such as Google Calendar or Google Docs. Select the right options, and your application appears in a window that resembles traditional desktop application window rather than a browser; the tabs and the toolbars fade away so that all you see is the application itself, as demonstrated in Figure C.2. Even better, web-based applications run much faster in Chrome than they do in competing web browsers—more than 50 times faster than with Internet Explorer, or at least that's what Google's engineers claim.

FIGURE C.2

Running Google Docs in Google Chrome—no browser tabs or controls.

Chrome's speed is due partly to the stripped-down interface, but more likely is a result of the modern JavaScript engine used to run the browser. Chrome's engine, dubbed "V8," is designed to improve the performance of complex applications—just like the cloud computing applications that Google serves up to its millions of users.

Why is Google launching its own web browser? Isn't Microsoft Explorer (or Firefox or Safari or Opera) good enough? Apparently not—at least when it comes to working from within the browser. The folks at Google, like many users, spend much of their computing time not working with traditional applications, but rather working inside the web browser. Whether it's reading email via Gmail, checking appointments in Google Calendar, or working on documents and presentations with Google Docs, a lot of work gets done inside the browser. Unfortunately, today's major browsers are based on technology originally developed more than a dozen years ago—and that technology was designed for the process of loading traditional HTML web pages, not for running dynamic web-based applications.

Thus Google's interest in developing a new type of web browser optimized for running cloud applications. As I stated previously, Chrome is more of an application container or web-based operating system than it is a browser. To this point, Chrome doesn't compete with Internet Explorer; it competes, instead, with Microsoft Windows itself. And that is something that Microsoft ought to be worried about.

note According to Google the name Chrome derives from the "chrome," or bells and whistles, that accompany a typical user interface. Google sought to minimize the "chrome," which led to the browser's name. (Others have pointed out that "chrome" was the name of an ill-fated multimedia technology product from Microsoft that was killed just days before release; this has been interpreted as a Google slam against Microsoft.)

Installing and Configuring Google Chrome

You can download and install your copy of Chrome from www.google.com/chrome. Click the Download Google Chrome button, then sit back and let the installation take place.

After you have Chrome installed, you can import the settings and bookmarks (favorites) from your current web browser. Start by clicking the Tools menu and selecting Import Bookmarks & Settings.

note As of September 2008, Chrome works only with computers running Windows Vista (any version) and Windows XP (Service Pack 2 or later). It does not currently work with Mac or Linux computers—although those versions are said to be in development.

When the Import Bookmarks and Settings dialog box appears, pull down the list and select your web browser, check those items you want to import, and then click the Import button.

Chrome also lets you configure a few other options. When you click the Tools menu and select Options, Chrome displays the Google Chrome Options window, shown in Figure C.3. There you find three tabs:

- **Basics.** This tab lets you determine what happens when you launch Chrome, what page is used as your home page, which search engine is used by default, and whether Chrome is selected as your default web browser.

C

■ **Minor Tweaks.** This tab lets you select the default location for software downloads, choose whether to save the passwords you use, and select the fonts and language displayed in the browser.

■ **Under the Hood.** This tab contains some technical settings that you might need to adjust if you run into operational issues.

FIGURE C.3
Configuring Google Chrome.

Browsing the Web with Chrome

Most of us will get our first taste of Chrome when browsing the web. To that end, when you launch Chrome, it displays your nine most recently visited web pages, along with a list of your most recent bookmarks, as shown in Figure C.4. If you have pages bookmarked, they appear in bookmark bar at the top of the page.

FIGURE C.4
The Chrome start page.

Searching with the Omnibox

To go to another web page, you type that page's URL into what looks like a standard address box at the top of the browser window. This box is more than an address box, however; it's an *Omnibox* that you also use to enter search queries.

When you start typing in the Omnibox, Google suggests both likely queries and web pages you are likely to visit, as shown in Figure C.5. Just select what you want from the drop-down list or complete typing your URL or query, and then press Enter.

FIGURE C.5
Viewing URL and query suggestions in Chrome's Omnibox.

Using Tabs

If you've used Internet Explorer 7 or similar browsers, you're already familiar with the concept of tabbed browsing. With tabs, you can open different web pages in different tabs, instead of opening one page after another, or using multiple browser windows.

Chrome makes good use of tabbed browsing. To open a new tab, just click the "+" button next to the current tab. You can also open a link in a new tab by right-clicking the link and selecting Open Link in New Tab.

Also neat is the capability to detach a tab and open it in a new browser window. Just drag the tab outside the current browser window and a new browser window opens. You also can add that page back to the original browser window, again by dragging and dropping.

Downloading Files from the Web

Here's another thing at which Chrome excels—downloading files from the Web. With most other web browsers, downloading is a chore that involves multiple dialog boxes and a lot of "OK" button-clicking. Not so with Chrome. When you choose to download a file with Chrome, it just happens. Chrome downloads the file without opening any dialog box; a small bar at the bottom of the browser window, shown in Figure C.6, shows the download progress (along with other recent downloads). When the download is finished, you can save it in any location by dragging the button for that download to the desired folder on your computer.

FIGURE C.6
Viewing file download progress in Chrome's download bar.

Browsing Incognito

You may or may not know it, but most web browsers keep a record of every web page you visit. That's fine, but every now and then you might browse some web pages that you don't want tracked. To this end, Chrome offers what it calls Incognito mode, in which the pages you visit aren't saved to your browser's history file, cookies aren't saved, and your activities are basically done without any records being kept.

C

To enter Incognito mode, click the Page button and select New Incognito Window. This opens a new window with a little spy icon next to the first tab, as shown in Figure C.7. When you're done with your private browsing, just close the Incognito window and no one will be the wiser.

note Chrome lets you run both normal and Incognito windows simultaneously.

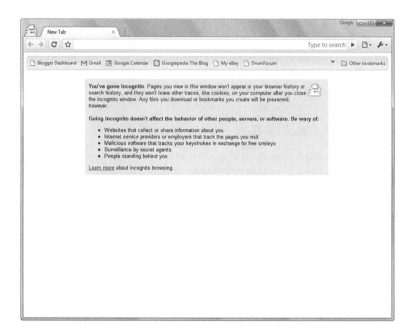

FIGURE C.7
Browsing anonymously in Incognito mode.

Running Web-Based Applications with Chrome

To me, the best thing about Chrome is how it runs web-based applications. Not only is it fast, it also lets you make a web-based application look and feel like a traditional desktop application.

To make a web-based application function like a desktop application, start by opening that application in a Chrome tab. Then click the Page button and select Create Application Shortcuts. When the Google Gears dialog box appears, select what type of shortcut to create: Desktop, Shortcut menu, or

Quick launch bar. When you click OK, not only will a shortcut be created, but the application will open in a new "chromeless" window, like the one in Figure C.8.

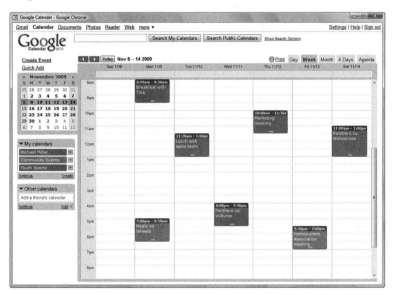

FIGURE C.8

Google Calendar in a "chromeless" window.

This window functions like any traditional desktop application window. It can be resized, and when you next open the application, the window opens to the previously saved size.

In the future, you don't even have to navigate to the application's page on the web. You can open the application by clicking the shortcut you just created; the application opens whether you're online or offline, just like a desktop app.

And here's another great feature, especially if you're running Google apps: Chrome has Google Gears built in, so you can run your applications whether you're online or offline. This feature alone makes Chrome a worthwhile choice.

note Learn more about running web-based applications offline in Chapter 19, "Using Google Docs." Learn more about the technology behind Google Gears in Chapter 46, "Using Google Gears."

The Bottom Line

Google Chrome is a very important development for both web browsing and cloud computing. Whether you look at it as a sophisticated web browser or a technology enabling cloud operating system, Chrome is definitely a game changer. Microsoft is well advised to keep an eye on Chrome; it could end up affecting both its web browser and its desktop applications!

C

Index

SYMBOLS

NUMBERS

A

F

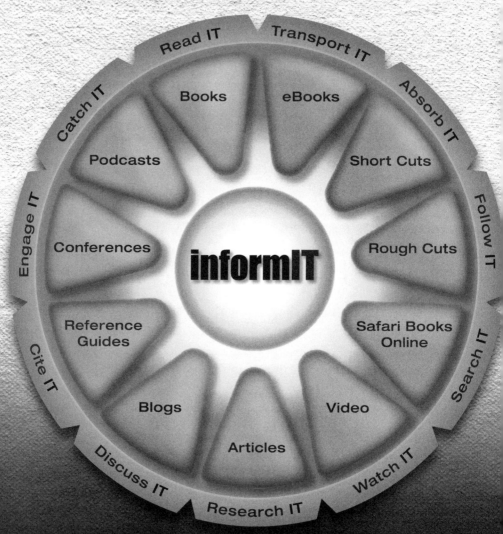

Third Edition

Michael Miller

The Ultimate Google Resource

Google.pedia

FREE Online Edition

Your purchase of **Google.pedia: The Ultimate Google Resource, Third Edition** incl
access to a free online edition for 45 days through the Safari Books Online subscri
service. Nearly every Que book is available online through Safari Books Online, al
with more than 5,000 other technical books and videos from publishers such as
Addison-Wesley Professional, Cisco Press, Exam Cram, IBM Press, O'Reilly, Pren
Hall, and Sams.

SAFARI BOOKS ONLINE allows you to search for a specific answer, cut and past
code, download chapters, and stay current with emerging technologies.

Activate your FREE Online Edition at
www.informit.com/safarifree

> **STEP 1:** Enter the coupon code: AZXOAAA.

> **STEP 2:** New Safari users, complete the brief registration form.
> Safari subscribers, just log in.

If you have difficulty registering on Safari or accessing the online edition,
please e-mail customer-service@safaribooksonline.com